The Morning Chronicle's

LABOUR AND THE POOR

Volume VII

THE RURAL DISTRICTS

The Morning Chronicle's

LABOUR AND THE POOR

Volume VII

THE RURAL DISTRICTS

ALEXANDER MACKAY & SHIRLEY BROOKS

Edited By
Rebecca Watts & Kevin Booth

Ditto Books
www.dittobooks.co.uk

First Published by Ditto Books 2020

A catalogue record for this book is available
from the British Library

ISBN 978-1-913515-07-2 (hardback)
ISBN 978-1-913515-17-1 (paperback)

Cover Image:
Labour
Engraving by J. Cousen after J. Linnell
Image courtesy of the Wellcome Collection

"We have not," the eldest daughter said, "tasted any bread for two days. We have had nowt but turmuts (turnips) to eat. We boil 'em for dinner, but the children are so hungry that they won't wait sometimes till they're biled, but eats 'em as they are."

Contents

List of Illustrations

Preface

This work attempts to be a faithful reproduction of the "Labour and the Poor" letters as printed in *The Morning Chronicle*. Only obvious typographical errors and omissions have been corrected. Variations in the spelling and hyphenation of words have largely been retained. We hope any such inconsistencies prove to be of some historical interest to the reader.

As much as possible we have tried to recreate the original layout and styling of the text and all factual tables have been reproduced as closely to the originals as possible with only minimal alterations made where necessary to improve readability.

Not all letters were titled. Where missing we have added titles to the Table of Contents to assist navigation and explanation of content. The letters themselves are as per the originals.

A handful of illustrations have been added to each volume. These did not appear in the original text but hopefully provide added interest.

R. W.
K. B.

Introduction

In 1849 a leading London-based newspaper, *The Morning Chronicle*, undertook an investigation into the working and living conditions of the poor throughout England and Wales in the hope that their findings might lead to much needed change.

The reputed catalyst for their "Labour and the Poor" series was an article written by Henry Mayhew recording a journey into Bermondsey, one of the most deprived districts of London, which was printed in September 1849. Following this it was proposed that an in-depth investigation be carried out and "Special Correspondents", the investigators, were selected and distributed around the country. The first article or "Letter" appeared on the 18th of October 1849 and the series would run for almost 2 years and 222 letters.

The well-known and respected writers and journalists recruited for the task included Henry Mayhew who was assigned to the Metropolitan districts, Angus Bethune Reach to the Manufacturing districts, Alexander Mackay and Shirley Brooks to the Rural districts and Charles Mackay to investigate the cities of Birmingham and Liverpool. The author of the letters from Wales is as yet unknown.

It is clear from references made in the letters that Alexander Mackay commenced his investigation in the counties of Buckinghamshire, Berkshire, Oxfordshire and Wiltshire, before examining the south western counties of Devon, Cornwall, Somerset and Dorset. He then proceeded eastward through Hampshire, Surrey, Sussex and Kent. He began an inquiry into the counties of Gloucestershire, Monmouthshire, Herefordshire, Worcestershire and Shropshire, but only one letter of this was published. In 1850 he accepted the task of travelling to India to investigate the viability of expanding the cotton producing areas and trade in the East Indies.

It is most likely that Shirley Brooks commenced his portion of the investigation in the eastern counties of Norfolk, Suffolk and Essex, continuing on to cover Hertfordshire, Bedfordshire,

Huntingdonshire and Cambridgeshire, before proceeding to the midland counties of Northamptonshire, Leicestershire, Rutland, Nottinghamshire and Derbyshire.

The "Labour and the Poor" letters were extremely popular at the time, being widely read throughout the nation and even abroad. The revelations in them caused quite a stir amongst the middle and upper classes of Victorian society. *Letters to the Editor* poured in with donations for specific cases of distress that appeared in the letters and also for the general alleviation of the suffering of the poor. A special fund was set up by *The Morning Chronicle* to collect and distribute these donations.

These *Letters to the Editor* have been included in this series, predominantly in the Metropolitan district volumes whose letters elicited the majority of responses. They provide a unique window into the thoughts and sentiments of the Victorian readership as they react to the incredible accounts of misery and desperation being unveiled.

The Morning Chronicle's extraordinary and unsurpassed "Labour and the Poor" investigation provides an unparalleled insight into the people of the period, their living and working conditions, their feelings, their language, their sufferings and their struggles for survival amidst the poverty and destitution of 19th century Britain. An investigation of such magnitude had never before been attempted and the undertaking was truly of epic proportions. Its impact at the time was profound. Its historical importance today is without question.

LABOUR AND THE POOR.

—◆—

THE RURAL DISTRICTS.

[FROM OUR SPECIAL CORRESPONDENT.]

THE NORTHERN COUNTIES—DURHAM, NORTHUMBERLAND, CUMBERLAND, AND WESTMORELAND.

LETTER XXIII.

To ascertain the state and prospects of the working-classes and the poor, especially of those who depend for their bread on agriculture, throughout the North of England, is the department which has been assigned to me in the prosecution of the important investigation that you have undertaken; and I now proceed to furnish your readers with such evidence on the subject as I have been able to collect, in the hope of thereby laying a solid foundation for a just judgment. I have spared no pains to collect information of every sort bearing upon the question, and I shall detail it fully and freely—with no bias, I trust, to one-sided views of any kind, and with an anxious desire to treat fairly every point of this very complex topic.

Before coming to the marrow of the matter, however, it is necessary to define the limits of our field of action, and to give a passing glance at its physical characteristics, and at certain internal relations subsisting unaltered through the revolutions of centuries, which must in every case materially modify the conditions of a social problem. The four northern counties—Durham, Northumberland, Cumberland, and Westmoreland—(together with the town or dominion of Berwick-on-Tweed)—cover an area of 5,253 square statute miles— about one-eleventh of the area of England and Wales, which is 57,812 square miles. Their population, by the census of 1841, was 809,064, or less than one-eighteenth part of the total population of England and Wales, which was 15,906,741. It thus appears that, whereas the population of England and Wales gives nearly 275 souls to a square mile, that of the four northern counties gives 154—showing a density of little more than one-half. To assign the proportion of inhabitants to statute acres is a more difficult matter, for it appears that though we have fixed, or consider ourselves to have fixed, with accuracy, the number of square statute miles in England and Wales, we have not yet been able to determine with the same precision the number of square statute acres. Two different sets of numbers are given by the standard authority—which is, or should be, that of greatest mark and likelihood on the subject—the Population Returns. In the summary of the county of Durham (Enumeration Abstract, p. 88), the area in English statute acres is stated at 679,530; but the following note is subjoined:—"The area of the county of Durham is 1,097 square statute miles, and consequently 702,080 acres; while the area assigned to the several parishes amounts to no more than 679,530 acres; but no attempt to reconcile this apparent discrepancy has been deemed allowable." And so with all the other counties. I think most people will be disposed to agree with me that this is not merely an "*apparent discrepancy,*" but a real difference, of no small magnitude and consequence; and that in official statements put forth by the authority of Government, and professing to convey to the world the latest, most accurate, and most trustworthy results of scientific investigation and statistical research, the public have a right to look for less loose and unsatisfactory data. It is to be supposed that the two varying computations were made on diverse principles and methods; but as to the why and the how, we have no further explanation than is given in the following paragraph of the preface to the volume:—"The area, as assigned to the several parishes in England in the Abstract of 1831, has been adopted in the present Abstract. Attempts have been made without success to obtain authentic information whereby the apparent inaccuracies which exist in this computation of the area might have been remedied; but nothing short of an actual survey would be calculated to give a more accurate result than has been here obtained by the labours of the late Mr. Rickman." I draw attention to this point, partly on account of its intrinsic importance (for in some cases the diversity is still wider than in that which I have particularised), but chiefly as an illustration of the difficulties which one encounters in the search after truth, on the very threshold of the inquiry. If, in a document such as I have quoted, men cannot find exact information, where are they to look for it?

Taking, however, the statement embodied in the census as our basis, and leaving its framers to account for this glaring anomaly as best they may, it would appear that, whilst upon the whole area of

England and Wales there are nearly 2¼ acres for every individual of the population, there are in the northern counties (containing a population of 809,000, and a superficies of from 3,300,000 to 3,400,000 acres) about 4 1-12th acres for every individual. In Durham the number of inhabitants to 100 statute acres may be taken at 46; in Northumberland, at 20; in Cumberland, at 18; and in Westmoreland, at 11 only. This is, of course, to be accounted for by the wide extent of unimprovable moorland (from which, indeed, one of them derives its name) included within their boundaries. Whilst, therefore, their population might at first sight seem placed in happier circumstances, with reference to the amount of land available for their support, than that of any other district in England, it should not be forgotten that this amplitude is rather apparent than real. Much of the soil possesses little or no capability for the sustentation of man, and the population derive scarcely any further advantage from this territorial latitude than that of having near their own doors large tracts in which the sportsman may take his pleasure, ranging uncontrolled over the dun heath, or in which the admirer of nature may court her in her sylvan solitudes. The geographical conformation and ethnological peculiarities of the northern parts of England closely resemble those of the southern districts of Scotland, with which, indeed, they were long conjoined under the same dominion. The region is alike a land of mountain and fell, with fertile dales that stretch by rushing streams, and that afford many a broad strath, or sloping inch, or well-sheltered nook at the break of the holm, the value of which, for pasture or tillage, the farmer well knows how to estimate. On the east it stretches to the sea in the wooded dells and open downs of Durham, broken up by the untiring activity of the miner, and launching on the sea, through a score of crowded havens, its stores of wealth snatched from the bowels of the earth. The Cheviots bound it to the north, with the wide tract of moorland which, in the later times of the middle ages, formed the boundary between the dominions of the English and Scottish crowns; but from the Tweed to the Tees the plough, the axe, and the mattock rest not, and the land is vocal with the sounds of industry. In the west, from merry Carlisle to royal Lancaster, there is less of busy movement and enterprise, except along the course of the Solway; but here the lakes and streams and mountains combine, in shapes and groups of unsurpassed variety and beauty, to form the most picturesque portion of England. The territory that stretches from the slowly rolling Humber to the winding Forth is peopled by men for the most part of Scandinavian extraction—the children of indomitable Northmen, in whom the blood of their ancestors yet runs strong; a hardy, enduring, stubborn race, accustomed beyond any other natives of the British territory to struggle with the elements, and to extort a subsistence more or less abundant from the niggard bounty of nature. The popular tongue still bespeaks its origin more strongly than all the testimonies of ancient chroniclers; numberless words are still in use which have long perished from the southern speech of England—or which, perhaps, never had existence in it—but which a kindred race who dwell in the great Northern Peninsula, and amongst the islands of the Baltic, would be at no loss to interpret. Of the romance with which mediæval reminiscences invest the country and its inhabitants, I need say little. It is the true heroic ground of England: many are its battle-fields, and many the tales and songs of old times with which the peasantry cheer their winter firesides. Northallerton, Neville's Cross, and Otterburn, with twenty other fields less renowned, are still peopled by the imagination with the shapes of skilled captains of the host, bold champions, and steel-clad warriors. The names of Douglas and Percy here at least retain their charm. "In the merry old times of our ancestors, when the Saxons and the Danes ruled here," Danish princes of Northumbria, at the bidding of Alfred, endowed St. Cuthbert with his ample patrimony; and the territory formed a principality, independent in all but name, down to, nay beyond, the coming of the Normans. For years its inhabitants opposed a stern and pertinacious, though fruitless resistance to the shock of the robber chivalry of William the Conqueror, and much of the best blood of the invaders was shed at the terrible sieges of York and Durham. In more than one family of the northern gentry, some of its earliest ancestors are thus honourably commemorated in the genealogical table, "*Cæsus in prælio contra Gulielmum Ducem, ex parte Regis Haroldi.*" The Conqueror's host encountered the army of the Scots, and defeated the Saxons under King Malcolm and Prince Edgar, on the Northumbrian border, at Stanemoor, in Westmoreland—where a pillar was raised by way of solemn demarcation of the territories of the two crowns, the limits remaining the same for a century or more afterwards.

The four northern counties, and the larger portion of Yorkshire (despite the assertion of Mr. Rickman, which induced the Census Commissioners to believe that the boundaries of English counties have remained unchanged since the time of the Conquest), are not included in the survey of Doomsday. On the western coast the Celtic element enters largely into the composition of the blood of the race, and is even probably predominant. There is no evidence to show that the counties of Lancaster, Cumberland, and Westmoreland, were ever incorporated in the kingdoms of Northumbria or Mercia, though they occasionally acknowledged a vassalage which they were ever ready to throw off at the dictate of convenience or caprice. At Carlisle, the princes of the ancient Britons kept their court in such regal state as the rudeness and imperfect civilization of the age permitted; yet those times were not altogether barbarous, since they furnished apostles and martyrs of the Christian faith to the benighted Pagans of the East and South—of the West, too, I might add, since St. Patrick, the apostle of Ireland, was a Briton of Strath-Clyde, and the name of Kilpatrick remains to indicate the seat of his ministrations and his probable birthplace. The sway of those British potentates stretched to Al-Clyde on the one hand, and (through Cheshire) extended to Wales on the other. Celtic bards chanted their power and heroism; Merlin and Thaliessin, twin peers of Cymric song, adorned their palaces, and flourished under royal patronage. Such was the state of this tract of country during the Heptarchy, and in the later times of the Saxon monarchy; whilst, down to a far more recent period of the middle ages, we know that Galloway, and perhaps Cumberland (*lit.* the land of the Kymri) for some time continued separate principalities, and in some parts of the south-west of Scotland, a Celtic dialect continued to be spoken until the time of the Reformation.

I have offered this brief retrospect of some of the least known portions of British history, because we cannot reason with confidence as to the character and condition of a people, unless we have ascertained something of their origin, and are acquainted with their historical antecedents. I do not mean to pretend that original characteristics which have so often passed through the crucible of time and change in the mutations and revolutions of ages, subsist in their pristine vigour at the present day; in many cases their influence may be faint, and hardly, or not at all, appreciable; but still we must search in the annals of former times to obtain a true explanation of many social or moral phenomena now observable amongst a population made up of so many heterogeneous elements. I am even disposed to think that a perfect system of educational culture should vary with the generic or national peculiarities of those who are to be its subjects; and certainly I cannot sympathise with those who would crush all provincial character and every local peculiarity under the iron or leaden sceptre of centralization. Amongst the agricultural labouring population of this part of England, I believe, from all I have observed and heard, that the standard of comfort is considerably higher, and the means of enjoyment less stinted, than in most parts of the south and west. I know not to what cause this circumstance can be ascribed with any degree of plausibility, if the energetic, pertinacious, and determined character which they have inherited from their origin, and by which they have been distinguished almost since the first settlement of the country, is to count for nothing. They are a resolute, hard-headed, and above all, an independent set of men, who will not be trodden upon, and whom it is not easy to trick out of their rights. A thrifty, frugal, and industrious people, too; not given to squandering or junketing, and who can make little go far at need.

The great secret of knowing how to make both ends meet, however, is not more easy (nor perhaps so easy) of discovery in this than in other districts of England. A climate, raw, moist, and cold, beyond that of the south—and a soil poor and wet, though light and friable in its better aspect—oppose obstacles to the agriculturist which can be surmounted only (and as yet they are but very partially surmounted) by increased care and skill, by the attentive application of science, and by the liberal but judicious employment of capital. The state of agriculture, and of those labourers who depend upon it for subsistence, varies considerably—governed as it must be by the nature of the soil and the condition of the vicinity, the extent of farms, the greater or less opulence of the proprietors and tenantry, and the more or less perfect modes of culture pursued in different localities. These variations are generally observable between different counties, though sometimes subsisting in equal breadth and distinctness within the limits of the same county. Nowhere, indeed, can it be said, that agriculture has approached perfection. In some localities it is in a backward and unprosperous state; in all much remains to be done to make it not only what it should be, but what it easily might be. The general character of northern, as distinguished from southern agriculture, may, however, be pronounced good. The fields are invariably cleaner, freer from weeds and stones, and better drained; no space is lost, no sun and air are excluded by a thicket or hedge-row. The fences, in the pastoral districts, are often of rough stone or paling; but though more generally the ordinary thorn fence is seen, it is always confined to the smallest possible proportions. There are some parts of our southern and western counties in which I do not hesitate, from my own observation, to pronounce the state of agriculture behind that of Italy, or even that of France—not to mention Belgium. No such reproach, however, can in any instance be cast upon that of the north. It is true that the march of improvement often lingers, from the limited means within the command of the cultivator. But resistance to improvement, as innovation, or on the ground of mere aversion to change, is unknown in the North; and everywhere a disposition is evinced to make the most of existing facilities, and, where practicable, to go ahead. Some parts of Northumberland, and especially the more northerly districts of Berwick, Glendale, Belford, and others, have been long renowned, and with justice, for high farming and advanced science. In this county farms are generally large, and the farming business is in the hands of men of considerable capital; in Durham, large farms are comparatively rare—they never, I believe, exceed five hundred acres. It is in the way of drainage, I should say, that most still remains to be done in Durham—though I have observed that much is doing, and I would not be thought to imply that this point is neglected. There are few grazing farms, except in the western or upper district of the county, of which I shall speak by-and-by. On the whole, though Durham can hardly boast that it equals its northern neighbours in the introduction and prompt employment of scientific methods, its farmers have no reason to be ashamed of the assiduity and practical skill with which they follow out their methods, nor of the disposition which I believe generally prevails amongst them to live and let live, and to deal liberally with those in their employment. This disposition, however, I am bound to add, appears lately to have undergone some diminution. Under cover of the outcry raised as to the low prices of agricultural produce, advantage has been taken in some cases, in the southern and south-eastern districts, to effect—and still more frequently to attempt—a reduction of the wages of labour. I shall speak more fully of this hereafter; at present I wish to indicate the existence of systems of tenure peculiar to this county, and which interpose serious obstacles to the amelioration and perfection of agriculture. I allude to the leasehold tenure of lands held under the Dean and Chapter of Durham, which constitute no inconsiderable portion of the soil of the county. I am informed that these leases are for very short terms, generally only for seven years, renewable upon one year's fine. No security can be felt by the tenant under such a system, and instances have even been mentioned to me in which parties who had laid out money in improvements have found their situation very materially changed for the worse, in consequence of a greatly increased rent being exacted from them. On the large properties of Lord Londonderry, the Duke of Cleveland, the Earl of Durham, Lord Ravensworth, and others, the tenant-at-will system for the most part prevails. On the Seaham estates, about Stockton, some of the farmers have been encouraged to make considerable outlay under the able management to which they are entrusted; in other cases the farms are generally too small (no doubt partly in consequence of the land being so much broken up by collieries and mines) to enable agriculture to be pursued on such a scale as we often see it when the liberality of the outlay of capital is commensurate with the extent of the holding.

Generally, it is to be remarked that agriculture in the North is supported by, and leans upon, a vigorous and flourishing manufacturing industry. Large towns—for such may Sunderland, Shields, Newcastle, and Carlisle be called, though inferior in size to the growths of the factory system—are by no means rare; smaller towns, of from 10,000 to 15,000 inhabitants, such as Durham, Darlington, Berwick, Whitehaven, and Stockton, are still more common; whilst of places under 10,000, though still of some size and consequence, such as Hartlepool, Bishop's Auckland, Barnard Castle, Morpeth, and Alnwick, the number is considerable. In the sea-ports all the branches of trade connected with navigation—such as ship-building and carpentry, rope-making, sail-making, iron-works for the manufacture of chain cables, anchors, and other ship's furniture—are pursued on an extensive scale, and generally with adequate success. Besides these, some branch of manufactures is to be found established in almost every town. Thus, at Durham there are carpet-weaving and paper-making; at Barnard Castle, carpet-weaving, shoe-thread spinning, and flax-dressing; at Darlington, wool-combing and flax-spinning. Machine-making is followed in more towns than one—especially the construction of railway engines; for it is one of the peculiarities of Durham, that it contains more railways than any other county in England—though by this time Lancashire must be running it hard. Another branch of industry pursued more largely in Durham than anywhere else, is the manufacture of coke for railways, for which the abundant supply of coal, and the ready means of transport, present unequalled facilities. At Newcastle and Gateshead there are glass-houses and potteries, chemical and alkali works, manufactories of fire-bricks and grindstones, &c. At Shields, there are various establishments of the same class; the alkali works here employ 800 labourers, furnace-men, and mechanics, whose wages are 12s. 6d., 18s., and 22s. 6d. a week. At Tynemouth there are iron, glass, copperas, alkali, brick and tile, linseed-oil, and salt works. All these branches of industry were, a few months back, in a state of great depression; and numbers of men were unemployed, or only partially employed. They have now recovered; the men being almost all at full work and in receipt of good wages. The business of retail traders, however, and some branches of manufacture, continue to suffer partially from the depression which still affects the coal trade. In the western part of the northern district, the movement of industry is less varied and active, though far from languid or life-less. Whitehaven, at the extreme north, and Ulverston in the south, are the two chief centres of manufactures. At the former place there are sail-cloth weaving and flax-spinning, besides other employments connected with the shipping, coal, and iron trades; at the latter there are cotton, flax, and saw mills, iron mines, slate quarries, copper mines, and smelting furnaces. I have been thus particular in enumerating these, because it is necessary to look at the condition of the whole industry of a district in order to arrive at a just opinion as to the state of any of its great divisions. It is vain to suppose that the condition of agriculture and agriculturists will not be materially influenced by that of manufacturing enterprise. It is the money amassed in trade, and the foreign and domestic commerce which manufactures call into action, that give agriculture the sharpest stimulus for exertion. Again, it is evidently a fortunate circumstance for the farm-labourer—should hard times, slack employment, or insufficient wages overtake him in his original occupation—to be able to betake himself to a large town, to carry his labour into its busy marts, and to obtain some employment where practised skill is not required. To what but to the absence of such facilities are we to attribute that hopeless prostration and despair which palsies the unfortunate labourer in less advantageously situated districts? Agriculture, again, is often pursued, though on a small scale, in combination with other employments, in counties noted for the vigour of their industrial operations, by the manufacturer, the professional man, the tradesman, the innkeeper. This affords a larger number of openings for the labourer, and must evidently have an essential influence on his general condition. With the views above stated, it may be well, before proceeding further, to consider more minutely the proportion of persons engaged in agriculture to those engaged in trade, commerce, and manufactures, within the limits of the northern counties—and also to glance briefly at some very interesting general considerations which connect themselves with this topic.

By the last census the total number of persons, young and old, of both sexes, throughout England and Wales, engaged in trade, commerce, and manufactures, was 2,619,206—engaged in agriculture, 1,261,448. Excluding commerce and trade, and looking separately at the numbers engaged in manufactures, we find that they were 1,140,906. The proportion of persons engaged in trade, commerce, and manufactures, to persons engaged in all other occupations, was 40 per cent.—that of persons engaged in agriculture was 19 per cent. The persons engaged in trade, commerce, and manufactures, throughout the four northern counties, were 116,301—the agricultur- ists, 53,878; the proportions to all other occupations therein being, for trade, commerce, and manufactures, 36 per cent.—for agriculture, 18 per cent. The mass of the remaining population was composed of those coming under the somewhat vague head of "labourers," which includes all those working in mines of coal or metal. In Durham the proportion of these latter to the whole occupations is not less than 22 per cent.; in Northumberland, it is 15 per cent. The comparative numbers and proportions of different occupations vary considerably in the several counties, as will appear on analysis. Durham, by far the most thickly peopled of them all, contains a population of 324,284, on an area of 679,530 acres; 45,179 persons are engaged in trade, commerce, and manufactures; 14,362 in agriculture. In this county the disproportion between those two great divisions is greatest, the relative per centage on the total occupations being 37 and 11; whilst throughout England and Wales, as will be recollected, they are as 40 and 19. Of persons engaged in trade, &c., in this county, 33,691 were males of twenty years and upwards; 7,815 males under twenty; 3,058 females of twenty years and upwards; 615 under twenty. Of persons engaged in agriculture, 11,850 were males of twenty years and upwards; 1,284 under twenty; 954 females of twenty years and upwards; 274 under twenty. I may observe in passing, however, that the numbers of females engaged in agriculture are to be understood only of those permanently employed as farm-servants and labourers; there being necessarily regular employment for but few women in this branch of industry, and the number of those who obtain temporary employment in the course of the year being notoriously much larger, though probably nowhere exactly ascertained.   To proceed, Northumberland contains a population of 250,278, on an area of 1,165,430 acres—37,298 persons being engaged in trade, commerce, and manufactures—17,339 in agriculture; the relative per centages on the total occupations are 37 and 17.   Of persons engaged in trade, &c., there were 27,451 males of twenty years of age and upwards, 5,769 under twenty.   Of persons engaged in agriculture, there were 14,036 males of twenty years and upwards, 1,900 under twenty; 1,113 females of twenty and upwards, 290 under twenty.   Cumberland contains a population of 178,038 on an area of 969,490 acres; of these 26,053 were persons engaged in trade, commerce, and manufactures, 15,611 in agriculture—the relative per centages on the total occupations being 36 and 21, showing a greater approximation to equality of proportion than either of the two former cases. Of the persons engaged in trade, &c., 16,969 were males of twenty and upwards, 3,659 under twenty; 4,111 were females of twenty and upwards, 1,314 under twenty.   Of those engaged in agriculture, 12,613 were males of twenty and upwards, 1,121 under twenty; 1,519 were females of twenty and upwards, 358 under twenty. Westmoreland, the last on our list, and the most thinly peopled of all, is also one of the smallest of the English counties; there being only three—Rutland, Huntingdon, and Middlesex—of which the superficies is less. It contains a population of only 56,454 souls, on an area of 485,990 acres; of these 7,771 persons were engaged in trade, commerce and manufactures, 6,566 in agriculture; the relative per centages to the total occupations being 32 and 27, showing the nearest approximation to equality of all the cases passed under review. The North Riding of Yorkshire, it may be added, shows a similar approximation, the per centages being 29 and 34; whilst the East Riding of Yorkshire, and the counties of Dorset and Bucks, exhibit still closer approaches to equality of proportion in this respect. Of persons engaged in trade, &c., in Westmoreland, 5,259 were males of twenty and upwards, 1,152 under twenty; 1,067 females of twenty and upwards, 293 under twenty. Of those engaged in agriculture 5,481 were males of twenty and upwards, 728 under twenty; 297 were females of twenty and upwards, 60 under twenty.

For the sake of showing in a more general point of view the relative distribution of employment to various ages and sexes, furnished by the two great divisions of occupation, it may be advisable to advert to another topic appearing on the face of the returns. Of the

924,096 persons engaged throughout England and Wales in manufactures alone (excluding trade and commerce), 479,774 were males of twenty and upwards, 130,443 males under twenty; 191,968 were females of twenty and upwards, 121,911 females under twenty. Of the 1,269,941 persons engaged in agriculture, 1,049,255 were males of twenty and upwards, 162,378 males under twenty; 48,949 were females of twenty and upwards, 9,359 under twenty. With reference to the latter numbers, the remark introduced above relative to the employment of females in agriculture should be borne in mind.

The disproportion at present existing between the sexes in the population of this country is well known, but it seems worthy of remark that this is not caused by a corresponding disproportion in the births, as will appear by a short statement of figures. Of the 15,906,741 persons making up the population of England and Wales at the last census, 7,771,094 were male, and 8,135,647 female—the latter thus exceeding the former by nearly 400,000. But male births are more numerous than those of females. In the seven years, 1839-45, there were 1,863,892 males, and 1,772,491 females, born alive—the proportion in the whole country being nearly 20 boys to 19 girls. The proportion of boys born is greatest (1.0617 to 1.000) in the northern division, least (1.0455 to 1.000) in the south midland division. It becomes, then, an interesting subject of inquiry, to what this existing disproportion in the number of the sexes is to be ascribed. In some degree, no doubt, to the larger number of males who emigrate, but in a much greater degree, I am inclined to think, to the larger mortality amongst male children. The extent of this will be evident from looking at the comparative number of male and female deaths, in the years 1838-44. In that period the male deaths under one year ranged from 41,081 to 45,183; the female deaths under one year, only from 32,535 to 34,903; the male deaths under five years, from 70,990 to 77,988; the female deaths under five years, from 61,947 to 67,332; the male deaths at five years, from 8,306 to 10,199; the female deaths at five years, from 7,832 to 10,008; the male deaths at ten, from 4,278 to 4,722; the female deaths at ten, from 4,382 to 5,044, when the balance of mortality inclines against the female side. This is a curious branch of inquiry, which, however, rather falls within the province of the medical statist and the actuary.

In regard to the general mortality of its inhabitants, I find that the northern division is as favourably situated as most other districts of England. The general mortality of England (exclusively of Wales) taking the mean of the years 1838-45, is 2.176 per cent.—or, in every year, there are 46 persons living to one who dies. The greatest mortality is in the northern district, including Cheshire and Lancashire, where it is at the rate of 2.591 per cent.—or there are 39 persons living for one who dies every year. In the metropolis it is 2.527—or there are 40 living for one dying; in Yorkshire the rate is 2.177—or there are 46 living for one dying. In the northern district, again, the rate of mortality is 2.087—or there are 48 persons living for one dying. The healthiest districts of all are the Welsh, south-western, and south-eastern. In the latter the rate of mortality is 1.901—or there are 53 persons living for one dying; a considerable superiority as compared with the general rate of England.

This seems the proper place to call attention to another point, established by the returns issued from the office of the Registrar-general of Births, Deaths, and Marriages, and which throws a curious and significant light on the distribution of education through the different districts of England, and amongst the various classes of its population. In the years 1839-45, the number of marriages ranged from 118,825 to 143,743. In each of these years a formidable proportion of persons, varying from 40 to 42 per cent., signed the marriage register with marks—thus clearly evincing (in the vast majority of cases, it may at least be assumed) their inability to write. Thus, in 1839, out of 242,000 persons married, 40,767 men, and 59,949 women—in all fully 100,000 persons—signed with marks; in 1845, out of 247,000 persons married, 47,665 men, and 71,229 women—in all nearly 119,000 persons—signed with marks. It is well worth while to advert to the proportions of persons signing with marks in some of the different districts into which England, for the purposes of eleemosynary, educational, and registrational inspection and regulation, is divided. In the metropolis, for the years 1839-45, the proportion of men signing with marks ranges from 11 to 12 per cent.; that of women signing with marks from 28 to 24,—the mean proportion for all England during these seven years, being, of men 32.9, or nearly 33 per cent., and of women 49.2, or more than 49 per cent. In the south-eastern division (Surrey, Kent, Sussex, Hants, Berks) the mean proportion for the same seven years was, of men 32.1 per cent., of women 39.4 per cent. In the south midland division (including Middlesex, Hertfordshire, Buckinghamshire, Oxfordshire, Northamptonshire, Huntingdonshire, Bedfordshire, and Cambridgeshire) the mean proportion of those signing with marks is, of men 42.4, or nearly 42½ per cent.—of women 52 per cent. In the eastern division (embracing Essex, Suffolk, and Norfolk) the mean proportion is, of men 45.9, or nearly 46 per cent.—of women 51.6, or more than 51½ per cent. In the three latter districts, the agricultural population greatly preponderates. In the western district, where the population is agricultural and manufacturing, mixed in pretty nearly equal proportions (it embraces Gloucester, Hereford, Shropshire, Worcestershire, Staffordshire, and Warwickshire), the mean proportion is, of men 37.9, or nearly 38 per cent.; of women 51.9, or nearly 52 per cent. In the north-western district, comprehending Lancashire and Cheshire, the great seats of our manufactures, the mean proportion of men signing with marks is 38.7—of women 65.9, or nearly 66 per cent. The ignorance of Wales is yet more marked. But by far the most respectable figure of all is made by the northern division (comprising the four counties that form the immediate subject of our consideration), in which the mean proportion of men signing with marks is only 21.1 per cent., and of women only 41.6 per cent. These statistics of ignorance, fearful in one light, are very instructive in another. They teach us to estimate at its true value the pretensions to exclusive or special enlightenment occasionally put forward by those who assume to speak on behalf of a particular section of our population. Profound darkness is not always the lot of those who inhabit rural districts—nor is all illumination confined to great towns, or rather to large agglomerations of houses. I leave to others the duty of drawing the inferences which obviously present themselves to the mind on considering these tell-tale figures. I must hasten onwards with my appointed task.

The mean proportion per cent. of persons married under 21 years of age is less in the northern districts than in any other division, the metropolitan and Welsh excepted. In the northern it is 7.7, in the north-western 8.7, in the eastern 11.2, in Yorkshire 12.2, in the south-eastern 8.6, in the western the same, in the south-midland 13.5—the mean for all England being 8.7. The proportion of illegitimate children is also less in the northern than in some divisions, though greater than in others. Over England and Wales the proportion is 6.7, in the northern 7.4, north-midland 7.7, north-western 8.8—whilst the Welsh and western districts are 6.8, and the south-western 5.7. This latter figure, by-the-bye, shows, that in spite of the inadequate house accommodation of the south-western peasantry, the restraints of morality have not lost their force amongst that portion of our population.

Illegitimate births, among the peasantry, are in almost all cases followed by the marriage of the parents.

I now proceed to give a succinct sketch of the agricultural relations of the four counties with which we are dealing—shunning, however, minute details for the present, in order that your readers may have it in their power to institute some comparison between the relative condition of each. First, with regard to the relative amount of land in each—cultivated—uncultivated, but improvable—and unimprovable. It is calculated that Durham, upon a superficies of nearly 680,000 acres (I take the estimate of Mr. Couling, civil engineer and surveyor, given some years back in evidence before a select committee of the House of Commons, appointed to inquire into the subject of emigration), contains about 500,000 cultivated—100,000 uncultivated, but improvable—and upwards of 79,000 unimprovable, lying chiefly in the western portion of the county. The proportion of cultivated (or enclosed) to waste or unenclosed land is thus seen to be as 5 to 1—to land which may be pronounced wholly unimprovable in the present state of our agricultural knowledge, as 5 to 0.8—and to both together, as 5 to 1.8. The only large enclosures now proceeding in this county are those of Cornsay Common, a tract of 611 acres, situated eight miles westward of the city, for which powers were obtained three years ago; and of Cockfield Fell, a tract of 573 acres, near Staindrop, in the southern and least thickly populated part of the county. Northumberland again, upon a superficies of 1,197,400 acres (that is, as estimated by Mr. Couling), contains 900,000 acres of cultivated or enclosed land—160,000 acres entirely uncultivated, but capable of cultivation—and 137,000 which may be deemed wholly unprofitable. The proportion of cultivated to uncultivated soil in Northumberland is thus shown to be as 9 to 1.6, or 1 3-5 (rather less than in the former case)—to unprofitable land as 9 to 1.4, or 1 2-5 nearly—and to both together as about 3 to 1, or considerably less than in the case of Durham. There appears to be but one large enclosure in progress in Northumberland, that of East Coamwood, containing 1,580 acres, which I have not yet had an opportunity of seeing. The act authorizing its enclosure is the 10 Vict., c. 25, passed two years ago. Cumberland, upon a superficies of 946,000 acres (as estimated by Mr. Couling), contains 670,000 cultivated acres, 150,000 uncultivated, and 126,000 unimprovable. The proportion of cultivated to uncultivated or unenclosed land in this case is thus seen to be (nearly) as 7 to 1½—to unprofitable land as 7 to 1¼—and to both together as about 7 to 2—something less than in the case of Northumberland, and very considerably less than in the case of Durham. In Cumberland there are several enclosures proceeding, some of them of considerable magnitude; by far the largest is that of Greyfell-common, containing 4,000 acres, powers for which were obtained two years ago. Those of smaller extent are Langwathby-moor, a tract of 507 acres, waste of a manor, in favour of which the Enclosure Commissioners reported in their fifth report, presented last session; Whitrigg-marsh, containing 272 acres, authorized by the act 10th Victoria, c. 25; Gamblesby-fell and Viol-moor, containing 1,268 acres, waste of a manor; Gamblesby and Biglands-common, 179 acres, waste of a manor; Talkin-fell, 1,700 acres, also described as waste of a manor (this does not appear to have been yet reported on); Ellenborough, 104 acres; Crosby and Birkby, 131 acres; Ponsonby and Calder, 200 acres, &c. The progress of enclosure appears more active in Cumberland than in any other part of the northern division. The last county on our list is Westmoreland, which, on a superficies of 488,000 acres, contains 180,000 cultivated—110,000 uncultivated, but supposed to be improvable—and 198,000 unprofitable. The proportion of enclosed and cultivated to waste but improvable land, is thus shown to be rather less than 2 to 1—to land believed altogether unprofitable nearly 1 to 1—and to both together nearly as 2 is to 3—showing by far the greatest proportion of waste and unimprovable land in any of the four counties. The enclosures proceeding, or recently effected here, are those of Sleddale Forest, containing 993 acres, authorized by the commissioners three years back; Asby Mask, containing 1,248 acres, waste of a manor; Smardale Fell, containing 643 acres, waste of a manor (in this township there are but 35 inhabitants, the farms being cultivated by the farmers and their families, with servants residing in their houses), authorized, as well as the preceding case, by the Act 11 and 12 Victoria, cap. 27; Newbiggin-moor, containing 500 acres, authorized by the Act 11 and 12 Victoria, cap. 109; the Low and High Intake, together 280 acres, authorized by the commissioners in 1847; Crosby Garrett, containing 434 acres, authorized by the commissioners in the course of last year; and Firbank Fells, containing 1,200 acres, authorized last session. The spirit of improvement appears thus to be active in Westmoreland, though the large proportion of land naturally valueless must restrict its sphere of operation within comparatively narrow limits.

With reference to the rate of increase of population in the four northern counties, as compared with each other and with that of England and Scotland respectively, some interesting particulars are to be noted, and may as well be mentioned at this stage of our progress. In the ten years included between the census of 1831 and that of 1841, the actual increase per cent., of the whole population of England and Wales, was 14.4; that of the population of Scotland was 10.7; that of the whole of Great Britain, 13.1; that of Westmoreland (the smallest county on our list) was only 2.5—being the smallest rate of increase of all the English counties, with the exception of Hereford, where the rate was 2.4; that of Cumberland was 4.9; that of Northumberland was 12.2, or not quite equal to the rate of general increase; that of Durham was 27.7—showing the largest increase within those ten years of any county in England, Monmouth alone excepted, where the increase was 36.9 per cent.; the increase of Lancashire, I may mention, for the sake of comparison, being 24.7—of Cheshire 18.3—and of Stafford 24.3. The very large increase of 27.7 in the case of Durham is, of course, to be set down to the account of persons immigrating to work at the mines—the natural increase for the same period being only 13.2—about the same rate as those of Bedford and Cornwall.

The general observations which suggest themselves under this head, as necessary to complete the sketch which I have attempted to draw, may be brought into a short compass. Beginning with Durham—the appearance which the soil and its cultivation present to the eye corresponds with the impression which the reader of the above statistical details would be likely to form from their consideration. There are fewer tracts of land of any considerable extent entirely uncultivated than in any of the other counties, and a smaller proportion (according to the size of the county, and the area of unreclaimable land that it comprises) very well cultivated. The strictly rural part of the population of Durham is comparatively small, since the inhabitants of the "pit villages," as they are commonly called, which are scattered over the greater portion of the county (many of them more like towns than villages) can scarcely be said to belong to it. Many of the farm labourers occasionally work at the coal pits, and the fluctuation of trade in the collieries has a tendency to cause an irregular demand for labour in agriculture. A considerable proportion of the men employed in agriculture are hired into the farm-houses by the year and half-year—in the former case generally as hinds (I shall consider this subject more fully hereafter). When the coal trade is depressed, and the pitmen have not employment for more than six, seven, or eight days in a fortnight, they often seek work upon the land, and glut the agricultural labour market; but as the regular pitmen are very inexpert, except in a few branches of farm labour, the countrymen have the advantage over them. In summer time the pitmen's wives are also employed a good deal in field labour. In Durham the accommodation for the labouring poor may be pronounced decidedly good—far superior to what appears to exist in some of the southern districts. A clay soil, but cold and wet, prevails in this country. Though some outlay of capital has already taken place, much more would be required in order to draw the greatest possible amount of advantage from a soil which is often of indifferent quality. I have already alluded to the obstacles to improvement which arise, whether from the fact of the tenants being very generally persons of scanty means, with small holdings—or from the peculiar tenure under which a considerable portion of the ground is held. In Northumberland the soil is generally a light friable loam, the farms large, with wealthy occupiers, who are in many cases disposed to a liberal outlay of capital; the crops are frequently luxuriant, the live stock abundant, and its quality excellent. This is particularly the case along the east coast, by Morpeth and Alnwick. To the south and west, in the neighbourhood of Rothbury, Bellingham, Hexham, and Haltwhistle, the land is chiefly in pasture, with extensive tracts of moorland, but the soil is capable of being much improved by thorough drainage and the use of artificial manure. Generally over the four counties the proportion of waste land in meadow and pasture, to land under the plough, considerably exceeds the average, which is three-fifths. The condition of the Northumbrian peasantry—or "bondagers," as they are otherwise termed—is one of great general comfort, though the cottage accommodation is inferior to that found in Durham. In Cumberland, the farms—though their size and destination vary with the nature of the district—generally consist of moderate holdings, the proportion of pasture to tillage being large. In many localities, as Carlisle, Bootle, and Penrith, agriculture is conducted on a liberal and advanced system, the farmers being in easy or affluent circumstances. Neither in this county nor in Westmoreland can the labouring population be said to be redundant; and employment, with fair wages, is to be had. But this is not the place to enter minutely on these topics, which must be postponed to another letter.

I have left myself but little space for treating of a very important subject, which cannot be left out of sight in any general description of the social condition of the northern counties—that of pauperism. On a future occasion I may go at greater length into it; but the working of the present poor-law, and the amount of poor receiving parochial relief at the most recent period for which any official returns have been received, will be best shown by the following table, which is entitled to the utmost reliance. It shows the population of Durham, Northumberland, Cumberland and Westmoreland, according to the census of 1841—the number of paupers in the workhouses of each county—the number and cost of out-door paupers (exclusive of lunatics in asylums), for the week ending the 9th of September last, and also for the corresponding week in 1847, and the comparative increase or decrease. No statement of the amount of in-door maintenance, I am informed, has been returned since the introduction of the new order of union accounts in March, 1848. The table has been framed with the view of showing the state of things in the last quarter, and the calculations are made from the tenth week, because in the last week of the quarter; the cost of lunatics in asylums is added by many unions to the usual out-door relief returns—in some instances more than doubling the week's expenditure, and thus leading, if adopted, to erroneous conclusions.

Counties.	Population in 1841.	Number of In-door Paupers relieved week ended on the 9th September, 1847.	Number of In-door Paupers relieved week ended on the 9th September, 1849.	Increase.	Decrease.	Number of Out-door Paupers relieved week ended on the 9th September, 1847.	Number of Out-door Paupers relieved week ended on the 9th September, 1849.	Increase.	Decrease.	Cost of Out-door Paupers week ended 9th September, 1847.	Cost of Out-door Paupers week ended 9th September, 1849.	Increase.	Decrease.
										£ s. d.	£ s. d.	£ s. d.	£ s. d.
Cumberland ..	177,912	1,206	1,154	...	52	7,112	7,061	...	51	496 0 0	452 14 0	...	43 6 0
Durham	325,997	905	1,072	167	...	15,464	16,824	1,360	...	1,105 0 0	1,126 11 9	21 11 9	...
Northumberland	265,988	1,226	1,242	16	...	14,156	15,395	1,239	...	1,042 0 0	1,132 12 1	90 12 1	...
Westmoreland .	56,469	333	362	29	...	2,044	2,619	575	...	169 10 1	183 5 10	13 15 9	...

From this table it appears that during the last quarter the proportion of persons in the receipt of parochial relief, out-door or in-door, to the entire population, was—in the county of Cumberland 1 in 22, in Durham 1 in 19, in Northumberland 1 in 16 nearly, and in Westmoreland 1 in 19 nearly. The inferences to which these data lead, as compared with the circumstances of other parts of England, will be considered in a future letter.

LABOUR AND THE POOR.

THE RURAL DISTRICTS.

[FROM OUR SPECIAL CORRESPONDENT.]

THE FOUR NORTHERN COUNTIES—DURHAM.

LETTER XXIV.

In my last letter I offered you a sketch of the social economy, internal relations, and industrial state of the four northern counties, with some remarks upon their historical conditions, and the foundations of their polity in the middle ages. In this letter I shall proceed, after brief preface, to consider at greater length the condition of the working classes in the county of Durham, and with especial reference to the question of wages.

"The bishoprick of Durham, or Duresme" (says Camden—still the best authority on British topography)—for so old writers denominate the County Palatine—"bordering upon the north side of Yorkshire, is shaped in fashion of a triangle, the utmost angle whereof is made up, toward the west, where the northern limit and the spring-head of Tees do meet. One of the sides, which lieth southward, is bounded in with the continued course of the river Tees running down along by it; the other, that looketh northward, is limited first with a short line from the utmost point to the river Derwent, then with Derwent itself, until it hath taken into it Chopwell, a little river, and afterward with the river Tyne. The sea-coast fashioneth out the base of the triangle which lieth eastward, and the German Ocean, with a mighty roaring and forcible violence beateth thereupon.

"On that part where it gathereth narrow to the western angle, the fields are naked and barrain, the woods very thin, the hills bare without grass, but not without mines of yron. As for the vallies, they are reasonably grassy, and that high ridge, which I termed the Apennine of England, cutteth in twain this angle. But on the east part, or base of the triangle, as also on both sides, the ground being well manured, is very fruitful, and the increase yeeldeth good recompence for the husbandman's toile; it is also well garnished with meddowes, pastures and corn-fields, beset everywhere with townes, and yeelding plenty of sea-coale, which, in many places we use for fewell." And herewith our great antiquary and topographer declares it to be his opinion that coal is nothing else but bitumen, or "a clammy kind of clay hardened with heat under the earth, and so throughly concocted; for it yeeldeth the smell of bitumen, and if water be sprinkled upon it, it burneth more vehemently, and the cleerer; but whether it may be quenched with oil, I have not yet tried."

"All this countrie (he proceeds), with other territories also thereto adjoining, the monasticall writers term the Land or Patrimonie of Saint Cuthbert. For so they called whatsoever belonged to the church of Durham, whereof St. Cuthbert was the patron; who, in the primitive state of the English Church, being Bishop of Lindesfarne, led all his life in such holinesse and so sincerely, that he was inrolled among the English saints. Our kinges also, and peeres of the realme, because they verily persuaded themselves that he was their Tutelar Saint and Protectour against the Scottes, went not only in pilgrimage with devotion to visite his bodie (which they beleeved to have continued still sound and incorrupt), but also gave very large possessions to this church, and endowed the same with many immunities. King Egfride bestowed upon Cuthbert himself, while he lived, great revenewes in the very citie of Yorke. King Alfred and Guthrun the Dane, whom he made Lieutenant of Northumberland, gave afterwards all the lands betweene the rivers Weare and Tyne unto Cuthbert, and to those who ministred in his church, to have and to hold for ever, as their rightfull possession (these be the very wordes in effect of an ancient booke), whence they might have sufficient maintenance to live upon, and not be pinched with poverty; over and besides, they ordained his church to be a safe sanctuarie for all fugitives, that whosoever for any cause fled unto his corps, should have peaceable being for thirty-seven daies, and the same liberty never for any occasion to be enfringed or denied."

The city of Durham, planted on a commanding eminence on the finely-wooded banks of the Wear, overlooks the country for miles around with the towers of its noble Minster, which affords, I may observe in passing, the single specimen of the pure early Norman, or, more properly speaking, Byzantine style, which we possess amongst our English cathedrals. Durham (a corruption of the Saxon name Dunholm, signifying "a dark wooded height," which perfectly describes the spot), was founded in the year of grace 995, and in the reign of Ethelred, by Aldune, Bishop of Lindisfarne and a colony of monks, driven from their insular seat by an incursion of the northern

Pagans, at the close of those wanderings which have been commemorated by the muse of the great minstrel, who sings—

> "How, when the rude Dane burned their pile,
> The monks fled forth from Holy Isle;
> O'er northern mountain, marsh, and moor,
> From sea to sea, from shore to shore,
> Seven years St. Cuthbert's corpse they bore."

It now contains a population of 15,000 souls, with some manufacturing establishments of moderate extent. It is the centre of the northern and midland agricultural districts of the county, as Darlington is of the southern, and Stockton of the eastern. The towns of the county, I may observe, being in almost every case situated on the banks of rivers or on the sea, are very favourably situated for purposes of drainage, and, except in the sea-ports, the filth natural to which is allowed to accumulate through mere negligence and slothfulness, no complaint is to be made of the arrangements in this respect. In spite of the plenty of streams, however, they are very inadequately supplied with that greatest necessary of life, health, and cleanliness—water. That of the rivers is not available to any great extent for domestic purposes; for the Tyne, the Wear, and the Tees are generally turbid currents, discoloured by the particles worn from the red clay soils through which they pass; whilst the water of the springs and draw-wells, at this season of the year at least, has a villanous earthy smack of the soil, muddy as it is, and saturated with rain. So true is it that, in respect of the commodities and appurtenances of civilization, our urban economy is still in its infancy, despite our experiences of a thousand years. And this reminds me of another particular, which ought not to be passed over—I mean the miry state of the streets, even in our small towns, and the world of petty misery and discomfort thereby occasioned to all whose necessities or unfortunate pursuits of business oblige them to be foot passengers. A few showers cover causeway and pavement alike with a coating of dirt six inches thick, and leave them in a plight little better than the high roads, which, neglected as they have been since the establishment of the railway system, are now reduced by two or three days' rain to the consistency of a puddle. Scavengers you never see at work by any chance, nor can it be pretended that the streets are cleaned during the night, for the state in which you find them by morning too surely demonstrates the vanity of this supposition. Considering the number of poor with little or no regular employment, who are ever to be found hanging about, one would think that a better purpose than that of street cleaning, for which to apply their labour, could not be found or devised. Yet if you ask in the streets of a busy town, why there are any able-bodied poor idle and hungry, you will be told that it is because there is no work for them. Making sweet the thoroughfares would find many an outcast in useful employment for more than half the year round, with such a climate as ours. A few years ago, Englishmen used to pique themselves on a character for cleanliness; but if no measures are taken to remedy the too apparent evils which affront us at every step, we shall establish our unquestioned pre-eminence for dirt over every other European nation. If parsimony is the true objection, might it not be suggested to boards of guardians and commissioners for paving, lighting, and cleansing, that the outlay of a few pounds, for health and cleanliness' sake, would be true economy?

In the county of Durham there were by the last census rather more than 10,000 agricultural labourers, male and female, of all ages; 7,886 of these were males of twenty and upwards; 1,203 were males under twenty. The former, supposing nine-tenths of them to be married, would of course represent a population of about 28,000. There are three classes of agricultural labourers in this county, the case of each of which I shall now proceed to lay before you—the hind, the farm servant, and the ordinary labourer by the day or the week, or, as he is expressively called here, the *daytillman.* I put aside women, who, when regularly employed, are almost always inmates of the farmhouse, their occupation partaking equally of the nature of the domestic at-tendant and the farm servant, and boys—as the instances of their working independently apart from the families of husbands or fathers are extremely rare. Confining myself, then, for the present, to male la-bourers, I begin with the hind. He is the farmer's right-hand-man of all-work, acting also as a man of authority among the labourers. He is almost always married, with a family generally of moderate numbers, for Scottish household maxims are as rife here as north of the Tweed. His cottage, which he holds rent-free, is either near the grange, or forms a portion of the garth or farm-inclosure (*gard* is a Norse word, still existing among us in the forms of *garth* and *yard,* and connec-ted also with *gird*). There is no precise limitation of his hours of la-bour, for he is understood to be ever ready at the farmer's behest, and works occasionally both late and early, tending the cattle at even and night, and repairing to the threshing-floor or the mill with lanthorn alight in the early winter's morning. Hence he is occasionally termed a *bondager*, being as it were the farmer's bondman; though, if we go back to Saxon times, we shall find that *bond* or bondager truly signifies a free peasant or yeoman, but the word speedily lost its proper sense, and changed its meaning when the Saxons were themselves reduced into bondage, and even Esau became a stranger in the tents of Isaac. The hind, however, bears no serf's heart in his breast; intelligent and simply educated, I have spoken with many of this class, and have learned to estimate their admirable qualities aright, and to know that "the might which slumbers in a peasant's arm" may often be equalled by his natural nobility of soul. No little tyrant of his fields would have a chance with him; with a hay-bill in his hand (a weapon of formidable aspect, used for cutting hay from the stack), you might take him for the master himself. The hind's wages, as I have learned from themselves, are from 10s. to 12s. a week; he is entitled, besides a cottage rent-free, to other "privileges," as they are styled, which generally consist of twenty bushels of potatoes in a year, and his fuel carted; if he gets the milk and butter of one cow for himself and family, this is reckoned at 4s. weekly. This at first struck me as being an exorbitant estimate of its money value, and I remarked the circumstance to one of them employed on a farm near Middleton-one-row. He answered that he had tried both ways, the full money wages, or the reduced standard and the cow's milk, and seemed to think there was no appreciable difference. His own wages, he said, were 12s. a week; he had a wife and five children. The hind's wife and children are, of course, employed in preference to any others; indeed some farmers (and mostly all in Northumberland) will not hire a hind except on the express stipulation that his wife shall be ready to do farm work in summer and harvest time. This, of course, enables him to look with certainty to a sometimes not inconsiderable addition to his earnings. The hind may be paid by the week, but the agreement is generally by the year, though sometimes by the half-year. The hind's cottage, from its locality, is sometimes without a garden, for which he has less occasion than other labourers. On a farm of two hundred acres there are generally two hinds, but, of course, other labour is required. This class of labourers, except when they forfeit position and character by misconduct, are rarely in distressed circumstances; yet the last few years have somewhat modified their status, and the new law of settlement, introduced by the passing of the Poor Removal Act, which confers irremovability after five years' residence, has seriously affected their interests in some instances. To evade the operation of the law, and obviate the possibility of the hind ever acquiring a chance of settlement by residence, some farmers will not keep them longer than four years, at the utmost, and have new hinds every year or two. This course shows but a mean spirit, and I should hope is not often taken by respectable farmers.

The denomination of farm servant is applied to unmarried men, oftenest youths, who are lodged and boarded at the farm, and hired by the year. The wages of adults in this situation vary from ten to eighteen, or even twenty pounds, according to the work of the workman, and the duties required of him; this year, however, has left few at the latter standards, and a common rate even for smart hands is £14. Boys and very young lads obtain only their clothes, or a sum of £3 or £4, in addition to their board. The condition of this class of labourers, of course, depends in a great measure on the character and disposition of their employer; in a well-regulated family, and under a well-principled master, they are placed in the situation most desirable for their own interests, and a farmer has it in his power to be a real benefactor to them. Farmers of deficient means and capital, however, are shirking the employment of this class of men, and engaging mere boys and girls in their stead. The wages of a good woman-servant in a farm-house are from £8 to £12. They are, I believe, always the daughters of labourers or small farmers.

I now come to the *daytillman,* or ordinary day-labourer, the most numerous class of all, and, it must be added, the most precariously situated. It is here where the shoe really pinches; not but that a large proportion, I may say the largest proportion, are comfortably enough situated, but it is a class which includes all, from the man in receipt of regular wages at 12s. 6d. a week, to him whose employment is the most temporary or uncertain. The wages of independent labourers, as this class is styled, are 2s. 6d. per day; nominally they are 12s. or 12s. 6d. a week, and this rate has often been, and at this moment no doubt is paid, but the tendency of the times is to reduction, and in most districts the farmers have succeeded within the last year or two in establishing rates of 11s., 10s., nay, 9s. or 8s. a week, according to circumstances, when the understanding is that the party hired is to remain a long period. Still at such rates, as I shall presently show, a man may maintain himself and a wife and moderate family in decency or comfort—though with the lowest I have named it is a close shave indeed in some cases. The question of wages, instead of being a simple one, as is often supposed, and as some foolish doctors of political economy have endeavoured to inculcate, is really one of the most complex imaginable, and is modified by a hundred different conditions. Perhaps I shall best illustrate the subject by taking particular instances which have presented themselves in the course of my investigations, and which may be set down as the types of so many different classes, there being nothing extraordinary or anomalous in the circumstances. I shall give you the details, and leave you to draw your own inferences.

Case 1, which I shall mention, was that of a day-labourer, past the middle age of life, married, but with his children provided for in various ways. On inquiry I found that he was originally from Essex, but had been resident in the county of Durham for sixteen years. Here I may mention a fact with which any one visiting the north of England must be struck, but which, in fact, corresponds exactly with the conclusions to be drawn from the statistics of the country in reference to population, as fully explained in my last letter. Fully the half, I should say, of the labouring people with whom you converse are merely denizens, not natives, of the locality, having immigrated into it in search of employment; very frequently they will tell you that they are strangers in the neighbourhood, having only been there a few weeks or months. This is the case more or less all over England, for the habits of our labouring population are no longer stationary, but migratory—nowhere, however, so much so as in the north. I found this individual at work not far from the bank of the Tees, rather more than a mile from the little town of Yarm, on the borders of Yorkshire; he had worked as a day-labourer in all the usual capacities, on and off farms, and was then employed in excavating the foundations of a house. The wages he received were 15s. a week (or at the rate of 2s. 6d. a day), and in his then position he had, of course, no other aids or appliances to look to. He was an intelligent man, more so than the generality of his class; he was well acquainted with the provisions of the new law of settlement, with the operations of the railways (perhaps he had been a "navvy," but I forgot to ask him), and their influence on the labour market. He was a reader also of newspapers, and referred to an account he had seen of the condition of labourers in the southern districts, which had no doubt originally appeared in *The Morning Chronicle.* He seemed to think the lot of men who hardly tasted meat from one year's end to the other a very pitiable one, and assured me that he had it every day. In this neighbourhood there has been ample employment for some time back, on the Leeds, Thirsk, and Hartlepool Railway, which passes by the town; the viaducts at this spot are of beautiful construction, and models of brickwork. At Yarm there is also a paper-mill, and some minor establishments of manufactures of flax and wool.

Case 2 was that of a *daytillman* employed on a farm in the same neighbourhood. He was at the time at work on *"gripping,"* as surface-drainage is here commonly termed, and worked by piece-work. He was paid 1½d. a rood, and made from 12s. to 13s. a week. Thorough drainage he considered less profitable and too heavy work; he also was an elderly man, married, but his children were "off his hands." He made the same amount at hedging or ditching. The piece system, I should say, is fully as general in Durham as the ordinary plan of paying fixed wages. It has the advantage of effectually preventing anything like unfair play on either side. The labourer cannot idle away his time or shirk work; the farmer cannot show undue preference to one man over another. I should mention here, that the practice prevailing in the south, of systematically giving higher wages to men who have families, and the manifold discontents and heartburnings thus occasioned are utterly unknown in any part of the north with which I am acquainted. So, also, as regards the truck system, which has no existence so far as agricultural labourers are concerned. With pitmen I have nothing to do. This man was also enabled to have meat regularly.

Case 3 was that of a young farm-servant, unmarried, one of the class described above. His wages were sixteen guineas, but he thought himself worth eighteen, and wished me much to engage him at that rate.

Case 4 was that of a farm-labourer in regular employment at 11s. a week. A wife and three children; one child earning 2s. a week nearly all the year round; the wife and another child employed in summer and harvest-time, the former occasionally making 3s. or 4s. a week.

Case 5 is that of an aged couple, whose working days were now past; the man, who is so weak-sighted as to be nearly blind, had been employed regularly as a hind, or daytillman, at 12s. and 13s. a week, assisted, of course, by his wife's earnings. They had, he told me, an allowance of 6s. a week from the parish; this seemed unusually large, but I could discover no particular reason for it. They occupied a cottage, of which the rent was £2. It was in all respects adapted for the abode of labour.

Case 6 is that of a man who should in strictness be included in the class of small farmers; but his condition was perhaps not superior to that of the better class of labourers. He farms seven acres, the property of Lord Eldon, for which he pays a rent of £3 per acre. This struck me as an exorbitant rate, but, on inquiry, I was told that, being situated at no great distance from two or three rural villages, it was considered as in the nature of "accommodation land." Accommodation land is so called from lying near towns or villages; it is either garden or pasture land, and often let to butchers for the convenience of grazing their beasts, or to publicans to keep horses on. This man kept four cows on his ground, selling the milk and butter. He had two calves, which he was going to sell, as the stock was as much as the land could maintain without them. He was a widower, with only one daughter, for whom sufficient occupation was found at home. His cottage was an exceedingly comfortable one: on a plot of ground kitchen vegetables were grown.

Case 7 is that of a peasant inhabiting the village of Stainton, in the south-western part of the county. He had been a farm servant, in the receipt of £15 per year, three years boarded with the same master, whom he had left, simply, he said, because he would like to change. He had not been able to get a hiring at the Martinmas term, and had been six weeks out of employment. Knowing the declining tendency of the market, I remarked to him that I thought he had not acted wisely, and he seemed to be much of the same opinion. He could not, or would not, give any other distinct reason than I have stated. He was unable either to read or write (a comparatively rare instance in this quarter of England), but told me he went regularly to church.

Case 8 is that of two brothers in the same village; one occupying a small farm of 15 acres, on which four cows are kept, turnips and vegetables grown; the other acting as his hind, or labourer. In this and similar cases I found it impossible to obtain clear details of household economy, as no regular accounts are kept. But the amount of necessaries and comforts within the command of men of this class, after paying their rent and providing for the trifling repairs of farm-buildings, or implements which may be required, does not exceed that within the reach of an ordinary well-employed labourer.

Case 9 was that of a labourer at weekly wages, employed on a farm near Barnard Castle. At one time he had worked at a tan-yard in the town, where he had earned 13s. a week, but was tempted, as he told me, to desert his occupation by the offer of employment for three days, at 5s. a day, as a placard-bearer at the county election. On returning to work he was refused employment, and had taken to farm labour. I asked him what the rate of wages in this quarter was. He said, "Nae one that ca'd himsel' a man wad gang out to work at less than 12s. a week;" but by-and-by he confessed that if there were a prospect of long service, some deduction might be enforced. He was married, and had five children—none of the latter able to work; the age of the eldest was seven, the youngest was an infant of three months old. He had been seven years in service at his present place, employed on a grazing farm of 130 acres, and acting as the factotum of the farmer during the absence of the latter at a larger farm, also in his occupation, in another part of the county. His money wages were but 8s. a week; he had, in addition, the privilege of growing as many potatoes as he required on his employer's land, providing the seed at his own expense, and being of course not at liberty to make any other use of them than in his own family. This year he had planted thirty bushels, of which only ten were good, the others being unfortunately diseased; one year he had been able to save but a bole, or two bushels. He had also his fuel carted to him gratis; coals are 5s. a ton, or 3d. a cwt., at the mouth of the pit, and are sold at 6d. a cwt. in Barnard Castle—the carriage for ten miles and the retailer's profit causing a rise in price of 100 per cent. He estimated his wages, with these additions, at about 9s. 6d. a week; his wife had earned only 18s. for three weeks' harvesting this last time, having been prevented from earning more by her confinement, but had generally made 2s. a day for some weeks. He paid 50s. a year rent for his cottage, a snug little tenement in good repair, consisting of one well-sized room below, used as a kitchen, and also serving the purpose of a sleeping-room; above was the garret floor, of corresponding dimensions. There was also a hutch adjoining, in which he kept his fuel, and sometimes a pig. In one corner of the lower apartment stood a large bed, which had probably served more than one generation of his ancestors, with curtains of many colours—dingy, but not ragged, and good flock mattresses (feather-beds, however, are not unknown in the dwellings of the peasantry, for it appears they do not always despise the effeminacy); a bright fire blazed in the grate, and the place seemed neither dirty nor "dowie." What a blessing to the poor man to live in a county where coals are cheap; and in a climate like ours, how much does not this one item add to the comforts of labour in the coal districts! This man, who stated that he had maintained himself from the age of seven, was far from being a first-class labourer, as will appear clearly from his own accounts, here literally given. He avowed that, in these hard times, he was not above accepting "broken meat" from those who would assist him in this way. No signs of want, however, were perceptible about his household economy; his eldest boy, a fine-looking child, with sleek flaxen hair, and a winning frankness written on his clear open face, was discussing with great zest his evening meal, a bowl of that most nutritious of all vegetable aliments—peas brose. A colly, or shepherd's dog—one of the most good-natured creatures of the canine race I have ever fallen in with, and not too big for the house—stretched his limbs on the earth, a cat and two kittens tumbling over him in as full confidence of fraternal affection as could be shown by any members of the "happy family." The master of the household could neither read nor write (it was my odd fortune to encounter two men in this category on the same day), but thought that the experience of the world and practical skill might sharpen a man's faculties as well as the mastery of these arts would do. Having known many examples which made good his proposition, and remembering the ways of the world in old times, when men managed to get through life very creditably even in high places, though ignorant of either, I was not inclined to controvert him. He was determined, however, that his sons should be scholars in some sort, though himself was none, and stated that he had missed more than one comfortable birth from his want of learning.

The next man whom I may mention was a canny Scot, from Duddingstone, near Edinburgh. The number of Scotchmen in the northern districts is considerable. He had resided fourteen years in the county, performing various sorts of unskilled labour, and was now employed at the brick-works and cinder-kilns (as coke ovens are here called), near Brancepeth, a village a few miles west of Durham. His wages (so much was paid him for every oven he "drew") ran from 16s. in winter to 24s. in summer, but the work, he said, was very hard, and the labourer is exposed to extremes of heat and cold. He walked, besides, every day five miles to his work and five miles back, occupying a cottage (larger-sized than those of the strictly rural districts) not far from the city of Durham, for which he pays a rent of £5 a year. His wife, who was a native of this district, sometimes earned a trifle at indoor or out-door work; he had four children, one of them an infant. He had two children at the day school; for the schooling he paid 3d. if by the week, or 3s. (2s. if for one child only) when by the quarter. He could not say he had reason to complain, as they never wanted at meals. He regretted his own want of "lear," being able to read, but writing with great difficulty, which had sprung from idleness in boyhood. He said he had made about as much at home, ascribing his removal to a disposition to roam a little.

Case 11 was that of a man whom I hardly know how to describe. I suspect he was some loose hanger-on about the skirts of society—a stray waif floating on the billows of life. He was at work on the road, about two miles from Durham. He told me he had been living near since last Mayday, and had had but two days' work during the whole time. I asked him how he had maintained himself then? To which he answered that he had a little, though not just enough; whether from public or private alms he did not state, and as I thought he might feel a delicacy upon the point, I forbore to press it. I then inquired how it was he had found no work? "Well, I hardly know," was his reply; "there's so many Irish now. I think they generally get all the work, except it be just some kind of stacking, thatching, or mowing, which they cannot do."

I might multiply cases of a similar kind ten or twenty fold; but as you may be of opinion that I have already instanced enough, and as no essential difference between them was perceptible, it will be better that I should compress the result of my individualized inquiries into a general portraiture of the labourer's condition, taking the average, and noting the variations of feature in species, or defining the margins on either side, of penury or plenty, as well as possible. Before doing so, however, I must specify two cases which could not be properly introduced under the foregoing head, as the parties in each were strangers—vagrants, in fact; but which are of importance, inasmuch as the number and frequent occurrence of personages of the same sort materially affect the condition of the home-bred labourer in many cases for good or evil.

The first was that of a young labouring Irishman, with his wife and child, who had left Dublin some three weeks before, and come into this country by way of Leeds, in search of work. I found them cowering by the road-side, under the shelter of the hedge, on a sleety December's day. It was bitterly cold, the child had the hooping-cough, and in spite of the snow flakes, they had contrived to kindle a little fire of thorns, which was giving out smoke, but little heat. They had a little tin can, with some broth or gruel in it, which they were trying to make their infant swallow, but I thought it doubtful if the poor thing would live through many days of such weather. The man was really handsome, with the vivacious, sensitive, arch expression of face peculiar to the better specimens of the Irish peasantry; the woman also was formed in the luxuriant mould of Irish feminine beauty. I regretted my inability to give them any effectual aid. They asked me eagerly how far it was to the town, where they were going to apply at the vagrant-house for some relief.

The next case, met on the same day, was that of two male Irish vagrants travelling in company—one a shoemaker from Dublin, the other a ropemaker from Cork. Their clothes were squalid tatters, and their whole appearance as loathsome and repulsive as that of the other man had been engaging. The shoemaker had been in England for some months, and had had some work, but seemed not to have settled at it. Generally, I have remarked that the Irish peasantry and poor are either decidedly handsome or decidedly ugly: their organization seems more flexible and impressionable than that of the English or Scotch, and the types of feature are much more strongly contrasted.

The condition of the labourer, it will be gathered from the details given above, so far from being either uniform or simple, as we are usually apt to conceive it, in reality includes a hundred different classifications and shades. It is modified through so many channels and by so many diverse influences that its varieties are almost infinite. There is a not inconsiderable proportion, the first-class hands, who are little affected by extrinsic causes of fluctuation, inasmuch as they will always command their price from employers who know their own interest. But it cannot be doubted that, in so far as the mass is concerned, causes extraneous to the sphere of rural life, such as the abundance or scarcity of other kinds of employment, do most materially affect their interests, and heighten or lower the rate of wages. Four years back, for example, when the construction of railroads was still proceeding with unabated vigour, and the field of future railway operations seemed interminable, employment was to be had by all who would work, wages were universally high, and a man must be a ninny indeed if he could not earn his 15s. or perhaps 20s. a week. The labour of "navvies," however, is much more severe and continuous than that of the ordinary run of farm-work, and all but the youngest and strongest preferred their quiet rural life and more regular employment, even though their earnings might be a shilling or two less in amount. Still wages were kept up, and rarely fell below 12s. or 13s. Now the complexion of things is altered; the railways are pretty well finished or abandoned, and the proportions of supply and demand in the labour-market are inverted. The farmers, who, for the most part, never possessed capital or means to prosecute agriculture as it should be prosecuted (for the estimate of required capital at £1 per acre is certainly not exorbitant), now profess to be hard pushed by the present prices of agricultural produce, and are anxiously contracting their outlay by every possible method. The consequence has been, in the northern districts, a reduction of wages to the extent of 1s., 2s., or, in the case of inferior labourers, 3s. a week. The industrial capabilities of a man of course make his value to the farmer, and they vary just as much in agricultural as in other descriptions of labour. The labourers of the north, however, still possess advantages which are denied to those of some other divisions of England. The fervid and busy movement of industry which animates both town and country is very different from the languid depression of the south and west; commercial, mining, and shipping enterprises are prosecuted with activity, and agriculture is itself conducted with more of the spirit of improvement. The relative demand for labour, therefore, must evidently be more brisk, and the chances much more in the labourer's favour. The lower price of fuel, again, is a great benefit and blessing. It rarely exceeds 10s. a ton, and is generally considerably less; in the towns 7s. is a common price.

In spite, however, of all the variations to which I have adverted, there must still be an average rate of wages for the agricultural labourer, and it should now be our endeavour to fix it as nearly as possible. From all the observations and inquiries I have been able to make, I am inclined to conclude that the present average for the earnings of a male agricultural labourer cannot be less than 10s.; nor does this include those of his wife and child, or children, which may often amount to 5s. a week for the whole year. If unmarried, of course he has no burden, and no extra assistance to look to; if married, without family, he is perhaps more favourably situated in all respects than if single. The wife, unless hindered by sickness, is employed during the hay and corn harvests, and occasionally at other times; her earnings during the former period, are at least 10d. a day, or 5s. a week, and sometimes double. The eldest boy, if he has children, is sent to work at the age of eight, or sometimes seven, and soon pays for his own board and lodging. This may in some degree interfere with his education, but that subject, as well as the particular employment of women and children in agriculture, will be considered by and by. Sometimes, if unable to do out-door work, the labourer's wife may earn a trifle by washing and sewing, but this is not a very common case. I mention it, however, in order fairly to estimate the amount of his available resources. All things considered, the man of ordinary health, strength, and common sense, has a comfortable home in the north, where his children may grow up in habits of regular industry, and his own days wear away in peace to the grave.

With respect to the character of the cottage accommodation, so far as I have observed, it may be pronounced good on the whole, or, at least, not bad. I doubt whether such a thing as an *occupied* cottage in ruins is to be found from the Humber to the smoke of Auld Reekie. In the northern district the cottages are substantially built of brick, or as often of rough stone, containing two, or sometimes three rooms, which furnish sufficient accommodation for all, excepting large families, and large families are not common here. It would, of course, be impossible to accommodate in such a cottage half a dozen lads and lasses with due regard to the restraints imposed by delicacy, but the labourer's children are not all of the same age, and they do not remain about him long after they can shift for themselves. We have seen the shameful consequences which result in the southern districts from a different state of things and style of living, induced by the neglect of those who should have obviated it. I may remark, from my own observation, that the old rural manners of England permit a degree of liberty or laxity in this respect which strangely contrasts with the fastidious delicacy of urban habits and modern tastes, but which still subsists to this day in some parts, uncensured, because no decent person thinks of abusing it. It even now sometimes happens that several grown-up persons of different sexes (probably only when the parties are connected by blood, or affinity, and perhaps all in the married state), will occupy the same large room at a country inn. I have myself seen instances of this within the last month. Exactly the same thing prevails in the country parts of Italy, though I cannot say that I have observed it anywhere in France. How else, indeed, are we to account for the use of those enormous beds, capable of holding three people with ease, and of which you often find two in the same room? Enough of this. I mention it to preserve some record of a feature in our domestic manners which is gradually becoming obsolete, and which will probably in time entirely disappear.

It falls now to consider the effect of the reduction in the prices of the necessaries of life on the condition of the labourer and his family. The farmers contend that this reduction is sufficient to compensate for an abatement of wages in the cases where it has taken place, and where the measure was forced upon them, they aver, by that corresponding reduction. Butcher meat is now at 5d. a pound, instead of 6d. or 7d.; the bushel of wheat is at 4s. 6d. instead of 9s. or more, where it stood two years ago. Upon these grounds a reduction of wages has been successfully attempted in some of the southern districts of Durham; near Darlington and Stockton they have been in many instances lessened from 10s. or 11s. to 9s. Where no reduction has taken place, the labourer's condition has been of course improved, and distress, where it existed, materially alleviated. Labouring people in this county consider that if they can earn a boll of wheat (two bushels) in a week, their condition is tolerable, and this has passed into a kind of proverbial saying. The aliment of the northern labourer includes substances unknown to the daintier palates of the middle classes, but which are, nevertheless, fully as nutritious as any of the staples in use amongst other classes. Oatmeal and pea-meal are both used to some extent, in the form of crowdy, brose, and cakes. The latest results of scientific experiment and research have amply confirmed the opinion, long current in the simple lore of the northern workmen, as to the excellence of these vegetal products. They are now supposed to furnish a more abundant recruit of muscular strength than any other vegetal substances.

It will have been seen from the foregoing statements and reasonings, that the employment of wife and children, and the earnings which they are constantly enabled to bring into the common store, is often a main resource looked to by the agricultural labourer. The indoor work of a farm is generally done by female servants, who are the daughters of agricultural labourers, in conjunction with the wife and daughters of the farmer; but women thus employed speedily marry, and their savings go rather to find clothing and furniture for themselves than to eke out the necessities of the paternal household. In out-door work, the wife and children of the labourer are employed in hoeing turnips, weeding, or "couching," as it is sometimes called, clearing the ground from stones, manuring it, tending cattle, &c. But their great sources of employment are the hay and corn harvests, when the earnings of a woman rise from 8d. and 10d. a day to 1s., or even 2s., according to the quantity of work performed and the rate of price at the moment. There were days when in harvest-time the reapers of the field poured out in numbers from the small towns of the rural districts; and at Darlington there are persons who recollect when from 200 to 300 lasses and lads would leave the town of a morning to gather in the harvest, transported to the scene of their labour in wains, and marshalled by the rustic music of tabor, pipe, and fiddle. In the town I have just named, as well as in others, all this has disappeared, the young people of the place being generally employed in manufacturing establishments; but something of the kind still exists in places of smaller size. Women are generally employed for a fortnight at the hay-harvest, and for a month at the corn-harvest, and the produce of their labour during that time may add a sum of £2 or more to the labourer's yearly earnings. Boys are employed in most of the above lines; but the great branch of occupation for the youngest is in scaring birds from the corn, at which they will earn 1s. 6d. a week, or for other things 2s. Upon a farm of 200 acres, two men and three boys will be employed, rather a less average, perhaps, than in some districts in England, but less work is required on pasture-farms, and in Durham the proportion of land in pasture is about one-third, which is rather more than usual. The indoor work of the dairy is often felt to be severe by women; churning, in order to produce butter, and also the making of cheese, are most laborious occupations, perhaps as much so as any description of out-door labour, and they sometimes occasion complaints arising from over fatigue and exhaustion. But of this more fully in future occupations. I advert to it here in order to complete the estimate of resources available for the maintenance of the labourer and his family.

The field of agriculture, in such a county as that of Durham, the theatre of a vast mining industry, is after all comparatively limited. But there is some satisfaction in reflecting that the same county which contains so many memorials of ancient grandeur, and episcopal and aristocratic power, from the princely magnificence of Raby to the chivalrous splendours of Hilton, Lambton, and Brancepeth Castles (the latter one of the most perfect, if not the most perfect modern restoration of a feudal castle in the world), should also present examples of comfort in the humble abode of the labourer. The farm-houses have an air of substantial plenty in most cases, though never perhaps of opulence. They have, however, a trim well-kept air about them which evidences care and attention to domestic economy. I know not a more pleasing spectacle than one of them, with its well-stocked yard, containing some dozen or twenty ricks. Stone is a common material in building here, there being excellent quarries at Brusselton and Dunhouse, in the county. I had an opportunity of admiring the stone drawn from them in a new church just completed at Darlington, in the purest style of early English architecture, from the designs of Mr. Middleton, an architect of that place. At the Roman Catholic College of Ushaw also, near Durham, the same stone may be observed; it has there been used in the construction of a chapel, which forms another monument of the genius of Pugin, and is at present being used for the completion of a common hall and library. These and other buildings in progress through the county keep quarriers and masons in activity. With reference to Ushaw, which I visited, I may mention in passing, that it is a flourishing educational seminary, containing about 130 students, many of them belonging to old families of Roman Catholic gentry in the north of England. The methods of education followed have something of a foreign character, bearing a closer resemblance to those pursued in the universities of Italy than to those which are for the moment in vogue in England.

As an evidence of the progress which agricultural science has made, even in the outlying districts of the county, I enclose a list of lately invented implements, which I found on sale in one of the second-rate towns. It is as follows:—

"THE TWO-WHEELED PLOUGH.—This plough had the society's prize of 10*l.* at York, 1848; and a prize of 5*l.* at the meeting of the Yorkshire Agricultural Society, held at Leeds, in 1849. Price 4*l.* 15s.; with skim, 5s. extra. Extract from the Royal Agricultural Society's Report:—'The land was of excellent character for testing the merits of these ploughs; there were twenty-two in number, some with two wheels, some with one; while others worked as swings. We directed these ploughs not to work less than 8 inches deep, and what width of furrow the makers chose to take. Those with one wheel and also the swings gave us very little trouble in deciding where to place them. The land was strong, and whilst most of those with two wheels were doing their work pretty well, the former were working very indifferently, not one of them turning the furrows in the style we approved. We considered Mr. Busby, of Newton-le-Willows, to deserve the first prize. His plough worked 9 inches deep, with a 13-inch furrow slice, four horses drawing it in very good style, whilst others, which were not ploughing either so deep or so wide a furrow by 1 to 2 inches, could scarcely be drawn at all by the same number of horses. This plough cut the land side clean, made a level sole, kept the furrow more together, and turned it in better style than any other in the field.'"

"LIGHT TWO-WHEELED PLOUGH, adapted for all descriptions of soils, with a movable nose-piece upon which the shares are placed, and which can be set more or less to land; and also at more or less pitch. This has been found to be of great advantage where cast iron shares are worked, for as they wear down, the plough may still retain the same hold upon or inclination towards the soil. Price 4*l.* 15s. This implement obtained a prize of 7*l.* at the meeting of the Yorkshire Agricultural Society, held at Scarborough, in 1847; and the silver medal at Beverley, in 1845; and a prize of 3*l.* at Wakefield in 1846; and also a prize of 10*l.* at Leeds, in 1849, for light and general purpose plough."

"Drilling Machines—Made on the most approved principle, avoiding all unnecessary complication, of well-seasoned materials, and warranted to perform the work in a satisfactory manner. The corn and manure drills are adapted to drill corn or seeds, with or without manure, in any required quantities. For greater convenience of using as a corn and seed drill alone, the manure box and apparatus may be entirely removed, if required, by a farm labourer. They are all fitted with iron levers and two barrels complete. Corn and seed drills: Seven-row, 20*l.*; eight-row, 21*l.* 10s.; nine-row, 23*l.*; ten-row, 24*l.* 10s.; eleven-row, 26*l.*; twelve-row, 27*l.* 10s.; larger sizes, if required, at 30s. per row extra.—Corn, seed, and manure drills: 30*l.*, 32*l.*, 34*l.*, 36*l.*, 38*l.*, and 40*l.*; extra for every additional coulter to convey corn or turnip seed behind the manure culture, 7s. 6d."

"Machine for Breaking Rape and Linseed Cake, for beasts and sheep, and small for the purpose of tillage.—This machine has two pair of rollers, the bottom pair finer than the other. It will be found a most complete and easily managed machine, as it may be set to break cakes of every thickness, to any required size, for feeding stock or manure. The labour in working this machine is economized by allowing alterations in the speed according to the power applied and the hardness of the cake. Price 10*l.* 10s."

"Large Chaff-cutting Machine.—This machine is similar in most respects to Cornes's well-known chaff-engine, which took the prize at the Shrewsbury, Newcastle, York, and Norwich shows of the Royal Agricultural Society. It is arranged on an entirely new principle, to vary the length of cut, and will cut four different lengths. It is fitted so as to be worked by one man, or at double the speed by two men, and may be had for horse or steam power if required. It is strongly recommended as a most useful plain machine, and will cut a larger quantity with less labour than those on any other principle. Price for one or two men, 11*l.*; with extra spindle for the feeder to assist when one man is cutting, 11*l.* 11s.; extra strong for horse or hand power, 12*l.*"

"Improved Horse-Hoe.—Price 2*l.* 10s. This horse-hoe obtained the silver medal, 1848, and a prize of 5*l.*, 1849, at the meetings of the Royal Agricultural Society. Extract from the Royal Agricultural Society's report:—'A silver medal was awarded to Mr. Busby for his horse-hoe exhibited in this class, which worked very well. Its construction was simple, having a triangular sock in the centre, and two bent knives behind, followed by two sets of rowels on the principle of the Norwegian harrow. These had a good effect in clearing the soil from the roots of the weeds, and leaving them on the surface to wither. They also made the hoe run more steady.'"

"Grass Land Cultivator, or Hay or Stubble Rake.—(Obtained prize, the silver medal.)—This implement has a leverage attached to it, which allows the person working it the advantage of pressing the tines into the ground to any reasonable depth that may be required. It has been used by many extensive farmers in Yorkshire, for preparing old pasture land for the reception of any description of land tillage that may be applied. Extract from the Royal Agricultural Society's Report:—'The only one tried was exhibited by Mr. Busby, of Newton-le-Willows. It appeared to answer the purpose for which it is designed, and to clear off the moss and old grass roots in good style. It also, by the same operation, collects it into rows ready for carting off. All other grass land cultivators that we have seen leave the moss, &c., that they tear up, spread over the surface. Where an implement of this kind is required, we think this will prove very efficient. We gave it a medal.'"

The Western district of the county of Durham, comprehending the upper course of the rivers Wear and Tees, or Weardale and Teesdale, as they are called by terms of indefinite application, is an upland grazing country, with extensive lead mines, which support a population of several thousand miners. In this district the farms are generally small, from 20 to 100 or 150 acres, and often the property of the farmer himself, who, in some cases, does the work with his own family, with little or no extra assistance. The country rises gradually to the westward, from Barnard's Castle to the south, and Stanhope to the north. The former is one of the finest feudal ruins in England, so called from Bernard de Baliol, of the family which played so disastrous a part in Scottish annals, whose seat was at this place. It rises gradually over the rushing Tees, which here tumbles in a cascade over a ledge of rocks, and overshadows the swift stream with its gloomy ruins, like the shadow of death brooding over life. As you ascend, you come upon treeless green hills and large tracts of moorland, which stretch onwards into the expanse of Stanemoor. The course of the Tees offers many points of interest, of which the chief is the High Force, where the river, rolling through a spacious portal of precipitous black rocks, forms a grand waterfall of full forty feet in actual height, but which inclines back in such a manner at top, when viewed from below, as to appear still higher. *Forss* is a Norse word, signifying cataract; it is now commonly used in the Norse countries, and we here recognize it as surviving amongst us in its true sense, in the dialect of the people. All this district, indeed, abounds in Scandinavian memorials. Thorsgill, that is, Thor's Vale, or valley; Thorsgillbeck, the brook flowing through it; Thorsby, or Thoresby, the dwelling of Thor; Balder's beck, or brook, are found within it, recalling times when Odin ruled the popular faith, and testifying to the worship of ancient deities. Ascending yet higher, the relics of Celtic theism have been found here, and altars traced which once smoked with offerings to Belatucader, the British Mars, to Vitires, and to Magon. But without dwelling too long upon ancient recollections, this district offers sufficient wherewith to whet interest and reward curiosity at the present day. The two principal points are Middleton in Teesdale, and St. John's Chapel in Weardale, round which the scanty population congregate. Numerous lead mines are scattered round, which are worked by Colonel Beaumont and by the London Company of Lead Miners. I inspected the Cowshill mine, the largest in the district of Weardale, and sounded its depths, which extend downwards for nearly one hundred fathoms. The descent of a lead mine is a process infinitely more laborious and dangerous than that of a coal pit, where you are let down and drawn up in a basket, and may consider yourself safe if the rope is not rotten. In the other case, there are no such facilities, and you descend into and mount from the bowels of the earth by a series of crazy ladders, in some places half worn away, and from which a single false step would precipitate you to destruction. You first quit the realms of upper air by a lateral horizontal shaft, which is driven through the hill-side for a distance of nearly two miles, and has a second opening in some distant region. Along this shaft is laid a line of rails, on which waggons drawn by horses run with great velocity. Into one of these you must step, and traverse the narrow shaft, in imminent peril of your head, which, if you moved it a few inches to the right or left, would infallibly suffer by a collision. On each side of you, you catch a dim glimmering of rugged black rocks. You arrive, at length, at the top of the vertical shaft, and proceed to descend the ladders through galleries and landing-places dripping with wet, and foul with mire. Whilst descending, your attention is distracted, and fears for your personal safety suggested, by a tremendous sound of rushing waters, which, on inquiry, you find proceeds from a waterwheel and engine employed to raise the ore from the depths of the mine, the water moving which is supplied by springs in the mine itself. The upper drifts have long been closed and are blocked up with rubbish. At length you come upon the lower drifts, galleries that is, about seven feet in height and breadth, run through the rock, where the sounds of mattock and crow fall on your ears, and the miners, their swarthy-looking forms naked from the waist upwards, are busy grubbing out the ore. The ore found in some mines about this spot, contains a considerable proportion of silver, and is imbedded in beautiful though rather fragile spars. I do not know, by-the-by, if these spars are turned to much purpose at present, but they struck me as much resembling the stones of which the Italians make so much use in the composition of some kinds of their superb mosaics. The ore glitters and sparkles in its native state, before it is smelted, with a lustre not very inferior to silver. The ascent of the shaft is a most toilsome business, and there are many who faint on trying it for the first time. There are long lateral galleries below as well as above, in which lines of rails are laid, and the rattle of the waggons, as they are driven by reckless lads along the narrow passages, is ten times more appalling than an open air railroad. As my guide, one of the overlookers, remarked to me, "it is far to seek for a bit of bread" in these intestinal depths of the earth, but were it not for wet and dirt it would be less uncomfortable. I observed that most of the miners have haggard and somewhat corrugated features, from the high temperature at which they work below, and the sudden changes of atmosphere to which they are exposed. The shafts and drifts are ventilated by fanners driven by the water-engine. Accidents have been known to occur in the mine, but not from fire-damp. At the surface of the ground the work of washing, sorting, and crushing the ore is carried on, through a variety of stages. When the waggons emerge from the surface drift, spoken of at first, they are drawn along a line of rails raised on posts, like the "staiths" for loading coal-ships at the river wharfs, through one of the many openings of which they discharge their contents upon an ore-heap below. A number of stands are placed in rows, at each of which stands a washer, engaged in washing the small ore and dross as actively as if he were following his vocation in the diggings in California. The ore is washed and rewashed, some of it a dozen times over. There is a large crushing-mill, the iron rollers of which crush with irresistible force blocks of various sizes, separating the crystallized particles of metallic ore from the spar to which they adhere. A lead mine, like others, is known afar by the heap of rubbish and "plate," as the spar is called when the ore has been abstracted from it, thrown up near the mouth. There are three hundred persons, including a few boys, employed upon the single mine of Cowshill. The miners are divided into copartnerships of six each, to every one of which a separate portion of the drift is allotted. To every miner a sum of ten shillings a week (called by them lent, or lentern money) is advanced by the company; their further wages are dependent on the success they meet with in their search for ore, which is, of course, various. Many of them make 40s. a week, others barely cover their 10s. The average wages of the sorters and washers of the ore, who work at the surface, are 25s. There are schools in the dales for the education of their children, and a miners' reading-room has lately been established by Colonel Beaumont, at Newhouse, a spot about a mile and a half distant from the Cowshill mine. Some of those employed at the mines have bits of land which they cultivate; their cottages have much the same appearance and aspect as those of the agricultural labourers, though generally rather larger. None of them work longer than eight hours a day, that term being called a shift, and no more than five days a week, for no work in ordinary cases is done upon Saturdays.

It would be improper to dismiss the subject of the wages of agricultural labourers, without adverting to the fact (which I had forgotten to mention in its proper place), that in winter their hours of labour are considerably shorter than those of mechanics and artisans working in towns. Excepting the hinds and farm servants, whose case I have described above, they work only from the dawn to the close of daylight—or, at this moment, from half-past seven to half-past four. In summer, if they work longer than ten hours (or twelve hours, with two for meals), they are paid extra, 2d. or 3d. per hour.

The Morning Chronicle, Wednesday, January 9, 1850.

To the EDITOR of the MORNING CHRONICLE.

Sir—I have read with very great pleasure the admirable letter on the poor of Essex, published in *The Morning Chronicle*, and I feel satisfied that such interesting and impartial publications must be of immense service to the country at large.

I have for very many years been of opinion that the first requisite for improving the condition of the labouring population of this country is a better, a more general, and scientific education of their masters. To tell farmers that they ought to employ more labourers, and pay them better, are words thrown to the winds; you must show them that it is their interest so to act, or you make no progress in the work of improvement. I myself have seen all the essence washed out of the dung in farmyards, into horse-ponds and ditches, and thence into brooks, whilst the farmers themselves have been purchasing guano at a very high price, or barges of manure from London, or have even cultivated their lands with no manure at all; but seemed glad that it had run away of itself and saved them the trouble of carting it on their lands. Yet such men scrambled on, paid their rents and taxes, and deemed themselves quite perfect, because they farmed exactly as their forefathers did.

Now, as they could act thus under protection to agriculture, and it is notorious that they have so acted, it seems clear to me that under free trade they would do quite as well had they scientific information enough to teach them the value of their own manures, and how to employ them, and also how properly to perform all their other farming operations. I am no politician, but I am perfectly satisfied that protection has been a great drawback to improvements, as all monopolies ever are, and that free competition will accomplish what no reasoning ever could effect. Men of education and enterprise will stand their ground as farmers, whilst the uneducated must give place to better men. The average quantity of wheat grown in England per acre has not hitherto exceeded twenty-four bushels, and some authorities state the average not to be above twenty bushels; but it is clear to me that full forty bushels an acre will, at no distant period, be the average, and produced at much less expense than the twenty or twenty-four are now; and as with wheat, so with all other kinds of grain.

Animal physiology will also be studied, and in consequence of a knowledge of animated nature cattle will be fed at a much less expense than at present; for, although at a cattle show visitors are struck with admiration at what can be done by the few, they should go into the fields and farmyards to witness the operations of the many. In the former place you are compelled to admire all you see; in the latter to condemn the greater part.

Let farmers, therefore, obtain a knowledge of their profession, or let them prepare for it, as other professional men do, and my opinion is, that should this be done, they will court rather than dread foreign competition. The greater the amount of population the greater is the means for the growing vegetable food for the feeding of them. No country could compete with Great Britain in her own markets in the sale of corn, if agriculturists would take advantage of the resources within their reach and skilfully employ them. I know a union workhouse in the midst of a farming neighbourhood, the guardians of which are all farmers; the house has also nine or ten acres of poor land attached to it; yet the guardians know so little of the value of the manure of the establishment—human guano, better than any foreign— that they contracted with an adjoining landowner for 50*l.* to allow them to conduct it all away in drains, made at a great expense, on to his lands, though it is quite certain that the real value of it cannot be less in that house than 50*l.* a year, if not much more. And as with one house so probably with most others. But surely such sheer ignorance would be annihilated by an improved education amongst the conductors of such establishments.

The first step, therefore, towards general improvement must be the establishment of agricultural schools, where something more will be taught and learned than the mere rudiments of knowledge, as is the case at present in all parts of this kingdom, unless Scotland be an exception.

But farmers in general say, we do not want such stuff; we do not want what you call science, and chemistry; we farm as we always have farmed, and always will continue to farm. This, I observe, is their general language; but there are, I rejoice to know, many, very many, honourable exceptions to such ignorance; and necessity will bring others into their school, or they must sink into the condition of labourers, or perhaps into workhouses.

A Chinese gardener gives its proper food to every plant in his garden, but an English gardener or farmer has but one kind of pabulum for all the various vegetables he grows. Plants vary in nature as much as animals do, and there would be as much wisdom displayed in the feeding of sheep and oxen, as well as cats and dogs, with horse-flesh as there is exhibited by the farmer or gardener in the giving to all kinds of plants the same kinds of food; this comparison may appear to be stretched, but by a little reflection it will be found to be correct. When the Dutch sent some naturalists to China, and the botanists among them were looking in the Chinamen's corn-fields for some specimens of weeds among their corn, they could not find one, and indeed there was not one to be found. We esteem those people barbarians; but by their superior skill and industry, they feed four times the amount of population per square mile that we do, and without the least foreign importations of grain or cattle. We, it is true, surpass them in the manufacture and use of implements of war and destruction, but not in the cultivation of our fields and gardens; for therein, it is quite certain, we are vastly their inferiors. What England wants, therefore, I repeat, for her farmers is knowledge; with this she could undersell the whole world; but without it she must remain in the condition of being dependent upon nearly all the nations of the earth for daily subsistence. Now, this is the state of this country as it has been left by protection; can it grow worse under free-trade? Impossible!

G. W. WILKINS.

LABOUR AND THE POOR.

—◆—

THE RURAL DISTRICTS.

[FROM OUR SPECIAL CORRESPONDENT.]

NORTHERN COUNTIES—DURHAM AND NORTHUMBERLAND.

LETTER XXV.

I have now nearly completed what I have to offer to you on the subject of the county of Durham, and the condition of its working population. On reviewing the course of my inquiry, and looking back at the many steps which have conducted me to the conclusions already communicated to you, I am struck with the variety of circumstances which investigation showed to exist, and with the infinite diversity of individual cases. Experience teaches me the difficulty of generalizing with safety and certainty. I am inclined to think that few questions are more complicated than that of the wages of labour. There is no such thing as one uniform rate; to put the matter thus would only be to deceive; and it is no easy task to ascertain the mean of a hundred different terms. It is probable that these diversities may exist to a greater extent in counties which are, like the one in question, the seat of a vigorous and varied industrial movement. Still the standard of wages must ever be influenced by individual character, both in the employer and the employed; whilst the sufficiency of its remuneration is a point partly determined by causes within the control of the labourer himself, and depending on his own habits of provident or improvident management. Few arts, again, appear to me to embrace a greater multiplicity of qualifying conditions, or to require for their successful prosecution a higher degree of practical skill and versatile accomplishment, than that which is the parent and foundation of them all—agriculture. Modes of cultivation and systems of farming are not only very various in themselves, but receive, in practice, a hundred modifications, from the nature and state of the locality, the character of the population, and the plentiful or stinted supply of articles required by the farmer.

A subject on which I have hitherto given but few details, is the rent of land. I have already alluded to the indifferent quality of the soil; rents, therefore, are not so high generally as the proximity of large towns and populous collieries would lead us to expect. I am induced to believe that 25s. an acre might be a fair average. A farm of 150 acres was taken the other day at 12s. an acre, but the land is far from good, and has been much neglected. I know a moorland farm of 350 acres which is let for £45. But 30s. and £2 are common rates in more favoured localities; whilst in particular circumstances a considerably higher rate prevails. In Weardale, near the lead mines, where the land is almost entirely pasture, and the farms generally small, I found much of it let for £3, £3 10s., and even £4. Accommodation land, near the towns—so called because subserving the convenience of some classes of tradesmen, such as the butcher, the innkeeper, or the greengrocer— often runs as high as £5.

The principal manufactures of this county are as follows, viz.: the carpet, employing 385 persons, of whom 65 are under twenty years of age; the flax and linen, employing 339 persons, of whom 43 are under twenty years of age; the rope and cord, employing 427 persons, of whom 122 are under twenty years of age; the sail and sail-cloth, employing 299 persons, of whom 85 are under twenty years of age; the woollen, employing (dyers included) 605 persons, of whom 186 are under twenty years of age; the glass and glass-bottle, employing 858 persons, of whom 184 are under twenty years of age; the iron, nail, anchor, and chain, employing 1,637 persons, of whom 408 are under twenty years of age; the earthenware, employing (painters and print- ers included) 520 persons, of whom 107 are under twenty years of age; and the paper, employing 235 persons, of whom 27 are under twenty years of age. There are 262 manufacturing chemists, 96 bleachers and dyers, 900 weavers and spinners of linen and woollen. The mines of this county employ 18,000 labourers, of whom 16,000 are coal-miners and 2,000 lead-miners.

The rate of mortality differs very considerably in different dis- tricts of this county. It is greatest in Gateshead, where it is 2.523 for males and 2.351 for females, and in Sunderland, where it is 2.703 for males and 2.287 for females. In the city of Durham and its neigh- bourhood, it is 2.206 for males and 2.122 for females. In Weardale and Teesdale—the country of the lead mines, but which enjoys the most pure and salubrious air to be obtained in the county, except on the border of the sea—it is 2.028 for males and 2.012 for females.

I have already alluded to the comparative state of education in the northern district, as illustrated by the number of persons signing the marriage register with marks. Applying this test to the year 1847, the latest for which returns are given, it appears that for all England and Wales the number of marriages was 135,845—that the number of cases in which both the parties signed with marks was 32,622, and that of cases in which one only signed in that manner, 39,062; in all more than 104,000 persons. In the county of Durham the number of marriages was 3,287; that of cases in which both signed with marks, 638; in which one only did so, 1,100; total of persons, 2,376. In Northumberland the number of marriages was 2,311; that of cases in which both signed with marks, 275; in which one only thus signed, 640; total of persons, 1,190. In Cumberland the number of marriages was 1,012; that of cases in which both signed with marks, 117; in which one only thus signed, 286; total of persons, 520. In Westmoreland the number of marriages was 431; that of cases in which both signed with marks, 48; in which one only thus signed, 124; total of persons, 220. But it is interesting to look at the number of men in the northern counties whom the possession of studious tastes and the acquisition of knowledge have elevated from the lowest and most obscure stations to eminence and fame. Emerson, the great mathematician, was one remarkable instance of this; and in the scientific world of London at the present day, more than one might be named. Nowhere, perhaps, in England, do excellent schools abound to such an extent as here; educational activity and a wish to learn pervade all ranks. Boarding-schools and day-schools for the middle classes are multitudinous. Every town contains its free grammar school and its charity schools. With regard to the educational institutions growing up under Government superintendence, and particularly to schools for the pauper children in the workhouse, fault may, perhaps, be found with some of the details, and much has been said in condemnation of the arrangements adopted. But it appears to me essentially unfair to press with severe censure on measures which are only in their initiatory stages, and which, as regards a system of education for workhouses, can hardly be said to be yet commenced. The report of Mr. Browne, inspector of workhouse schools in the northern district, is a document which shows that its writer is fully alive to the duties and responsibilities of his position. It abounds in sound and valuable suggestions on the subject of pauper education, as will be seen by the subjoined extracts on the subjects of the religious instruction and industrial training of the children, the qualifications of the teachers, &c.:—

"Religious instruction, as the subject of most importance, is usually most attended to, but it is often very imperfect, especially in those schools where no secular books are used, or where the teachers are paupers. In some workhouses, as at Chorley, Lancashire, where there is a very incompetent pauper teacher, the ordinary practice is to hear the children read the Testament, and ask no questions. The teacher expressly excused himself from questioning the children, on the ground that he was a Roman Catholic. Under such circumstances, the children read on mechanically, without attending to the subject-matter; and their ignorance of it when questioned, or when required to explain its meaning with the books open before them, is marvellous. One defect in examining a class I find common to all bad teachers. They cannot so shape a question as to compel the child to frame an answer in his own words. Thus, when the Scriptures are read, their questions can constantly be answered in the very words of the text. They do not teach the children to think, and the consequence is, that it appears to be quite an accident whether the answer suits the question or not. I have frequently found children, after repeating the Creed, unable to tell whose son our Saviour was; and could fill pages with such answers as, to the question, 'Who was Pontius Pilate?—Mary Magdalen.' It is obvious, that unless the matter of a child's lesson is made part of his mind by reflection, it is perfectly useless to him. The impression is almost as transient as that of a footstep on water.

"The cultivation of land is peculiarly desirable, as it renders the labour of the elder boys directly available towards the diminution of the expenses of the establishment, of which the manure would otherwise be wasted, or not made the most of; as a very healthful occupation; as furnishing the means of earning a livelihood with less interference with the labour market than by giving instruction in trades; and it is also more beneficial morally, for, as the work is hard, the thoughts cannot ramble in the same manner as in those employments where manual dexterity rather than strength is necessary; so that, when the fingers get accustomed to the task, the mind can be employed otherwise.

"Arrangements for the cultivation of land by the labour of the elder boys are nowhere as yet in a matured state in this district. It appears not unreasonable to anticipate that, by employing the boys, who have sufficient strength, in the cultivation of land attached to a district school; by rendering the manure of the establishment available, and thus growing larger and more frequent crops; and by the greater economy which is always practicable to a certain extent in a large establishment, where everything can be turned to some account, the expenses per head of each child in an industrial school may be reduced below the average of an ordinary workhouse. If so, the most common objection to the formation of district schools would be removed. With a little additional experience, it is probable that this point may be satisfactorily determined.

"In an industrial school the girls might be trained, as at Swinton and Kirkdale, to the duties of domestic servants, without the risk of corruption, to which they are liable, even in the better class of workhouses, from casual association with the adult females. They would also contribute to reduce the expenses of the establishment by doing the chief part of the household work, and by making their own clothes. But it seems to me that the advantages of district industrial schools are moral rather than economical, or economical because they are moral, as it is certain that the nation must gain, even in an economical point of view, by the greater influence of religion, by the more general prevalence of upright conduct, and by the diminution of crime, vice, and pauperism. I would, therefore, advocate the formation of such schools, mainly on the ground, that a better education is attainable in them than elsewhere, with less exposure to corrupting influences.

"The qualifications of workhouse teachers in the north of England are proved by their examination papers, transmitted to the Privy Council Office, to be generally low. Very few have received any regular training for their office. I have not been able to recommend a single schoolmistress for a higher certificate, as yet, than that of probation, and one only, the schoolmaster of Leeds, for a certificate of efficiency. He has since been examined by her Majesty's Inspector of Church of England schools, and has obtained, according to your lordships' minutes for 1848, a middle-class certificate, first division. The head-master of Kirkdale school, who was a Battersea student, has obtained a certificate of the same class; and another Battersea student, the schoolmaster of Cockermouth, has received the lower-class certificate, second division. The position of the teachers, generally, in the northern district has not yet been determined.

"Of some teachers whom I have examined, the ignorance was gross. One schoolmistress who had been appointed, though her duties had not actually commenced, did not know that King Saul and the Apostle Paul were different persons, and her spelling and penmanship were on a level with her scriptural knowledge: another, when required to mention some of our Saviour's principal miracles, answered, 'Those which He worked before Pharoah, king of Egypt, to deliver the Jews from Egyptian bondage.' These persons were not paupers, and are not now teachers.

"Schoolmistresses usually prove most deficient in arithmetic, and this is also the subject in which the inferiority of the girls to the boys is more uniformly manifest than in any other. It is easier, however, to attain a certain amount of arithmetical knowledge than to conduct a class satisfactorily: in this essential point I have rarely known an untrained teacher succeed. Good sense, however, to discriminate what is trivial from what is material, is a more valuable element of the schoolmaster's character than any acquirements. Yet a man of sense, principle, and acquirements may fail, or succeed very imperfectly, unless he also possess a ready perception of the characters of children, and tact in influencing them accordingly; since it is certain they will do far more for one person than for another. The common low estimate of a teacher's qualifications may have altered somewhat of late, but there is still practical proof that many consider a person fit for that office who is scarcely fit for any other.

"The desire of your lordships to raise the character of the teacher is now clearly felt, and will, I doubt not, be felt more extensively; but teachers constantly complain that want of leisure prevents them from improving themselves. At Chorlton, Northwich, and elsewhere, the teachers are occupied for about twelve hours daily, although the children are scarcely half the time actually in school. Sometimes teachers are employed in offices directly menial, as at Burnley, where the schoolmaster acts as porter; but the teacher's time is more commonly occupied with a succession of petty duties, not, perhaps, absolutely inconsistent with his office, but which a respectable servant might easily discharge. It appears essential that the teachers should be present when the children rise in the morning, and when they go to bed at night, in order that their devotions may not be omitted, and to secure due attention to cleanliness. But there does not appear to be the same necessity for the constant presence of the teachers during the children's meals, or for their superintendence of the children during play-hours. The consequence is, that the teachers have very frequently no time really at their own disposal until about eight o'clock at night, when they are naturally fatigued and ill-fitted for study. The position of a workhouse teacher is otherwise unpleasant, as he is constantly liable to be brought into collision with the governor; it is one of much confinement, and which a good teacher, easy as it now is for such persons to obtain situations of more comfort elsewhere, would feel often reluctant, not unnaturally, to occupy or retain. Under such circumstances, the qualifications and attainments of workhouse teachers are likely to continue of a mediocre description, and the schools to remain nearly stationary, when a certain point has been reached, by no means advanced, and below that where education may be expected to make a lasting impression upon the child, and, consequently, to operate as a check upon pauperism."

Desirous to sound the lowest depths of destitution and moral degradation in the district of which I have undertaken the inspection, I have visited, in most of the towns through which I have passed (Darlington, Durham, Bishop Auckland, Barnard's Castle, Stockton, Morpeth, Alnwick, &c.), the lodging-houses resorted to by trampers and cadgers, as the classes of vagrants and mendicants are commonly styled. I found, however, in these establishments little to excite surprise. Of the squalid misery of which I have often read, and which I know from my own observation to exist in the great metropolis of England, at a stone's throw from the most gorgeous abodes of opulent luxury and princely splendour, I have here seen nothing. Some of these abodes are fitted up in a style by no means uncomfortable, and with the single exception of the bed-sheets being occasionally dirty, there is nothing repulsive in the household economy. One of them, of which the matron was a returned convict, was remarkable for its regularity and tidiness of aspect. There are, however, considerable differences in the character of the accommodation. The charge made is low enough—3d. a night in all the cases where I inquired. The parties frequenting these include the extensive and indefinite class of persons of loose, vagabond, or disorderly habits. The most respectable are the drovers who are employed by the butchers in bringing up cattle to market, the hawkers of petty wares—pottery, articles of dress, printed pamphlets and broadsides—and labourers or mechanics, of an inferior class, in search of work. The less reputable characters are beggars, poachers, and petty pilferers. In many cases, these persons are as well provided for as the honest and intelligent labourer; and, on the whole, they may be set down as being fully as well off as they deserve. Still there are degrees of discomfort or misery, and in the lowest depth you will always find lower depths still. Upon the habits of this class of our population a most curious and instructive light is thrown by the story of a prisoner in the gaol of Durham, as given from his own mouth in the Fourteenth Report of the Prison Inspectors. I think it, on every account, well deserving of insertion. It is as follows:—

"J. G. S., a prisoner under sentence of transportation, examined: I am 29 years old. I am a native of Edinburgh. My father and mother are both dead. My mother died when I was a mere suckling. I do not know when my father died, and I cannot be quite sure that he is dead, but I believe he is. He deserted his family, I believe, soon after my mother's death, and went to England. The only time that I ever remember seeing him was one day in the streets of Edinburgh, when I was 15 years old. He tapped me on the back, and invited me to go and take some refreshment with him, which I agreed to do. He took me to a tavern, and after a while he told me that he was my father, and he appointed me to meet him again the next evening. I was at that time in the Orphans' Hospital at the D——. The next day I saw Mr. ——, a writer in Edinburgh, who was my mother's father, and I told him joyfully whom I had met the day before. He, however, desired me not to go to this person again, and he sent a letter to the teacher of the hospital to prohibit my going to him. My mother was an illegitimate child of Mr. ——. I obeyed Mr. ——'s directions, and I never saw my father afterwards, but I have heard that he died in London, from a person who represented herself to me as his second wife. I have been told that my father had some property at the time of his marriage, and that he received some with my mother; that he got through it all by drunkenness and dissipation. Till I was seven years old I was under the care of Mr. ——, who lived in —— street, Edinburgh. He was my godfather, and my grandfather Mr. —— paid him so much a-week for my board. I then went to the Orphans' Hospital, and there I remained till I was fifteen. I left a short time after I met my father. I have no brother, but I have a sister. I do not know where she is. The last time I saw her is about eight years ago. I do not know whether my grandfather, Mr. ——, is still alive. It is about eight years since I saw him also. On leaving the Orphans' Hospital I went to live with my grandfather, Mr. ——, and I used to go to Mr. ——, surgeon, living at —— street, to have lessons in anatomy. I was to be brought up as a surgeon. In about nine months, however, I had a quarrel with my grandfather, and left him. It was about my keeping company with a girl named ——. She was very respectable, but she was a Catholic, and my grandfather, who was a Presbyterian, did not approve of her for that reason. He was afraid that if I married her I should change my religion, which he said would be sacrilege. He expostulated with me, and tried to show me the difference between the two religions, but I would not give up Miss ——'s company, and he told me that I must either keep such company as he liked, or leave his house. I therefore left his house. One cause of my first losing my grandfather's favour was my getting the worse of liquor the first new year's day after leaving the Orphans' Hospital, but I did not form any habit of drinking till I went to live at Newcastle. My grandfather then lived at ——, but he afterwards went to live in ——. About two years ago I wrote to him according to that address, to ask for some assistance, as I was going out as mate of a vessel from Sunderland, and he sent me 5*l.* I have not written to inform him of my present situation. On leaving my grandfather's I went to Dunfermline to be out of his way, and intending to remain there till the father of Miss —— should find me a situation, which I hoped he would do when he knew how I was placed. My motive for wishing to be out of my grandfather's way was, that I had taken some money, about 8*l.* I think, which belonged to him, and which was kept in a writing-desk in my bed-room. The desk was locked, but the key had been left in the lock. This was the first theft I ever committed. I did not take the money till after my grandfather had told me that if I did not abandon Miss ——'s company, I must leave his house. After staying a short time at Dunfermline I went to the Rumbling-bridge, and remained at the inn there about four months. During the first six weeks I paid for my board, but during the remainder of the time I was allowed to remain without charge, on condition of giving some lessons every day to the landlord, Mr. ——, in reading, writing, and arithmetic. At the end of that time I returned to Dunfermline, and was six months there with Mr. ——, a master weaver. I kept his accounts. During all this time I heard nothing from Mr. ——. I left Dunfermline at the end of six months, because I had taken 30s. which belonged to Mr. ——. I went to Edinburgh, but Mr. —— followed me and found me at my sister's. He had me taken before Mr. ——, but on my paying back the money in court, and promising to return to Mr. ——'s employment, to whom by a written agreement I was engaged for four years, I was released. I returned that night with Mr. —— to Dunfermline, but I found that the people there looked down upon me for embezzling the money; and as I did not like the disgrace, I absconded the next week, and went to Newcastle. At Newcastle I went into a chemist's shop to buy some cough lozenges. I believe while I was there a person came in and asked for some medicine. There was no one in the shop but a boy, and I observed that this boy took down a bottle with the wrong medicine marked on it to give to this customer. I told him it was not correct. I forget just now the name of the stuff which the boy was going to give, but I remember that it was poisonous, and that it would have proved fatal if taken. While we were discussing the matter, the master of the shop, who overheard our conversation, came in. He asked me how I knew that the medicine was the wrong one, and whether I had ever been in a chemist's shop? I told him that I had not, but that I understood Latin, and was acquainted with the names of many kinds of medicines. He asked me who my parents were? and after some further conversation, he told me that if he should have a vacancy, and I liked to be bound to him for seven years, he would take me into his employment, provided my friends would give security for my remaining the whole time. This person's name was ——, and he lived in the ——. He wrote to my grandfather, and my grandfather and Mr. ——, the lord justice clerk, together, gave security to the extent either of 50*l.* or of 150*l.*, I forget which. I then entered Mr. ——'s service, and remained with him four years. At my birth my mother suckled one of Mr. ——'s children, which is the reason, I believe, that Mr. —— was kind enough to join in the security. At the end of four years I was obliged to leave Mr. —— in consequence of an improper intimacy which took place between me and his niece. Mr. —— did not, however, demand payment of my security, because it was his act for me to leave. At Newcastle, as I have already mentioned, I first fell into the habit of drinking. I became acquainted there with several people who were themselves addicted to drinking, and were in other respects of bad character. The street in which I lived, called the ——, is, I believe, the worst in Newcastle. A large portion of the inhabitants in it are of loose and drinking habits. On leaving Newcastle I went to Edinburgh, and after some time got a situation with a baker living in the ——, whose name I forget. I became bound to him, but at the end of six weeks I absconded, as I found that the employment did not agree with my constitution. I took some money with me, but I forget how much. The baker gave information to the police, and I was apprehended and sent to prison for sixty days. On leaving prison I wrote a note to my grandfather, saying that I had been ill, and begging him to pay the doctor's bill. This was done to gain admission to his presence; for in reality I had not been ill. He saw me for a few minutes, but he had found out that the story of my illness was a pretence, and he upbraided me for my conduct, and refused anything more to do with me. He sent me out, however, a sovereign by the butler. After calling on my sister, I set out for Newcastle. I remained a night there, and then went to North Shields, and finding a vessel in which an apprentice was wanted, I engaged myself to go one voyage on trial. I did not like the sea, and on the return of the vessel I gave up my situation. I then went to Sunderland, and got a place in another vessel, but this was only to get a passage to London. After remaining a few weeks in London, and trying in vain to obtain employment, I returned to Sunderland. There I engaged as a seaman on board a collier that was going to Cowes, in the Isle of Wight. At that place I enlisted into her Majesty's service, and went on board the Peak frigate. We sailed to Barbadoes, and there I was drafted to the Flamer, a steam brigantine. I did not like service, and soon deserted. I was, however, retaken, but on our passage from Barbadoes to Demerara I deserted again at St. Vincent's. There I remained about eighteen months in the employment of a Mr. ——, a grocer. At the end of that time I returned to England, on board a brig bound for London, in which I acted as steward. Soon after landing I fell in with a prostitute, and in the house to which she took me I was robbed by her; but a man who appeared to live in the house, and who had once met me before in the north, recognized me, and ordered the girl to return the money. He and I drank the money together, and from him I learnt the art of forging base coin, which has ended in bringing me here under my present sentence. This man's name is ——. He lived at that time in —— street, ——; but I do not know where he is now. This is about six years ago. He first taught me to make shillings by means of a mould of plaster of Paris. I found it difficult at first to make a good mould, but at the end of three or four months I could make one perfectly. I could make about 100 shillings in a night. We used, at that time to make them for sale to other parties. We sold some to people who took them into the country, and a good many we sold to keepers of public-houses. There were two men, named —— and ——, who bought large numbers of them, and we sold large numbers to the keeper of the public-house called the —— in —— street, and to the keeper of the —— public-house, in —— street-road. The name of the latter person was ——, but I forget the name of the other. We generally got five shillings for a pound's worth of base shillings; but if the parties would consent to give six shillings a pound, then we used German silver or Gates's metal in coining, otherwise we made the shillings of Britannia metal. Four of us worked together. We made different coins. I made shillings, two other men, named —— and ——, made half crowns, and —— made sovereigns and half sovereigns. The sovereigns and half sovereigns were made out of buttons. For the sovereigns we got 10s. a-piece. In making shillings and half crowns we sometimes used a metal called British plate, which is so close an imitation of silver that it is scarcely possible to distinguish it from silver. This is more expensive than the other kinds of metal which I have mentioned, and when we used it we got 10s. a pound for the coins. We generally worked two or three nights in the week; it depended upon what custom we got. When there was not much custom we used to go and pass some of the coins ourselves. —— did not pass any, but he got one-half of what we passed. We worked together in this way for six months, during the whole of which time we were never apprehended by the police, or in any fear of being apprehended. When we were not at work our tools were always either buried in the ground, or hidden in a hole behind a movable brick in the wall. During the whole time we did not hear of any one who had bought the coins from us being apprehended. At the end of six months I went to work by myself, as I found I could get more money than when I was with the others. I went to Gravesend, and there fell in with an acquaintance who followed the same pursuit as myself, and we travelled together to Portsmouth, where we remained a short time, and then returned to London, where I remained all the following winter, employed chiefly in coining; but I sometimes went out with members of the swell mob to take the dimensions of locks, in order to make false keys. After making the keys, I was sometimes engaged in the robberies. I some-times got as much as 50*l.* for my share of a robbery. One of these robberies was committed on the house of a gentleman at Plumstead, whose name I forget, and another on the house of Dr. Dodds, in the Commercial-road. Sometimes we robbed shops also. A robbery was frequently committed by one of us going into a shop, and engaging the attention of the shopkeeper, while another slipped in and took off something: or sometimes the other party would cut out a pane of glass, and take away articles. Many jewellers' shop were robbed in this way. My principal associates were named ——, ——, ——, and ——, one of my former associates in coining. I do not know where they are now. —— was once apprehended, but he was acquitted for want of evidence. A woman was living with me at that time; and I have no doubt, but one week with another, she and I made 5*l.*, by making and passing bad money, besides what I made by the robberies. Next spring she and I went to Gravesend, where she fell ill. I returned to London to get some more metal for coining, and on my road broke into a house on Plumstead common. I had been told that the house belonged to a miserly gardener, and that there was a chest with a good deal of money in it underneath the bed, but I found nothing in the chest but a suit of clothes and 15s. These I took; but as I was walking at a rapid pace into Woolwich, with the clothes in a bundle, I was met by a policeman, who stopped me, and finding that I could not give a proper description of the clothes in the bundle, conveyed me to the police-office. I was sent to Newgate, where I remained a month, and was then tried and sentenced to 12 months' imprisonment, which I underwent at Maidstone. Both at Newgate and Maidstone the prisoners have frequent opportunities of talking together, and the conversation was almost always about the robberies we had committed, and what robberies we might commit in future. There were the same opportunities in the trial ward in Durham prison, when I was in that ward, and the conversation was of the same kind. I had not been out of Maidstone prison more than a fortnight, when I committed another robbery at Shawn, a village near Gravesend. Between money and goods, I made about 35*l.* by that robbery. I was apprehended, but acquitted for want of evidence. I then went to Sunderland and broke into a ship-builder's office; there, however, I got only 6*l.* I soon after committed a robbery at Whitburn, but was caught on the premises by the squire's coach-man. When I was taken to the police-station and examined, it was discovered that I had committed the robbery at Sunderland by the cir-cumstance of part of my braces being missing, which part had been found in the ship-builder's office. For these offences I was tried by the magistrates at Sunderland, and was sentenced to two months' im-prisonment. The remainder of that summer and the winter following

I passed in the north of England, coining and passing bad money. I pretended to be a doctor to avoid suspicion, and had a man with me to pass bad money. I often really practised as a doctor. I bought several medical books, and dispensed medicine as well as I could. I got a good deal of money as a doctor, chiefly between Hartlepool and Scarborough. I got on better in the towns as a doctor than in the country. At the end of the summer, now two years ago, I got tired of this life, and determined if I could to reform and lead a new career. I engaged to go as mate in a vessel from Sunderland, which was bound for St. Petersburg, but was shipwrecked on the coast of Jutland eight days after we left the port. I returned to England, and in about a month got another situation as cook and steward on board another vessel, bound for Alexandria. Before sailing, I coined 50 dollars, with the intention of passing them at Alexandria, which I did. On my return to England, I went to Gisborough, with the intention of marrying a respectable young woman with whom I had become acquainted, but I there met with some of my old companions, and went with them to Sunderland. There I soon got through all my money in drink; and I sold my watch, a ring, and part of my clothes. I then borrowed a little money from a prostitute with whom I had become acquainted. With the money she lent me I purchased a small stock of goods, and went about as a hawker, but without a licence. This I carried on through the winter, but I made only barely enough to maintain the young woman who lent me the money (and who lived with me) and myself. I then determined to try the sea again. I wished, if I could, to drop coining altogether. I made three voyages to London, but in the last voyage I was washed overboard, and nearly lost. The young woman who lived with me was unwilling, after this, that I should go to sea, so I took to hawking again. I could, however, but barely support us; and some persons who knew I used to coin, and who wished to get a supply of false money from me, persuaded me to go again to my old business of coining, which I did. This was early in the present year. After I had been coining about two months I was apprehended on the charge for which I have now been sentenced to transportation. The cause of my apprehension was partly in consequence of my not being able to get good plaster of Paris at Sunderland to make a correct mould with, which caused the counterfeits to be inferior in make to those which I generally produced. I have no idea how many thousand counterfeit coins I have made altogether, but the number must be very great. I believe there is a deal of counterfeit money in circulation, especially in this part of England. I know several people at Newcastle and Sunderland who supply it wholesale. There is one man, who is called —— the ——, who, as I understand, has followed the business twenty or thirty years. He is generally at Newcastle or Sunderland. I do not know his real name. There is another man, named ——, at Newcastle, but I do not know where he lives in Newcastle. Indeed, persons in this trade have no fixed place of residence, and change their lodgings very frequently. I could, however, give such a description of —— the —— as would lead to his apprehension. He both coins and sells. If counterfeits are made with German silver mixed with British plate, they cannot be detected either by the ring or the weight; but they may by the feel, or by scraping them. Counterfeit coins have always a smooth surface, and the more the surface is rubbed the smoother it is; whereas the more genuine coin is rubbed, the rougher it is. Counterfeits which are not well made have also what are called a hill and a hollow; that is, one side projects a little, and the other goes inwards. I have seen bank-notes forged, but I never forged any myself, though I have passed forged notes. There is a considerable manufacture of forged notes in London. The notes generally forged are five-pound Bank of England notes. In passing base money the usual way is for two persons to go together. One enters the shop, while the other remains near, to observe what goes on. The person who goes into the shop, after he has made his purchase, and is going to pay for it, tries to take away the attention of the shopkeeper from the coin by talking about the weather. But if the shopkeeper suspects the forgery, and gives a signal to any one to fetch an officer, then the associate comes in, buys something with a good piece of money, and makes a signal to the first man to leave. I should never be able to lead an honest life if I remained in this country."

Remarks the inspector in his report:—

"Supposing the foregoing history to be true—and, under the circumstances of the case, I am disposed to believe that in the main it is so—it is instructive in various particulars. In the first place comes the wrong act by the prisoner's grandfather and grandmother, which causes the boy's mother, his first natural instructor, to enter the world as an illegitimate child, and with all the difficulties in the path of virtue which that state creates. Next, are the drunkenness and dissipation of the man who becomes the husband of this girl and the father of the prisoner, and the consequent waste of both his own property and his wife's. Then comes the abuse of a charitable institution, by sending to it, as an orphan, a child whose father was living, and who, even if his father had been dead, had a much greater claim on another party— his grandfather—than upon any funds that had been bequeathed for charity. The next stage of the history brings us to an act of religious bigotry, by which a young person is compelled to leave his home unless he will consent to break an attachment which he was forming with a respectable girl of another creed. Under the temptations and fear of poverty now presented, the boy appears to have committed his first theft, the offence being palliated, however, by the circumstance that the money was taken not from a stranger, but from a person on whom the boy had great claims. The barriers of morality, however, being once broken, and the boy thrown into a position of difficulty and temptation, his principles, probably never very firm, gradually give way, and in the course of time he becomes a daring and habitual offender; and, among other acts, commits the very one in which his grandfather had given him an example. The vast number of separate offences which may be committed by a few persons is shown by the prisoner's statement of the rate at which he and his associates coined base money. Each of the four, it will be seen, could produce a hundred separate coins in a night; and, supposing they worked, on an average, two nights in a week (his statement is 'two or three') not fewer than twenty thousand separate coins must have been forged by these men in the six months which they were together, a period forming but a small portion of their whole career as coiners."

In reference to the amount of crime in this part of England, the following statement is made by the Prison Inspector of the Northern District, which, it should be observed, includes not only the four counties which form the immediate subject of our present inquiry, but Lancashire, Cheshire, Yorkshire, and a part of Wales:—

"I am sorry to say that there has been again a considerable increase in the number of prisoners. In 1846 the average number of prisoners in the district was about 3,300; in 1847 it was about 4,000; and in 1848 about 5,100: thus showing an increase last year of 27 per cent. as compared with 1847, and of 54 per cent. as compared with 1846. This increase became greater and greater as the year advanced; the number in the last quarter having been considerably larger than the general average for the year. Last year, like 1847, shows an increase in the number of prisoners at every large prison in the district without exception. The chief causes of the increase which has taken place appear to have been the continued depression in trade (with the idleness and temptations arising from it), and the continued influx of Irish. It must be remarked, however, that a certain portion of the increase has no reference to the amount of crime in the country, as it has been caused by an unusual delay in removing convicts under sentence of transportation."

The same document from which I have already quoted contains other statements which strikingly illustrate the working of the present system of prison discipline, and its effects on that class of the population which is brought within its influence. There can be no doubt, the

Inspector observes, that as regards vagrants at least, some of our prisons are not at present sufficiently deterring; nay, that they are made positively attractive. In confirmation of this opinion, the last report of the chaplain of the county prison at Northallerton states:—

"The situation and feelings of this vagrant class of persons, who, in the North Riding, at least, constitute the great bulk of our criminal population, seem to set at nought all attempts at their improvement. They are undeterred by the zeal and activity of the police-officer—they are not reclaimed by the discipline of the prison—they are uninfluenced by any advice or instruction that can be given them; and, consequently, when liberated, they resume their former habits, their crimes, and their associates. The chaplain would further observe, that with respect to the gaol there is at present something very anomalous. By many it is not, as formerly, regarded with aversion, but as a place of refuge for the sick, the houseless, and the destitute, for those, in short, who have none to help them. Whether or not this be a healthful state of society in which such an anomaly prevails, or whether there may not be in it something requiring the correcting hand of a paternal Government, the chaplain is at a loss to determine."

The following appears in the last report of the chaplain of the prison at Kendal:—

"Clean apartments, and a sufficiency of wholesome food, contrast agreeably with what they call the late bad times, and cause them to settle down with remarkable complacency under their calamities. The deprivation of liberty is doubtless, at first, a source of fitful annoyance to the oldest offenders; but congenial companionship (the indulgence of which cannot be effectually checked under the present system), which is seldom found wanting, rapidly reconciles them to their periodical home; while beginners, who really are bowed down beneath a sense of their disgrace, are soon laughed out of their novitiate, and become as shameless and hardened as the rest."

The governor of the City Prison at York stated as follows:—

"When any prisoner comes in with clothing containing vermin we burn the clothing, and when this prisoner goes out we give him some second-hand clothing in place of that which has been burnt. When a prisoner's clothes are very ragged also, or are deficient in any article, such as shoes, we frequently give him other clothing, or a pair of shoes, as the case may be. The prisoners in want of clothing, and who are thus supplied, are generally vagrants, and especially Irish vagrants. Besides clothing we often give such prisoners money to help them on their journey. In this way we often give a prisoner on his liberation as much as 5s., in the form of clothing and money, and frequently more than that. The great majority of the vagrants are not sent to the prison for more than a week. I have no doubt that many people would be glad to come to the prison for that time, or even longer, in order to get the clothing and money which are given to those who appear to be destitute. About a month ago three men were sent to this prison for stealing a coat. Although it was an undoubted case of theft, they were committed under the Vagrant Act, and for one week only. This I understood was in consequence of the party from whom the coat was stolen being unwilling to prosecute. It appeared from the statement of the police-officer who apprehended them, that the men, in the most public manner, took the coat from a hook at the door of a woollen-draper in the town. The coat was hanging there exposed for sale. When charged with the theft they at once acknowledged it, and said they had taken the coat on purpose to be sent to prison, that they might get something to eat. This they afterwards repeated to the magistrate who examined them, and when they came to the prison, to myself also. I have no doubt whatever of the truth of the statement. Two of them were nearly naked. On leaving, all three were clad afresh from head to foot at the expense of the prison, and each of them had 3d. in money given to him. The cost of the clothing was about 6s. 6d. each, on an average; so that, altogether, more than 1*l.* was expended on these men at their liberation. The men had not been sentenced to hard labour, and, as none others are required to do any work in this prison, they had passed their week in idleness, having all the time been well fed and comfortably lodged. Three or four days after these men had been received into the prison, and while they were still with us, another man was committed for the very same offence, namely, stealing a coat. When this man was taken into the yard where the other three were, he was immediately recognized by them; and, on my putting a question to them on the subject, they admitted that he was a companion of theirs. I have no doubt that this man, having seen that the others had been so lightly dealt with, and that they had gained what they wished, had committed the same offence in the hope and expectation that he should fare as they had done. The person, however, from whom he stole the coat, was not like the other, unwilling to prosecute, and the magistrates, therefore, committed this prisoner to take his trial at the next quarter sessions; and he is now in confinement, waiting for the arrival of that period. These are far from being solitary cases of persons committing offences to get into the prison. Last winter there were many such cases. In March last a Scotchman, named W. H., was committed for seven days as a disorderly vagabond. He passed the time in idleness. At the end he was liberated, and was supplied with a shirt, jacket, trowsers, and shoes, and 6d. in money. When he left us he said that he should go off to Scotland, but he did not, in fact, leave the town; and in four days after he was committed again for exposing his person. It appeared that he had sold the jacket which we had given him, and had torn the rest of his clothing to pieces. I have no doubt that the jacket went for drink, and that he had torn his other clothing that he might get back again to prison. Being again committed for simple imprisonment without hard labour, he again, in accordance with what has hitherto been the practice of this prison, passed his time in idleness. At the end of another week he was again discharged, clad once more at the cost of the prison, and left with 6d. in his pocket. Five days afterwards he was committed a third time, the offence being again that of exposing his person. This time, except that he had a rug wrapped round him, he was quite naked. He said that he had again torn up his clothing to get back to prison. This time he was committed for two months, and sentenced to hard labour. At the expiration of this third imprisonment I told H——— that if he was committed again the magistrates would certainly have him severely flogged, and this time he left the town, and I have not seen him since. It had been suggested to me by one of the visiting justices, that I should try to frighten him away."

The inspector adds:—

"To render a prison deterring, it is not, in my opinion, necessary to resort to artificial punishments, such as flogging, tread-wheel labour or other unproductive work, or constant silence. Nor is that the most effectual plan. A system of treatment, whose purpose is the moral improvement of the offender, and the formation of good habits, carries with it, if pursued with a just regard to economy, as much pain as artificial punishment. Early rising, hard work, plain fare, punctuality, and cleanliness, are naturally painful to those to whom indolence, irregularity, and vicious indulgence are habitual, and are well known to be, in fact, more terrible to the criminal class, and therefore, more deterring. Further, this discipline confers upon the offender, habits and powers which greatly smooth his difficulty upon his release, in gaining his livelihood by honest means. It therefore must tend to prevent the deterring influence from being in his case overpowered by the stern pressure of want."

Pauperism, in all its manifold ramifications, moral and social, is a subject so immense that one feels some embarrassment in approaching it. I have already enabled you to fix the precise condition of the northern district, with reference to the amount of pauperism and its pecuniary cost, as existing in the years 1847 and 1849. Before entering further into detail on these heads, it may be well to advert to some general results bearing on the condition of the poor throughout England and Wales, as established by the evidence of official returns, which are in every point of view highly worthy of arresting our attention. The first point which strikes us is the very serious increase in the number of paupers relieved, and the cost of their relief, which has taken place during the last six years. It appears that the total number of able-bodied paupers relieved, in-door and out-door, increased from 411,890 in the quarter ended Lady-day, 1842, to 666,338 in the quarter ended Lady-day, 1848. The progressive increase in the number of the able-bodied poor which has taken place, excepting during the prosperous years from 1844 to 1846, is manifest from the following comparative statement of the number of adult able-bodied paupers relieved in England and Wales during each of the quarters ended Lady-day, 1842 to 1848 inclusive, distinguishing those relieved on account of temporary sickness or accident:—

Quarters ended Lady-day.	IN-DOOR.			OUT-DOOR.			Total Number of Able-bodied Relieved, In-door and Out-door.
	On Account of Temporary Sickness or Accident.	All other Causes, including Vagrants.	Total In-door.	On Account of Temporary Sickness or Accident.	All other Causes, including Vagrants.	Total Out-door.	
1842	10,922	74,249	85,171	134,641	192,078	326,719	411,890
1843	10,888	88,308	99,196	146,704	220,685	367,389	466,585
1844	11,458	86,327	97,785	158,280	175,419	333,699	431,484
1845	11,407	76,216	87,623	167,277	165,196	332,473	420,096
1846	11,258	74,413	85,671	144,394	152,352	296,746	382,417
1847	13,485	109,739	123,224	202,403	236,728	439,131	562,355
1848	15,084	140,795	155,879	203,373	307,086	510,459	666,338

The result is established with additional clearness, on taking the whole year instead of the quarter, and extending our view to all classes of the pauper population, inclusive of children. The total cost of relief, in-door and out-door, increased from £3,739,414 in the year 1840, to £4,956,119 in the year 1848, whilst the total numbers of in-door and out-door poor (relieved, as before, during the quarter ending Lady-day) increased from 1,199,529 in 1840, to 1,876,541 in 1848. This result

is sufficiently afflicting. It is evidenced by the following tabular statements, showing the amount of money expended for in-maintenance
and out-door relief for each of the *years*—and the total number of in-
door and out-door paupers relieved in England and Wales, for each
of the *quarters*—ended at Lady-day, 1840 to 1848 inclusive; together
with the estimated population for each year, the rate per head of such
expenditure, and the ratio per cent. of the number of paupers relieved,
on the population, with the average price of wheat per quarter in each
year:—

Years ended Lady-day.	EXPENDITURE.					Average Price of Wheat per Quarter, in each Year.*	Rate per Head of Expenditure for In-Maintenance and Out-Relief on the Population.
	In Maintenance.	Proportion per Cent. to Total.	Out-relief.	Proportion per Cent. to Total.	Total In-Maintenance and Out-Relief.		
	£		£		£	s. d.	s. d.
1840	808,151	22	2,931,263	78	3,739,414	68 6	4 9¾
1841	890,883	23	2,995,330	77	3,886,213	65 3	4 11¼
1842	934,158	23	3,090,884	77	4,025,042	64 0	5 0½
1843	958,057	22	3,321,508	78	4,279,565	54 4	5 3½
1844	833,856	21	3,223,618	79	4,057,474	51 5	4 11¼
1845	844,816	21	3,272,629	79	4,117,445	49 2	4 11½
1846	804,101	20	3,207,819	80	4,011,920	53 3	4 9¼
1847	899,095	21	3,467,960	79	4,367,055	59 0	5 1½
1848	1,102,822	22	3,853,297	78	4,956,119	64 6	5 8¾

* The average price of wheat per quarter was obtained from the
Comptroller of Corn Returns.

Year	Population for each Year, estimated according to the Ratio of Increase.	Number of Paupers of all Classes Relieved (including Children).					Ratio per Cent. of Total Number of Paupers relieved to Population.
		In-door.	Proportion per Cent. to Total.	Out-door.	Proportion per Cent. to Total.	Total In-door and Out-door.†	
1840	15,562,000	169,232	14	1,030,297	86	1,199,529	7.7
1841	15,770,000	192,106	15	1,106,942	85	1,299,048	8.2
1842	15,981,000	222,642	16	1,204,545	84	1,427,187	8.9
1843	16,194,000	238,560	15	1,300,930	85	1,539,490	9.5
1844	16,410,000	230,818	16	1,246,743	84	1,477,561	9.0
1845	16,629,000	215,325	15	1,255,645	85	1,470,970	8.8
1846	16,851,000	200,270	15	1,131,819	85	1,332,089	7.9
1847	17,076,000	265,037	15	1,456,313	85	1,721,350	10.1
1848	17,304,000	305,956	16	1,570,585	84	1,876,541	10.8

† These numbers are for the quarter ended Lady-day in each year.

NOTE.—The above expenditure is for In-Maintenance and Out-Relief only, and does not include salaries to paid officers and other establishment charges, or workhouse loans repaid. An estimate is made for places not under the Poor Law Amendment Act.

The information, as regards pauperism and expenditure, was extracted from the Quarterly Abstracts received from the clerks to the guardians of the several unions.

The year 1818 exhibits the maximum of poor-law assessment and expenditure since the commencement of the present century. In that year (with a population less than the present by one-third, be it recollected) the total amount of money levied for poor-rates in England and Wales was £9,320,440, and the amount of money expended in relief £7,870,801. The succeeding year, 1819, showed no great diminution in the total of public misery; the amount of money levied for poor-rates being £8,932,185, and that expended in relief of the poor £7,516,704. In 1834, the year ending Lady-day—being the last of the old system of poor-laws—the amount of money levied for poor-rates was £8,338,079, and that expended in relief £6,317,255. The year 1837 exhibits the minimum of poor-law assessment and expenditure, as 1818 does the maximum; the amount of money levied for poor-rates being £5,294,566, and that expended in relief £4,044,741. In the last year to which the returns extend, namely, 1848, the amount of money levied for poor-rates was £7,817,430, and the amount expended in relief £6,180,764—a sum only £150,000 less than that expended during the last year of the old system! It should be observed, however, that in 1834 the population of England and Wales was 14,372,000; whereas in 1848 it is estimated, according to the ratio of increase prevailing between 1831 and 1841, at 17,304,000, or 3,000,000 more. The rate per head of the cost of poor relief, for the estimated population, was, in 1834, upon the amount levied, 11s. 7¼d.; upon the relief expenditure, 8s. 9¼d.; in 1835, upon the amount levied, 10s. 1½d.; upon the relief expenditure, 7s. 7d.; in 1848, upon the amount levied 9s. ½d.; upon the relief expenditure, 7s. 1¾d.; being the highest rate of any subsequent year. The rate in the pound of expenditure for relief to the poor in each year, calculated on the annual value of rateable property in 1847, was for the year 1834, 1s. 10½d.; for the year 1835, before the new system had come fully into operation, 1s. 7¾d.; for the year 1836, 1s. 4¾d.; and for the year 1848, 1s. 10d.; being the highest rate of any subsequent year, and considerably higher than in 1835, and within a trifle of the rate for 1834. It will be acknowledged that such results are in a high degree curious and interesting.

Coming now to the branch of the subject more immediately concerning our present inquiry—the comparative state of the various unions included within the counties of Durham and Northumberland, and the number of in-door and out-door paupers in each, during the autumn quarter (ending upon the 30th of September) of the years 1847 and 1849 respectively, will be ascertained from the following tables, which I am enabled to submit to you, showing the return of the number of paupers relieved, in-door and out-door, for each week of the quarter.

1. For the year 1849, being the number of in-door paupers relieved in each of the unions undermentioned, in each of the thirteen weeks of the quarter ending September 30, with the total for the quarter, the average for each week, and the increase or decrease on the corresponding quarter of last year:—

IN-DOOR PAUPERS, 1849.

DURHAM.—Weeks	1	2	3	4	5	6	7	8	9	10	11	12	13	Total.	Average.	Increase.	Decrease.
Auckland	57	56	61	62	64	65	60	65	63	62	55	59	60	789	61	18	..
Chester-le-Street	59	54	56	55	55	55	53	52	52	52	51	55	54	704	54	..	..
Darlington	97	95	96	96	95	97	97	97	78	93	92	85	80	1,198	92	11	..
Durham	84	79	81	83	90	90	86	88	89	91	95	96	99	1,151	89	24	..
Gateshead	172	172	167	168	177	171	171	175	183	179	178	170	173	2,256	174	7	..
Houghton-le-Spring	14	14	12	13	10	11	11	11	14	13	13	12	13	161	12	..	5
Lanchester	59	61	54	60	52	52	53	53	55	52	56	58	61	726	56	23	..
Sedgefield	29	29	22	22	29	26	22	23	22	21	21	23	23	312	24	..	4
South Shields	146	146	146	140	140	142	137	135	140	147	144	135	130	1,828	141	10	..
Stockton	67	65	69	59	58	54	59	57	58	55	55	50	50	756	58	14	..
Sunderland	231	224	228	228	236	224	224	225	225	231	234	250	253	3,022	232	17	..
Teesdale	60	62	54	52	59	58	58	57	59	52	55	51	49	788	56	..	1
Weardale	35	32	33	33	32	31	27	27	35	28	31	30	25	399	31	8	..
										1,072							
NORTHUMBERLAND.																	
Alnwick	72	69	70	64	70	74	65	67	64	61	66	68	73	883	68	..	11
Belford	16	17	18	20	19	19	20	22	19	21	20	19	16	262	19	..	1
Bellingham	23	23	25	32	30	30	29	30	29	29	20	21	22	343	26	..	2
Berwick-on-Tweed	108	107	102	106	104	109	108	109	111	110	107	102	105	1,388	107	..	2
Castle Ward	69	62	65	65	69	70	71	71	67	72	79	84	74	918	71	6	..
Glendale	36	38	36	36	36	34	34	35	34	34	34	35	35	495	35	..	1
Haltwhistle	25	25	26	26	24	24	24	24	22	22	22	22	23	309	24	..	28
Hexham	168	171	164	164	164	161	165	155	139	135	137	136	140	1,999	154	..	2
Morpeth	56	51	51	53	53	51	51	47	46	50	46	49	51	655	50	..	..
Newcastle-on-Tyne	426	426	435	438	431	427	436	435	438	433	429	431	432	5,617	43	..	17
Rothbury	26	26	27	27	27	27	28	27	26	32	26	27	24	381	27	1	..
Tynemouth	262	267	260	266	256	252	252	250	247	243	245	246	245	3,291	253	18	..
										1,242							

2. SIMILAR RETURN AS REGARDS OUT-DOOR RELIEF.

DURHAM.—Weeks	1	2	3	4	5	6	7	8	9	10	11	12	13
Auckland	1,019	1,007	1,019	993	1,020	995	989	979	1,142	1,100	1,074	1,153	1,107
Chester-le-Street	1,295	1,295	1,291	1,291	1,290	1,290	1,256	1,256	1,240	1,240	1,184	1,184	1,181
Darlington	776	771	777	789	802	823	811	801	804	814	816	816	803
Durham	1,013	985	1,036	998	959	951	1,043	1,020	1,038	1,016	1,009	993	979
Easington	729	750	738	756	728	750	748	738	729	746	730	756	723
Gateshead	1,930	2,001	1,968	2,008	1,986	2,297	2,001	2,172	2,042	2,071	2,121	2,159	2,082
Houghton-le-Spring	811	859	815	787	830	796	827	798	803	778	832	805	830
Lanchester	336	336	338	338	347	347	352	352	357	355	375	375	368
Sedgefield	280	321	312	308	300	308	290	293	296	308	292	290	289
South Shields	1,507	1,524	1,516	1,566	1,543	1,563	1,537	1,543	1,519	1,551	1,506	1,539	1,507
Stockton	1,421	1,657	1,570	1,214	1,447	1,661	1,501	1,418	1,286	1,442	1,352	1,460	1,325
Sunderland	4,058	4,055	4,056	4,064	4,092	4,080	4,026	4,008	3,991	4,009	4,004	4,004	4,012
Teesdale	711	693	696	794	791	796	788	691	769	706	738	738	798
Weardale	618	733	616	686	636	704	634	718	623	686	623	678	626
										16,824			
NORTHUMBERLAND.													
Alnwick	928	928	981	914	944	911	978	902	950	909	950	910	933
Belford	293	291	291	282	286	284	289	287	277	274	274	269	267
Bellingham	378	382	366	380	369	370	379	371	369	371	379	379	374
Berwick-on-Tweed	1,222	1,241	1,251	1,172	1,160	1,188	1,168	1,155	1,153	1,181	1,168	1,166	1,163
Castle Ward	618	609	615	604	614	610	606	603	622	605	605	604	627
Glendale	733	729	727	744	739	741	736	750	747	755	752	750	749
Haltwhistle	144	144	133	133	134	134	138	138	139	139	136	136	146
Hexham	1,224	1,251	1,230	1,265	1,248	1,246	1,252	1,242	1,251	1,248	1,250	1,261	1,251
Morpeth	826	840	828	823	815	783	781	803	795	787	799	813	808
Newcastle-on-Tyne	6,137	6,067	6,099	6,147	6,140	6,069	6,080	6,044	6,034	6,075	6,056	6,084	6,095
Rothbury	366	367	367	369	364	364	376	376	379	379	378	378	382
Tynemouth	2,701	2,718	2,707	2,710	2,613	2,647	2,580	2,659	2,622	2,674	2,736	2,739	2,723
										15,395			

In the case of out-door relief, it is impossible to ascertain totals and averages with accuracy, many being returned twice under the heads of non-resident and non-settled relief.

3. Similar return of in-door relief for the year 1847, quarter ending September 30.

IN-DOOR PAUPERS, 1847.

DURHAM. Weeks.	1.	2.	3.	4.	5.	6.	7.	8.	9.	10.	11.	12.	13.	14.	Total.	Average.	Increase.	Decrease.
Auckland	66	50	44	51	49	55	53	55	59	63	59	61	60	60	719	55	34	..
Chester-le-Street	110	54	46	47	44	47	46	47	46	45	46	45	44	45	602	46	..	1
Darlington	154	63	61	62	62	61	59	59	59	63	59	58	62	61	789	61	3	..
Durham	125	85	85	78	83	85	84	86	85	80	84	83	92	97	1,107	85	9	..
Gateshead	276	161	157	162	160	164	163	161	165	168	164	158	158	158	2,099	162	23	..
Houghton-le-Spring	44	14	14	14	14	14	17	16	15	14	14	14	13	13	186	14	..	4
Lanchester	40	32	37	34	38	43	35	36	35	34	33	34	34	34	459	35	11	..
Sedgefield	50	34	36	36	37	37	37	32	25	25	26	26	26	26	403	31	4	..
South Shields	260	130	130	135	134	134	137	132	134	132	130	130	129	128	1,745	134	18	..
Stockton	80	41	42	48	51	54	59	59	53	36	33	36	33	35	520	43	7	..
Sunderland	300	225	223	233	244	247	211	224	215	225	217	219	219	232	2,934	226	49	..
Teesdale	160	73	70	74	65	60	58	58	60	58	60	62	63	65	826	64	6	..
Weardale	70	34	33	32	25	21	25	26	27	29	26	27	34	25	364	28	2	..
											905							
NORTHUMBERLAND.																		
Alnwick	110	100	98	101	91	89	79	75	82	84	79	73	78	80	1,174	90	37	..
Belford	..	15	16	16	16	17	16	16	16	15	15	14	14	15	197	15	..	6
Bellingham	53	21	21	21	19	19	22	24	23	24	23	23	19	21	280	23	..	11
Berwick-on-Tweed	160	112	101	108	90	81	76	85	86	78	83	81	80	81	1,142	88	10	..
Castle Ward	90	79	76	73	76	73	77	69	71	69	69	73	69	74	948	73	2	..
Glendale	70	41	39	33	34	34	39	32	35	34	41	46	42	45	495	38	10	..
Haltwhistle	30	30	30	34	34	30	30	27	27	27	27	28	28	30	382	29	5	..
Hexham	264	158	159	164	178	182	171	170	174	165	170	162	161	160	2,174	167	39	..
Morpeth	92	66	61	68	64	66	67	69	65	62	61	64	75	74	862	66	13	..
Newcastle-on-Tyne	500	374	382	389	375	385	388	383	375	373	367	369	357	361	4,678	360	3	..
Rothbury	52	30	28	28	28	27	29	28	41	27	26	27	29	25	373	29	6	..
Tynemouth	290	284	261	263	271	275	268	270	270	273	265	264	257	253	3,474	267	39	..
											1,226							

4. Similar return of out-door relief for the same quarter of the same year, excluding totals and averages for the reason above stated.

Durham. Weeks.	1.	2.	3.	4.	5.	6.	7.	8.	9.	10.	11.	12.	13.
Auckland	884	836	929	922	925	891	886	901	848	896	860	1,173	853
Chester-le-Street	964	964	964	962	962	960	960	960	961	960	962	964	964
Darlington	839	851	837	810	843	845	829	831	839	881	877	824	876
Durham	856	851	908	811	839	820	852	848	853	844	878	864	838
Easington	528	513	520	538	524	540	518	532	521	528	510	521	503
Gateshead	1,934	1,913	1,950	1,972	1,993	1,939	1,987	1,928	1,943	1,910	1,973	1,936	1,811
Houghton-le-Spring	795	709	691	805	785	812	785	822	772	808	790	790	814
Lanchester	295	283	282	260	260	265	265	268	268	276	276	310	310
Sedgefield	308	306	306	298	290	293	282	276	275	277	275	277	272
South Shields	1,243	1,242	1,254	1,248	1,251	1,246	1,253	1,226	1,258	1,252	1,267	1,263	1,310
Stockton	1,244	1,004	1,074	1,035	1,176	1,071	1,236	1,106	1,123	1,242	1,123	1,164	1,208
Sunderland	4,249	4,240	4,256	4,232	4,221	4,222	4,226	4,203	4,199	4,213	4,217	4,211	4,222
Teesdale	881	922	913	788	779	807	789	810	802	732	748	770	756
Weardale	659	615	613	619	698	625	658	640	683	645	652	601	660
										15,464			
Northumberland.													
Alnwick	831	1,121	862	1,055	852	850	1,119	871	1,112	871	872	861	1,014
Belford	515	883	509	286	286	286	289	287	285	285	479	289	302
Bellingham	342	342	345	345	345	344	350	349	349	335	336	350	350
Berwick-on-Tweed	1,041	1,044	1,042	1,035	1,042	1,044	1,029	1,033	1,035	1,096	1,095	1,094	1,037
Castle Ward	585	607	605	611	607	604	612	605	592	595	597	591	588
Glendale	668	718	667	754	675	747	654	806	664	788	661	762	666
Haltwhistle	163	163	175	175	171	171	173	173	178	178	178	178	154
Hexham	1,158	1,183	1,136	1,159	1,151	1,150	1,147	1,144	1,139	1,137	1,142	1,139	1,138
Morpeth	656	656	667	659	677	673	703	698	707	703	712	707	694
Newcastle-on-Tyne	5,065	5,150	5,287	5,254	5,232	5,151	5,258	5,269	5,282	5,385	5,463	5,513	5,394
Rothbury	355	354	354	355	354	354	355	355	355	355	355	351	351
Tynemouth	2,693	2,588	2,619	2,628	2,619	2,623	2,606	2,599	2,587	2,588	2,566	2,571	2,553
										14,356			

LABOUR AND THE POOR.

—◆—

THE RURAL DISTRICTS.

[FROM OUR SPECIAL CORRESPONDENT.]

NORTHERN COUNTIES—NORTHUMBERLAND.

Letter XXVI.

Northumberland—though the region thus designated is much narrowed in its dimensions since the days when it comprehended all the land on the east coast lying northward of the Humber—is still an extensive and important district, with a distinct and strongly-impressed character. It abounds with architectural remains of the middle ages, amongst the grandest to be found in any European country. At Newcastle, the visitor sees the huge Norman keep which the Conqueror reared to curb the bold Northumbrians, frowning over the crowded haven to which the ships of all nations repair, and over the flourishing streets which attest the modern civic grandeur of the town, and watching, as it were, over one of the most superb constructions of modern engineering science—the high-level bridge of Stephenson, across which the express trains of the Great Northern Railway whirl the throngs of passengers that flit between the capitals of England and Scotland. Other and even more imposing relics of former times are found in the minster church of Hexham, towering on its hill (Hagulstad, the holy place), above the fertile vale of Tyne; in Alnwick, that princely seat and stronghold of the Percies; in the vast feudal ruin of Warkworth, seated on its river-circled crags, and overlooking Coquetdale, with its blythely brawling stream, so dear to anglers; and, greatest of all, the steep of Bamborough, the Flame-bearer's gift to his queen, where the voyager yet sees—

> " King Ida's castle, huge and square,
> From its tall rock look grimly down,
> And on the swelling ocean frown"—

a pile that has seen fifteen centuries roll over its head, and is still strong and serviceable to the uses of man. The triangular shape of Northumberland, though naturally defined by the Cheviot hills and the Tweed, is yet not without a meaning that speaks of political relations existing in ancient days, when the island contained two hostile and warring nations, who delighted in indulging their mutual antipathies; it was a wedge projected by England amidst the Scots, and running up towards the heart of the enemy's territory. Camden says that "the ground itself, for the most part rough and hard of cultivation, seemeth to have hardened the inhabitants, whom the Scots, their neighbours, also made more fierce and stubborn, while sometimes they keep them exercised in warres, and otherwhiles in time of peace intermingle their manners among them." No county in England has made more real or solid progress in all the elements of social prosperity than Northumberland: commercial and mining enterprise goes hand in hand with skilled cultivation, and supplies a various and extensive field to industry; a sound and healthy, if limited, education, is generally diffused amongst its inhabitants; and the hard-headed shrewdness and intelligence of the peasantry form a remarkable contrast with the apathy and stolidity observable amongst them in some other quarters.

The coast district, by Morpeth, Wooler, and Belford, is generally level, and its aspect differs little from that of the North and East Ridings of Yorkshire, except that it is poorer and comparatively devoid of wood. A few miles to the west the country rises into uplands of moor and fell, which furnish scanty pasture for sheep and cattle; but tillage is active along the margin of the streams, and is pushed up the hill sides. The ure-ox, the bison, and the elk, once roamed undisturbed in these spacious tracts; and still the wild bull, with shaggy mane, and hide as tawny as the Nemean lion's, makes his lair in the woods of Chillingham, where the hospitality of the ancient house of Tankerville finds him a corner sheltered against the ruthless march of improvement. Though expelled from the territory of Douglas and Hamilton, this denizen of the Caledonian forests is still secure from molestation here.

Agriculture is less advanced in the southern division; and farms, except in "Hexhamshire" and the vicinity, are in general of moderate size. Amongst the chief proprietors are Colonel Beaumont and Mr. Silvertop, both noted for liberal dealing and enlightened views. The Duke of Northumberland has also large property here, though more in the north. Most people are loud in praise of his intentions and actions since his accession to the estates of his family. His tenants are stimulated to improvement, and large advances for draining or other operations are never withheld. The system on which his land is let is commended for its equity, and doubtless works well. In cases where complaint is made as to the tenure, leases are granted, and when objections are made to the rent as too high, the matter is referred to valuers. Should the farmer decline to stand by their award, the land is of course opened to competition. On the duke's own domain of Alnwick, employment has been found for labour to a greater extent than in the time of his predecessor, as I was informed; yet it appeared to me that more may be done with advantage, as it still has rather a neglected look. The Duke of Portland has also considerable property in the middle district of Northumberland, and its management is likewise much commended. In the northern division, farms generally run to a large size, those of 1,000 acres being met with in all parts. The homesteads are here of an extent rarely seen; indeed, with their rows of cottages adjoining, their immense farm yards with ranges of stacks, their thrashing machines worked by steam, and the brick chimney for the engine that drives them, they have much the air of corn-factories. But enter, and you will be struck with the order and science that pervade every part of the system, the large scale on which the arrangements are made, and the precision with which the work is distributed and performed. Tweedside and the Lothians can alone show the like. Still it is evident even to a passer-by who examines the appearance of the land, that improvement has nowhere reached its acme. You admire the large expanse of one newly ploughed field, the beauty of the furrows, the neat and clean look of the land; and the next minute perhaps you come upon a large piece which seems to have lain fallow for years, its balks and ridges steeped in wet, and even the clumps of rushes not extirpated. Some Northumbrian farmers have retired from their vocation in the course of the last twenty years with large fortunes—the best proof of the skill with which it had been pursued. Yet intelligent business habits are not universal amongst them. I know a farmer who holds seven hundred acres, and who confesses to never seeing a newspaper, which I should think can be no advantage to him in calculating the turn of the market. Northumberland contains a large proportion of indifferent land, on which the grain-crops do not run higher than from 12 to 16 bolls (24 to 32 bushels) an acre. Its wheat bears a much lower price in the market than that of Norfolk,

Essex, and Lincoln, and is inferior in substance and nutritive qualities. This is strikingly enough evinced in the character of the bread, which is thin and poor indeed, compared to the London-made loaf or roll. The farmer is here freed from some drawbacks to which he is exposed in other districts that might be specified. Although a sporting county, the crops sustain comparatively little injury in consequence; fox hunting is not so much the rage as in some parts of Yorkshire, where I have known a farmer have forty turkeys killed by foxes at Christmas, for which he would only be indemnified to one-half their value. There are few non-residents amongst the Northumbrian gentry. No men are more awake than the Northumbrian farmers to the necessity of applying capital and energy to the cultivation of the soil.

Before I proceed further, I may as well advert to the obstacles which are thrown in the way of such an inquiry as that on which I am engaged, by the utter want of any system for the collection of agricultural statistics. This obliges one to speak much in generalities, and even those who are best acquainted with the condition of agriculture, and who have been longest versed in its practice, can often do little more. How strange that a matter on which so many things depend, and for which a ready-made machinery may be said to exist to the hand, should be utterly unprovided for—and in that which is in many respects the first agricultural country in the world. How is the farmer to regulate his operations with certainty and satisfaction—how is the tradesman to guess the character of an approaching season, and his chances of conducting business with profit or loss—how are the people to calculate the probability of the future and to proportion their expenses with reference to its exigencies—whilst all exact knowledge as to the supply and amount of the articles which constitute the staff of life is beyond their reach? What value is to be placed on the deductions of statistics, whilst the most important department of all presents nothing but a blank? Through want of this, we have been led into a thousand miscalculations, absurdities, erroneous notions, and prejudiced theories. No man in his senses who really knew anything of the condition of the great mass of the people, could otherwise ever have believed that they ate nothing but wheaten bread to their beef and mutton—the facts being, that flesh is very often, except in favoured districts, reserved for the Sunday dinner, and that in the north of England the people are as far from despising oatmeal or peasmeal crowdy (sensibly enough too in this particular), as their neighbours beyond the Tweed.

Northumberland possesses the greatest stock-market in the north-eastern quarter of England—that of Newcastle. Its establishment dates no further back than 1830. For ten years it made comparatively little progress, but it has now absorbed all lesser circles of business in this branch into its own sphere. The show of cattle on several occasions lately has been considered unequalled for number and quality. Its condition and circumstances will be best understood from the subjoined extract from a report recently addressed to the magistrates and town council of the borough, which I am enabled to present to you through the kindness of the able and intelligent official by whom it was drawn up:—

"The seventh annual report of this market shows a considerable increase in the number of both cattle and sheep, as compared with those of former years; and also a corresponding increase in their weight and quality.

"The numbers of stock presented for sale at this market from March 28, 1848, to March 20, 1849, being fifty-two weeks, have been as follows:—Fat beasts, 30,752; keeping ditto, 3,951; sheep and lambs, 255,356; swine, 10,823; being an increase of 8,053 fat beasts; 219 keeping ditto; 21,434 sheep and lambs; and a decrease of 1,095 pigs, as compared with last year. I ought to state that the smaller kinds of the latter description of stock have sold at higher prices than were ever known.

"The following is a statement of the numbers of fat cattle and sheep and lambs offered for sale at this market during the last seven years:—

Year.	Cattle.	Sheep and Lambs.
1842	5,974	117,010
1843	8,686	141,581
1844	17,086	212,601
1845	19,098	211,172
1846	25,943	222,959
1847	22,699	233,932
1848	30,752	255,356

"It will be seen from the above, that the only interruption in the progressive improvement of this market was in the disastrous year of 1847.

"I am, gentlemen, your most obedient servant,
"FRANCIS SINTON.
"Cattle Market House, Sept. 11, 1849."

The lot of the tiller of the soil in Northumberland, though far from being exempt from hardship and vicissitude, is yet one of comparative comfort on the whole. I have already given you an account of the "hind," or as it is commonly called, the "bondage" system, as partially prevailing in Durham; it is much more widely spread in Northumberland, where it may be considered as the general condition of the labourer. But this difference is to be noted—that whereas in Durham the hind generally receives the greater portion of his wages in money, in Northumberland he is paid chiefly, and sometimes wholly, in kind. There are many degrees of variety in the condition of hinds; perhaps the best paid men—as they are those of greatest trust and mark—are the drovers employed on the large cattle-farms and sheep-walks, and charged with the care of the numerous and valuable flocks and herds which roam on the upland pastures. The drover, or head of the herdsmen, is, in fact, part holder of the stock; he has sixty sheep for every six hundred he tends, and pasturage for two horses and his cow, together with his wheat, oats, and potatoes. The drovers are a fine class of men, who dress picturesquely with their plaid (the originators, in fact, of the costume now so much in vogue with railway travellers); let the readers of the Ettrick Shepherd's works say whether they are deficient in intelligence. Their life is one of toil and exposure to bleak skies and inclement winds; yet its rustic pleasures are not the less keenly enjoyed for being few and hastily snatched. Terrible fellows, too, to quarrel with, some of them would be, and a man must wrestle well indeed to throw them. The Roman wall runs across their pastures, and may suggest to those of them who are inclined that way a world of historical reflections and poetic musings. The Cheviots rear their heads in the distance, and may remind them of days when the wild riders of the border poured down from their fastnesses, to chase the deer in Earl Percy's woods.

Having glanced in passing at rural pleasures and sports—a theme surely not unfitted for Christmas times—I may here mention one which exists only in the north of England, and which is, on many accounts, too curious a relic of other days to be passed without notice. I allude to the sword-dance, as exhibited by the guisers or mummers, who at this season quit the hay-knife and spade, or emerge from the coal-pits, to show their rustic gallantry. It is now much more rarely witnessed than it was twenty years ago. This dance is a most beautiful and animated saltatory performance, executed by parties of six men, quaintly garbed in feathered or tufted caps, and spangled jerkins; it includes a considerable variety of postures and evolutions, in which the weapons are grouped with very ingenious combinations, in star-like cluster, vertical poise, and horizontal radiation. A pipe and tabor furnish the music; and there is a spokesman of the party, who does the oratorical prelude in uncouth periods or doggrel rhyme, to repeat which would not greatly tend to edification. It is an indubitable heir-loom from the Scandinavian ancestors of our northern population; the dance is frequently celebrated by the Norse Scalds and Saga-writers, and I doubt not that after a thousand years the veritable measure and tune is still preserved to which it was performed by the Sea-Kings of Ragnar Lodbrock and Harold Hardrada, the two most redoubted champions of the North. These games flourish here at Christmas-tide—as morris-dancers in Yorkshire still circle the May-pole in the early days of summer; and may I not be excused for this brief record of toys which a few short years may blot out from the catalogue of visible things? Other amusements, of a less picturesque character, are long-bowling, the excellence of which consists in the smallest number of stone-throws to a mile (quite a different amusement from nine-pins, on a trim bowling-green), and cock-fighting—a barbarous pastime, which has now well nigh died out. But the sword-dance has escaped mention at the hands of almost all the antiquarians who have undertaken to describe the sports of the English people, and, therefore, I think it deserving of mention here.

There is one peculiarity in the aspect of Northumberland to which I may here advert. Villages are rare, and the eye is not offended by those aggregations of rickety hovels so common in some districts of the south. Small towns, from 1,000 to 5,000 inhabitants, are comparatively numerous—clean, pleasant-looking places, well and substantially built, generally of the whin or free-stone, plentifully found in the north of England and the south of Scotland. This feature of the social arrangements of the district arises, no doubt, from the insecurity of life and property caused in old times by the turbulent and predatory habits of the border population, and which admitted of safety only under the shelter of the feudal castle, or in the streets of the walled town. This, doubtless, has its effect in maintaining the old-fashioned system of lodging the farm-servants and labourers in or about the homestead. The extended cultivation of the soil is here of comparatively recent date; a great portion of the county consists of reclaimed moorland, which has been enclosed and brought under tillage within the last hundred years. The district under the Cheviots naturally was the last to receive cultivation, both from the poorness of the soil and from the memories of ancient ravage and depredation.

Some most excellent farms have been created here within fifty years—
the farm-steadings being on such a large scale as to be in fact hamlets,
and the buildings of a very superior description. The cottage accommodation in many localities was formerly indifferent, from the fact
of the dwellings being held rent-free, and therefore often neglected,
and left without repair; and in some places it still continues to be so,
but in no respect has the march of improvement been so rapid as in
this. This result is to be ascribed, I am informed, to the excellent example set by the Duke of Northumberland and Sir Walter Riddell,
a magistrate and proprietor of the county, who also presides in the
duke's court-leets. It is doubtful, indeed, whether in some cases improvement is not being pushed to extremes. New cottages are now
almost always built with four rooms (some of the old cottages had
but one); the consequence is, that the labourer cannot, for some considerable time at least, furnish them, and this leads to the temptation
of subletting.

Drilling and Harrowing

I come now to consider the condition of the hinds, who in
Northumberland constitute the mass of the agricultural labourers.
Hinds do not work for weekly wages, but are hired by the year or the
half-year. Each of the married men is provided with a cottage and
small garden on the farm for himself and family, several of whom

are in many cases engaged by the year as well as himself. The wages
of the hind, as I have said, are paid chiefly in kind; those of his sons,
either in money, or partly in money and kind. He is bound also to
find the services of a woman, who, of course, is almost always one
of his family. The conditions of the engagement vary somewhat in
different parts of the county, and will best be illustrated by taking a
series of particular instances. The first I shall take is that of a hind
employed on the Greenwich Hospital estates, once belonging to the
Derwent-water family, near Hexham, in the south-western district
of the county; he receives 36 bushels of oats, 24 of barley, 12 of peas,
3 of wheat, 3 of rye, 36 to 40 bushels of potatoes, and 24 lbs. of
wool; he has besides a cottage and garden, a cow's keep for the year,
carriage of coals from the pit, and £4 in cash. The next is that of one
employed on a farm near Morpeth, in the central district; he receives
10 bushels of wheat, 30 of oats, 10 of barley, 10 of rye, and 10 of peas;
he has besides the potatoes grown on 800 yards of ground, a cow's
keep for a year, a cottage and garden, his coals led, three hens, or
two bushels of barley as an equivalent, and £3 10s. in cash. The next
case I take from the neighbourhood of Wooler, in the northern part
of the county; this hind receives 36 bushels of oats, 24 of barley, 12
of peas, and 6 of wheat, with the potatoes grown on 1,000 yards of
ground, a cow's keep, a house and garden, coals led, and £5 in cash.
A pig also is kept in most cases, and is a source of considerable profit,
being killed for the market in winter; at 20 stone it will bring (at the
present price of pork) a sum of £5 or £5 10s. The conditions of the
agreement are in writing—sometimes, indeed, a printed form is used.
It is to be observed that the recent reduction in the price of grain
has partially affected the money value of the hind's earnings. Of
course the greater part or the whole of what he receives is consumed
in his own house, when he is married and has a tolerably numerous
family. There is, however, often a considerable surplus, and this will
fetch less in the market now than it did three years ago. Hence the
reduction of prices has in some cases affected them; and I heard
a husbandman employed in the midland district of the county (an
unmarried man, however, which is not frequently the case) regret
the tenor of his bond, and express an opinion that the condition of
the hinds and other labourers near Newcastle, where the payment
is made chiefly in money (14s. and 15s. a week, with cottage and
garden, potatoes and fuel carted) was now preferable. In some cases,
as I have stated, the hind is paid wholly in kind; he then receives 12

bolls, or 24 bushels, of wheat, with the other articles in pretty nearly the same proportions as above; in cases where his cow is not kept, he receives 5s. a week instead, which thus appears to be considered the money value of a cow's keep. I have thus given you the average wages of the hind; of course, however, these do not include the earnings of his wife and family. The latter will often amount to a sum of £20 in the year—sometimes considerably more, sometimes less. The female bondager, who is the hind's wife or eldest daughter, is paid 10d. a day for what is called small-work, and 1s. a day in harvest. This is the stipulated price, in cases where the employment of the woman is regular during the year; but when she is only casually employed, in harvest time, the amount is from 2s. to 2s. 6d. a day. Children's earnings are very various in their nature and amount; they run from 4d. to 6d. a day, and 1s. in harvest time. In one case of which I had cognizance, the man's family consisted of six persons, including his father; the half-yearly earnings of all these persons were £19 7s. None of the three daughters was employed in domestic service.

It will be admitted, I think, that in such a state of things as I have described, the condition of the hinds is one of general comfort. The system is one well adapted to a simple rural population, and especially to the Northumbrian character. It has not, however, escaped censure or condemnation, though upon no very rational or intelligible grounds. The name of the "bondage" system, as it is commonly termed, seems to have been the chief objection brought against it. Cobbett, towards the close of his life, attacked it, and his example has since found imitators, who have denounced it as a species of serfage, which it in no respect resembles. It surely argues a confusion of ideas, amounting almost to imbecility, to speak of a voluntary engagement for a year, upon specified terms, as a sort of slavery; yet this has been done. I have explained in a former letter that the true meaning of the word "bondage," if we recur to its original sense—and no doubt it is in this sense that a people of Danish descent continue to use it—is simply *husbandry; bonde* signifying to this day, in the Swedish, Danish, and Norse tongues, a free peasant, or yeoman. An outcry, however—on this ground chiefly or solely—was raised some years back against the system, and many of the hinds were led away by it. Mr. Jobson, of Chillingham Newton, one of the largest farmers in the northern district, yielded to the wishes of his men, and hired them at certain wages, with regular employment for the year, but before the year was out they unanimously desired to be replaced on their original footing. In fact, as has been well remarked, there can be no doubt that, owing to the thinness of the population, the great farmers who have suddenly sprung up on the borders found some such system necessary in order to carry on their agricultural operations, and the labourers receive an equivalent for submitting to tie themselves by the year. One of these farmers estimated to me the yearly value in money of the earnings of his hinds—not including, of course, their families—at £35 to £36 a year, which I am far from thinking an over-estimate. Unmarried farm-servants, who are lodged in the farm-house or (now more generally) in some cottage adjoining, were paid till lately £10 for the summer half-year, and £8 for the winter half-year. There has however, I am sorry to say, been a reduction in the recent hirings, and the general rate for the past year was £8 or £9 for the summer half, and £5 or £6 for the winter. The daytillmen, or husbandmen at weekly wages, regularly employed in Northumberland, are comparatively few; but there is always a class of labourers whose exact occupation is not easily definable, and who generally work on a farm during a portion of the year. The rate is 2s. 6d. a day, or by the week 12s. to 15s. Men employed in the quarries were, till lately, paid 17s. a week; their wages have been reduced within the last three months to 15s. Millers were formerly paid 16s. to 18s.; at present a general rate is 15s. In this county are some of the largest mills to be found in England. At one fine establishment of the kind, near Lesbury, belonging to Mr. Thew, 700 bolls (1,400 bushels) of grain can be ground in a week. Both water-power and steam-power are generally used in the same establishment.

Here it affords me unmixed pleasure to be able to bear testimony to the high, manly, and independent character of the northern labourer. In this respect the natives of the district with which I am dealing yield to those of no country upon earth. They face their lot, whatever it may be, with stern endurance, and bear it without murmuring. In no case, even where real hardship existed, have I heard them complain; their nature is too full of energy and resolution to be querulous. Under an aspect externally cold, deep-seated feelings, strong passions, and the enthusiasm which makes men martyrs or heroes, are hidden, not lightly to be revealed. They are also to the full as loyal and well-disposed a set of people as the island contains; and though thorough-going Liberals in politics and Puritans in religion, they are by no means disposed to speak evil of dignities. Such is the true northern type—and long may it flourish.

I have already spoken of the general diffusion of education in the county. Good schools are to be found in all the towns, and most of them have mechanics' institutes and subscription libraries. I think it to little purpose to trouble you with many details on this head; one or two points, however, deserve specification. At Chevington there is an agricultural school for the training of labourers, established and supported by Earl Grey; the boys have allotments of about 122 square yards each, for which they pay 1s. 6d. per annum, and they are stated to realize 17s. in the year by their labour. In Bamborough Castle is located the munificent charitable institution founded by Lord Crewe, Bishop of Durham in the early part of last century. The trustees of the charity deserve every praise for the care and taste with which they have restored the fabric of the castle, which was a mere ruin at the commencement of their occupation, but is now perhaps the most curious building of the kind in the world. The educational provision, however, seems hardly so extensive as was designed by the princely liberality of the founder; forty girls and the same number of boys, generally the children of labourers or small tradesmen in the neigh-bouring parishes, are all who at present are admitted to its benefits. The quality and amount of the knowledge imparted are of course reg-ulated by the destination of the pupils in life; the greater number in this case have little other prospect before them but that of a life of la-bour, though the trustees (ten clergymen of parishes in Durham and Northumberland, appointed under the will of the founder) occasion-ally send a lad to the universities. It is a curious fact, however, that the original object of the institution was to benefit shipwrecked sail-ors, and it might be a subject well worthy of inquiry how the founder's intention was so completely lost sight of, and whether some portion of the funds administered by the trustees might not be made available for the relief of the class contemplated by him, than whom more de-serving objects of bounty could hardly be found. Bamborough Castle contains a choice library of 9,000 volumes of old books, admirably selected, bequeathed by Lord Crewe and Dr. Sharpe, to which any respectable householder within 20 miles round has free access. It is to be hoped, however, that the educational arrangements of the trustees may receive some extension; in their present state they hardly appear commensurate with the very large funds at their command.

With regard to the education of the labourer, it is complained by many persons that the time allowed for school is broken in upon by the employment of the children in field labour, whenever that is to be procured, as at harvest or other seasons. I am, however, rather inclined to regard it as a benefit that the agricultural labourer is enabled by the earnings of his children to add something to his own gains, however scanty; and I cannot think that the time thus subtracted from the school (which, after all, is not more, perhaps, in most instances, than a six weeks' holiday) is any real loss. Upon this subject, one who has written well on the condition of the husbandman says, that "the employment of children in agricultural labour must limit the time and opportunities for instruction, but that it should do so is necessary in a pecuniary point of view, and, indeed, in an educational one also; for labour is the agriculturist's special education, as school is his general education. That such discipline is needful from an early period, seems undeniable, when we consider the accomplishments which he must possess in after life, as well as the manner in which, at present, he is obliged to acquire them. We know the skill and exercise required to make a good swordsman, to give the masterful use of a single weapon, either for war or amusement; none acquire this without practice; some, in spite of practice, never attain it. But the agriculturist, before he can claim work throughout the year, as an able-bodied labourer, must, especially in those counties where the cultivation is varied, honestly profess the use of very many implements which require a peculiar mode of handling, and, in spite of their more vulgar form and purposes, no inconsiderable skill to manage them with effect. The spade, the scythe, the hoe, the axe, the sickle, the flail, the beck, the bagging-hook, and the other implements of husbandry, all require a cunning and handicraft of their own, not exceedingly intricate or finished, but differing from each other—none to be attained without practice, and all, if possible, to be possessed by one able-bodied man. The materials, too, upon which he is called to work, and the process of labour which he must perform upon them, differ in kind and number as much as the tools themselves. With all these there is the best and the worst way of dealing—a right and a wrong method—so that their familiar management requires much practical address and discrimination. I was told by a very intelligent occupier of land, that the general skill of an able-bodied man decidedly increases so long as his strength lasts. For a man to turn his hand to all the works of the various seasons, he must be versatile and accomplished; and without this capability, his occupation is not secure and steady. As population increases, the labour of the field, in a purely agricultural district, becomes more and more a subject of competition, and consequently an exercise of adroitness, as well as of honesty and steady habits. When we add the peculiar manner in which all this ability must be attained, the necessity for an early apprenticeship becomes still clearer. The use of the different implements of husbandry in the most effective manner depends unquestionably upon general rules, as much as the use of the sword and musket. There is in the nature of things a flail exercise, and a scythe and plough exercise—as real as, though ruder than, that of less peaceful weapons; but as the use of these instruments has never been analysed, the novice is not drilled and instructed in their management; he must learn entirely by experience—by his own mistakes and successes. The knowledge which he obtains, too, is of the same nature—not imparted generally and together, but snatched up piecemeal and imperceptibly, resulting entirely from familiar intercourse with the subject, and amalgamated so completely with his practical habits as often to take no intellectual form at all. His powers of imitation are much needed; and as these last are in their fullest perfection in the early years of life, it is not entirely without reason, even as a matter of training, that he begins his labours as soon as the development of his bodily strength will permit him to do so." In corroboration of these views I can state that many farmers declare, that a boy who begins work later than six or seven never turns out worth anything as a labourer. There are first and second classes of labourers in agriculture, as well as in all other occupations. Those who can turn their hands to all kinds of work as the seasons draw round, naturally do best, and are always most secure of employment.

I have not hitherto given you any account of a different, but very interesting class of labourers, who are spread all along the north-east coast from Whitby to Tweedmouth—I mean the fishermen. The chief fishing port between these two places is Hartlepool, now also the seat of a vast coal-trade, where docks of immense extent have been constructed to accommodate the shipping thus engaged. When I visited the place, now about a fortnight ago, I beheld the melancholy spectacle of no less than nine coal-laden ships sunk or driven ashore on the beach near the mouth of the harbour, in the violent gale that occurred at the time. Greaves, in his "History of Cleveland," thus speaks of the antique mode of fishing:—"Truly it may be said of these poor men that they are lavish of their lives, who will hazard twenty or forty miles into the sea in their small trough, so thin that the glimpse of the sun may be seen through it; yet at ten or eleven of the clock in the morning, when they come from sea they sell their whole boat's lading for 4s., or if they do get a crown, they suppose to have chaffered faire. Three commonly come into one boat, each of them having two oars, which they govern by drawing the one hand over the other. The boat itself is built of wainscoat, for shape exceeding all models for shipping. Two men will easily carry it on land between them, yet are they so secure in them at sea, that some in a storm have lived aboard three days. Their greatest danger is nearest home, where the waves break dangerously, but they, acquainted with those seas, espying a broken wave ready to overtake them, suddenly oppose the prow, or sharp end of their boat into it, and mounting to the top descend down, as it were into a valley, hovering by until they espy a whole wave come rowling, which they observe commonly to be an odd one, whereupon, mounting with their coble, as it were upon a great furious horse, they row with might and main, and together with that wave drive themselves upon the land." Most of this is true at the present day; there are no fishermen more daring than those of Hartlepool and the ports along this coast, who brave, in their little cockleshell cobles, seas that make one stand aghast to look at them. The poetry of a fisherman's life will be appreciated by all who have read the "Antiquary," or heard the late lamented Wilson sing one of the most glorious songs existing in any language—I mean that of "Caller Herring." The cobles used by the fishermen are about 25 feet long, and five in breadth, with a flat bottom and a sharp stem (the principle of the Venetian gondola), about two tons burden. Each carries three men, one sitting at the stern using a pair of oars, the others having each one oar. Each man has three lines coiled on an oval flat piece of wicker called a rip; each line is about 200 fathoms, with 400 snoods of horse-hair (a snood is a short hair-line fastened to the main-line, with hooks attached), placed at equal distances from each other, with well-secured hooks baited with mussels, or sometimes with limpets, sand-eels, or worms; the lines are all fastened together, sunk at equal distances, and secured by perforated stones where the coast is rocky, or on sand by grapnels, or creepers, as they are styled by the fishermen. The lines are shot across the tide, and remain about two hours before they are hauled. Another method, practised in summer, is called shooting the haavers, that is, the sea-lines—*haaver* comes from the Norse word *haf*, the sea. The haavers are strong lines of 300 fathoms in length, with snoods of 4½ feet tied at distances of three fathoms; they are shot in thirty fathoms water, where they remain for several weeks, and are fresh baited as occasion requires. Ling, cod, skate, halibut, &c., are caught with these lines. Soles are caught by the plaice lines, about 240 fathoms long, with 400 snoods; they are shot in the evening and hauled next day; the bait is the small worm; the depth for soles and plaice is from six to fourteen fathoms. They are also taken by a trawling net fastened to the stern of a coble, or drawn rapidly along a smooth sandy bottom. Mackerel are occasionally found in the herring nets, but are generally caught by dor lines of fifteen fathoms and only two or three snoods, baited with the silvery part of the mackerel or other fish. The lines are hung over the side of the coble and drawn rapidly along in a fresh breeze or "mackerel gale." The gurnard or rather gurnet—called the "snorer" from the peculiar noise it utters—is taken in the same way. Herrings are taken from August to March; the nets are provided with corks at the top, and remaining upright on the water, are driven by the current. Turbot are caught in a slight net of one hundred yards by seven, the meshes being six inches from knot to knot. They are buoyed by corks at the top, and being sunk by small stones remain as a perpendicular wall in the water. Crabs and lobsters are taken by a bag-net fixed to an iron hoop twenty inches in diameter—the bait, generally, being the entrails of fish. The net remains some time in the water, generally near the rocks, and is then hauled out rapidly. Lobsters are found in winter in deeper water, fourteen or fifteen fathoms; they are also caught in summer with an iron hook at low water. Both crabs and lobsters are kept alive in large boxes, moored in harbour, called "gallies." The bait are mussels, herrings, ten-tails (the *sepia loligo*), limpets, whelks, sprats, (the *lumbricus terrestris*), and worms. In July and August the fishing is unproductive, as the dogfish abounds on the coast. When the lines are hauled the fishermen immediately return, as the lines require fresh baiting before they can be used again. The general fishing distance from land is ten to twenty miles in summer, and eight to fifteen in winter.

Northumberland has often been afflicted by periods of such disaster and depression that its present condition may be considered in comparison as one of ease and prosperity. In 1799, for example, the dearth caused by the combined pernicious influence of the war and a bad harvest was such that wheat sold in Newcastle at one guinea per Winchester bushel! At the end of the same year and the commencement of 1800, no fewer than 69 out of 71 vessels laden with coals from Shields and Sunderland were unhappily wrecked on their passage to London. The corn and provision riots of last century show how intense were the sufferings sometimes caused by want and high prices. But this is a subject which I may consider more fully hereafter.

———

LABOUR AND THE POOR.

THE RURAL DISTRICTS.

[FROM OUR SPECIAL CORRESPONDENT.]

NORTHERN COUNTIES—CUMBERLAND AND WESTMORELAND.

LETTER XXVII.

The western division of the northern district offers fully as many points of contrast as it does of resemblance to its eastern counterpart. The surface of Northumberland and Durham is generally flat, or gently undulating, except towards the west, where the country rises into that vast tract of moorland which reaches from the Cheviots down to Staffordshire, maintaining a nearly equal distance from the two seas that wash our eastern and western coasts. Cumberland and Westmoreland, on the other hand, include within their limits the most mountainous portion of the English soil; in the fastnesses of their hills and lakes the aboriginal population of our island found a refuge from Saxon and Danish invasion. Both compartments are alike rich in mineral products—coal and lead being found in abundance, and iron in smaller quantities; both also are distinguished for activity in commercial pursuits. In agriculture, however, the west must yield the palm to the east; its ruder husbandry shows nothing to match the skilled cultivation of Northumberland and the Scottish border. The ethnological diversities observable even in the present day are strongly marked, and furnish a striking testimony to the truth of ancient narrations. In the east no one can help being struck with the Scandinavian features, character, and customs of a race sprung from the Danish colonists of old Northumbria; in the west the Celtic type is not less strongly impressed on the population, and may be read in their lither forms and darker complexions, as well as in the straight aquiline features and black eyes common on this side of England. This holds true generally, in spite of a large intermixture of the Teutonic or Norse element, as evidenced by the number of names ending in *by,* which signifies, in the northern tongues, a settlement or habitation; such are Appleby, Kirkby, Lazonby, Corby, and Newby, and very many more. But Carlisle (properly *Caer-leol* or *luel,* "the castle for the army by the wall") and Penrith ("the red hill," so termed from the colour of its soil) are old British names; and the very appellation of Cumberland (more properly Cymmerland, as the word is to this day pronounced north of the Tweed) attests the true character of its population. Honour to the old and noble blood of the west! Percys and Tancarvilles—Neville, Greville, and Grenville—Beaumonts and Beauchamps—St. Maurs and St. Clairs—came in with the Conqueror, and led the redoubtable chivalry of Normandy; Forsters and Featherstonehaughs—Hilton, Vane, and Lambton—Radcliffe and Rokeby—deduce their origin from men who fought at Hastings in the fated host of Harold, or waged war with the invader through succeeding years of deadly strife. The Howards are a Danish house (their true name is Havard or Haward), though the head of the British aristocracy—I speak it merely in praise—is of modern and plebeian extraction. The Gordons are Frenchmen of Guienne—Campbells, perhaps Italians of Lombardy, of Piedmont, or Tuscany. But Graham, and Douglas, and Lowther, like Caradoc and Llewelyn, were before the Normans, before the Danes, before the Saxons—nay, before the world-conquering Romans themselves. Gog and Magog, the princes of the Goths, keep watch over the passes of the Caucasus in their enchanted castle with walls of brass and gates of burnished steel: but Arthur's tomb, in the vale of Avalon, is tended by loftier fates and more potent spirits; the dragon line is first and last of English dynasties; and even now his blood asserts its right to rule on the throne once filled by the Cymric champion.

"Westward and northward of Westmoreland," says Camden, "lieth Cumberland, the utmost region this way of the realme of England, as that which on the north side boundeth upon Scotland; on the south side and the west the Irish sea beateth upon it; and eastward, above Westmoreland, it butteth upon Northumberland. It took the name of the inhabitants, who were the true and natural Britons, and called themselves, in their owne language, Kumbri and Kambri. For the histories testifie that the Britons remained here a long time, maugre the English Saxons, howsoever they fretted and stormed thereat: yea, and Marianus himself recordeth as much, who termed this country *Cumbrorum terra*—that is, the land of the Cumbri or Britons, to say nothing of the places that everywhere here beare British names, which most evidently declare the same, and as cleerely prove mine assertion. The country, although it be somewhat with the coldest, as lying farre north, and seemeth as rough, by reason of hilles, yet for the variety thereof, it smileth upon the beholders, and giveth contentment to as many as travaile it. For, after the rockes bunching out, the mountaines standing thicke together, rich of metal mines, and betweene them greate meeres, stored with all kindes of wild-fowle, you come to pretty hilles good for pasturage, and well replenished with flockes of sheepe; beneath which again you meet with goodly plaines spreading out a great way, yeelding corne sufficiently. Besides all this, the ocean driving and dashing upon the shore affordeth plenty of excellent good fish, and upbraideth, as it were, the inhabitants thereabouts with their negligence, for that they practise fishing no more than they doe. The south part of this shire is called Copeland or Coupland, for that it beareth up the head aloft, with sharp-edged and pointed hills, which the Britons term cope."

In the county of Cumberland, 3,640 persons are returned as employed in mines, of whom 825 are under twenty years of age; 3,836 in the cotton manufacture (bleachers, dyers, and printers included), of whom 1,065 are under twenty years of age; and 388 in the flax and linen manufacture, of whom 153 are under twenty years of age. In addition to the above, 2,088 persons are returned simply as weavers. The manufacturing and mining interests of Cumberland are now in a state of high prosperity, which, as I shall explain by-and-by, has had a favourable influence on the condition of the labourers. Carlisle is the seat of flourishing establishments for the spinning and weaving of cotton, and I gladly embraced the opportunities of inspecting them which were afforded to me by the kindness of the proprietors. The Messrs. Dixon alone employ, besides spinners, 3,000 weavers, of whom about 2,000 reside in and near Carlisle. These are chiefly hand-loom weavers, employed in the manufacture of ginghams, a description of goods in the fabrication of which manual labour is employed with advantage. In this town the power-loom has not yet superseded it to any extent. Messrs. Dixon's factory, however, contains 240 power-looms, some of them on the double-shuttle principle, by which checks and other patterns of two or more colours can be woven. In the wages of hand-loom weavers an advance to the extent of not less than 20 per cent. has taken place within the last three months; the ordinary earnings of an adult male are now 12s. a week, and in some cases even more; those of women and children from 5s. to 8s. It is a circumstance which curiously illustrates the working of the enhanced rate of wages, and attests at the same time the existence of rather a low standard of *morale* in this particular class of labourers, that, in consequence, the keeping of Saint Monday is very general amongst them. The weavers who tend the power-looms earn less than the above amounts; the average wages of the men (of whom, however, there are but few) are 8s., of the women and girls 6s. There are also piecers, reelers, and warpers, who are in some cases paid as high as 16s. The wages of the other great class of workmen employed in the cotton manufacture—the spinners—are at present 16s. to 17s., considerably lower than they were a few years back, when 24s. and 25s. were generally earned. A reduction, varying from 5 to 10 per cent., took place in the calamitous year 1847, from which they have not yet recovered; though several employers expressed to me an opinion that the prosperous state of trade—a continuance of which may fairly be calculated upon with present prospects—and the brisk demand for labour consequent upon this, would have the effect of raising them to former rates in the course of the ensuing spring. No definite opinion seems yet to have been formed in this quarter as to the working of the Ten Hours Act; in fact it has hitherto been practically inoperative, as, since it became law, the mills have universally been working short time. The apprehension of a deficient crop of cotton in the United States was mentioned to me as the cause which had prevented a rise of the spinners' wages in the past autumn.

The coal district of Cumberland extends along the western coast, and an active trade in this great staple of the north is carried on in the towns and harbours of Maryport, Workington, and Harrington. But the great seat and centre of this branch of industry in Cumberland is Whitehaven, a place which now contains a population of more than 16,000 souls, and which is in some respects one of the most remarkable of our seaports. The average quantity of coals yearly exported hence (chiefly to Ireland) from 1781 to 1792 was 80,000 chaldrons; for the five years ending 1814, 100,000; in 1826 the amount was 135,000; in 1827, 115,000. In 1846 the quantity entered at the Custom-house for Whitehaven, Harrington, and Workington was 321,835 tons of coal, and 4,832 of culm. Iron ore is also sent in considerable quantities to the Welsh furnaces from the mines of Egremont and Alston, and pig-iron to Liverpool. In the sixteenth century, Whitehaven was a hamlet so obscure and inconsiderable as not to be mentioned by Camden; it is now a flourishing and well-built town, with broad and straight streets, the houses generally constructed of stone, and roofed with slate. The numerous piers raised for the improvement of its harbour have involved an immense expenditure of money. That most recently erected, called the New West Pier, is one of the finest in existence, and surpasses the most ambitious constructions of this kind which were planned by the genius of Napoleon. It was commenced in 1824, and finished in 1839; it is a noble work, of vast strength and magnitude, extending to the length of three hundred yards, and terminating in a circular bulwark or tower, raised high above the waves of the Irish Channel, on which a lighthouse is placed. The harbour was fast being silted up, and this pier was constructed with the view of preserving it; but I regret to learn that it is considered to have little or no practical effect in obviating the evil. Whitehaven owes its creation and aggrandizement wholly to the noble family of Lowther, whose ancestor obtained from King Charles II. a grant of the adjacent land, then a waste, and commenced the mining enterprises which have since been prosecuted so successfully. Sir John Lowther, we are told, having laid the foundation of the future importance of Whitehaven, lived to see a petty village (which in 1633 consisted of only nine thatched cottages) grown up into a thriving and prosperous town. The population increased so rapidly that in 1713 it consisted of 800 families, or about 4,000 souls. Sir James Lowther, son of Sir John, prosecuted with great energy the plan of his father, and lived, it is said, to see his coal-works and the rents of his buildings at Whitehaven yield upwards of £16,000 a year, though his grandfather never received above £1,500 per annum from the same source. Under his patronage the population of the town was augmented by numerous strangers from different parts of the three kingdoms—"there being at that time employment and encouragement for every one, genteel and rational entertainment and amusement for gentlemen, commerce for the merchant, and plenty of work for the mechanic and the labourer."

The first *iron* railway in the kingdom was laid from a pit near the town to the harbour. The principal collieries are those of How-gill and Whin-gill, in the immediate neighbourhood of the town; the William and Wellington pits are worked to a depth of 150 fathoms and upwards, and the workings extend for miles under the bottom of the sea. In these mines every practicable provision has been made to ensure the safety of the labourers, and to alleviate the inevitable discomforts attendant on their lot; the solidity of the works and the accuracy of the finishings are worthy of admiration, if compared with the ricketty and insecure aspect of many other places in which the miner pursues his dreary vocation. The Wellington pit has three workable coal seams—the Bannock Band, seven feet thick—the Main Band, eleven feet—and the bottom seam, about six feet. The charitable and educational institutions of this town are upon a footing not inferior to those of any other place with which I am acquainted. Of the latter I may specify a few particulars, in corroboration of this opinion. The National-school affords education to no fewer than 450 boys and girls; the school buildings, which are large, and include all requisite accommodation, were substantially repaired some years back, at the expense of a resident of the town. The Marine-school was founded in 1817 by Mr. Piper, a member of the Society of Friends of this place, who endowed it with £2,000 Five per Cent. Annuities, vested in the hands of fifteen trustees, for the education of sixty poor boys, resident in the town or neighbourhood, in reading, writing, arithmetic, gauging, navigation, and bookkeeping. The school-house was built by the late Earl of Lonsdale, and was opened in 1822. St. Nicholas's Infant and Sunday-school, erected in 1846, and capable of holding 500 children, is attended by 300, who are placed under the charge of a school-mistress and two assistants. Trinity Church-school, in Newtown, is a neat and commodious building, erected in 1847, and capable of containing 800 children. It is attended by 120 boys, and 60 girls, who pay a penny each for reading, and three-halfpence for writing, arithmetic, and geography. These and other institutions of lesser extent supply ample means of instruction for the children of the poor. The town possesses a subscription library of more than 10,000 volumes, and a mechanics' institute, established only so recently as 1844, to which a judiciously selected and increasing library is also attached.

The lead mines of Cumberland are extensive and important—producing yearly, on an average, about 7,600 tons of lead, each ton yielding nine or ten ounces of silver. They are situated in Alston parish (anciently Aldenstone), a district about nine miles in length from north to south, and eight in breadth from east to west, forming the eastern angle or nook of Cumberland. It is a region of dreary wastes and narrow dales, pent in on the west by Cross Fell, Hartside Fell, and Thackmoor Fell, and on all other sides by high lands and heaths in the counties of Northumberland, Durham, and Westmoreland. The mines of Alston Moor at one time yielded 30,000 bings of ore yearly (a bing is 8 cwt.); at present the quantity does not exceed 17,000 bings, producing about 4,200 fothers (a fother is 21 cwt.) of lead. The Hudgill Burn Mine, said to be the richest ever opened in the kingdom, has been known to yield in one year 12,000 bings. The entire number in the parish, great and small, is sixty. Copper ore is also found in the same veins with the lead ore—the latter then generally containing a large proportion of silver. Iron ores are also found throughout this district, containing from 30 to 60 per cent. of metal of very superior quality. The lead ores lie in cracks or fissures of the strata; the small fissures, and such as have not altered the level of the corresponding strata on each side, are called by the miners *strings;* those which are so large as materially to affect the coincidence of the strata, by raising one side or depressing the other, are called *veins;* hard and heavy stone veins, which are sometimes found intersecting the mines, are termed *riders;* the horizontal drifts or galleries, in which the miners work, are styled *greaves* (an old English word, signifying ditch or dyke, the correlative of the German *grabe*). Large caverns are often found in the mines, forming picturesque grottoes, resplendent with crystaline spars of various sorts, dressed in all the colours of the rainbow, which imagination sometimes peoples with the elves and dwarfs to whom ancient mythology assigned the guardianship of subterranean treasures. Among the most remarkable of these are Tutman Hole, in Gildersdale Fell, a vast cavern of unknown length, which has been explored to the distance of more than a mile—and another on Dun Fell, in Westmoreland, with chambers and passages so intricate as to rival the Cretan labyrinth, and the explorers of which have actually found it advisable to revive the contrivance of Dædalus, by taking with them a clue of thread to guide them on returning.

The mines are worked on the principal explained in a former letter, and the condition of the labourers closely resembles that prevailing in the adjacent districts of Durham and Northumberland. In 1841 the parish of Alston contained 6,063 inhabitants, and the town 1,650. "Most of the men," says a local annalist, "are miners, and, by long continuance in the works, they show a simplicity of manners rarely found amongst other labouring people. They are strong in limb, and, when in liquor, a vice too frequent, they are quarrelsome and resolute, but when from home, are remarkably tractable, and steadfastly attached to their countrymen and fellow-labourers." Kindness, hospitality, and courtesy to strangers, are pleasing features in the character of this upland population, to which even a passing visitor may bear testimony. The occupation of mining is generally supposed not to be a healthy one, and to have a tendency both to retard the period of manhood, and to induce premature old age. I turned, therefore, with curiosity and interest to the reports of the Registrar-General, with the view of testing, by correct data, the average rates of mortality, and ascertaining the number of persons living at different ages. But in all the three counties of Cumberland, Durham, and Northumberland, the mining districts are lumped together with others, of which the conditions are entirely different, and no attempt is made to discriminate between the different classes of the population; so that it is utterly impossible to attain satisfactory or reliable results in this respect. Thus it is that the most useful lines of inquiry may be frustrated by the negligence of those whose duty it is to supply materials for them. As the matter stands, big blue-books, containing interminable columns of figures from which the utmost ingenuity can extract little or nothing to the purpose, may be pronounced somewhat worse than useless. In this district there are also several large smelting mills, belonging to the London Lead Company and others, with smelting hearths, reducing and refining furnaces, and separating-houses, in which the various processes of purifying and sorting the ores are carried on.

Cumberland possesses one mineral product of which no other example is found in England—the black lead, plumbago, or wad. The mine is situated in Borrowdale, about nine miles south by west from Keswick, on the eastern side of the steep and lofty mountain of Seatollenfell, in full view of the billowy ridges of Glaramara, and surrounded by the most magnificent scenery of the lake districts. It has, however, been utterly barren for the last six years, and the search for the mineral can be carried on only in a very haphazard fashion—the wad not lying in regular veins, but being found in "sops" or "bellies," formed by the intersections of strings or small rake veins, often lying at considerable distances from each other. Nine persons only are employed in the mine. The wad with which the public are now supplied is the surplus stock of previous years on hand, or imported from abroad. The manufactory of black lead pencils in Keswick, under the management of Messrs. Banks and Foster, was unique, until the establishment of the manufacture of late years in London, and it is still said to produce a larger quantity of the article than all the other manufactories in England combined. Some processes of the manufacture—including the cutting of the cedar slips, and the rounding of the case which encircles the black lead—are carried on by machinery, simple in its principle, but of complex and highly ingenious construction, which was contrived by Mr. Jackson, wheelwright, of Keswick. The slips are cut, and the channels in which the lead is to be lodged are hollowed out, by one and the same operation; two circular saws of small dimensions, of which the planes are at right angles to each other, and which can be made to revolve 2,000 times in a minute, working in combination. By this means 1,200 cases ready for the reception of the black lead can be prepared by a single workman in one hour. There are about fifty men, women, and children, employed in the manufactory—the former at wages averaging 20s., the latter at various rates, from 5s. to 15s. The miners are paid 18s.

I now come to the condition of agriculture and of the class dependent on it; and with reference to this subject I find more diversity of circumstances prevailing in Cumberland than in any other case which has yet come under my notice. From my own observation I should be inclined to conclude that a large proportion of the cultivable soil is farmed in a very indifferent manner—judging from the small fields (of shape and demarcation often the most quaint and fantastic), the scraggy and unclean appearance of the fallows, and the wet and untidy look of the fields generally. In the two western wards of Cumberland and Allendale, below Derwent, this aspect of things is very prevalent. But there are other districts in which a condition of things very different is found to prevail, and where, as in Eskdale and Allendale, above Derwent, the example of enlightened and improving landlords has given a stimulus to the backward and slothful. Of the agriculture of these districts, a competent witness says—"Every species of improvement and melioration of the soil that industry, skill, and capital could accomplish, has been brought into action; the excellent system of tile-draining especially has been assiduously attended to; irrigation is often used when the situation is suitable" (this measure has been found of great advantage for producing heavy crops of hay), "and lime, bones, gypsum, and all other kinds of manure, are used in fertilizing it." Cumberland boasts some proprietors who yield to none in the kingdom in liberal enterprize and active exertion to benefit those around them; I need only mention Sir James Graham, the improvements effected by whom have entirely changed the appearance of his estate—and Lord Lonsdale, who is said to have invested no less a sum than £60,000 to £70,000 within the last few years in draining operations, under the Act passed for that purpose. Farms in this county are extremely various in size; but the proportion of those of 500 acres or upwards is very small, though in the lake district a farmer may have moorland pasture almost *ad lib.*, to add to his tilled land. There is a class of landowners in this county, who, if not absolutely peculiar to it, far exceed in number and relative importance the ordinary proportion; I allude to the small proprietors or yeomanry, who are here known by the appellation of "statesmen," that is, men of estate. Most of these occupy estates worth from ten to fifty pounds a year, either freehold, or held of the lord of the manor by customary tenure. It is said that this class has been decreasing in numbers during the last seventy years; they are still estimated, however, at nearly 7,000. There is also a large class of small farmers not proprietors, whose holdings are from 40 to 100 acres. The cattle of Cumberland, being intermixed with the Galloway breed, are generally small and long-horned, and in the sheep the face is often black and piebald—in both cases with the air of stock bred on the mountains. The quality of the beef and mutton, however, is hardly inferior to the primest Scottish and Welsh.

The value of land in this county ranges between two extremes, which are more widely divided than in most other districts of England. This will be best exemplified by particular instances, specifying the number of acres, and the rateable value in each parish. Stanwix parish, lying on the north side of the river Eden, opposite and close to Carlisle, is about seven miles long from east to west, and from one to two miles in breadth, comprising an area of 5,535 acres, of the rateable value of £12,359, or nearly 45s. an acre, with a population of 2,088 souls, by the census of 1841. This parish, however, includes a large village of the same name, which may be considered as a species of suburb to Carlisle, with handsome terraces and elegant houses, inhabited by the merchants and tradesmen of the adjoining city. Kirk-Bampton, a purely agricultural parish, a few miles to the south-west of Carlisle, contains 3,681 acres, and is rated at £2,868, with a population in 1841 of 536 souls. Dalston parish, also purely agricultural, contains 12,413 acres, of the gross value of £15,129, consisting in general of a dry loam—except near Dalston village, where it is gravelly, and is mostly laid down in grass for pasturage and meadow, though all kinds of grain thrive well—with a population in 1841 of 2,874 souls; the average value per acre being in this case 24s. 8d. Bowness parish, about six miles in length from east to west, and two miles in breadth north to south, occupies a large peninsular head-land, stretching westward into the Solway Firth, from the mouth of the Eden and Warnpool rivers. The soil in some parts is very fertile, in others moorish and barren, the broad and flat grounds being heavy and marshy in aspect, and the parts rising gradually presenting a mixture of reddish clay and gravel; it comprises about 11,500 acres, with a tract of waste; its rateable value is £6,570, and its inhabitants in 1841 were nearly 1,500. This parish contains many vestiges of the great Roman wall, and its two extreme stations, Gabro-Teutum and Tunnocelum. Alston parish, above-mentioned, containing 40,000 acres of meadow, pasture and common, the rateable value of which is £9,792, or under 5s. an acre on an average. Hesket-in-the-Forest (so called from having anciently formed part of Inglewood or Englewood, which once covered the greater part of Cumberland, and which is described as "a goodly great forest, full of woods, red deer and fallow, wild swine, and all manner of wild beasts") contains 14,492 acres of the rateable value of £14,474—the average as nearly as possible 20s.—and a population of 1,206 persons. The parish of Egremont contains 2,708 acres of the rateable value of £5,055—average nearly 40s.—with a population of 1,515. Millom parish, in the same ward, contains 18,600 acres, of the rateable value of £1,060—average little more than 1s. per acre—with a population of 1,497. I need not further multiply instances.

The numerous class of small proprietors and tenants, alluded to above, in some degree restricts the employment of agricultural labourers in this county; the extra labour required on a small farm, beyond that of the occupier and his family, being inconsiderable—at least upon the very imperfect system of culture which universally obtains in such cases, except where the tenant is a man of ample means, who keeps the farm chiefly as an amusement or hobby. Generally, in this county, the labourers are lodged in or near the farm-steading, where they are boarded also, as in a large proportion of instances is the case. Their present wages are from seven to eight guineas for the half-year, which is a reduction on the rates prevailing three or four years back, when they were from nine to ten. The wages of day-labourers are in general 2s. a day, but it is customary in this county for this description of labourers to receive their daily dinner at the farm-house, and in this case the wages given do not exceed 1s. 3d., and are in many cases not higher than 1s. The advantages of this arrangement are very questionable—in as much as, though the labourer may thereby obtain a better dinner than he would eat at home, the amount disposable for household expense, when the man is married and has a family, is materially lessened. This arrangement, however, subsists by the consent of both parties; and I am bound to say that I have not heard it complained of by the one principally concerned. The cottage accommodations on this side of England are, upon the whole, except in unfortunate cases of stinted means on the part of the employer, which occur more or less in all districts, not inferior to those of the north-eastern counties. The different style of building in use, as well as the different physical conformations of the country, cause the aspect of the rural districts to vary materially from those of Northumberland and Durham. The farm-houses and cottages are, for the most part, rough-cast and whitewashed, or else built of that reddish sandstone found in more or less abundance over the whole western district of our island from Cornwall to Clydesdale; in the east, brick, whinstone, or sometimes a superior freestone, are the ordinary materials. The day-labourers of this county are more exposed to suffer than those of the east, from the competition of Irish immigrants—a source of depression from which the farm-labourers of Northumberland are protected by the bondage system. During the last year numbers of "navvies," discharged from the railroads, have sought employment in farm-work in Cumberland, and in the neighbourhood of the larger towns, often with success. These men have executed the drainage of some tracts of land at a rate of remuneration not exceeding in the whole 1s. a day.

I have alluded in former letters to the comparatively high standard of education prevailing in the northern district, as evinced by the relative numbers of persons signing the marriage registers with marks, or with their names in full—which, in spite of any cavils that have been raised in depreciation of this test, I must regard as one of the most decisive that could be selected for determining the comparative amounts of ignorance and knowledge existing in a given district. I cannot conceive any motive which could induce one person in 1,000, out of those who marry in a state of sanity, to sign with a mark if he could muster up sufficient acquaintance with the art of writing to subscribe his name, as other people now-a-days do. I find that in this respect, of all the northern counties, Cumberland is the most favourably situated. During the years 1839-45, the mean proportion per cent. signing with marks was, in the county of Durham—of men 25, of women 48; in Northumberland—of men 19, of women 37; in Westmoreland—of men 20, of women 35; in Cumberland—of men only 16, of women 36. No county in England, I believe, contains a larger proportion of free endowed schools than Cumberland. The number of parishes in the county is 108; of free or endowed schools, 60. Of these a few examples, illustrative of their nature and operation, may be specified. The Grammar School of St. Bees was founded, in 1583, by Grindal, Archbishop of Canterbury (who was born in the village of Hensingham, near Whitehaven), under a charter from Queen Elizabeth. The founder's will stipulated that there should be seven governors, including the Provost of Queen's College, Oxford, and the Rector of Egremont, in the former of whom the nomination of the master was to be vested. The founder's donation was £50 a year—viz., £20 to the master, five marks to the usher, £20 to the master of Pembroke Hall, Cambridge, five marks to an exhibitioner at Queen's and Pembroke alternately, the residue to be appropriated in repairs and other charges; the head master to be a native of Cumberland, Westmoreland, or Yorkshire, and the scholars to be educated gratuitously, excepting 2s. 6d. entrance. In 1604, King James I. granted, in augmentation of the endowment, a number of messuages and tenements in the adjoining parishes, value £28 8s. yearly. Sir John Lowther, who died in 1705, gave a valuable library to this school, which has since been augmented by other donors. The site of the school and the master's house was given by Mr. Challoner; the late Earl of Lonsdale expended a large sum in repairing and enlarging it, and in its present state it is a building with some pretensions to magnificence. The intentions of the founder have been departed from in the lapse of ages, and it is no longer a free grammar school, though offering many valuable privileges to those who are educated in its precincts. There are twelve exhibitions to colleges at Oxford, and the amount of its resources, accruing from rents and dividends in the funds, is returned to the income-tax at £1,580. The number of boys in the school is 150, of whom 35 are on the foundation, and they pay an amount of about £700 yearly. At Parton (a considerable fishing village and bathing place of ancient standing), there is a school, endowed so recently as 1818 with freehold property of the value of £45 a year, besides a free house for the residence of the master—who is to teach sixty free scholars under the superintendence of eight resident trustees, who hold an anniversary meeting in July to scrutinize the master's conduct and the proficiency of the pupils. In this instance the intentions of the founder are carried out with exactitude, the master being allowed to take twenty scholars for his own benefit. There are a great variety of minor endowments in aid of schools existing beforehand.

The remains of antiquity (in an endeavour to ascertain the circumstances and relative condition of the mass of the people, some allusion to their state in ancient times cannot be thought misplaced) existing on the soil of Cumberland, attest its former importance as one of the bulwarks of England on the northern frontier. Such are the castles of Naworth (so lamentably reduced to ruin only a few years back by a fatal conflagration), Cockermouth, Millom, and Dacre—the last of which, like some others of minor importance in the northern counties, is now converted into a farm-house. Cumberland also contains the relics of one of the most curious monuments of past times to be found in our island—the Roman wall, still distinctly traceable at many parts of its course. "Verily I have seen the tract of it" (says Camden) "over the high pitches and steep descents of hills, wonderfully rising and falling; and where the fields lie more plain and open, a broad and deep ditch without, just before it, which now in many places is grounded up; and within, a bank or military highway, but in most places interrupted. It had many towers or fortresses about a mile distant from one another, which they call castle-steads; and more within, little fenced towns, termed in these days *Chesters,* the plot or ground-works whereof are to be seen in some places four square. But that I may follow the track of this wall more directly in particular, it beginneth at the Irish sea, hard by Blatum Bulgium, or Bulnesse (the present Bowness), and goeth on along the side of Solway Frith, and so by Burgh-upon-Sands unto Luguvallum, or Carlisle, where it passeth over Eden. From thence it runneth forth, and hath the river Irthing beneath it, crossing over Carnberk, a little brook running crooked, with many windings in and out, where are great tokens to be seen of a fortification. After this, having cut over the rivers Irthing and Poltross, it entereth into Northumberland, and, among the mountains huddled together, goeth along by the side of the river which they call South Tyne, without any interruption (save only that it is divided by North Tyne, where, in ancient times, there was a bridge over it), as far as to the German Ocean. Yet this admirable work could not arrest and keep out the tempestuous storms of foreign enemies; but when the Roman armies were retired out of Britain, the Picts and Scots, assaulting the wall upon the sudden with their engines and hooked weapons, plucked and pulled down the garrison soldiers, brake through the fence, and overran Britain far and near, being then disarmed and shaken with civil broils, and most miserably afflicted with extreme famine. But the most awful and lamentable misery of those heavy times, Gildas, a Britain, who lived not long after, pencilleth out lively in these words:—'As the Romans were returning homeward, there appear striving who could come first out of their barges—in which they had crossed over the Scottish seas, like unto dingy swarms of worms coming forth out of their little caves, by narrow holes, at noonday in summer when the heat of the sun is at the highest—a rabble of Scots and Picts, in manners partly differing, but united in one and the same greedy desire of bloodshed. And having knowledge once that our allies and protectors were retired home, and had denied ever to return again, they with greater confidence and boldness than before time attempt to wrest all the north side and uttermost part of the land from out of the inhabitants' hands, as far as to the very wall. Against these invasions, there stands, placed on high, in a keep, a lazy crew, unable to fight, unfit (God knoweth) for service, trembling and quaking at heart, which, night and day, sat still, as benumbed, and stirred not abroad. Meanwhile, their naked and bare-shanked enemies cease not with their hooked engines, wherewith the miserable defenders are plucked from the walls, and dashed to the ground. This good yet did such untimely death unto those that thus lost their lives, that by so quick a despatch and end they were freed from the view of the piteous pains and imminent afflictions of their brethren and children. What should I say more? When they had left the cities and high wall, they were again driven to fly and hide themselves; and being thus dispersed, in more desperate case they were than they had been before. And even as lambs are torn to pieces by butchers, so are these lamentable inhabitants by the enemies; insomuch as their abode and continuance together might be well compared to wild beasts.'"

I may now pass to Westmoreland, respecting which, however, I have little to add—inasmuch as, though its agricultural conditions differ from those of Cumberland, and large farms are more common, the lot of the labourer is as nearly as possible the same in both. "The more southerly part of this shire," says Camden, "contained in narrow spaces between the River Lone and Winandermere, is reported fruitful enough in the vallies, though it can show many fells with rough and stoney rocks, lying ever bare, without grass, and is all termed by one name, the Baronny of Kendale, or Candale, that is, the dale of Ken; for it took the name of the River Ken, which, running rough upon stones, cutteth through it. On this west bank hereof standeth Kendal or Kandal, called also Kirkby Kendale, a town of very great trade and resort, with two broad and long streets crossing the one over the other, and a place for excellent clothing, and for industry so surpassing, that in regard thereof it carrieth a great name; for the inhabitants have great traffic and want of their woollen cloths through all parts of England." Kendal is at this day one of the neatest and most beautifully built of our smaller towns. Indeed, throughout nearly all the Lake district the smallest villages have an air of elegance which is really charming, and which no doubt is attributable to the multitude of strangers resorting to them in the fine season to enjoy the pleasure of contemplating some of the grandest scenery of our island. But here I feel that I am approaching dangerous ground—for, with a vivid re-collection of the poetry of Wordsworth and the prose of Wilson, who would venture to dilate on the beauties of the lakes and mountains of Cumberland and Westmoreland? I question, however, if, when viewed beneath the effulgence of a sun of August or July, they are more grand and imposing in their aspect than on a clear frosty day of winter, with their noble heads crowned with a snowy diadem, and their enormous sides clad in robes of virgin white. Skiddaw, Blen-cathra, and the mighty Helvellyn, mirrored in the pure waters that sleep at their feet, wear now an aspect of Alpine grandeur, and may well tempt the admirer of nature to quit the noisome smoke and dirt of our great cities for a day or two, and exchange them for the delicious quiet and clear bracing atmosphere of Keswick, Rydal, or Ambleside.

LABOUR AND THE POOR.

THE RURAL DISTRICTS.

[FROM OUR SPECIAL CORRESPONDENT.]

THE STONE QUARRIES OF SWANAGE.

LETTER XXVIII.

Before proceeding to describe the condition of the agricultural labourer in the counties forming the south-eastern angle of the kingdom, it may not be amiss that I should present the reader with a brief account of the quarries and quarriers of Swanage. Such a task may appear to be somewhat episodical in a series of communications having more especial reference to the state and circumstances of the agricultural labourers, with whom the parties in question cannot properly be classed. But if they cannot be strictly so classed, it requires no very great latitude of construction to bring their occupation within the category of labour in the rural districts. It is only thus that, like the miner and the fisherman, they can be brought within the range of the present inquiry; whilst their singular position, peculiar habits, and antiquated fashion of transacting business, render them more interesting as a study than even the laborious excavator in the mine, or the hardy adventurer who braves all weathers in pursuit of the mackerel, the herring, and the pilchard.

A little to the east of St. Alban's Head the coast of Dorset trends suddenly in a northerly direction. From the north side of the entrance to Poole Harbour it makes again to the eastward, stretching towards the Isle of Wight in a waving line, that terminates with the long point of sand on the extremity of which, commanding the entrance to the Solent, stands the historic fortalice of Hurst Castle. The town of Swanage, which is in the bight of Swanage Bay, is situated about midway between St. Alban's Head and Poole Harbour, having thus an easterly look-out, with the Isle of Wight visible in the distance, when the day is at all clear. The district of high land which rises abruptly behind the town, and stretches back for some miles in the direction of Corfe Castle and Kingston, is also known by the name of Swanage. This district comprises the stone quarries in question.

On approaching Swanage from the direction of Studland, the whole district behind it, sloping rapidly up from the sea, presents to the stranger the appearance of one huge rabbit-warren. It has a varied aspect, from the surface being in some places tolerably well cultivated, and in others still covered with down. But what strikes one most is the number of holes with which it appears to be perforated, and the quantity of rubbish which has been thrown up in the immediate vicinity of each. These are to be seen, in all directions, scattered not only over the face of the downs, but also amongst the fields which have been enclosed and cultivated. They impart to the district the singular appearance alluded to; and the stranger, ignorant of its real character, might, on approaching, fancy it a spot in which game of all kinds had enjoyed a succession of jubilees, ever since the establishment of the New Forest itself.

But these are far from being the tokens of the abandonment of the land either to game or vermin. They are the signs of busy industry, the results of the toil of generations of honest and hard-working men. The chief value of the district is not in its surface, but in that which is beneath. The holes which so thickly stud the hill side are the means by which the quarriers get at its hidden treasures. The small mounds beside the holes consist partly of the produce of their labours, and partly of the debris which they necessarily accumulate in the conduct of their operations.

The district in question is part and parcel of the Isle of Purbeck, so long celebrated for its marble and its different varieties of stone. The most southerly of the chalk ridges, which dips into the sea at the Needles, emerges from it again at the point known as Old Harry, immediately to the north of Swanage—this point, indeed, forming the northern boundary of the bay. From this point it proceeds inland towards Corfe Castle, stretching towards Dorchester and the borders of Devon, near which some of its spurs again dip into the sea. The strip of land lying between this chalk ridge and the Channel, and including Swanage, the greater part of the Isle of Purbeck, and the whole of the Isle of Portland, is rich in sandstone, and here and there in that peculiar species of marble which has entered so largely into the ornamental part of our ecclesiastical architecture. About Swanage and the Isle of Portland, the sandstone comes near the surface, and is easily quarried. Proceeding northward from the coast, it soon dips under the chalk—where, of course, it cannot be worked.

Swanage has long been celebrated for its quarries and its quarriers. Almost from time immemorial has stone been extracted from the hills which sweep around the bay, until now the whole country, for miles back, is so perforated and undermined as to resemble one huge catacomb. From the earliest period, too, the quarriers have existed as an organized body—bound together, not only by the tie naturally created amongst those engaged in common pursuits, but also by a number of ancient and revered articles, which they have invariably treated as a charter of incorporation. Indeed, for centuries they were known in their corporate capacity as the Company of Marblers. They still retain the articles, to which even to this day they pay especial reverence, and they still keep up to some extent the organization of former times. That to which they now cling, however, is more the form than the substance of bygone privileges—the skeleton of their organization being still perfect, although the flesh and muscle have long since dropped away from it. But much as the general objects of the original association have been departed from, there are still some points in respect to which they are to this day rigidly enforced.

Originally, the body of stone quarriers constituted a species of copartnery—each member being interested in the profits, and liable, *pro rata,* to make good the losses of the body. When such was the case, wardens were annually elected, under the articles, whose business it was to exercise a general supervision over the interests of the body, to dispose of the produce of its labour, and divide the proceeds amongst its members. The wardens thus chosen by the quarriers were invariably members of their own body; and during their tenure of office they were relieved from all duties, except such as pertained to the post which they were called upon to fill. Some of these are still performed by the wardens—for, to the extent of electing these ancient officers, at least, the old organization is still kept up. They are not, however, so numerous now as formerly, for the simple reason that their duties are more limited. The number now elected does not exceed two, who, with the secretary (whose position is permanent), constitute the entire official staff of the body. The quarriers have still common interests to watch over and promote; and in the furtherance of these they still act in their united capacity. But the general partnership of past times no longer exists—each, so far as his labour is concerned, being at liberty to promote his own individual interests, whilst it is competent for as many as please to unite in groups for the same object.

One of the main objects of the original association was to secure a monopoly of the quarrying trade of the district. To effect this it was made one of the articles that none but such as were made free of the company should be permitted to enter its works, or to have any share whatever in the business which it pursued. As it scarcely ever happened that any were made free of the company but the children of its existing members, it followed that strangers were effectually excluded, and that the business of stone quarrying, in that neighbourhood at least, remained a complete monopoly in the hands of a certain number of families. If antiquity be an essential element of true nobility, there are families at this moment in Swanage, with unbroken genealogies, extending back far beyond those of half the nobles in the realm. One can understand both the institution and the jealous maintenance of such a provision, so long as the whole body constituted one company with common interests and liabilities. But now that the partnership is effectually broken up, and the business is pursued individually, and not as a corporate concern, it may be easier to account for, than to justify, their continued adhesion to the rule for the exclusion of strangers from the quarries. They themselves have free warren of the wide field of competition around them, of which many of them, impatient of labour in the quarries, take advantage, and obtain employment in the metropolis, or wherever else Government works may be in progress—for it is generally to these that they flock. Should they tire of this, or should occupation elsewhere fail them, the quarries at Swanage are open to them on their return—for "once a quarrier always a quarrier" is the rule. It is this that renders so invidious their jealous exclusion of the stranger from their own peculiar field. They avail themselves of the right to compete with him on his ground, but will not suffer him to meet them on theirs. They have, of course, no legal right to exclude him. Any man who chooses may, if he can get a lease from the lord of the soil, take a quarry at Swanage, and work it. But there are a thousand ways in which they could annoy him and put him at a disadvantage; and to remain, under such circumstances, for any length of time amongst them, a man would require to be possessed of some means, and of an uncommon stock of fortitude. They are particularly jealous of the Portland men, who, on the other hand, are equally jealous of them. If a master-quarrier employs any stranger in his quarry, he is liable to a fine of £5—the mode of exacting which will be afterwards alluded to. In some cases there might be a mitigation of the penalty, but the fine would, in all instances, be inflexibly enforced if the interloper could be traced back to Portland. Indeed, the rule is, never to remit, and seldom to mitigate, the fine— a knowledge of which, on the part of the quarriers generally, renders the necessity for its imposition a matter of rare occurrence. An amusing instance of the extent to which the jealousy in question is carried, and particularly as regards strangers of their own order elsewhere, was related to me by a Swanage man who had attempted to smuggle himself into the quarries in Portland. When they find a stranger at work in the latter place they generally permit him to work for a week, at the end of which time they presume that he has earned enough to carry him out of the island. They then, when circumstances will admit of it, present a very ugly alternative to him—namely, to walk a plank, partly projecting over a cliff, or to quit Portland, never to return to it. My informant told me that, for the first week, he was treated with every possible consideration; indeed, he could not conceive of greater kindness than that which he experienced, particularly from the man who worked next to him—"Yet that was the very man who laid the plank for me when the week was out," said he; giving me to understand that the alternative alluded to was then quietly, but seriously, offered to him. As a sensible man, he preferred quitting the island to walking over a cliff into the sea. "And would you serve a Portland man in the same way?" I asked him. "Well, I am not sure that we would," said he; "but we would lead him such a dog's life of it, that he would soon be glad enough to be off." The system of exclusion is, perhaps, not now so rigidly adhered to in Portland as in Swanage—the Government works which have recently been carried on at the former place having tended, more or less, to break it down, from the large and constant influx of strangers which they have occasioned.

A quarrier cannot be made free of the company until he is twenty-one. He may be apprenticed at any age at which he may be found capable of working; but at whatever time that may be, his probation does not cease until he comes of age. It is to his father that he is generally apprenticed, or, if the latter is dead, to his nearest male relative, being a quarrier. It is not necessary, however, that the master should be at all related to the apprentice. It is to the father, however, that in the great majority of cases he is apprenticed, the business regularly descending from father to son. Indeed, the veriest infants, when males, are generally treated by their parents as the raw material for future quarriers. The father is entitled to the whole profits of his son's labour during the entire period of his apprenticeship. Should the father die during the term, the apprentice does not necessarily become his own master. In that case, the mother's interests are provided for—she being conditionally entitled to the profits of his work until he attains the age at which he can be admitted a freeman. The condition on which this right is secured to her is a very simple one, and one easily performed, being neither more nor less than the payment of a shilling into the funds of the company on the day of her marriage. This condition, which is within the reach of every couple, is almost universally complied with. The ceremony of admission takes place but once a year. The grand gala-day of the quarriers is Shrove Tuesday. On that day they meet at Corfe Castle for the admission of new members and the general management of their affairs, so far as they are still regulated in common. The apprentices who have completed their term, and are otherwise unexceptionable, are then admitted, and on payment of 6s. 8d. are enrolled freemen of the company, being thenceforth entitled for life to all the privileges which that honour confers upon them. On this occasion, the quarriers manage to combine festivity and amusement with business. I have already alluded to the condition on which the mother, in case of the father's death, is entitled to her son's earnings whilst he remains an apprentice. The last couple married during the year have to provide a foot-ball, which is regarded as tantamount to the shilling paid by others—the woman who provides the foot-ball being entitled to all the privileges of those paying the shilling. As soon as the young men who are found qualified have been admitted and enrolled members of the company, they are sent out to amuse themselves with a game at foot-ball, in which they very heartily engage. The articles of the company, some of which are supposed to date back as far as the reign of Richard II., are then read by the secretary to the seniors, who remain in conclave behind, the newly-made members not being admitted to so great a privilege until the following year. If there are any matters of general interest to be talked over they are then discussed, after which the elders adjourn to join the young men at their game. The festive board is not a feature overlooked amongst the ceremonies of the day, which generally, however, to the credit of those concerned, closes without riot or disorder. Such is the principal ceremony enacted at these annual meetings—a ceremony which has now reference more to the commemoration of past privileges than the maintenance of present ones.

The secretary is a man of no little authority with them. The influence which the present incumbent of that office wields is more of a personal than an official character. His name is Webber. He is at present chief clerk and book-keeper in the office of the Messrs. Pike, formerly alluded to as the principal clay merchants in the neighbourhood of Wareham. His original occupation was that of a stone-mason, which he still occasionally pursues, during his leisure hours, by way of recreation. His labours on such occasions generally take a funereal turn—the carving of gravestones being his forte as regards the chisel. Having received some education in his youth, he has turned it to the best advantage; not only thereby improving his own position, but acquiring an almost unbounded influence over the body to whom he originally pertained. He is not only their chief official, but also their friend and counsellor. "Mr. Webber," they will tell you, "is an understandin' man. He knows more about us than we do ourselves. He keeps us all right. Whenever we get into difficulty we always go to he." To the qualities of the intelligent observer and shrewd man of business, Mr. Webber superadds some touch of the poetic fire, as the file of the *Poole Herald* can testify.

The quarriers are now divided amongst themselves into two classes—the master-quarriers, and the ordinary quarriers, who give their labour for hire. This classification goes evidently no further back than the termination of their original arrangement, by which all the quarriers were upon an equal footing. The difference between a master and an ordinary quarrier is purely accidental—the two classes not existing as distinct orders amongst them. A master-quarrier is he who takes and works a quarry; and there is nothing to prevent an ordinary workman from taking a quarry if he pleases, and if the lord is willing to give him a lease. Many of the quarries are taken and worked by a single quarrier, all the aid which he receives in his operations being in the shape of hired labour. In other cases, several join together in a kind of partnership, working a quarry between them—being sometimes employed alone, and at others having hired labour in aid of their own. When one or more intend to take a quarry, the first thing to be done is to obtain a lease from the lord. This is generally granted without much difficulty, the lessees selecting their own ground, unless some good reasons exist for confining them in their choice. By the terms of the lease the landlord becomes, as it were, a partner in the adventure; his rent depending, as to amount, upon the quantity of stone yielded by the quarry. At

Swanage the stone produced is generally of two kinds—the solid block and the flat paving stone. The lord's dues are regulated by the number of superficial feet excavated in the one case, and generally by the number of cubic feet excavated in the other. They amount to a shilling for every hundred superficial feet of paving, and the same for every hundred cubic feet of solid stone. The lord has thus an interest not only in the goodness of the quarry, but also in the industry of the quarriers. One of the conditions of the lease, therefore, is, that the quarry shall be worked—a condition sometimes only complied with as regards its letter, when it is not the interest of the lessee or lessees either to work it constantly, or to give up the lease. It is seldom that anything in the shape of a written document passes between the parties, the leases having been verbal ones from time immemorial. And when a lease is once granted, the lessees cannot be dispossessed so long as they comply with the condition already alluded to. As to the scene of operations, too, they are only limited as regards the shaft; but, having sunk the shaft at the point selected when the lease is granted, they are at liberty to work under ground in any direction they please, and as far as they please, provided they do not transgress the bounds of the landlord's property, nor come within a hundred feet of another quarry which is being then actually worked. If they go beyond the bounds within which it is competent for the landlord to license them to work, and trespass upon another man's land, the party thus aggrieved has his remedy, as in ordinary cases. If they go within the forbidden distance of another quarry, the parties whose rights are thus invaded look not for their remedy to the law of England, either common, statute, or ecclesiastical, but to the code peculiar to the locality, and which may be designated as Swanage law.

For, amongst the other peculiarities of this singular district, it must be borne in mind that its people have their own code of laws, and their own mode of giving them effect. It is possible, no doubt, theoretically, that an English writ might issue into a Swanage quarry; but English law has, generally speaking, very little to do with the practical administration of Swanage justice. When a party is suspected of trespassing in the manner alluded to upon the rights of his neighbours, a meeting of the whole body is called, by whom the accusation is heard, and if a *prima facie* case is made out, a deputation is appointed to descend into the quarry and examine into the real state of the case. This deputation is not a mere committee of investigation, whose simple duty it is to inquire and report—for it is contingently armed with administrative powers, which it is enjoined to put in force, should such a course be necessary, to do justice between the parties. Thus combining ministerial with judicial functions, the deputation descends into the quarry, provided with compasses and other appliances necessary for ascertaining the truth. If there is no ground for the accusation, the charge is dismissed, and the matter goes no further, unless the accusation be repeated; but if there is ground for it, and a trespass has actually been committed, a fine is imposed upon the delinquent party, according to the extent of his transgression. If the trespass is one which is likely to be persevered in, it is the business of the deputation to take such steps as to render it impossible that it should be so. To effect this, it is armed with very summary powers, which it invariably exercises, whenever a necessity arises for putting them in force. The mode of proceeding in such case is to destroy the portion of the quarry in which the offence is otherwise likely to be continued. This is done by breaking down the roof, or otherwise destroying the "lane" or level from which the stone is being excavated. When this process is not likely to answer the purpose, or when its execution might be attended with considerable risk or trouble, the end is more speedily effected by walling up the lane with mason work, and thus preventing the delinquent from having further ingress into it. It is seldom that the offence is repeated after this, at least in the same direction; for the culprit is not certain that, should he again be caught trespassing in the same quarter, he himself might not be walled bodily in as a warning to others. So tenacious are the quarriers of the privileges which remain to them, that I am not sure that public opinion in Swanage would not sanction such a mode of procedure with one who should prove himself incorrigible in their infraction. One reason for enforcing the rule in question is that, if they approached nearer each other, they might mutually endanger the stability of their works, as will be seen when their mode of working is described. One would think that their interest being thus mutual in the observance of the rule, they would all be anxious to observe it. And so they are, unless strongly tempted to infringe it. Thus, a vein of stone which is being worked may be found to be both improving, and getting more and more easy to work, when the prescribed limits are reached—and then the temptation to transgress them is sometimes too strong to be resisted. When the rule is being violated, the trespassers sometimes work at night, so as not to be overheard. An amusing story is told of two parties who were lately thus trespassing upon each other. They generally worked within the forbidden limits at night, until at length one of them drove his crowbar through the thin partition which separated them. The surprise of both may be imagined at seeing each other's light gleaming through the aperture which thus unexpectedly revealed them to each other. Mutual recrimination would have been worse than useless, so for a time the matter was prudently hushed up between them; but at length it leaked out, to the great scandal of the whole body.

For all purposes of action as a body, their organization is essentially democratic. They settle nothing by delegates—all matters of common interest being canvassed and determined in their primary assemblies. It is only when the time for action comes that they delegate their powers. Whenever a question arises which it is necessary for them to settle, the two stewards or wardens of the body go round to all the quarries—not exactly with the fiery cross—but with a notification to all the members of the body to attend a general meeting thereof at a time and place then mentioned. Nor is this a notification to be disregarded with impunity, the attendance being compulsory. The absentee, unless detained by sickness or other unavoidable cause, is liable, for non-attendance, to a fine of 3s. 4d.; and this being more than the average value of a whole day's work, it is seldom that any who can attend are absent for the sake of gaining half-a-day, which is the time usually occupied by such meetings. The place of meeting is generally the neighbourhood of some well-known quarry in as central a position as possible. At the mouth of most quarries there is a capstan used in drawing the stone out of the mine. The meeting is constituted under the presidency of the session warden, whereupon the business of the day is immediately entered upon. The assembly is usually addressed from the capstan, which is mounted by the different orators in succession. Sometimes the utmost order is preserved; at others, the assembly is somewhat disposed to be disorderly. "At times, sir," said one of them to me, "they do be all talking at once, except the warden, who keeps all the time calling 'silence!'" The matter, whatever it may be, being fully laid before the meeting, the next thing to be done is to come to some resolution respecting it. That being attained, the last business of the meeting is to devise the means of carrying its resolution into action. When the case is one of trespass, the mode of procedure is generally such as has been already described. When the body is called together to adjudicate upon the case of an interloper, the master-quarrier charged with having employed him is regularly put upon his trial. Should he be found guilty, he is condemned, as already intimated, to pay a fine of £5. Should he afterwards refuse to pay the fine, another meeting is convened, at which the whole matter is re-heard—when, if the former judgment is affirmed, the power of levying the fine, per force, if necessary, is delegated to a certain number of the body. These, after having given him sufficient time to reconsider his determination, proceed, if they find him still contumacious, to his quarry—and, without further warrant than the behest of the tribunal which appointed them, seize all the stone they can lay their hands upon, to the value of the fine imposed. A more lawless proceeding can scarcely be imagined—rendering, as it does, every man engaged in it liable to a civil action at least, if not to be criminally indicted, for the part he takes in it. Yet it is generally regarded in Swanage as one of the ordinary channels through which justice takes its course. Again, the body may be called together to consider respecting some real or fancied invasion of their privileges, or some nuisance which may have been instituted to their injury. The question then to be determined is, whether they will resist the innovation or abate the nuisance? If the case is one which admits only of passive resistance, the result is a simple resolution to resist; but if it is one calling for active measures, the means for taking them are immediately provided. It is but a short time ago since a case of this kind occurred. The grievance assumed the double aspect of the invasion of a right, and a positive nuisance. The offending object was neither more nor less than a weigh-bridge, which had recently been established upon a road over which the quarriers had long enjoyed the right of conveying as heavy loads as they pleased. They looked with the greatest suspicion upon the appearance amongst them of this appliance of civilized life, and immediately summoned a meeting to canvass its nature and consider its tendencies. The one they soon determined to be at least suspicious, and the other to be indisputably bad; so they resolved, by one and the same act, both to vindicate their right and abate the nuisance. The course determined upon was the very energetic one of demolishing the weigh-bridge, to effect which an executive commission was extemporized on the spot. This commission, armed with sledge hammers, was proceeding in the most orderly manner to the execution of its duty, when it was met by the *merchants* of Swanage—a set of men who will be afterwards alluded to—who did all in their power to divert it from its purpose. But all their entreaties were of no avail, until they at length pledged themselves that the offending object should be removed. On this the commission desisted, and the weigh-bridge was afterwards removed. The quarriers thus carried their point, and to this day they convey their loads over the road in question without being subjected to the annoyance of having them weighed, and of virtually paying a double toll—one for passing through the gate, in the neighbourhood of which the obnoxious machine was placed, and the other for the purpose of weighing. This may suffice to show how primitive is the state of development which society has as yet reached in Swanage.

When a quarry is taken, whether by one or more lessees, it of course requires several hands to work it. The number generally engaged in and about a quarry varies from six to twelve. When the adventurers themselves are in sufficient force to work it, no hard labour is called for. But it is seldom that you see a quarry where all those at work are master quarriers. It is not uncommon that you find two or three of them working a quarry in partnership, having five or six hired men about them to aid them in the work. The father is frequently found thus in partnership with his grown-up sons. In other cases a man, if his family is pretty numerous, may work his quarry with the aid of his sons alone, who may yet be all in their apprenticeship. The first practical operation is the sinking of the shaft, which is the only portion of the work requiring a little money capital on the part of the adventurer. The expenditure of this capital is, generally speaking, the best guarantee that the lord has that the quarry will be properly worked. The shaft is not sunk perpendicularly, as in most other mines, it being generally constructed at an angle of about 45°. It presents the appearance of a large hole in the form of a parallelogram, nearly perpendicular at one end, but slanting down at the other, at about the angle named. It is by the slant that access is had to the quarry, and the stone extracted is elevated to the surface. Along one side of this slant, or inclined plane, rude steps are constructed for the ascent and descent of the men. The rest of it is paved with flags, up which a truck is dragged with the stone which is being brought to the surface. Sometimes the motive power is a capstan—at others it is a horse. When the latter, the horse is, in some instances, joint property, and does duty at more than one quarry. The depth of the shaft is regulated by that of the vein under the surface. There are three veins of stone lying parallel to, and at pretty regular distances from, each other. To reach the first vein, the shaft, according to circumstances, must be sunk for from 40 to 70 feet. It is at the bottom of the shaft, when the vein is reached, and right under the perpendicular end of the shaft, that is to be found the real entrance to the quarry. It looks precisely like what it is—being neither more nor less than the entrance to an artificial cave. A horizontal passage is first driven from the foot of the inclined plane into the vein, from which "lanes" are struck off in different directions, in which lanes the quarry is worked. Generally, to get at the vein, a superincumbent stratum of solid but worthless stone has to be penetrated. Under this, and separated from it by only a very thin layer of clay, lies the first vein, in working which, the stone above forms a safe and substantial roof for the different lanes. They do not trust to it entirely, however, for as the lanes are widened, the roof is propped up by the rubbish which is accumulated. Thus, if a lane is originally constructed about eight feet wide, it is never permitted to exceed that width, for, to the extent to which the solid mass is excavated on the one side of it, the roof is propped up by the rubbish on the other. In some places the vein is six feet in depth, in which case it is all worked, when the men have sufficient room to stand at their labour. In others, however, it does not exceed three feet in thickness, when no more of the mass above or below is removed than is absolutely necessary to enable the men to work it. Thus, while some lanes are six feet high, others are not more than four, and the smaller the space, of course, the more laborious the occupation. Whenever they choose they can sink to the second or third veins. Many have gone to the second, but few to the third. Such as have done so have their shafts from 100 to 150 feet deep. The stone is excavated with comparative ease, lying as it does in horizontal layers, in contact with each other, and having numerous perpendicular fractures, which enable the men to detach it in blocks of different sizes from the mass. If the layers are thin, the produce is paving instead of block stone. Most quarries produce both, whilst in some the layers are occasionally found so thin that a species of slate stone is extracted from them. The stone is brought to the surface in the rough, where it is dressed and made ready for market by workmen who seldom descend into the quarry at all. This is frequently also the work to which apprentices are first put. The highest grade of work is that under ground. The work below is, of course, all conducted by candlelight; which, as may be supposed, does not add to the purity of the atmosphere in the lanes. Sometimes the quarriers complain very much of the "damps," particularly during the summer season. When the lanes are run very far back—and they are sometimes so run for hundreds of feet—it becomes advisable, as well for the additional working facilities which it will afford, as from sanitary considerations, to construct an additional shaft. Sometimes, for the sake of proper ventilation, a lane will be run through to an old quarry, which may be close at hand. At others, the owners of two contiguous quarries will agree to run a lane from one to the other for the same purpose.

When the stone is dressed and ready for market, it is conveyed in waggons to the harbour. The farmers who lease the surface under which the quarries are worked, claim the right of carriage between them and the beach. This claim is acquiesced in, but the result is that the quarriers pay a much higher freight than they would otherwise do. If in any case the farmer should decline the carriage, the quarrier can then look where he pleases for his means of transport.

All the means and appliances of labour about the quarries are of the rudest description. Main force is the element principally relied upon, but little aid being derived from machinery. Long as the district about Swanage has been quarried, and immense as has been the quantity of stone shipped from it, it does not, even to this day, possess a pier or jetty of any description. The vessels which receive the stone lie at anchor in the bay. The stone is dragged from the shore by very tall horses, in carts with very high wheels, as far into the sea as such an apparatus can venture with safety. From the carts it is consigned to the vessels, by means of barges, which are constantly plying to and fro. Could there be a ruder contrivance than this? Yet it is in perfect keeping with everything around.

But the most extraordinary characteristic of this singular social development still remains to be described. The world has long been divided on the subject of the standard of value, and the question of the currency is one that has baffled the most profound statesmen and the most astute economists. In Swanage these questions have received a very easy solution. The virtual standard of value is the article chiefly produced in the district—stone. But as silver is to the only standard of value, gold, in the national currency—so is bread to stone, the recognized and accepted standard in the currency of Swanage. This may be very new to the reader, but it is very ancient in this remote nook of Dorset. Stone is virtually in Swanage the standard of value, and the currency is composed of stone and bread. There is scarcely any coin in circulation in the district. All payments which are not made in actual money—those so made being very few—or in goods, are made either in stone or in bread. The workmen in the quarries are paid in stone, and it is for stone that they receive in exchange such articles as they consume. It is quite true that there is a money value put on everything, but stone is almost the universal substitute for money. Thus when a master quarrier takes a quarry, and hires workmen to assist him in his operations, a money value is put upon their labour, and they are engaged at so much per day, or so much per week. But when the time of payment comes, no money passes between the master and his workmen, but a portion of the stone produced, equal in value (taking its current value for the week) to the sum at which the workmen were in each case hired, is set apart for them. Thus, if a man was hired at the rate of 3s. a day, instead of getting 18s. at the end of the week, he would get 18s. worth of stone. The stone so apportioned to him would in that case constitute his sole means for commanding the necessaries of life for himself and family. Sometimes, instead of the stone, the quarrier gives his workmen orders upon the merchant with whom he has credit. But still it is the stone that does it all, for it is upon the credit of the stone that the orders are executed. The course of dealing between the master quarrier and the merchant will serve to explain the whole system.

It is necessary to premise that the word *merchant* has, in Swanage, a peculiar local signification. There are here two classes of merchants in the ordinary acceptation of the term. There is, in the first place, the class of independent dealers who sell their goods for ready money, when they can get it, or for bread, which they afterwards convert into money, but who never deal in transactions having the transfer of stone for their basis. There is, in the next place, the class to whom the term *merchant* is exclusively applied, who keep a general assortment of goods, which they exchange for stone. Each merchant has a bakehouse attached to his establishment, the bread baked at which is one of the chief articles which he exchanges for the stone. His shop is thus, in one sense, a bank of issue; for he manufactures in it that which forms half the currency of the district—and its entire currency, in the way of small change. Every quarrier must have his merchant, as every man of business elsewhere has his banker. To establish a credit with a merchant, the quarrier must deposit stone with him, and the extent of the credit is regulated by the quantity of stone deposited. The merchant has what he calls his *banker*, which is neither more nor less than the spot of ground on which the stone left with him is deposited. The banker is like the vault, and the stone like the bullion deposited in it.

The quarrier may make his deposits in the banker when he pleases and to what extent he pleases, until the merchant, for reasons of his own, refuses to receive any more. An account is kept by both parties of the quantity deposited, as well as of the goods taken by the quarrier, or on his order, from the shop. When he wants to know how he stands he takes an account, and the balance, in the shape of stone, which remains to his credit in the banker, indicates the extent of his worldly means. When the stone is deposited a money value is set upon it, according to the current price of the day, that price being now about 21s. 6d. per hundred superficial feet of paving stone. The goods are also sold at a money value, so that the accounts between the parties are, as elsewhere, kept in money. When the quarrier pays his men in stone, they must have their merchant, as he has, to turn it to account. When he pays them by order on his merchant, he of course takes all the stone and deposits it, to his own account, in his merchant's banker. The merchants dispose of it as they best can, Southampton being one of their best and most accessible markets.

So far the system savours considerably of transactions based on credit. But there are, as it were, ready money transactions, in which stone figures as currency. A pair of boots, for instance, is sometimes paid for at once in stone. At some of the public-houses they take stone in deposit; at others, if a man wants a pint of beer, he must wheel a barrowful of stone to the house to pay for it. But in the great majority of transactions of the ready money kind, bread is the currency in vogue. Although the merchants keep a pretty varied stock, it is generally in the shape of different articles of food, bread being the principal. If a quarrier therefore, wants a coat, a pair of shoes, or anything else for himself or family which his merchant has not got, he has to go to one of the independent dealers who can supply him. But they not dealing in stone, and he having no credit with them, he is obliged to procure from his merchant that which they will take in exchange for what he wants. This is generally—in fact almost invariably—bread. He, therefore, draws for so much bread upon his merchant, which he carries to his clothier or his shoemaker, and gives in exchange for what he procures. It is in transactions like these that the system works with peculiar hardship to him. The result of the whole system is to make almost every necessary of life 15 to 20 per cent. dearer in Swanage than elsewhere in the neighbourhood. Thus the loaf which can be got for 5d. in Poole, is valued at 6½d. in Swanage. But it is only so valued to the quarrier when he takes it from his merchant. When he exchanges it for anything else, at the independent dealer's, he can only get 5½d. for it, or 5½d.'s worth. He thus loses a penny on every loaf which he turns to the purposes of currency. A quarrier in whose house I was seated, conversing on the subject, sent, during the interview, for some ale. His wife took with her a 6½d. loaf, and brought back 5½d.'s worth of beer. The stranger, ignorant of the purpose to which bread is thus applied, would be utterly at a loss to account for the quantity which he would see carried about in all directions. If a woman wants a piece of ribbon she must take a loaf with her to the shop. The dealers afterwards convert the bread into money at the price at which they receive it—those who ultimately consume it thus getting it at a penny a loaf less than the value at which it was originally issued from the merchant's establishment, and all at the cost of the poor quarrier. But this is not the only disadvantage under which he labours, for whilst his stone is taken from him at the lowest—and the bread and other articles which he receives from his merchant are given to him at the highest—possible rate, such commodities as he afterwards purchases from the dealers, by means of his bread, are highly overcharged; whilst that in which he pays for them is reduced at the counter fully 16 per cent. in value. Thus although the wages of a quarrier may nominally be 3s. a day, they are virtually reduced to 2s. by the series of peculations to which he is subjected. But even of the master quarriers, few can be said to average 3s. nominally a day. The average nominal wages of the working men, as contradistinguished from the masters, are from 2s. 3d. to 2s. 9d. a day. This, in reality, is but from 1s. 6d. to 1s. 10d. a day. They are also subjected to another great inconvenience by the length of time which sometimes elapses ere the merchants will balance their accounts with them. Some are careful to have a balance struck every year, but there are cases in which years elapse without any settlement of accounts. This leads some of them astray as to their real standing, whilst it begets reckless habits in the more thoughtless of them. These latter, so long as they have credit at their merchants, care little how they stand, so long as the day of reckoning is postponed. Others again, meaning to stand well, find themselves at last unexpectedly in debt, when they thought they had a balance in their merchant's hands.

There is little money in circulation in the town and district; house rents are exacted in money, and so are the lord's dues. To enable the quarriers to meet these demands, and also the rates which are levied upon them, the merchants, instead of goods, allow a certain sum of money to be drawn each week by their depositors. It is seldom that this sum exceeds 2s. 6d. per week to each depositor. This enables them to meet the demands in question, and also occasionally to buy a little fresh meat, which they do not often enjoy, and for which they have invariably to pay money.

They bitterly complain of the inconvenience and losses to which they are subjected from the almost total absence of money from their ordinary every-day transactions; and they are most anxious that some merchants would come amongst them, who, taking their stone at even a lower valuation than now, would pay them money instead of giving them goods for it. In this respect matters do not seem to be improving with them, the more advanced in life amongst them saying that there is less money in circulation now than formerly. But their universal desire is, at any reasonable sacrifice, to commute their present earnings into money. If a money system were established amongst them, instead of the present system of limited barter, not only would the price of the necessaries of life fall, and their physical comforts be thus increased, but the habits of some of them would be greatly improved.

Taking their condition throughout the year, they are, on the whole, considerably better off than the agricultural labourers throughout the country. Their houses are, generally speaking, vastly superior as regards accommodation, and consequently as regards cleanliness and healthiness, to those of the labourer in the fields. There is an abundance of the best material for constructing them at hand, and they are in many cases provided with four or five rooms. With the exception of Hop-about-lane, the houses in which are of a very inferior description, the dwellings of the quarriers in Swanage may be characterized as spacious, clean, and comfortable. Their furniture and bedding are also abundant and clean. They generally pay from £4 to £4 10s. in the shape of rent, in addition to which they pay rates amounting to nearly £1 more. Their diet, too, is also, in the main, better than that of the farm-labourer. They seldom eat fresh meat, but they consume more bacon than he does. But even of this they have a very insufficient supply, considering the laborious character of their occupation.

They are generally very ignorant, and in the majority of cases almost entirely illiterate. If any of them attend school, they are sent too early to work to derive much benefit from it. The boys, at about nine years of age, become useful about the quarry, and they are sent below as soon as they become strong and skilful enough for underground work. The bulk of the quarriers adhere to the Church, the rest being chiefly divided amongst the Methodists and Independents. On the whole, they are considered an orderly and well-regulated set of men.

But few, perhaps, of those who read this account were aware, before perusing it, that so rude and primitive a state of society is to be met with within a few hours' ride of the metropolis.

LABOUR AND THE POOR.

THE RURAL DISTRICTS.

[FROM OUR SPECIAL CORRESPONDENT.]

THE SOUTHERN AND WESTERN COUNTIES.

Letter XXIX.

Having disposed of the counties of Somerset, Devon, Cornwall, and Dorset, I proceed to give some account of the state and prospects of the labourer in Hampshire, Surrey, Sussex, and Kent. In doing so I shall first describe him as I found him in various parts of Hampshire, and in the western division of Sussex. I take these two together, because the prevailing industry in both is the same—farming, in its ordinary acceptation, being carried on, to the almost total exclusion of other kinds of rural employment, throughout the whole of the one county and the western moiety of the other. It is true that in some portions of Hampshire (as the neighbourhood of Petersfield), hop-gardens are to be met with; but, taking the county generally, the cultivation of the hop is rare and exceptional. It is far more general in the county of Surrey, whilst in East Sussex, and throughout almost the whole of Kent, it is carried to such an extent as to exercise a material influence over labour and the general condition of the labourer. For the present, therefore, I shall confine myself to the portion of the district comprised by the four counties in which farming, in the usual sense, is almost exclusively carried on.

The south-eastern section of Hampshire, comprising somewhat more than one-fifth of its whole area, is almost as isolated from the main body of the county as is the Isle of Wight itself. On the east and south it has Southampton Water, the Solent, and Christchurch Bay—whilst to the west it abuts upon Dorset, and to the north upon the south-eastern angle of the county of Wilts. Between the upper end of Southampton Water and the Wiltshire line is a narrow strip of land, by which alone the district has a direct connection with the main body of the county.

This part of Hampshire is chiefly famous from so large a portion of its surface being occupied by what is known as the New Forest. The wild and picturesque tract thus designated, so long a royal domain, occupies almost the whole of the central portion of the district. It is surrounded on nearly all sides by a belt of cultivated or cultivable land, which separates it from Wilts and Dorset, and which interposes, except at a very few points, between it and Southampton Water, the Solent, and the Channel. Throughout the whole of this cultivated belt—but particularly the portion of it stretching to the south of the Forest, from Boldre Church to Lymington, and thence to Christchurch, and to the west of it, from Christchurch to Ringwood, and thence on to Fordingbridge—the condition of the farm-labourer is, in almost all respects, similar to what I have already described it as being in the adjoining counties of Dorset and Wilts. Between Lymington and Boldre, which is the south-eastern angle of the Forest, the land is good, and in parts highly cultivated. The labouring population is, therefore, denser in that direction in proportion to the surface than it is immediately to the west of Lymington, between which and Christchurch there is a good deal of high down-land. In places in which this high down-land stretches back any distance from the sea, large tracts may be seen without the faintest trace of a human habitation upon them. The coast is high, cold, and shelterless, vegetation along it struggling in many places very hard for an existence. The trees, when they are to be met with, are all bent inwards at a considerable angle from the perpendicular; their branches stretch inland from the sea, whilst at top they are cut smoothly off by the keen wind, as if a huge scythe had been swept over them, at elevations varying according to their distance from the shore. Proceeding inland, the cold, cheerless, and naked downs merge gradually into the vast heathy tracks of the Forest, with patches of land in a state of tolerable cultivation sometimes dividing them from each other. On these, and on the borders of the heath, humble tenements may be seen at somewhat long intervals. The country improves, and population increases in density, as you approach Christchurch—from which, up to Ringwood and Fordingbridge, stretches a narrow belt of land, about twelve miles in length (and separating the Forest from Dorset), the greater portion of the surface of which is in a state of comparatively high cultivation. Taking the whole of the portion of Hampshire now under consideration, it is along this last-mentioned belt that population is to be found pressing in the greatest numbers upon the area. In 1841 the

Ringwood division of the county, with an area of about 67,000 acres, and comprising, amongst other districts, the hundreds of Christchurch and Fordingbridge, had a population of upwards of 18,500 souls, being about one for every 3¾ acres. The population of the Lymington division was, at the same time, only about 11,500 to an area of about 80,000 acres, being about one person to every 7 acres, or a little more than one-half the population of the other division. The population of the Petersfield division, which lies inland on the eastern side of the county, and is tolerably well cultivated throughout, was only about 10,600 to an area of about 62,000 acres, or about one person to every six acres—or from 30 to 40 per cent. lower, in proportion to the surface, than that of the Ringwood division. The disparity between the Ringwood and Lymington divisions is easily accounted for by the extent of the latter, which lies waste and unproductive; but it is not so easy to explain that existing in this respect between the Ringwood and Petersfield divisions—seeing that, in both cases, the greater portion of the surface is occupied and cultivated in one way or other. But whatever may be the reason for this disproportion, the fact is that it is as great now as it was in 1841. No one can traverse the tract of land of which Ringwood is, longitudinally, the centre, without being struck by the extent to which it is pressed upon by population. Most of the county districts, taking them separately, are considerably below the average ratio of population to surface throughout all England, comprehending, of course, the entire population—that of the towns, as well as that of the rural districts. But the Ringwood division of Hampshire comes, in this respect, within a fraction of the average rate. The disparity between the Ringwood and the other divisions is, if anything, greater now than it was in 1841; for both the latter districts have received more relief from emigration than the Ringwood one.

As may be supposed, so comparatively dense a population, in a district almost exclusively agricultural, will furnish a very large proportion of cases of casual and permanent distress. It is in the hundred of Fordingbridge that that distress is, perhaps, seen most constantly and to the greatest extent. In 1842 the amount of poor-rates levied in the Fordingbridge division of the hundred very nearly equalled one-third of the whole assessed value of its property. In Lymington, during the same year, the poor-rates did not amount to one-seventh of the assessed value of property; whilst, although they fell rather heavily upon the town of Petersfield itself, the ratio in the hundred in which it is situated did not much exceed one-tenth of the assessed value of the property. In Ringwood, on the other hand, within the same division as Fordingbridge, they exceeded one-sixth of the declared value of the property assessed. The same relative proportion, as regards rates, is still kept up between these places. There is a larger actual amount of employment given in the Ringwood division than in the others—but not so much as in them, in proportion to the numbers to be employed. Hence the comparative weight with which the rates fall upon that division. The great bulk of the land is brought under cultivation, between Dorset and the Forest, and between the border of Wilts and the Channel, but much of it is appropriated to the purposes of dairy farming, which gives rise to far less employment than tillage does. A dairy farm of considerable extent can be managed by a man and his family without any extra aid—whereas, to get crops from an ordinary farm, even of small size, it is in ninety-nine cases out of a hundred necessary to call in the aid of hired labour. It is true that there are but few dairy farms so economically managed, but, as a general rule, the more land is laid out in dairy farms the smaller is the population of the district, or the greater the number of paupers. In districts, indeed, where dairy farming has been long pursued, as in portions of Buckinghamshire, Berkshire, Oxfordshire, Somerset, and Devon, the relative proportion of paupers to population is not greater than elsewhere, because the effect of such a system has been to keep down population. But in places in which arable farms have recently been turned into dairy farms, the proportion of paupers to population is generally found to be larger than elsewhere, inasmuch as time has not yet been given to the system to develop its necessary tendency towards the diminution of population. This is the case in some parts of the counties just named, and in many parts of Wilts and Dorset. It is also the case, to some extent, in the portion of Hampshire now under consideration. Here and there arable land has been resolved into grass farms for the feeding of cattle, with a view to dairy produce. Wherever this has been done many labourers have been thrown out of employment, and the wages of those continued at work have been reduced. In other cases, in which the change has not yet been made, it is talked of, and wages have been reduced in anticipation. Many farmers complain that they cannot go on at present prices, without a reduction either of rents or wages. A reduction of rent is what most of them look to as most likely to immediately benefit them; but this being more difficult to secure than the diminution of wages, which is a course more in their own power, they resort to the latter at once.

Whilst in conversation with one of them, in Dorset, in reference to this subject, he informed me that he paid away about £500 a year in the shape of wages. He had been lately reducing the wages of his men to the extent of about a shilling a week each. On making a calculation of the saving which this would secure to him in the course of a year, I found that it would amount to about £35. I asked him if he expected to be able, with £35, to meet the exigencies of his position? "What can I do?" he asked, "I can't get a reduction of rent." "I'll tell you what I'll do," he continued, "if I can manage it; I shall make an arrangement to let my farm go to grass. Dairy farming costs less money, and is likely to be the most profitable going." "How does it cost less money?" I inquired. "It employs fewer hands," he answered. "But the hands are with you, and you must feed them," I suggested. "That's true," he replied; "but the more of them there's out of work, the more likely it is that we'll get them emigrated." This is the direction in which, at this moment, the minds of many farmers are being bent, not only in Hampshire, but also in the interior of Dorset, where land is at present extensively tilled. They would like, in the first place, a reduction of rent, of from 20 to 25 per cent. When they find they cannot have that, they next press upon the labourer, and seeing that they have but little margin for reduction in that quarter, they look to a new system of disposing of the land, which will require less labour and outlay in maintaining it. It is thus that, in the west of Hampshire, as elsewhere, even where they have not made actual preparation for converting their arable into dairy farms, they have already reduced wages, and talk of eventually having resort to such a course.

As may be inferred, therefore, wages are, in this part of Hampshire, but the counterpart of what they are in Dorset. Seven shillings a week I found to be about the maximum rate paid to the ordinary day labourer. Carters have 8s., and sometimes, but very rarely, 9s. And when I say that 7s. a week is about the maximum paid to the ordinary labourer, I mean the labourer steadily employed. The employment of many of them is of the most precarious description, and it is only some of them that are paid, whilst they are at work, even at the rate of 7s. a week. I met a labourer near Fordingbridge, who told me that he had had but three days' work during the previous week, at 1s. 2d. a day, or at the rate of 7s. a week. Thus his earnings for the week were but 3s. 6d., and he had four children to support, house rent to pay, and fuel to purchase. His existence at all was a mystery to himself. He could not tell me how he got along. Nor could anybody else do so. And so it is with the great bulk of his class. How they manage to eke out an existence is a puzzle to everybody, and everybody will frankly tell you so. Nothing could more forcibly show that there is somewhere something very seriously wrong, than the fact that one class of society is thus at a loss to account satisfactorily for the mode in which another class manages to exist. Nor is the man who is only occasionally employed always so fortunate as to be paid at the same rate per day as the man steadily employed. To numbers who have casual work by the day, only 1s. a day is paid, being at the rate of 6s. a week. These are generally, however, such as are not deemed able-bodied, or capable of a full day's work. But still both they and their families are capable of consuming the same quantity of food as before, and the amount of privation suffered by those so circumstanced is shocking to witness. Besides, there is no one to decide who is and who is not able-bodied; and many are put upon the incompetent list at 6s. a week, who appear to be quite as capable of going through a day's labour as others receiving more constant work and higher pay. Nor is it always that the lowest rate is confined to such as are declared not able-bodied. When the numbers of the labourers are considerable in a district, the farmers frequently take advantage of their being so to lower the wages of those who are indisputably able to perform a good day's work. Thus I have seen young and athletic men labouring for 1s. per day, who were compelled to accept that rate by being told that if they did not do so, there were others that would. "Do you give your employer more than 6s. worth a week of the work that is in you?" I inquired of one of them thus circumstanced. "I'm sure I don't, and fool would I be if I did," was the answer. Here, after all, is the mistake. Nominally cheap labour, in the case of able-bodied men, is not the cheapest labour that a farmer can employ. Unless he exercises the most stringent supervision over his workmen, and keeps them constantly at their work, it is impossible for him to get a full week's work out of them for 6s. Indeed, it is questionable if he gets even the value of his 6s. Lord Fortescue was led to conclude, by experience, at South-molton, that labour at 12s. a week was, in the end, more profitable to him than labour at 8s. The hiring of the best available labour, at a comparatively high rate, is almost invariably the example set by those who boldly embark upon a system of improved and efficient cultivation. It is the course adopted by the Rev. Mr. Huxtable, in Dorset.

He hires no man simply because he is a dweller in the parish, and because, if not employed, he may be thrown upon the rates, but because he is a good workman—and being so, he is hired at good wages. The wages paid by Mr. Huxtable are considerably higher than those paid around him, yet there is reason to believe that his is in reality the cheapest labour in the neighbourhood.

The diet of the labourers in this part of Hampshire is as low as their scale of wages would lead one to expect. Its staple consists of bread, cabbage, and turnips. As a general thing, butcher-meat is out of the question. The failure of the potatoes has been severely felt throughout the district. Those immediately on the borders of the Forest are, for obvious reasons, better off, as regards diet, than those living nearer the Dorsetshire line—having sometimes considerable quantities of venison carefully stowed away in their larders. Fortunately for them all, provisions are cheap; but for which, they say, there would be no living in these times. In many parts, throughout this district, the 4 lbs. "seconds" loaf was selling for 5d.

Having, one market day, been informed by a farmer at Wareham, that he could scarcely dispose of his wheat at a penny a pound, or about 5s. a bushel, I was curious to know how the 4 lb. loaf could be sold, as it was in some cases, for 4½d. The additional halfpenny seemed to constitute the sole margin for the expense of grinding the wheat, for the payment of the baker's labour, and for his profits. On inquiry, however, I discovered that this margin was somewhat greater than I had supposed it to be, inasmuch as a 4 lb. loaf can be made out of little more than 3 lbs. of flour. But, with wheat at a penny a lb., 3 lbs. of flour must cost more than 3d. There is then the cost of the yeast to be taken into account, and the outlay of the baker, in the shape of labour, fuel, and rent. In addition to this, it must be borne in mind that the whole of the wheat does not enter into what is called "seconds" flour—a portion of it being thrown aside in the process of grinding, for other purposes which are in general not very profitable. The margin is, therefore, still small on which the baker has to fall back for his profits. At Blandford, where the price of wheat and of bread was about the same as at Wareham, I inquired more particularly into this, and found that it was only to the union that the bread was sold at the rate of 4½d. a loaf. To private customers in this town the "seconds" loaf was charged 5d. The baker who informed me of the exact state of the case had himself but recently fulfilled a contract for the supply of the workhouse at 4½d. a loaf. He told me that he paid

28s. a sack for his flour, and sold it to the union for 30s. in the shape of bread, having thus but 2s. a sack wherewith to cover his expenses and realize a profit. "Did you realize a profit?" I asked. "No, sir," said he, "I didn't cover my expenses." "Then you would not take such a contract again?" I suggested. "I should be very sorry to do so," he replied; "and no one can take it without loss if he acts honestly by the union." "Is the union now supplied at that rate?" I then asked. "I believe it is," replied he.

As regards house accommodation, the poor throughout the Ringwood division are rather badly off. In the Lymington division their condition in this respect is superior to what it is in that of Ringwood. In 1841, when the population of the Lymington division was 11,478 persons, the number of inhabited houses which it contained was 2,295. This gave almost exactly one house for every five persons. There were at the same time, in the division, twenty-five new houses in process of erection. In the Ringwood division the proportion was about one house for every six persons. Notwithstanding this, there were at that time but thirty-eight new houses being built throughout the whole district. Nor have things in this respect improved since the last census was taken. Since that time influences have been at work, which did not then exist to the same extent as now, to cause the disappearance instead of the erection of cottages. In the town of Ringwood and its immediate vicinity the pressure is not so great, rents being there tolerably moderate, and the houses, although some of them are inconveniently crowded, not being generally so. But in the outlying hamlets, particularly around Fordingbridge, and between Ringwood and Christchurch, cases of this kind, quite as bad, and attended with as pernicious results as any in Dorsetshire, came but too frequently under my observation; indeed, the characteristic of the whole district is the pressure of population, both upon surface and upon house accommodation.

From the district in question I passed directly into the New Forest.

It is not my purpose here to enter into any of the political questions connected with this royal domain. And it is well that these matters are foreign to my present inquiry, for the means of obtaining information respecting the management and condition of the Forest are by no means facile or abundant. Those connected with it—that is to say, those who live both in and upon it—are extremely jealous of anything assuming the form of inquiry concerning it. It is astonishing, when you ask them a question, how utterly ignorant they are of the subject to which it pertains. No one seems to know anything of what is going on in the Forest, whilst some meet your inquiries in a manner which might lead you, if not on your guard, to infer that they were entirely ignorant of its very existence. Others, again, will affect a very warm sympathy with your object, and, deeply regretting their own inability to furnish you with the information required, will politely refer you to some one else, who, they assure you, will be as delighted as he is competent to answer any questions which you may put to him. Now, in many cases, the very existence of the party to whom you are thus referred is highly problematical—whilst, on consulting your map to ascertain the position of the point to which you are directed in order to find him, you generally discover it to be at one of the remotest extremities of the Forest. It fortunately requires but little experience to put one on his guard against such practices, for if it were not so a man might be sent for a whole twelvemonth on a series of wild-goose chases, and emerge after that time from the Forest quite as wise as he was when he entered it. Most of those living in and upon it treat you as if they felt that their position was equivocal, and that the slightest inquiry tended to endanger it. This being the prevailing feeling, different parties have, of course, different modes of expressing it. Some receive you with a courtesy formal and conventional, but nothing more. Others again get rid of you by referring you, as already stated, to real or imaginary parties at a distance—whilst there are others who know not how to disguise their real feelings. These last are, generally speaking, the foresters of the rougher sort, many of whom assisted, some time ago, in burning in effigy Major Freeman, the Government Commissioner; and to do them justice, some of them looked as if they longed for a decent pretext for performing the same kind office for your Correspondent *in propriâ personâ*—so jealous are they, one and all, of anything savouring of investigation.

My main object being to ascertain the physical condition of the lower class of foresters, I soon found that my best plan was to take counsel of no one, but to traverse the district and observe for myself. In doing so, I wandered over it from Fordingbridge to Minstead, and thence to Burley, near Ringwood—from Burley down towards Christchurch, and thence east to Lymington—from Lymington towards Boldre and Beaulieu—from Beaulieu to Brockenhurst—and from Brockenhurst, by Lyndhurst, back to Minstead again. I thus took, as it were, the entire circuit of the forest, whilst, from Beaulieu through Brockenhurst and Lyndhurst, my route led me almost through the centre of it. The whole district presents to the tourist, in traversing it, a succession of landscapes, which—particularly in summer, when the forest is in leaf—are as greatly varied as they are strikingly picturesque. Now the road wanders over long stretches of heath, here covering tracts of rich and generous land, and there cold and intractable soils. Then it plunges into the thick wood, through which it leads—sometimes in straight and sometimes in winding lines—amidst gnarled and hoary oaks, whose branches overhang you as you pass. From the wood it emerges again upon the open space, covered as before with heath, or short grass, or both—to plunge into the wood again, or into the copse, the young wood of which may yet flourish for centuries, after the older denizens of the forest have disappeared. Thus alternating from wood to open space—with numerous roads, sometimes very indifferent in their character, intersecting it in all directions, and with, here and there, a primitive-looking little town, village, or hamlet—the forest presents itself in a rapid succession of wavy undulations, calculated alike to charm the eye and stimulate the fancy. In some places, it is so wild and lonely that it appears to be part and parcel of that domain,

"Which mortal foot hath ne'er or rarely trod;"

and in traversing these, one would be in no hurry to attribute it to a trick of the imagination if he thought he saw a troop of satyrs in their more sequestered glades. The traveller would feel quite as easy in the presence of them, in one of these lonely nooks, as in that of a troop of foresters—some of whom are rather uncouth and unprepossessing, when suddenly encountered so far from the haunts of civilized men, and, as it were, in the very depths of nature. The beauties of the forest seem to culminate in the vicinity of Stony Cross, where William Rufus was mistaken for a stag.

In its moral aspect, the New Forest is about as wild, without being as attractive, as it is in its physical features. The population included within what may be regarded as the circumference of the forest is considerably greater than that of what is, strictly speaking, the forest itself. Large encroachments have, from time to time, been made upon this public domain—its surface being, more or less, interspersed with numerous patches of cultivated land, in the hands of private individuals. These patches vary very much in size—from a very few acres to

A Scene in the New Forest—The Rufus Stone

thousands in extent. Some of those in possession of these encroachments occupy the position of large landed proprietors, whilst others
are like so many squatters on small patches of land, which they cultivate either exclusively themselves, or with the aid of very little hired
labour. The possessors of the larger encroachments are very bold in
the assertion of their rights, and maintain, that if a thorough adjust-
ment of conflicting claims were to be come to, the Crown would lose
at least two-thirds of what it now possesses in the district. Yet, like
the more insignificant encroachers, they are not ambitious of court-
ing inquiry, nor are they in any hurry to push matters to an issue. The
whole space which can alone be now, strictly speaking, regarded as the
forest, comprises from sixty to seventy thousand acres. The encroachments in some places, such as the large one at Minstead, project into it
from the circumference—whilst in others they are dotted over its surface in isolated patches. As they are generally more or less cultivated,
it follows that the population of the forest comprises, in addition to
those strictly termed foresters, a small class of agricultural labourers.
On the larger encroachments these are tolerably numerous; on the
smaller ones, they are the squatters themselves, together with such
persons as they employ to cultivate the land with them. The class

strictly termed foresters are those in the employment of the Woods and Forests—this body frequently comprising some of the smaller class of encroachers. Those who are field labourers in and about the forest are but little better paid than the labourers around them; but the foresters are much better paid, many of them receiving from 13s. to 15s. a week, and some even more. They have frequently, however, to walk very far to get at their work. The general condition of the foresters and of those about them is very much influenced by the extent to which they take advantage of what are termed forest rights. These sometimes resolve themselves into rights of common, for the pasturage of cattle—and at others, it is to be feared, into killing deer for the supply of the larder. It is almost impossible to conceive that the deer, with which the forest abounds, were safe, when timber was being purloined to the extent of £5,000 worth a year. And although the keepers are numerous, and the look-out more vigilant now than formerly, it is by no means probable that the deer are yet treated by the foresters as things sacred, on which it would be sacrilege to lay hands. Indeed, that they are not so is evident from the fact, that in some of the towns within and on the borders of the forest there are parties who can procure you venison, to order, like mutton. In this way the foresters, as a body, manage to fare better than the poorer classes elsewhere. If they have not more butcher-meat than the poor have elsewhere, they are not altogether destitute of animal food. Their command of fuel is also better than that of the farm labourer, whilst their houses are, in the main, warm, comfortable, and tolerably roomy. They generally build them themselves—the fabric being constructed in most cases of mud, or of that composition of sand and clay which, when other circumstances are favourable, is by no means a bad material wherewith to build. I found some houses rather inconveniently crowded, both in Brockenhurst and Lyndhurst; but, in general, as compared with the labourers' houses elsewhere, overcrowding is not the fault of those within the forest.

From these considerations, taken in connection with their higher scale of wages, it is obvious that in point of physical condition the forester is considerably in advance of the farm labourer. In using the term forester here, I include those who work in the forest in the cultivation of the soil (wherever it is cultivated), inasmuch as they partake, more or less, of the comforts at the command of the foresters more strictly so-called. The life led by the denizens of the forest is, on the whole, rather a lawless one, and a somewhat lax morality pervades the entire region. Indeed, it can scarcely be otherwise—general demoralization being the necessary characteristic of a community a large proportion of whom are systematically engaged in poaching. It is seldom, however, that they will molest a wayfarer, meet him where or when they will. I have more than once been benighted in some of the most lonely spots of the forest, when I have met them prowling about in twos and threes. On one occasion one of them remarked, whilst passing me, "I wouldn't like to be travelling alone through the forest at such an hour;" but with this exception, they have generally passed me with a simple "good night." So far as I could manage to hold any intercourse with them, I found a degree of ignorance prevailing amongst them which indicated but too plainly that, whoever else may have traversed it, the schoolmaster has not as yet taken very extensive walks through the forest.

From the forest I proceeded to Southampton, and thence to Winchester and Basingstoke. This led me through the central region of the county—a district almost exclusively agricultural. It is to the north-east of Basingstoke that the country assumes that aspect of wild sterility which characterizes so large a portion of the weald of Surrey, of which this tract of Hampshire is but a prolongation. From Basingstoke to Southampton is one stretch of almost unbroken cultivation, the whole district between these two extremes being almost exclusively a farming one. The hop districts of Hampshire, which are small and not very numerous, are generally found near the eastern line of the county. The condition of the farm labourer in the districts in question may be taken as the type of his condition throughout the entire county. In the immediate vicinity of Southampton and Winchester—as in that of all tolerably active markets—the wages paid are somewhat in advance of those received in the circumjacent parishes; but, throughout the whole of this central division of the county, 8s. a week is the highest average of wages—including the higher rates paid here, as elsewhere, to carters and others in employments more or less confidential. Numbers are in receipt of only 7s. a week, and many who were not considered altogether equal to a day's work, I found toiling from daylight to sunset for 1s. a day. Sometimes you find a labourer with a house free; but this is the exception, not the rule. Near the waste, to the north-east of this district, they are a little better off, having some privileges which are not enjoyed by those living in the more arable tracts. As regards their dwellings, they are better provided in point of room than the labourers in some of the counties further to the west. In connection with the last census, this portion of Hampshire was divided into the three districts of Basingstoke, Winchester, and Southampton. It then appeared that, in point of room, the labourers were best off in the Basingstoke division, and worst in that of Southampton; but, even in the latter, the average number of people to each house did not exceed six. In too many cases, however, the tenements themselves are of a most miserable description. The worst I met with were in some of the parishes between Basingstoke and Winchester. In the neighbourhood of the latter town they are tolerably good.

From Winchester I passed to the eastern borders of the county, by Bramdean and Petersfield. For fully half the way to Bramdean the road is flanked on either side by successive sweeps of down. This tract is consequently very thinly peopled, nor are the traces of human habitations visible but at long intervals. Indeed, the only living things apparently inhabiting it are the rabbits, which swarm upon the estates of Lord Northesk. From the high land you at length rapidly descend upon a more sheltered and cultivated tract. This continues on to Bramdean, and thence, through an undulating and picturesque region, to Petersfield, from which it also stretches, with but little intermission, for two or three miles more, to the borders of Sussex. Here population again becomes scarce, and the farm labourer is to be found, as before, in his village, his hamlet, and his isolated hut, but with no perceptible change for the better in his condition. Seven shillings a week is again the average of his earnings; nor is it always that this rate is paid for a full day's work, the pernicious practice prevailing here of making a distinction between married and single men. The consequence is, that many single men, who do not choose to be under-paid for their labour, take to poaching, instead of to regular employment.

From Petersfield I entered West Sussex, by way of Rogate and Midhurst, and shortly afterwards proceeded to Petworth. From the Hampshire line, all the way to Petworth, the country is, with but few exceptions, highly cultivated. The chief proprietors of the neighbourhood are Lord Egmont and Colonel Wyndham—the seat of the former being near Midhurst, that of the latter close to Petworth. In the immediate vicinity of both seats the labourers are comparatively well off, both proprietors finding a good deal of work for the labourers about their respective parks and mansions, and paying them somewhat higher than the farmers in the neighbourhood. Lord Egmont, I was informed, pays most of his labourers who are engaged in operations connected with the soil from 8s. to 9s. a week. Colonel Wyndham pays them about the same. But the ruling rates around them are lower than this. From 7s. to 8s. a week is all that the farm labourer is receiving who is in the employment of the farmer. Some get 8s., but most only 7s. The farmers say they cannot pay more—and many of them talk of giving up their farms, as they say it is impossible for them to go on at present prices, with swarms of game to support in addition. A few, I was told, had surrendered their farms, assigning as their reason the insupportable burden of the game. The proprietors in this neighbourhood are game preservers on the most extensive scale; and on all hands you hear complaints of the mischief done by the game, except from the poacher and those whom he supplies. "We have a rare lot of poachers here," said a labourer to me, whilst speaking to him on the subject—"and the more keepers they put on, the more poachers get about." "Do they catch them often?" I asked. "They're keen old fellows, some of them," said he; "but they do get catched sometimes." "And what is done with them?" I inquired. "Oh, they get about three months in Petworth gaol," said he. "Does that do them any good?" "No; they come out worse than ever." Lord Egmont gave compensation to some of his farmers for the mischief done by the game, but still there are great complaints. The game preservers of this neighbourhood have been much scandalized, I am told, at the proceedings taken by Mr. Cobden, who has purchased a small property near Midhurst. He has two or three tenants, to whom he has given unlimited license to kill the game upon their farms. Throughout the whole district, the able-bodied labourers are almost all kept employed, but it is apprehended that many even of these will be denizens of the workhouse before next spring. In some cases, the able-bodied have only been kept at work, by their consenting to take 6s. a week. Such is the result of the competition for employment in a densely populated district. In numerous instances throughout the line from Petersfield to Petworth, the houses occupied by the labourers are of the most squalid and miserable character. The characteristic of all of them is that they are overcrowded. Emigration has been actively promoted from this district; but notwithstanding this, the population has greatly increased, and, as I was informed, it presses now much more upon the house accommodation of the district than in 1841. The few houses on Mr. Cobden's property, when he purchased it, may be taken as the type, in this respect, of the labourers' dwellings in this part of Sussex. He is building new cottages, however, with a view to giving his labourers more roomy and wholesome dwellings. When the approach of the cholera was feared, something was done in the neighbourhood of Petworth, to mitigate, if not altogether to avoid, both the danger and the inconvenience of over-crowded dwellings. The labourers on many parts of Colonel Wyndham's property are now in a much better position, as regards their dwellings, than they were some time ago. Formerly they rented the cottages of the farmers, to whom they paid high rents, and who generally took from them the fruit which grew in the little gardens appended to their dwellings. In many cases the proprietor has taken these cottages into his own hands, letting them to the labourers for about half the rent formerly paid by them, and giving them the fruit into the bargain.

That which I have stated respecting the labourer in the neighbourhoods of Midhurst and Petworth may be taken as illustrative of his condition throughout the greater part of West Sussex. As you find him in the district stretching from Petersfield to Petworth, so do you find him in that lying between the latter place and Arundel, and thence on to Brighton. As elsewhere, you see him in some cases with steady work, in others with only casual employment, but in all with low wages. Owing to the cheapness of provisions, he nevertheless manages to live better now than he used to do when his wages were a little higher, and when even the potatoes were far more plentiful than now. But his staple diet, like that of the labourers in Dorset, is bread and vegetables. It is rare indeed to find either him or his family partaking of animal food. "I have known some of them," said a farmer to me, "who hav'n't tasted meat for the last six months." On questioning him, I found that by this he meant, that although "once in a way" they might get a bit of "broken meat" from those employing them, animal food had not appeared upon their tables, as a regular part of the family diet, for the length of time specified. I happen to have by me several dietary tables of different unions in the west, which furnish a very striking contrast to the labourer's diet in Sussex. In the Liskeard union, I find the inmates of the workhouse receiving bread and milk every morning for breakfast—the men seven, and the women six ounces of bread. In the Penzance union they have the same—both men and women getting seven ounces of bread; and in that of St. Germans the same, but with a scantier allowance of bread to the men, who have only six ounces. For dinner, in the Liskeard union, they have animal food three times a week, viz. on Sunday, when they have, men and women, four ounces of boiled meat, with one pound of potatoes each; on Tuesday, two ounces of boiled meat each, with a pound and a half of potato stew, which is prepared and enriched with meat; and on Friday, three ounces of boiled pork or bacon, with one pound of potatoes. On the Thursday they have fish—pilchards, no doubt—and 1 lb. of potatoes. On the intermediate days they have bread and broth, and bread and pea-soup. In the Penzance union they have meat on Sunday and Wednesday, with 8 oz. of vegetables and 5 oz. of bread. On Tuesday they have fish, with 8 oz. of bread. On other days they have bread and meat soup, bread and pea-soup, and bread with rice and milk; and on one, Friday, they have vegetables, bread, and meat soup. In the St. Germans union they have meat twice and fish twice a week, with very substantial potato stew three times a week. For supper they have, in the Liskeard union, bread and cheese three times a week, bread and suet broth twice, and bread and gruel twice. In that of Penzance they have 7 oz. of bread, with milk gruel, every day of the week; and in that of St. Germans, bread with rice milk five times, and bread and meat broth twice a week. But it may be said that, as the diet in the workhouse has, as regards its quantity and character, some reference to that of the labourer out of doors, that in the Cornish unions is comparatively high, as is the physical condition of a tolerably large class of the labourers in Cornwall, for reasons stated by me when treating of the subject of Labour and the Poor in that county. Let us, however, come nearer home, and compare with the diet of the independent labourer in Hampshire or Sussex that of a workhouse situated in a district in which the condition of the labourer is analogous to his own. In the Wareham workhouse I found bread and gruel the fare every day for breakfast—the men getting seven and the women five ounces of bread. For dinner the inmates have animal food—four ounces each when it is meat, and three ounces when it is bacon, with a pound and a half of potatoes or other vegetables, three days in the week; for three more they have bread and soup, and on Sunday they dine on suet or rice pudding, of which the men get fourteen and the women twelve ounces. For supper they have bread and cheese every night in the week. As already stated, the staple diet of the independent labourer and his family is bread, turnips, parsnips, cabbage, and potatoes. He rarely tastes meat—occasionally tastes cheese—but seldom has a meal of it. What an anomaly is here!

And, strange to say, although the union, by purchasing its edibles by contract, can procure them about 20 per cent. cheaper than the independent labourer can, who buys no more than he needs at a time, yet the independent labourer and his family manage to eke out an existence on about one-half that which it takes to support a pauper and his family in the workhouse. The wonder is, that every labourer in the land is not eager to pauperize himself.

The Morning Chronicle, Monday, January 28, 1850.

THE SWANAGE STONE QUARRIES.

To the EDITOR of the MORNING CHRONICLE.

Sir—I have read with great interest your communication of to-day, being No. XXVIII. in the series of letters upon "Labour and the Poor," and containing an account of the stone quarries of Swanage. I trouble you with this note, feeling it to be a duty to aid you by whatever can be contributed to render more complete your admirable reports, which are so well calculated to diffuse correct information on the state of our population, and thus to enable all better to understand, what very few now can appreciate—the real meaning of the words "Labour" and "Poor."

The details are so accurate and the facts so well related, that I cannot forbear requesting that, if the papers should appear in future in any other form, the error you have made in the description of the stone may be rectified. The stones of Swanage and Portland are lime stones, and not sand stones. Moreover, the articles of barter or currency, as you call them, are not always bread; but butter in red pans—or crocks, as they are called—and bacon in the side, form frequent media of exchange; articles of food generally, though bread and butter most frequently, being the currency.

There is another fact in connection with the position of the merchants, which, in estimating their power and position, is by no means unimportant.

The bankers are the only place of deposit on the beach for errot stone, and from this circumstance the owners exercise complete control over the trade; because, the freehold of the beach vesting in them, they keep to themselves the whole access to the water; and instances have occurred in which parties possessing every other means of establishing a trade have been ruined by the exercise of this power.

The "truck" system has so injurious an influence upon all this population, that I rejoice to find public attention thus awakened and directed towards a place where for so many years it has had uninterrupted sway.

There is a considerable manufacture of straw, in bonnets and hats, carried on by the female population; but this is all dealt with in the same manner as the stone.

Some years back the late Mr. Morton Pitt, who owned a large district in this neighbourhood, commenced extensive operations in building and road-making, with the view of converting the town of Swanage into a watering-place. The public, however, very feebly supported it, and although the late lamented Sir W. Follett resorted to this place in his last illness, but very few of his rank or position are aware of the great beauty of the surrounding scenery and the delightful retirement it affords.

The difficulty of access from the metropolis has prevented its becoming a place of much resort; but as there is now railway communication to Wareham, it is to be hoped that the public may have an opportunity of informing itself, and that thus this interesting locality being brought under the influence of public opinion, the result of more extended acquaintance with the district will be, that the condition of the inhabitants will be improved by their having a fair opportunity to receive and economize the well-earned reward of their toils.

Within the memory of many now living, all the streets of the metropolis were paved with the stone of Swanage only. It became gradually displaced by that of Yorkshire, which (being a laminated sandstone, quarried in open air, and hence more uniform in thickness and larger in size) has now altogether superseded it.

So that, while in former times the supply of London was a very important part of the trade of the town of Swanage very few freights are at this time sent in that direction; and of paving, not 20 vessels in a year reach London.

I am, sir, yours respectfully,

London, Jan. 23.   T. P.

LABOUR AND THE POOR.

THE RURAL DISTRICTS.

[FROM OUR SPECIAL CORRESPONDENT.]

THE SOUTHERN AND WESTERN COUNTIES.

LETTER XXX.

I now propose to take a general survey of the condition and prospects of the labourer, in what is pre-eminently the Hop-growing district of the kingdom.

This district comprehends the whole of Kent, the whole of Surrey, and the Eastern moiety of Sussex. It comprises an area of a little upwards of 3,000 square miles, or about 1,950,000 acres. The hop is not, however, cultivated to an equal extent throughout the whole of this region. It is far more prominent as a feature in the agriculture of Kent than in that of either Surrey or Sussex. There are few parts of Kent in which it is not more or less produced. In Surrey a less quantity of it is raised in proportion to the area of the county than in Kent, but its culture may be regarded as general throughout the county. In Sussex, on the other hand, it is chiefly confined to the eastern division—farming operations, in their ordinary acceptation, almost exclusively engaging the attention of the occupiers of the soil in the western division. In Kent the chief scene of the hop cultivation is the vicinity of Maidstone, and indeed the whole of that portion of the valley of the Medway which lies between Tonbridge and the chalky ridge that intervenes between Maidstone and Rochester. In Surrey, it is, perhaps, in the parish of Farnham that its cultivation is carried to the greatest extent. In East Sussex it is grown, to some degree, in the neighbourhood of Lewes, but the principal scene of its cultivation in this county appears to be Rye and its vicinity.

Nowhere, perhaps, even in Kent, is the hop exclusively cultivated. Its growth is a feature, and nothing more, in the agriculture of the district in question. In Kent there are large tracts of cultivated ground on which the hop is not to be seen. Nor are these, in every instance, tracts on which it could not be successfully raised. It is true that there are many districts in Kent, and in the other counties grouped with it, in which the culture of the hop could not be advantageously carried on—but even in Kent, where its cultivation is most prevalent, there are large tracts in which it has never been raised, or from which it has disappeared, although they are in all respects well adapted for its production. And you usually find its cultivation exceptional to the general agriculture of the district. It is only in a very few instances that you see farms of any size converted *in toto* into hop gardens—certainly in fewer instances now than formerly. To cultivate the plant on a large scale would require more capital than the great majority of the hop growers possess. A few wealthy capitalists have appropriated considerable tracts, not far from Maidstone, exclusively to the production of the hop, with great success, I am informed, in times past, but with very dubious prospects for the future. In the great majority of cases in which the plant has been and is still raised, the hop garden is merely an appendage to the farm. And it is the same in Surrey and East Sussex. The exceptional character of the business may be inferred from a glance at the farmsteadings, in the districts in which hop growing is most attended to. You almost invariably find the apparatus used for drying the hops, a mere addendum to the ordinary appurtenances of a farm. The Occupation Returns of the last census, too, clearly show that hop-growing is not regarded as an exclusive pursuit. The number returned for all Kent, as exclusively hop growers, in 1841, did not exceed seven. In Surrey and Sussex none were returned as such. And whilst in Kent there were only seven returned as exclusively hop growers, the number returned as agricultural labourers was close upon 40,000. If we look for the employers of these men, we find that they consist of from 5,000 to 6,000 farmers and graziers, amongst whom are the cultivators of the hop. In treating of the general subject of labour, therefore, in these counties, it is with farm labour, in its usual acceptation, that we have chiefly, as elsewhere, to deal; although in parts of them that labour is so influenced by the cultivation of the hop, that it is impossible to treat separately of the two in pursuing an investigation like the present. Even in districts which are exclusively appropriated to the ordinary purposes of tillage, and which are, comparatively speaking, far removed from the hop-growing sections of the counties, its cultivation has a sensible effect upon the condition of the labourer. This, of course, applies more particularly to Kent, where the growth of the plant is more general than elsewhere.

Taking the same basis of calculation as on former occasions, we find that in Kent the number of those employed as agricultural labourers, or otherwise dependent upon agricultural labour for support, was in 1841 about 130,000 souls. This, in a population of 548,000, gives but about 23 per cent. of the whole. We have seen that, in other counties, the proportion was 33 1-3 per cent. of the whole population. This, indeed, is the case in one of the counties of the present group—Sussex. In that county, the population in 1841 was within a fraction of 300,000. The number of agricultural labourers was about 30,000; making the whole number dependent for support upon farm labour little short of 100,000. In Surrey, the proportion was still smaller than in Kent; for, out of a population of 583,000, only 70,000 were dependent for their maintenance upon agricultural labour—or about 12 per cent. of the whole. But the causes of these varying proportions are obvious. Sussex is a purely agricultural county—for, although it has a few ports, it cannot be said to have any commerce. Indeed, some of its ports have long had more political than commercial importance attached to them. Both Kent and Surrey may, on the other hand, be regarded as metropolitan counties—a portion of the metropolis being situated in each of them. The whole of the southern district of the metropolis, with the exception of Greenwich, is comprehended within the limits of Surrey—that portion of London alone (forming but one-fourth of the whole metropolis) containing a larger population than any of the capitals of Europe, except four—viz., Paris, Constantinople, Naples, and St. Petersburg. It is here that the great masses of the labouring population of Surrey find employment, as mechanics, artisans, and otherwise. The number returned as labourers in this county, in contradistinction to agricultural labourers, was from 30,000 to 35,000—who, with those dependent upon them, would make about 120,000, or more than a fifth of the whole population. The number of the corresponding class returned in Sussex was but 10,000, who, with those dependent upon them, would make about 35,000, or somewhat more than one-ninth of the whole. What applies to Surrey applies also to Kent, but in a less degree—there being but a comparatively small portion of the metropolis within the latter county. But it is surrounded by a belt of busy seaports—such as Woolwich, Gravesend, Sheerness, Chatham, Margate, Ramsgate, Deal, Dover, and Folkestone—which, as the scene of great Government works, as fashionable resorts, or as commercial stations, give rise to a considerable demand for labour other than agricultural. It is, however, with agricultural labour that I have here chiefly to deal; and, in speaking of it, I shall—considering the influence which it exercises over the circumstances of the labourer generally in these counties—first draw the reader's attention to the subject of hop cultivation.

There are many who regard the cultivation of the hop as a great, if not an unmixed, evil to the district in which it is produced. As it is in Kent that its production is carried to the largest extent, so it was there that I found this opinion most prevalent. Many think that it would be a great boon to the counties in question if the hop altogether disappeared from their surface. It is not denied that great profits are sometimes realized from it—the complaint is, that it injuriously affects the general interests of the districts in which it prevails, by (amongst other things) greatly deteriorating the ordinary agriculture of those localities. It is alleged that the cultivation of the hop "starves the land." There is perhaps no other county in the kingdom the soil of which varies so much in respect to its capabilities as that of Kent. With the exception of the large central tract known as the Weald, and the chalky ridge which sweeps through the county from the South Foreland, across the valley of the Medway, and on almost to Gravesend, the whole of Kent presents to the eye the appearance of a garden. The ridge alluded to is in many places bare and unproductive, with stretches of woodland here and there at its base. Throughout the Weald the woodland is interspersed with the naked wild, the two forming together the district known by that name—a district not confined to Kent, but stretching through Surrey into Hampshire, and into the centre of Sussex. Here and there portions of it have been brought into cultivation, but vast tracts are yet unreclaimed—although the spots are exceptional in which it is irreclaimable. To the superficial observer the cultivated portion of Kent, which comprises the great bulk of its surface, is equally productive throughout. It requires, however, but little observation to detect the error of this conclusion. It is only here and there that the soil is really rich and heavy. It is to be found in many places constantly alternating between chalk, sand, gravel, and rich fertile loam. The quality of the soil is pretty well indicated by the timber which it bears. In many parts of Kent it is small and stunted—whilst sometimes a ridge of heavy timber, showing the course of a vein of rich loam, may be seen between two belts of much lighter wood, indicating the presence of more meagre soil. In other places small isolated clumps of heavy wood are to be met with, surrounded by a more stunted vegetation—the latter supported by a soil through the thin coating of which the sand comes frequently peering to the surface. But in other parts of Kent, as towards its eastern extremity, there are large tracts of heavy and rich land, on which corn is raised regularly and in abundance. The quality of the land, in some portions of the interior, and towards the south and south-west of the county, may be also inferred from the average rental which it commands, which is not much above 14s. or 15s. an acre. In some places—as, for instance, in the neighbourhood of Tunbridge Wells—there are farms now in the market for which there is no offer even at that rate. It so happens that it is chiefly in the districts in which the land varies most in quality that the hop is most generally cultivated; and it is almost always the best lands that are appropriated to its production. The inferior parts are left for the growth of corn and grass. Take a particular farm, for instance, and you find the hop garden, if it includes one, occupying the best part of it as regards soil. It is from the inferior portion that the cereal returns are looked for. And not only is the part of the land given up to the hop generally the best on the farm, but it is also that on which the farmer bestows his chief attention. The land must be kept in good heart to produce this plant, and it too frequently happens that the manure which should be applied to the corn-field is transferred to the hop-garden. Even were the land generally heavy and rich, this would be bad treatment of it, so far as regards the production of grain crops. But it is not so; and the evil of the system is, that this practice of impoverishing the corn land is prevalent in districts in which the latter, from its quality, requires a great deal of manure to enrich it, and keep it in heart. It is seldom that, in these cases, the land is sufficiently kept up to get good wheat crops from it. It is systematically neglected just where it should be systematically cared for. Even when it is properly dressed, and brought up to the right point for wheat, it soon falls back "out of repair," unless manure is constantly applied to it. Yet such is the soil which is robbed of its proper quantity of manure to enrich the hop-gardens. And if the soil in these districts is not sufficiently kept up for white crops, it will be readily inferred that it is certainly not so for green crops. Such is the case. No one can travel through the interior of Kent without having this fact forced upon him. The cultivation of green crops enters but very slightly into the agriculture of this part of the county. Here and there you may see a turnip or a potato field, or one set apart for the production of mangold wurzel. But they are few and rarely met with, the soil being chiefly divided between the hop-garden, the corn-field, and the meadow. When a hop-garden is converted into a corn-field the most luxuriant crops are generally got from it; but even in such a case the land must be well kept up, or it soon becomes meagre and comparatively unproductive. Yet such cases show what the land could do if it were properly treated; for in many instances in which the hop-gardens are thus dealt with, the soil which forms their basis is no better than that which has been stinted for their sake. This is the evil of which many in Kent complain—an evil which injuriously affects almost the entire agriculture of the county; and on this ground it is contended that the entire abandonment of the hop cultivation would be fraught with benefit instead of evil. Had these views been presented to me only in a few isolated instances, I should not have deemed them worthy of so much notice. That I have here laid any stress upon them, is simply because I found them very generally entertained.

Weald of Sussex

Another objection offered to the continued cultivation of the hop is the gambling character of the business. It is only occasionally—say once in three or four years— that it turns out a favourable speculation. But then the profits are sometimes so great that many are lured into the pursuit whose means do not justify their embarking in it. Like the business of tanning, as formerly conducted, which made but a slow return upon the capital invested in it, that of hop-growing should only be undertaken by those who can afford to wait patiently for returns on the portion of their capital so applied. But it is not confined to such—small farmers, with little capital, rushing eagerly into the adventure. It is by the splendid prizes which are sometimes drawn that they are enticed to take a share in the lottery. This will be readily understood when it is remembered that—under circumstances, however, which cannot be expected to occur again—the hop has fluctuated in price from £30 to 40s. a cwt. Many small farmers in Kent are constantly paying too much attention to their hop-gardens, and too little to their fields. Even when agricultural distress has not been complained of elsewhere, numbers of the hop-growing farmers have been floundering in difficulties. And so it is at the present moment. Last season was pre-eminently disastrous to the plant, and so large was the stake that even the comparatively ample returns of the fields have scarcely sufficed to make good the losses of the hop gardens.

It is not easy to determine what effect upon the general interests of labour in the county the diminution of the hop cultivation would have. There can be no question that it would be injurious, unless the improved cultivation of the fields gave rise to an additional demand for labour in that direction, equivalent in extent to the amount of labour left unemployed by the abandonment of the hop. Whether an improved cultivation would or would not result it is not necessary for me here to discuss, as I have put forth no opinion of my own in favour of the relinquishment of the hop. This, however, is certain, that were it abandoned, a good deal of capital which is now bound up in a very precarious pursuit would be released, and rendered applicable for other purposes. It is also obvious that the land in such case would not be starved as it is now, inasmuch as the manure which the hop garden now monopolizes would then be more generally distributed over its surface. It is likewise probable that were high farming resorted to, for which Kent is as well adapted as most counties in the kingdom, the demand for additional labour would more than cover the *hiatus* left in employment by the cessation of hop-cultivation.

It is not to be denied that, with the exception of gardening and nursery work—of which it is, in fact, but a branch—hop-growing is, of all agricultural pursuits, one of the most general and constant dispensers of employment. It furnishes work during the bulk of the year to people of both sexes and of all ages. Economy in the work of production has, indeed, embraced the hop-garden as well as other scenes of human industry; yet still, the average expenditure per year upon an acre of hops is fully seven times as much as the average outlay per acre upon corn land, even where farming is not pursued in a slovenly manner. The average outlay per year upon the hop garden is from £20 to £22 per acre. This expenditure represents employment under a favourable aspect—that is to say, it represents a great deal of it concentrated within a limited space. Not only can the father and mother and children be employed in the hop garden, but there are branches of the labour which they are each peculiarly adapted for undertaking. It is thus that not only may a whole family be employed, as in other agricultural operations, but the requirements of the hop garden are best attended to when the industry bestowed upon it is of that varying character which the labour of the different members of a family presents. Any serious disturbance, therefore, to an occupation so well adapted for administering to the necessities of the labouring poor, cannot be contemplated with indifference, unless a better mode of effecting the same object be at hand, and capable of being at once resorted to. On the other hand, it must not be forgotten that a pursuit which not only admits of, but is best promoted by, the employment of persons of different ages and sexes, is by no means attended with unmixed good. It but too frequently administers to the physical, at the expense of the moral, wants of the family. When children may not only go into the hop-garden, but their presence there is more desirable than otherwise, the business of their education, if attended to at all, is liable to frequent and very serious interruptions. Nor are even its physical advantages altogether without drawback. The mother of a family cannot be both in the hop-garden and at home—and home is her proper sphere. Her absence from it injuriously affects both the comforts and the interests of the family; and many a working man, both in Kent and elsewhere, have I heard deplore the necessity which seemingly existed for his wife betaking herself to the fields. You may prove to demonstration to them that they would be better off, even in a physical point of view, if their wives remained at home, and attended to their household duties—but the temptation presented by the few extra shillings which may be earned by the wife is, in most cases, sufficiently great to overrule all other considerations.

It may also here be remarked, that hop-work is generally done by the piece—a condition of work favourable to the labourer, until the competition becomes greatly disproportionate to the field for employment; and this gives rise to a relationship, in many cases, between the employer and employed in the hop counties, which is by no means prevalent in the other agricultural districts of the south. When a woman labours in the field in Dorset, for instance, she is generally hired directly by the occupier of the soil—being thus, as regards the employer, in precisely the same position as her husband, the only difference between them being that her work is usually the lighter, and her wages invariably the lower of the two; indeed, in many cases, husband and wife, and brother and sister, not only work in different fields, but also under different employers. In the hop districts it is seldom that you find a family thus dispersed. It is of course competent to a woman or any of her family to take work, here as elsewhere, directly from the employer, and in some cases this is done—more particularly in connection with those operations in the business of hop-growing for which women and children are best adapted. But, generally speaking, the practice is otherwise—the family usually working together, the husband taking the work, and his wife and children aiding him in the performance of it. This operates sometimes to the relief of the more tender members of the family, but at others it causes their subjection to very severe work. The wife is sometimes made to participate in the most laborious occupations of the husband—whilst in some districts the work is so distributed between them that she appears to have its severer part cast upon her. But it is the boy who is most frequently thus subjected to work to which his strength seems inadequate. He is frequently seen working by himself, but generally side by side with his father—either taking upon himself the lighter parts of the work, or sharing it, without regard to degree, with his father. If the latter apportions to his son the lighter work, he of course increases his own toil, by reserving to himself all that is heavy and laborious. If, on the other hand, he makes the son partake of the general work, whilst his own labour is not thus increased, the task devolved upon the boy is that which is only suitable for the man. In such cases, children are subjected to great hardships—not the least evil of which is, perhaps, the premature age and decrepitude that supervene. But in the majority of cases, although they are kept very constantly at work, they are not severely over-tasked, the parental instinct generally interposing between them and such a result. When the tenderer members of the family are thus not subjected to work beyond their strength, the system of the husband taking task-work, and being aided by his wife and children in the execution of it, seems much more favourable—at least as regards the conservation of morals—than the practice which elsewhere prevails, of each member of a family finding work for himself or herself, where and how he or she can, the husband working in one field, and the wife in another, the son in a third, and the daughter, perhaps, in a fourth, and sometimes under different employers. The system alluded to as prevailing in the hop districts has at least the merit of keeping the family together—a state of things more favourable to the exercise of a wholesome surveillance than the opposite practice.

The first business in the cultivation of the hop is of course the preparation of the ground. From this to hop-picking, which is the last out-door process, the hop-garden is the scene of almost constant industry. The ground may be prepared any time before February, when digging commences. The chief preparation is the manuring of the land. For this purpose rags and sprats are used, and, in the absence of these, ordinary manure. Occasionally, different kinds of manure are mixed together, and sometimes all these are combined. When rags are used, they are generally woollen ones, which, being composed of animal matter, make a very good manure. Before being used they are chopped very small upon a block, in which state they are fit for use. For chopping the rags a man gets from 12s. to 15s. a week. It is not exclusively men's work, it being such as boys may make themselves very expert in. They, of course, get lower wages than the men. The rags are also generally known as "hospital rags," being, in fact, the refuse of the metropolitan and other hospitals. Many complain of the pernicious results of introducing such a commodity into healthy localities. I have been told that the presence of small-pox in Tunbridge Wells has frequently been attributed to it. Whilst chopping the rags the workmen have often been sickened, and their appetites taken from them, by the offensive effluvia proceeding from them. "We don't like the work very well, but it gets us 15s. a week," said one of them, on being asked why he adhered to such an employment, especially after he himself had several times been made ill by it. When sprats are used, they are spread over the land to decompose upon it. When this is done, boys are in requisition to watch the fields and to act as peripatetic scarecrows to frighten away the gulls, which would otherwise come in great numbers from the coast to partake of a repast so temptingly spread for them. For this work a boy will sometimes get 6d. a day, at others not more than 2s. or 2s. 6d. a week. If the rags are objectionable in their way, so also are the sprats. I have been told in some places that the neighbourhood used to be regularly poisoned by the quantities of them which lay decomposing on the ground. They are used in but few places to the same extent now as formerly. The work of digging, with such manure on the ground, must, when the weather is at all warm and the work of decomposition incomplete, be anything but wholesome. Digging is generally the work of men aided by boys, when the work is not day-work. The boys are called in when the work is task-work, and, as such is undertaken by their fathers. A boy and his father frequently earn between them £1 a week at this work, the boy doing about a third of what the man does, or about a quarter of the whole work done. Digging is, as I have said, generally commenced in the month of February, when a brisk demand for labour succeeds the inactivity of winter throughout the whole of the hop districts.

The hole dug for the reception of the plant is an irregular one, being, generally speaking, about two feet in diameter, and from eighteen inches to two feet deep. It is desirable that the earth about the roots of the plants should be, for some distance around it, as loose and free as possible, and therefore it is that the hole is made of the dimensions specified. The nursery plants are then taken and put into the holes, there being generally but three of them to a hole. Care is taken that their roots are kept free, and that they are well spread out. After this, the mould which has been taken out of the hole is carefully replaced, having been first bruised and well pulverized. In this process the top of the plant is kept a little above the level of the ground, so that a slight hill can be formed around it, without smothering it. It sometimes happens that the hop bears the first year, and sometimes the second; but it is generally the third year ere it comes to bearing maturity. If circumstances favour it, the plant is ready, about the beginning of the second season, to undergo the operation of pruning. The first step in this process is that which is known as "opening the hills." This consists of removing the mould from about the roots of the plants, so as to get as low down as possible at the shoots of the previous season. The older shoots are then cut off with a sharp pruning-knife within an inch or two of the stem of the plant, after which the earth is restored carefully to its place, leaving the remaining shoots to grow. The opening of the hills is a species of work common to men, women, and boys; generally speaking, it is the work of men. They are frequently aided at it by the boys—whilst, in some places, custom, or something else equally arbitrary, has assigned it to women. It is seldom, however, that women are to be found doing this where the ground is comparatively heavy, as is the case around Brenchley and in the neighbourhood of Tunbridge. When the men and boys open the hills, the women generally prune the plants; when the women open them, the men prune. In some places, when the lightness of the soil admits of it, the women are put to the work of opening, because more reliance is placed on the skill and judgment of the men in the work of pruning. In some localities the work of pruning the plants, with its accompaniments, is given out by task; in others, it is almost exclusively treated as day-work. When the latter, the men may earn from 2s. to 2s. 6d. per day; and as the women and boys are then hired as independent labourers, they earn—the women from 10d. to 1s., and the boys from 6d. to 8d. a day. When the work is given out by task, the husband undertakes to do it, with such aid as he can get—generally that of his family. In such cases, the wages of the women and children are comprehended in the contract entered into by the man, which is usually to do the work at from 3½d. to 4½d. per hundred. The boys begin this work at twelve, when the opening of the hills is very severe labour for them. If they continue at it for two or three years, they may, when it is day-work, earn from 10d. to 1s. a day. When the work is given out by the day, the hours of labour are from six to six—hours which must be observed by boys as well as men. Women, in similar cases, work from eight to six, it being supposed that household duties prevent them from coming out at an earlier hour. When it is task work, they may select their own hours, always providing that they do not neglect their work. Half-an-hour is usually allowed to the men and boys for breakfast when labouring by the day, and an hour to men, women, and boys for dinner. Although the season of the year in which this process in the cultivation of the hop is attended to is not the most favourable for out-door operations, there are nevertheless circumstances attending it which render it in general a more healthy species of work than others that are performed at more genial periods of the year.

It is when the plant begins fairly to shoot that it undergoes the process of poling. The poles are forced into the ground to a sufficient depth to give them a firm hold. This being a work requiring almost exclusively muscular strength, is commonly assigned as task-work to men. But even in this they derive aid from their families, the women and children frequently assisting in laying out the poles for the men.

Boys can be thus employed at a much earlier age than either at opening the hills or digging in the hop-garden. They are not unfrequently thus occupied in the field at eight years of age. They are sometimes hired, when a little older, to assist others, when they earn about 6d. a day.

The remaining operations connected with the hop-garden I shall reserve for a subsequent communication.

LABOUR AND THE POOR.

THE RURAL DISTRICTS.

[FROM OUR SPECIAL CORRESPONDENT.]

THE SOUTHERN AND WESTERN COUNTIES.

LETTER XXXI.

In treating, in my previous letter, of the cultivation of the hop, I have alluded to the earnings realized by men, women, and children, in the various stages of digging, opening the hills, and poling. I have not mentioned these, however, as the wages at present received, but as the average rate of remuneration in former years, when hop cultivation was a less disastrous business than it has recently been, and when the prospects before it were of a somewhat more encouraging character than they are now. The rates mentioned are not to be taken as indicating the scale of the labourer's earnings during the past year. The declension of wages which has taken place elsewhere in the South and West has extended itself to the hop districts, giving rise to privations, on the part of the labourer, almost equalling those which I have already depicted as characterizing his lot in Dorset, Devon, Wilts, and Somerset. But to this matter I shall have occasion, hereafter, more particularly to advert; my sole object in here alluding to it being to apprise the reader that the rates of wages which I am now about to state, as well as those already mentioned, constitute the average of the past few years, the rates recently received being somewhat lower.

Tying the hop is the next step after "poling," and may, in fact, be regarded as part of that process. As soon as the plant shoots a little above the ground it requires the support of the pole. Its natural instinct is to climb; and to aid it in this effort it is tied, generally by means of rushes, to the pole. Three plants are usually tied to a pole, and the number of poles to a hill is frequently three. Tying the hop is a business which commonly devolves upon women; but it is by no means confined to them. Men sometimes take it, when driven to compete with the women from want of other occupation. Boys may make themselves very expert at it; but it is seldom that children of either sex are found thus employed, except as aids to their mothers or other adult female relatives, who have undertaken the work. It is almost invariably taken by the piece—a woman engaging to manage a greater or less quantity, according to the amount of time at her command, or of assistance on which she may reckon. Sometimes she takes a certain specified area, and engages to attend to it; at others she takes the work by the acre—the extent of surface which she will manage depending upon her own assiduity, and the aid which she receives. With a little assistance a woman can tie from two acres to two acres and a half per week. In the neighbourhood of Tunbridge, the wages received have been from 9s. to 10s. per acre—making this one of the most remunerative departments of female labour, connected with hop cultivation. In the neighbourhood of Maidstone the wages have been still higher—as much as 11s. and 12s. per acre having been paid. In Sussex the wages have averaged from 8s. 6d. to 12s. per acre, the lowest rates being paid for three-poled, and the highest for four-poled gardens. But the mere business of tying the hop is only the first part of the process. The plant has invariably to be rebound. In most cases this business of binding requires frequent repetition; and in Sussex it is very common for the women to undertake to bind the hop three times to the pole at least. Generally speaking, the plants are visited and rebound every four or five days, until at length they have grown out of reach—which happens in about five weeks.

Like all other out-door work, that of tying the hop is very much dependent upon the weather. Not only does very wet weather interrupt it, but boisterous days, even if perfectly dry, add very much to its amount. At such times, the plants have frequently to be tied over and over again, from having been detached from the pole by the wind, or twisted into positions unfavourable to their growth. Sometimes, too, the poles themselves are blown down, requiring the labour of men to replace them. This seldom happens, however, until the plant is far advanced, and the pole is more or less overloaded by its growth. Hop-tying is one of those operations which, when undertaken, must be performed speedily and briskly. The plant is tender, and the period during which it can be bound with safety is not of very long duration. The labour performed, therefore, is estimated less by the time occupied in executing it, than by its intrinsic value as regards the safety of the crop. It is further enhanced in value by the fact, that, whilst it is labour which must be performed briskly and within a given period, there is not that competition for employment which characterizes the hop-picking season, when there is a vast influx of strangers into most of the hop-growing districts. Hop-tying has all the disadvantages, with but few of the advantages, physically speaking, of out-door employment. It is an occupation requiring more nicety than exertion, and hence it is that it almost exclusively devolves upon women. The period at which it is undertaken is generally about the end of April and the beginning of May, when the weather is occasionally rough, wet, and boisterous. Unless it is altogether too stormy for the women to venture out, the more boisterous the weather the more necessity is there, at this critical period, for their presence in the hop-gardens— for the more dependent is the plant, on such occasions, on the process of binding. This frequently brings them out, when they would otherwise remain at home—and, being engaged all day in the open air, treading the cold, moist soil, without anything approaching to violent exercise to counteract the unhealthy tendencies of exposure in such weather, they very frequently contract diseases which never leave them, and which in many cases are aggravated to a fatal extent by the subsequent exposures of the hop-picking season. Not long since, 12s. per acre was the price at which the hops were tied; it has more recently ranged from 9s. to 12s.

As already intimated, it is seldom that, from the month of February to that of September, the hop-garden is free from occupants, male or female, old or young, employed in some process or other necessary to the rearing of the plant. It is essential to the well-being of the crop that the garden, when it becomes "foul," should be well cleaned— that is to say, cleared of weeds. This process is called "nidgetting" the hop. The operation, however, is designated by a variety of terms, such as "shimming," "nidging," or "breaking;" and in Surrey, sometimes, "becking" and "spudding." In general, the practice throughout the hop districts is to call in the aid of horses in performing this operation. It is sometimes performed by simple hoeing, which, although severe work, occasionally gives employment to women. It is unusual, however, to see women employed at all about the business of nidgetting—the work devolving upon men and boys. The implement used is the nidget or brake, which is drawn by horses. The man guides the implement, and the boy leads the horses. For this purpose boys of various ages are useful, although it is seldom that they are thus employed very young. Digging is severer labour; but they may become adepts at it before they are fit to be trusted with the command of the horses in the process of cleaning. It is not usual to see a boy under twelve in charge of a team thus employed. The process of guiding the team is rather a nice one; inasmuch as the hills, which are only six feet apart, must be carefully avoided—the object being not to disturb them, but to favour the growth of the plants by loosening the ground around the hills, and by clearing it of the weeds which would other-wise soon choke up the garden. In many parts of Surrey, this work is almost entirely of a manual description, the beck and spud supersed-ing the brake or nidget. In some parts, this work is also done by the piece, but it is now more customary to give it out as day-work. As in the case of all work in which horses are employed, the wages paid for this labour are higher than for other field-work, on account of the superior confidence reposed in those having charge of cattle; and as the work itself is sometimes as nice as it is always highly essential, the wages paid to those occupied in it are comparatively high. Some have told me that they have received as much as 2s. 6d. and 3s. a day whilst thus engaged, in addition to which the boy earns from 6d. to 8d. per day. When performed by the hand, the severity of the work is taken into account in apportioning the wages to be paid for it. In this, as in other cases, however, the wages of the labourer have materially declined.

Early in September commences the great business of hop-picking. The plant is, generally speaking, ready to be picked at the end of the third year of its growth. By the second week of the month above-named, hop-picking is universal throughout the hop-growing district. It thus follows the corn harvest—so that the labourers of Kent have, as it were, the advantage of two harvests. What this advantage is may be inferred from the fact, that it is generally to the extra earnings of harvest time that the labourers throughout the entire south look as the means of enabling them to buy clothing, &c., and to pay their "Christmas bills." Hop-picking is a work at which all can engage— old and young—men, women, and children. It is an important time for the poor of Kent, Sussex, and Surrey—the comforts of the ensuing winter depending, in the case of most of them, upon the joint earn-ings of the family during the brief time for which the work lasts. The hop, when ripe, is a precarious product, and must be picked with all possible expedition. Hence it is that all are pressed into the service— children, seven years old and upwards, being then of service in the hop-garden. Such of the schools as are open at the time are sure to be deserted until the hops are picked—when the children, after hav-ing added some shillings to the common stock of the family, straggle back again to enter anew upon the work of education. To meet the exigency of the case, most schools now time their holidays with a view to the hop-picking season. There are occasions, but they are few, on which hop-picking is given out as day-work, and I have been told by boys that they have earned 1s. a day whilst thus employed. But, considering the precariousness of the fruit when it is ripe, the great object of the grower is to have it picked and dried as soon as possible; and it is with this view that he gives it out as piece-work, and invites to his aid all the labour that his neighbourhood can furnish, as well as a portion of that which annually immigrates into the hop district at this period of the year. The picker is sometimes paid so much for every bushel that he or she picks—the price being sometimes as low as 1½d., and at others as high as 7d. per bushel. It is frequently 2d. and 3d. per bushel, but seldom rises to 7d. It is more general, however, to pay by the "tally"—a tally being so many bushels, according to agreement. The number of bushels in the tally depends upon the nature of the crop. If the yield is abundant, the number is comparatively large—say ten bushels to the tally; if, on the other hand, it is scanty, the number is smaller—sometimes not more than six or seven to the tally. It is obvious that the more abundant the crop is, the greater is the ease and rapidity with which a given quantity can be picked. This accounts for the variations occurring in the tally in point of quantity, for it is seldom that there is any variation in point of price. The sum paid is generally 1s. per tally, whether it be six, seven, or ten bushels. That it makes very little difference, in point of labour, to the picker, whatever the tally is, is evident from the fact that, whatever it may be, it is seldom that he can pick more than two a day. Thus, if it is ten bushels, the crop is so abundant that, with ordinary diligence, he can pick twenty. If it is seven, the crop is so scanty that, with the same diligence, he can only pick fourteen. It is by calculating what an industrious picker can achieve in a day, looking at the productiveness of the crop, that, in most instances, the amount of the tally is determined—most of the farmers being seemingly desirous to confine a picker's pay to that for two tallies per day. This is certainly but little for a long day's work, considering the great demand which exists for labour during this critical period for the hop-grower. But if the demand is great, so also is the supply; and the influx of strangers, competing with the resident labourers, enables the farmers to keep down wages at this season. But since, with a view to getting the fruit secured as speedily as possible, the grower generally gives the work out by the tally—paying the same per tally, whether large or small—it follows that when his crop is the least productive he pays the most for gathering it in. In former times, when he had a monopoly of the market, this was of little consequence, as high prices, if the crop was generally deficient, compensated him for large outlays; but now that the deficiency in the home supply is sure to be made up by foreign importation, it is questionable if he can in all cases afford to pay as much for the picking of a scanty as of an abundant crop. When fairly carried out, the system is as fair and as favourable as the labourer could desire. But it is not always fairly carried out—the pickers being sometimes in the middle of the garden, and through a great part of their work, ere they are informed what the tally is to be. Thus, sometimes, when they expect that it is not to be more than seven, they are told that it is to be ten bushels. There are circumstances in which a farmer can and does thus take advantage of his labourers, but there are others in which it is attempted without success. When the supply of labour is not over-abundant in the district, the attempt to do so might result in the complete desertion of the hop-garden by the pickers at the critical moment.

In average years a man, as already said, can pick about twenty bushels a day. A boy can pick from twelve to fourteen bushels, whilst a woman can pick even more than a man. The work is of a kind for which she is better fitted than the man—her figure being more flexible, her touch more delicate, and her fingers more nimble than his. When a whole family, therefore, are thus employed in the hop-garden, their aggregate earnings amount to a considerable sum per day. Taking a family of four thus employed—say a man and woman, and two children—they may earn among them from 6s. 6d. to 7s. a day. This favourable episode in their lives, however, is but of short duration—hop-picking seldom extending beyond three weeks in duration. But, at the rate alluded to, they may add about £6 to their means of subsistence for the winter; and this, too, after they have enjoyed the pecuniary advantages of the ordinary harvest. It is, therefore, no wonder that the hop-picking season is generally looked forward to by many of them with considerable anxiety, as being the turning-point as regards their means for the year. It interposes like a screen between many of them and the workhouse; and if it fails them, they have, too frequently, no alternative but to throw themselves upon the union for the winter. It is seldom, indeed, that you find them relying upon this alone for obtaining the necessaries of life. But they do almost universally rely upon it for supplying them with the means of meeting all the extra expenses to which they have been put, or may still be put, during the remainder of the year, such as for medical attendance, shoes, change of raiment, &c. If they fail in this, they must of course draw for these purposes upon the fund which they would otherwise apply to other purposes; and then the chances will be that they must become the recipients of public bounty before the month of February, when their labour is again briskly in demand. The past year was one of grievous disappointment to thousands of them, in consequence of the almost universal failure of the hops. The great majority of those whom I met in deep distress in Kent attributed much of the privation which they were enduring to having had their calculations falsified in respect to the usual earnings of the hop-picking season. In some portions of Surrey, where the yield was good, they were not disappointed—which was also the case with some labourers whom I met with, in comparative comfort, in the eastern part of Hampshire. I have already said that the hop is but partially raised in this last-mentioned county, but it so happened that, whilst the crop greatly failed in the districts to the eastward, the yield in it was exceedingly good.

I found somewhat contradictory opinions prevailing in regard to the effect which the cultivation of the hop has, in the main, on the health of those employed in it. It is not easy to get at the exact truth in reference to this matter—employment in the hop-garden being so mixed up with other out-door avocations, that it is difficult to trace results, as regards the health of the labourer, to their proper causes. There can be no doubt that, like all other out-door pursuits, when not carried too far, nor persisted in through all weathers, attendance in the hop garden is conducive to the health of those so employed. But the difficulty with regard to the hop is, that, at some stages of its growth, attendance upon it is imperative, without regard to the weather—and sometimes most so when the weather is inclement and inauspicious. Ordinary farm labourers have frequently complained to me that, without their being consulted, their work and wages were suspended on wet days, or even on wet forenoons or afternoons— many of them regarding it as a less privation to work in the wet than to be deprived of their wages by having their work interrupted. But in the hop-garden, it is frequently during inauspicious weather that they are obliged to work the longest and the hardest—and that, too, even in the case of women and children, to whom the hop-garden affords more constant out-door employment than the corn-field. Boys are exposed in the garden as early as January, when they receive but little damage, inasmuch as they can take what exercise they please, the duties which they are then called upon to perform being neither more nor less than those of a scarecrow. It is with the approach of the digging season in February that their trials really commence. But here, again, constant and violent exercise counteracts, to a considerable extent, the injurious tendencies of a damp soil and a chilly atmosphere. The hazard which the boys then run is that of being overworked, their fathers sometimes making them participate in the heaviest labour undertaken. It is seldom until the pruning season arrives that the women are engaged.

This occurs at a time when the weather is more variable, perhaps, than inclement. Their work, except when they are engaged in opening the hills, is in general of a sufficiently active kind to keep catarrhs and rheumatisms away from them. In opening the hills, except where the soil is very light, they run the risk, like the boys at digging, of being over-worked; but I have heard of but very few cases of anything like permanent injury having been sustained from an over-tasking of the strength at this species of labour. The operation of poling is generally conducive to the health of all engaged in it. But that of tying is sometimes very trying to the women and children employed at it. If the weather is favourable, but little difficulty is experienced, and the work is comparatively soon over; but if it is otherwise, the labour is peculiarly trying—whilst there is all the more necessity that the plant should be carefully and frequently attended to. It is at this work that the seeds of future disease are first implanted in many a constitution. The exercise is but slight, inasmuch as the work is more that of the fingers than of the limbs and body, whilst the exposure is frequently protracted and severe. In the next process—that of cleaning or nidgetting—the female does not participate; but the employment is conducive to the health of the men and boys engaged in it, although sometimes it over-fatigues the boy, and makes "his legs ache," as he will tell you. So far, the work involves little that is injurious to the health of the adult male; but the subsequent process—that of picking—is one in which he is as apt to suffer as any of the others engaged in it. Everything, in this respect, depends on the weather. It is commonly said that, when the weather is good, the pickers leave all their ailments behind them in the hop-garden. But, on the other hand, when it is not—and when there is all the more reason for securing the crop—numbers of them contract diseases which lay them up for the winter. How can it be otherwise, when they are sometimes compelled to stand upon boards as the only way in which they can keep their feet dry when engaged in an occupation which gives but little exercise to anything but the fingers? On the whole, although serious diseases do not appear to be more common in Kent than in the other agricultural districts which I have visited, I must say that in that county I have met with more of the peasantry "ailing," in proportion to their numbers, than elsewhere. Few of the medical men of the county admit that much of the disease which prevails amongst the labouring classes is attributable to the nature of their occupations—most of them tracing it to the malaria engendered by insufficient drainage, to the habits of the people themselves, and to the defective state of their dwellings with regard to ventilation. There can be no doubt that here, as elsewhere, insufficient drainage is a prolific cause of physical derangement—particularly in the valley of the Medway, which occasionally overflows large tracts of the country through which it runs. Of late years, means have been taken, and not without success, to confine these inundations to more contracted areas—and in other places, which are still subject to overflow, an effective system of drainage relieves the land of superfluous moisture, soon after the subsidence of the river. There can be no question, however, but that the work in the hop-garden, particularly in the lower grounds, is a cause superadded to those otherwise existing, of such disorders as ague, influenza, and rheumatism; and in some seasons it is not a minor one.

In corroboration of this, I find, on examining the very elaborate tables contained in the Eighth Annual Report of the Registrar-General, recently published, that the average mortality during each of the eight years from 1838 to 1845 inclusive, has been the greatest in that section of the hop-growing district in which the plant is most largely produced. In Kent the mean average for the eight years stands thus:—Out of every 100,000 males, 2,078 have died during each of the eight years in question; whilst out of every 100,000 females, the number who have died has been 1,838; taking both males and females, the mean average will give 3,916 deaths out of every 200,000 persons. In Sussex, on the other hand, the proportions stand thus:—Taking the same basis as above, the average number of deaths per year has been—males, 1,865; females, 1,766; and of both males and females, 3,631. In Surrey the following is the result—male deaths per year, 1,856; female deaths, 1,715; male and female, 3,571. I compare the three hop-growing counties together, because they closely resemble each other in their physical features, thus meeting the objection which otherwise might have been raised to the comparison, on the score of differences of climate, geological formation, and other circumstances. It will be seen that Kent, where the hop is most largely produced, exceeds the other counties in its average rate of mortality. It might be supposed that, on the same principle, the mortality should be greater in Surrey than in Sussex—the growth of the hop being at least more ubiquitous in the former than in the latter county. But it must be borne in mind that large tracts of Sussex are, as is the case with Kent, subject to annual inundations, from which Surrey is exempt; giving rise, from want of sufficient drainage, to a malaria which is very prolific of disease. And this makes the comparison, as between Kent and Sussex, at least, hold good. If the Medway overflows its banks, there are thousands of acres of meadow land between Petworth and Arundel annually under water—so much so that in travelling between these two points in winter one might almost fancy himself in the lake country. The sections of the metropolis falling within Kent and Surrey are of course excluded from this comparison.

I have already incidentally alluded to the effect produced on the rate of wages by the influx of strangers which annually takes place during the hop-picking season. It is not easy even to approximate to a correct estimate of the numbers who then pour from all quarters into the chief hop-growing districts. It is not so much to the population of the different counties in question that a great addition is then made, as to that of certain localities within them. Take Farnham, in Surrey, for instance, and the neighbourhood of Maidstone, in Kent—and the entire population which converges upon them about the beginning of September is, to a great extent, drawn from the surrounding towns and parishes. It is true that there is a great deal of what may be strictly regarded as imported labour—numbers of Irish, and of strangers from the purlieus of London, making their appearance in the hop districts on the occasion. They come in droves—sometimes whole families immigrating together—at others, only a portion of the family embarking on the adventure. When families thus appear in fractional parts, it is more commonly from the surrounding parishes that they come than from beyond the limits of the county. The mother and children will come, for instance, leaving the father at home, engaged, perhaps, in some other occupation. The new comers, so far as they can do so, obtain accommodation in the cottages of the resident population. In districts in which great numbers annually converge, sheds are frequently erected for their reception, since, with all the crowding to which they will submit, but a small proportion of them can be accommodated in the cottages. Not a few of them—the Irish immigrants in particular—bring with them contagious disorders, which sometimes spread and commit ravages amongst the resident population. Scarcely a year elapses, I am told, without small-pox and scarlatina appearing amongst them. The most prompt means are generally taken to check the extension of any malady so manifesting itself, by the removal of the patients. When the season is wet and unfavourable, the immigrants run even a greater risk of incurring disorders than the residents; for, bad as is, generally speaking, the house accommodation of the latter, that of the former is, in the main, worse. Such of them as crowd the cottages of the residents serve to render the latter more liable to disease than they otherwise would be. Their stay in the hop districts lasts altogether from five to six weeks. They begin to make their appearance from a week to ten days anterior to the commencement of the picking, and it is fully that time after the work is over ere they are fairly got rid of. Until the work begins they are frequently in a state of the greatest possible destitution. Depredations of all kinds are then committed by them for a supply of food and fuel. They are, in general, a somewhat unruly set, but it is usually admitted that the Irish are not the least peaceable and well-disposed amongst them. Indeed, in other parts of the country, subjected to an annual visitation of Irish migratory labour, testimony is readily borne to their industry and good conduct whilst the work lasts. If they break out at all, it is when they have got some money in their pockets—not when they are perfectly destitute, or are earning their wages. It is, indeed, generally observed by the captains of steamers plying between Ireland and Liverpool, that it is when they are returning home that they are the most riotous. They are, in most cases, quiet and subdued, when on their way to England, and tolerably well-behaved, until they are about to quit it with a few sovereigns in their pockets, when, in far too many cases, they become turbulent and troublesome.

But we have not yet done, either with the hops, or with the hopgarden. After being picked, the plant has to undergo the processes of drying and pocketing, which also afford employment to a considerable number of persons. This, however, does not last long, since, in addition to its being desirable that the hops should be ready for market as soon as possible, they must be dried (as they must be picked) within a limited period, or they run great risk of being spoiled. The

Hop-Garden, Farnham, Surrey

work afforded in the garden, after the picking is over, is that of pulling up the no longer useful plant, and stacking the poles. This is generally the work of men and boys, and is commonly undertaken by the piece, the price paid being usually from 5s. to 6s. per acre. The poles are pulled from their places in the hills, and put in stacks or upright piles together, in which state they remain until they are again wanted for the support of the plant. The garden is then deserted for a brief period, after which it is again manured—to be again dug, preparatory to receiving a new set of plants, to be tended and managed in the different stages of their development as their predecessors had been.

Such is the cultivation of the hop in Kent, Surrey, and the eastern half of Sussex. It is a department of industry which affords employment, where manufactures do not exist, to thousands who would otherwise be unemployed, or who, if occupied at all, would be so at tasks unsuited to their age or sex. It also furnishes employment to others at periods when their ordinary pursuits may be slack or interrupted; for the hop-garden has its seasons when it calls for the presence of the man, as at other times it requires that of the woman and the child. That a department of agriculture, furnishing so large a stock of employment to so great a number of people and distributing that employment over the greater portion of the year, superadded to the ordinary pursuits of an essentially agricultural district, should have a tendency to keep up the general rate of wages, including those of the ordinary farm-labourer, is too self-evident to be dwelt upon. It would be erroneous, however, to attribute the higher scale of wages paid for farm-labour in the hop-growing district exclusively, or even mainly, to the presence of an extensive and regular hop-cultivation. If the labour in demand in the hop-garden were in all respects such as competed with that chiefly in request in the field, its effect upon wages for field-work would be greater than it is. But the employment which it affords is such as devolves upon those who are, some of them, of but little use, and others wholly unavailable, in ordinary field labour. It, therefore, in the main, comes in addition to, instead of in competition with, ordinary farm-labour; and thus has the effect of enhancing the farm-labourer's means, without materially affecting the wages paid for farm-work. But there is a very great difference between the wages paid for farm-work in the hop district, and those paid in the counties to the west of it—a difference which is generally about 50 per cent. in favour of the former. What else is there to create this difference, if the cultivation of the hop but partly accounts for it? The great cause is the proximity of the whole district to the metropolis. Approach London from the south or west—and I speak of these directions only, because it is to them that my inquiries have been confined—and you find the scale of wages gradually rising from the moment that you enter within the circle of its influence. That circle embraces almost the whole of the hop-growing district—wages being similarly affected in such portions of it as may not be regarded as within the immediate range of metropolitan influence, by the different places of fashionable resort and of business which gird it from Brighton to Gravesend.

The Morning Chronicle, Thursday, February 14, 1850.

POOR-RATES LEVIED ON THE POOR.

To the EDITOR of the MORNING CHRONICLE.

Sir—It need not be remarked with what pleasure the thinking portion of the public have perused the able letters of your Reporter, relative to the condition of the "Rural Districts;" the truth of such letters and the faithful picture presented by them being their chief recommendation. In reading the one giving an account of this (the New Forest) district, it strikes me that one cause of grievance, and one that presses heavily on the labouring classes, has, amongst the multiplicity of details, escaped the notice of your Correspondent— and that is, the payment of poor-rates by persons who are not one remove from paupers themselves—by persons who endure the severest privations—by persons who are striving, by living in a state of half-starvation, to escape the necessity of resorting to the "dreaded union." This payment of poor rates is indeed a cruel burden on a class who can scarcely manage to live: live they do not—call it existing, and the term is more appropriate. On the political merits of thus rating an almost pauper population it is not my province to enter; but allow me, in conclusion, to give an illustration on the results of the working of the measure. In this neighbourhood an industrious workman, by the want of employment in his trade as a bricklayer, was reduced to a state of great destitution, but still keeping aloof from the parish, hoping that work would be obtained; he became in arrear of poor-rates; application is made for them; he states his case: he has no money— he is already a pauper, but struggling to keep his family off the parish. True, he had no money; but he had a few goods in his house: they are seized, and nothing remained but a remove to the union. There he and his family are—there they are likely to remain; and the man is now being absolutely relieved out of his own money. This is not a solitary case. Paupers are multiplied because they cannot pay the rates to keep other paupers. In many, many instances the rates are never paid; the fear of driving people on the parish forbidding the enforcing them. Surely, sir, this is an inconsistent state of things.

Sir, yours most obediently,

New Forest, Hants,   OMEGA.

LABOUR AND THE POOR.

—◆—

THE RURAL DISTRICTS.

[FROM OUR SPECIAL CORRESPONDENT.]

THE SOUTHERN AND WESTERN COUNTIES.

LETTER XXXII.

At the conclusion of my last Letter, I briefly alluded to the causes which tend to keep up the general scale of wages in the hop-growing district, as compared with that prevailing in the counties immediately to the west of it. I traced the circumstance of comparatively higher wages being paid for farm-labour throughout Kent, and in parts of Surrey and Sussex, than in Devon, Dorset, Wilts, and the more westerly parts of Hampshire, partly to the cultivation of the hop, but chiefly to the proximity of the district to the metropolis, and to the numerous centres of business and activity with which the greater portion of that district is begirt. There is nothing new in the influence here attributed to the metropolis. It appears from a table, which I have now before me, of the average rates of wages paid throughout the different counties of England in 1795, that whilst in the purely agricultural counties, remote from the capital, the average ranged from 6s. to 9s. a week, it was from 10s. to 12s. in those immediately to the west and south of the metropolis.

But, within the past year, wages in the hop districts, as in some other localities, have sensibly declined. In some cases the fall has been as great as in the counties to the west, and in others even greater, in proportion. It has not as yet, however, been as universal as it has been in Wilts, Dorset, Devon, &c. The complaint, therefore, in this respect, has been less general in the south-east than in the south-west. In some districts of Kent I heard no complaint whatever—no reduction having taken place in wages, although apprehensions were certainly rife everywhere that a calamity in this form was impending over the poor. Complaints of want of work were quite as common in

Kent as elsewhere; but it was not everywhere that I found the farmers disposed to take advantage of the number of hands out of employment, to make any great reduction of the wages of those kept at work. Indeed, instances have come under my observation, in which casual work has been given to the labourer, not because the employer really needed him, but because the latter wanted work; in which cases I have known as much as 2s. a day to be paid to the parties thus employed—that is to say, they were paid at the same rate as those kept permanently at work. But such cases were certainly exceptional, it being more common to find the farmer keeping a certain number steadily employed at undiminished wages, and paying for casual work at reduced rates, according to circumstances. In many instances, however, the farmer, as elsewhere, has taken advantage of the scarcity of work, and the consequent competition existing for labour, not only to get casual work done at reduced prices, but also to lower the wages of those permanently retained in his employment, and engaged in the work indispensable to the maintenance of the farm. Thus, whilst some employers are still paying as high as 12s. a week to their permanent and casual workmen—and many were to their permanent workmen only—others are paying as little as 8s. In the neighbourhood of Tunbridge-wells, Ashford, &c., I found the higher rates paid in numerous instances; whilst in the line from the town of Tunbridge to Brenchley I met with many cases in which 8s. and 9s. a week were the common rates. I speak of them, of course, as the rates paid to the ordinary labourer—carters, and others in employments more or less confidential, receiving from 1s. to 2s. a week in addition. Whilst, in the one case, the conduct of the employer cannot be traced entirely to benevolence, it cannot, in the other, be wholly attributed to selfishness. As a general rule, I found that, in Kent, where farm-wages were highest, labour was most in demand. This tended to keep up its general value, and the farm labourer, of course, benefited in consequence. After all, with some rare exceptions, it was but the market rate that was given in these localities. The same rule holds, in the main, in those places in which the lower rates are paid—the farmers regulating the price of the labour which they employ by the demand for employment. In such cases, it would be unreasonable to blame those who thus act, provided the diminution of employment, which lowers the value of labour around them, be not directly traceable to their own want of skill, judgment, enterprise, or means. But some go further than this, and take a positive advantage of the forced idleness of a portion of the labourers, to reduce still more the wages of those who are kept at work.

How far an improved system of agriculture would go towards absorbing the labour of the district, it is not for me here to inquire. But of this there can be no doubt, that there is far more labour in the district than can be profitably employed by the system of agriculture now in vogue. The consequence is, that the tendency of wages must be downwards, whatever the price of produce or the circumstances of the farmer. In seasons of extraordinary prosperity, he might, indeed, employ men largely in works which in ordinary times he would not undertake. But such seasons are from their very nature, of rare occurrence; and it does not follow that the farmer's prosperity would, in the main, enhance the comforts of the labourer, unless that prosperity were based upon an improved cultivation, which called more labour into operation. With the growing pressure of population, therefore, upon space, of which the south-eastern angle of the kingdom furnishes a striking example, the tendency of wages must be to decline, unless a great change come over the whole system of our agriculture. The struggle at present is amongst the labourers to find an employer, and the price which the latter will pay for labour is what the former are obliged to take for it. Were it otherwise—were the competition amongst the employer to obtain the services of the labourer—that which the latter would receive for his labour would be regulated by what the former would be compelled to pay for it. In many parts of England I have met with labourers who well remember when this was the case, and when wages were high in consequence. Even in the neighbourhood of Shaftesbury, where wages are at present very low, there are those to be found who remember the time when the farm-labourer had his 2s. a day. "But there's more men now, sir, than can do the work," said one to me, in recalling that time, "and they are obliged to take just what they can get."

So far as I could judge from statements made to me in different parts of Kent, the average wages now paid to the ordinary farm labourer throughout the county are from 9s. 6d. to 10s. a week. Ten shillings a week have for a long series of years back been the average paid in many parts of the county throughout the winter months. The localities from which the loudest complaints have come during the winter months are those in which a very serious reduction has been made below the average—a reduction to 8s. a week. This has been effected in many of the eastern districts around Canterbury, as well as between Tunbridge and Brenchley. In parts of the south-western section of Surrey, and in portions of East Sussex, in the neighbourhood of Lewes, and between that and Newhaven, the average is not so high. In connection with the hops, no very material diminution of the rates of remuneration heretofore prevalent has as yet taken place; but the experience of last year has taught the labourers to look to the farmer with apprehension, so far as their wages in this respect are concerned. The failure of the crop in 1849 occasioned a diminution of employment rather than a serious curtailment of the wages paid for such work as the hop-gardens afforded. What many labourers fear is, that the distress now pressing upon numbers of the smaller hop-growers, and the lesson which they learnt last year of the precariousness of the crop, will induce many of them to throw some of their hop land out of cultivation, and others to devise means of cheapening the cost of production which may, in some way or other, come into competition with manual labour. Yet it is not easy to see how this can be done, considering the peculiar nature of the work in the hop gardens. The average of wages for farm labour above alluded to has reference only to the winter season—2s. a day being very general all over Kent during the summer months. The more correct way, perhaps, to put it, would be to say that whilst from 1s. 6d. to 1s. 8d. is the average rate now paid per day, 2s. a day is very general during the summer months. In the one case the labourer will make from 9s. 6d. to 10s. a week, and in the other 12s., when employed for the whole week. But this many of them seldom or never are; whilst even those who may be regarded as having steady employment from a farmer have their wages stopped when their work is suspended by wet days, or by wet parts of days, or by other interruptions beyond their own control. This has been shown to be also the case elsewhere. The effect of it is, that in the aggregate these interruptions may reduce the wages of a labourer having steady employment at 10s. a week, to a little more than 9s. a week, for the whole year.

Nowhere have I encountered such difficulty in ascertaining the amount of a family's earnings as in the hop-growing districts. In counties where no other industry exists to compete, to any extent, for labour with the farm—or to superadd, to the demand for farm-labour, a demand for the labour of those who would otherwise be but little employed on the farm—there is not so much difficulty in coming at the aggregate of a family's means. The process is simplified by the fact, that, although more than one of the family may be at work, they all draw their earnings from the same source. But in Kent, the variety of occupations, the different kinds of work in which different persons are employed—and, frequently, the different kinds of work in which one and the same person is engaged—render it more difficult to ascertain the exact pecuniary condition of a family. In nine cases out of ten they are utterly ignorant themselves how they stand in this respect. Few of the labourers, or of their wives, sons, or daughters, keep any account of their earnings. Numbers of them would be at a loss how to do so, were they ever so willing—whilst others will not give themselves the trouble, no matter how capable they may be. I have frequently got them to try to give me some idea of what they made per week—when I have been astonished at its amount, particularly when the parties happened to reside near a town, where the boys occasionally picked up their sixpences and shillings, which were added to the family fund. In other cases I have got them to produce account-books, in which attempts had been made to keep accounts, and from which it appeared that 15s. had been made in one week, £1 in another, and perhaps £1 2s. in a third. In one instance, in which the account had been pretty regularly kept, I somewhat amazed the good woman of the house by telling her that the average earnings of her family had been about 17s. a week throughout the year. She could scarcely credit it, and she *naïvely* told me that, had she known they had received so much, she would have made them more comfortable. Such a thing as striking an average of their earnings, and regulating their expenditure from day to day by that average, had never entered into their heads. Whether the earnings of the week were 25s. or 10s., they always lived up to them; and when there was for a time a complete suspension of work, the only alternative before them was getting into debt or going into the workhouse. Where the highest wages ever earned by a labouring family are insufficient to bring their physical condition up to the line of comfort, they can scarcely be blamed for spending in each week the full earnings of the week. But such is not generally the case in Kent. Enough has already been said of the industry of the county to show that it affords a family far greater facilities for obtaining employment than exist in the purely farming districts. A family in Kent, therefore, frequently earn during the week far more than is necessary to keep them in comfort for the week. But, as in less favoured cases, the week's earnings generally go to supply the week's wants, and, therefore it is that at certain periods of the year those fast who feast at others, and distress as severe, and privation as great, are experienced in Kent, as any that are felt in Dorset. A case was brought under my notice of a man with a family, who sought for relief at the workhouse; being offered by one of the guardians, a farmer and hop grower, work for himself and family for the ensuing year at £1 per week, he refused the offer. The terms proposed showed the farmer's estimate of the value of the family's labour—while the man's refusal evidenced either that he put a still higher value upon it, or that he was too indolent to bind himself to anything like steady work.

So long as he is free from actual distress, the condition of the Kentish labourer is better than that of his brethren in the west. But it would be an error to suppose that his superiority in point of condition keeps pace with his superiority in point of wages. I have already shown that, but for the intervention of favourable local circumstances, the comparatively high wages paid in Cornwall would not place the labourer there in a better actual position than that in which the labourer in Devon is placed by the wages which he receives. And so, in Kent, the condition of the labourer is governed to some extent by other circumstances besides the mere amount of his wages. In some of the counties in which the lowest rate of wages is paid, farming is, generally speaking, conducted on a much better system than in most parts of Kent. The almost complete absence of green crops throughout large tracts of that county has a material effect upon the circumstances of the poor, especially in those parts where allotments are not generally granted, by which the deficiency of ordinary vegetables, thus occasioned, might be compensated. For instance, in some of the counties the circumstances of which I have already described, the turnip enters largely into the diet of the peasant. But neither the turnip nor the potato constitutes a very marked feature of the labourer's diet in Kent. Where allotments are granted, you may find him with his cabbage, his Jerusalem artichoke, and his white carrot; but where this system is not practised, his stock of vegetable food is extremely scanty. Owing to the want of ordinary vegetables, he is compelled to consume more bread than he would otherwise do. Along with his bread he will eat butter and cheese, in such quantities as he can afford, and occasionally a little bacon or fresh butcher's meat. I was struck with the contrast presented by the poor man's larder in Kent as compared with Dorset. In the latter county I found it generally to contain (when there was anything in it) a quantity of turnips and cabbages, a few potatoes, and perhaps a solitary loaf, or the fraction of a loaf—with, now and then, certainly not always, a bit of cheese, and, rarely, a piece of butter. In Kent, on the other hand, I found in it, when the family were at work, several loaves, and almost invariably some butter and cheese, and occasionally a piece of bacon or animal food of some kind, but very few vegetables of any description. If the Kentish labourer thus lives upon a better diet than that on which the peasant of the west subsists, it must be borne in mind that it is also a more expensive one. The consequence is, that when he has provided food for himself and family, his surplus, if he has any, is by no means equivalent to the superiority of his wages over those of the labourer in Dorset. The superiority of his condition chiefly consists in this, that he is a stronger and a heartier man than the other, because his wages suffice to procure him a more nutritious diet. He cannot feed his family as cheaply as the Dorsetshire labourer does, and have the surplus of his earnings in his pocket. But his wages enable him to feed his family better than the Dorsetshire labourer does. This is certainly a great point in his favour, although there is not that difference as regards money, after the wants of his family have been supplied, which at first sight there would appear to be. From the circumstances in which he is placed his more expensive diet is not optional but imperative with him.

Bread thus entering so largely into the diet of the Kentish labourer, it is obvious that he has very greatly benefited by the recent fall in its price. He feels this, and confesses that, bad as he may consider his wages to be, both he and his family are now better off, living upon a given sum per week, than they were seven years ago. In 1795 and 1796, his wages were but little higher than they are now. Yet those were years of scarcity, and consequently of high prices for corn. Wages, however, did not then rise in proportion to the price of bread. As illustrative of the effect upon a labouring family's comforts, of low prices, even when accompanied with low wages, I subjoin the two following statements, showing the expenditure of a family of six in 1837, and that of a family of the same number from sixty to seventy years ago. In 1837 flour was 1s. 1¼d. per gallon, and wages were a little upwards of 13s. a week. At the other period referred to, flour was but 6d. a gallon, and wages but 6s. a week. The expenditure in each case was as follows—the statements being taken from the very valuable report presented by Mr. Tufnell, in 1841, to the Poor-law Commissioners:—

Expenditure of a family consisting of a man, his wife, and four children, in 1837—

	s.	d.
5 gallons of flour, at 1s. 1¼d.	5	6¼
2 lbs. of butter, at 10d.	1	8
½ lb. of candles	0	3½
3 lbs. of cheese	1	6
Meat	2	0
1½ lb. of sugar	0	10½
2 ozs. of tea	0	7½
½ lb. of soap	0	3
Pepper and salt	0	2
1 oz. of tobacco	0	3½
Total	13	2¼

Expenditure of a family of the same number, from 60 to 70 years ago—

	s.	d.
4½ gallons of flour, at 6d.	2	3
Grinding, baking, and yeast	0	5
7 lbs. of beef, at 2½d.	1	5½
2½ lbs. of cheese, at 2½d.	0	6¼
(Or, instead of cheese, 1½ lb. of butter, at 4d.)		
Oatmeal and salt	0	2¼
1 oz. of tea	0	2
½ lb. of sugar	0	3
Firing (mostly heath-turf, cut free from the common or wood)	0	3
Candles	0	3
Soap	0	3
Total	6	0

It appears from this, that, in the case last cited, the family consumed two pounds of butter, half a gallon of flour, one pound of sugar, one ounce of tea, and half a pound of cheese less than in the other case—but, as a set-off to this, they consumed at least four pounds more of beef. On the whole, therefore, the difference was not very great in the amount of their comforts, although wages in one case were not half in amount what they were in the other.

In estimating the extent to which the higher wages of Kent place the labourer in an advantageous position there, as compared with the more scantily paid peasant of the west, there is another consideration which must be borne in mind, in addition to the higher price of his food—and that is, the comparatively high rent which he pays for his cottage. Throughout the whole of the hop-growing district house-rent is a far heavier drag upon the resources of the labourer than in the counties to the west, which are, in the ordinary acceptation of the term, purely agricultural. It will have been seen that, in the latter, the rent of cottages ranges from 30s. to 50s. a year, with a small garden included. In some cases it has been shown to be much higher, but in others it is somewhat lower. But throughout Surrey, East Sussex, and Kent—the last-mentioned county particularly—it ranges much higher than this. Mr. Tufnell reports that, in 1841, a cottage, the erection of which would cost only £40, was rented at 2s. a week, without a garden (this was in the island of Sheppy). This could not have been unless the demand had been much greater than the supply. But in addition to the disadvantage of high rents, there is the still more serious one, of the character of the tenements. Many of them have but one room—the family living by day and sleeping by night in the same apartment. In this respect I am given to understand that but little change has been effected in Sheppy since the date of Mr. Tufnell's report. There are, indeed, cottages of a better description on the island, and they are all occupied. Their cost of erection was, however, about double that of those just alluded to, and the rent is double also—the labourer who occupies one of them having to pay £10 and upwards. In the neighbourhood of Canterbury there are numerous cottages of a very inferior description—some with, and others without, gardens—and rented at from 1s. 6d. to 2s. 6d. a week. So far as mere money outlay is concerned, this is not so great a hardship, but many of the poor have bitterly complained to me of their want of accommodation in their houses. The overcrowding to which this gives rise, and the disastrous consequences which ensue, both in a physical and a moral point of view, are illustrated by what has already been said by me on this subject, when treating of it in connection with the more westerly counties. In the immediate vicinity of the town, and in the town itself, cottages of a better description have recently been built, containing two bed-rooms at least, with a family room and a washing room below. The average rent of them is a little upwards of 3s. a week, but the rent is, in too many cases, made up in whole or in part by sub-letting one of the bed-rooms, either to a single lodger, or to a man with a family. Between Canterbury and Dover, and on the eastern skirts of the Wold, the cottages are of a medium class in respect of accommodation, and they are generally moderately rented, as rents go in Kent. Between Canterbury and Faversham, particularly as you approach the latter place, they are decidedly superior as regards position and ventilation, and some of them likewise as regards room. Here also the rents are comparatively reasonable. I have seen some, with four tolerably good rooms and a wash-house, rented as low as 2s. and 2s. 6d. a week. The same may be said of the line between Faversham and Sittingbourne. In the immediate vicinity of the latter place there are numbers of commodious brick cottages, having four rooms and an out-house of some kind, which are rented at an average of 2s. 6d. a week. This includes some garden ground, usually about the eighth of an acre—the granting of a garden with the cottage being more frequent here than in any of the other places to which allusion has been made. To the north of Sittingbourne, however, as you descend towards the Isle of Sheppy, very miserable specimens are to be met with, occupied at high rents. From Sittingbourne to Rochester, there is little about the cottages calling for remark; and the same may be said of those met with on proceeding by the main road from the latter place to Maidstone, until you surmount the high chalky ridge dividing the two places from each other. In this part of the valley of the Medway the cottages are built of a material that is very conducive to their healthiness, chalk being chiefly used in their construction. Want of room is their chief defect, to which, lower down the valley, is superadded that of an unhealthy position. From Maidstone to Tunbridge the dwellings partake of the same general character as those on the other side of Maidstone. In the vicinity of that town rents average from 1s. 6d. to 2s. 6d. a week.

In the parish of Brenchley, to the south-east of Tunbridge, are some of the worst specimens of dwellings that I met with in Kent. This parish has long been notorious for the wretched state of its labouring poor. A manifest improvement has recently taken place, owing to the efforts of the resident clergyman, and of others who have zealously co-operated with him in the work of reformation. From Brenchley to Tunbridge Wells, passing through Matfield and Pembury, there are few cottages in which a family might not live comfortably and decently, were the inducement not so strong for the introduction of strangers. At a small place of fashionable resort like Tunbridge Wells, one would expect to find competence, comfort, and decent accommodation, the lot of all. But not so; for there is, perhaps, no other place in Kent which presents specimens of such miserable tenements and high rents combined. In one part of the town a private individual is erecting a line of very superior houses for the poor, small but neat in their external appearance, and extremely commodious in their internal arrangements. These are intended to supersede a cluster of the most wretched tenements, which are now occupied behind them, and which, when the new ones are ready, will be swept away. Unless this were done, the only result would be, that both the bad and the good would be occupied. The consideration that the building of new cottages only tends to increase the population of the place, unless the old ones are taken down, has given a check to the efforts of many benevolent persons, who would otherwise have aided in promoting their erection. Tradesmen, seeing the high rents paid for wretched accommodations, have been induced to build small tenements of a better class, in the hope of luring the tenants into them from their present filthy lairs. But the new cottages have generally fallen into the hands of new comers—or, if those inhabiting the bad ones have taken them, their places have been supplied by others, who immediately enter into the dens which they have vacated. For tenements of the most wretched description rents as high as from £10 to £15 are paid—and this, too, by those who have only the ordinary wages of labour to depend upon. For the most miserable, damp, and ill-ventilated abodes, 3s. and 4s. a week are commonly paid as rent. The same story may be told of Surrey, particularly in the districts of which Reigate and Godalming are centres. In East Sussex it is equally bad about Cuckfield, and along the low tract extending from Newhaven to Lewes; also in the vicinity of Hastings, and the district stretching back for some miles from Pevensey Bay. In the town of Hastings considerable improvement has, of late years, taken place in the tenements occupied by the poor. The rents are, however, still very high, as compared with the accommodation. In Rye and its neighbourhood the cottages are constructed on a decidedly better scale, and their inmates are accommodated with greater cleanliness, comfort, and decency.

This subject will be further pursued in the opening portion of my next letter.

LABOUR AND THE POOR.

THE RURAL DISTRICTS.

[FROM OUR SPECIAL CORRESPONDENT.]

THE SOUTHERN AND WESTERN COUNTIES.

LETTER XXXIII.

I propose, in the present Letter, to conclude the inquiry which I commenced some time since into the condition of the labourer in the Hop Districts.

It has been objected by some, that this investigation into the state and circumstances of the Poor has savoured too much of the character of a sentimental journey in search of the horrible. But, if I have made no particular allusion to that portion of the population whom I have found comfortably situated, it has been because I did not think it necessary to describe the circumstances of those whose condition was such as it should be. One of the main objects of the inquiry has been to ascertain if there are any classes in a situation, both moral and physical, in which it is improper that any British subjects should be placed. It is for this reason that less has been said of those who are favourably circumstanced than of those whose condition is the reverse. There is little to be done as regards the former, but to prevent them, if possible, from sinking to the condition of the latter—whilst the great object is to ascertain the true circumstances of the latter, with the view of elevating them, if possible, to the status of the former. Hence it is that I have not deemed it necessary to refer particularly to the circumstances of such of the labourers as I found in a position of comfort and decency. But it is desirable that there should be some allusion to such efforts as are now being made for the improvement of the condition of those who are not so circumstanced, and I shall therefore endeavour to show how far such efforts have succeeded, and are capable of still further succeeding, by what has been done in this direction at Tunbridge Wells.

Learning that there were in the neighbourhood of the town several model cottages for the poor, built by a local society, which is a branch of a general association in London, I went to inspect them. I found them situated about half a mile from the Calverley Hotel, on an elevated, airy, and healthy site. Leaving the highway, I entered, through a handsome iron gateway, upon a broad, smooth, well-gravelled road, extending about two-thirds of a furlong in length. On each side of this road it is intended that the cottages shall be built. As yet, those finished are all on one side, with the exception of one, larger than the rest, which stands across the road at its lower end, and directly opposite the gateway. The cottages, which are small and built of bricks, are exceedingly neat in their design, and I could not help admiring, as I approached them, the cleanness and neatness which characterized their external appearance. Anxious to know if what was within corresponded, in this respect, with that which I saw without, I entered the first that I came to. It was occupied by a family of the name of ——. On entering I found the house in some confusion, the cause of which was soon explained to me. There were but three persons at home, Mrs. ——, her daughter, a girl about nine years of age, and an infant, which the mother was then rocking in its cradle. The infant was but a fortnight old, and that was the first time that the mother had ventured down stairs since her confinement. She had been obliged to do so sooner than she otherwise would, by her nurse having been compelled to leave her, owing to some family affliction. The poor woman appeared quite in distress at the somewhat disordered appearance of her house, but hoped I would excuse it when I knew the cause. The explanation was scarcely necessary, her very appearance betokening a degree of weakness incompatible with the fulfilment of the active duties of housekeeping. On entering the house, I had to ascend a step, which led me into a small lobby. A door on the left led me from this into the principal family room. This arrangement added much to the warmth of the house, and to its healthiness, by keeping its temperature pretty equable throughout the day. In the case of the majority of cottages, you enter at once into the room from the external air. The apartment in which I found myself was large and lofty, as compared with the accommodation of the generality of cottages. Both the walls and ceiling were well plastered. The floor was boarded, and the house was quite dry, in consequence of its habitable part being elevated somewhat above the surface of the ground. The window was large, and admitted into the room a flood of light, which, of itself, sufficed to impart to it a more cheerful appearance than is generally possessed by the dwellings of the poor. In the fire-place was a small neat grate, flanked on one side by a "copper," full of hot water day and night, and on the other by a small oven for culinary purposes. Mrs. —— told me that she now found the oven very useful, but that at first she could make nothing of it at all. The same was the case with all her neighbours except one, whose oven worked well, and who used to accuse the rest of not knowing how to manage theirs. At length she went and carefully examined that of her exulting neighbour, after which she closely inspected her own. The cause of the difficulty was at once discovered. The oven was constructed of a double set of iron plates, between which the hot air from the fire was intended to circulate. With this view, it was necessary that there should be holes both above and below in the outer plate of the side next the fire. Mrs. ——, to her astonishment, discovered that these holes had yet to be made in her oven, and, as she said herself, one might as well expect a gun to go off without a touch-hole as the oven to work in such a plight. She accordingly set to work herself, and by means of a piece of a broken scythe, the edge of which was much serrated, she actually sawed a couple of holes through the thick iron plate. On my expressing my surprise at her perseverance and ingenuity, "Oh! indeed," said she, "I was at it all day from morning till night, and tired enough I was, but you would have laughed to see how astonished my husband was when he came home at night and saw what I had done." The experiment succeeded admirably. From that day forth, the oven has acted in a becoming manner, having proved itself adequate to baking a loaf, and to "doing a pie beautiful." The neighbours were electrified, and on ascertaining the cause of the sudden change, lost no time in having the necessary perforations made in their respective ovens. I mention the circumstance chiefly to show how light a matter an ingenious and thrifty housewife will make of difficulties from which others will shrink back, either through indolence or want of self-confidence.

In addition to the room in question, and the small lobby which led into it, there were below a tolerable-sized pantry, on the shelves of which were ranged, amongst other things, several large loaves of bread; a very commodious washhouse, with a copper and fire-place for boiling water; a small closet for holding coals, &c.; and a water-closet. The floor above was divided into three bed-rooms—all of them small, but still there were three of them—the parents occupying one, and the children the other two, the boys and girls being thus kept separ-

ate from an early age. On inspecting the washhouse I discovered that
the house was copiously supplied with water, in which respect it did
not differ from the other houses of the group. On inquiring whence
the water was supplied, I was informed that it came from a large elevated tank, into which it was daily pumped by a man paid for the
purpose—the sum which each tenant contributed being included in
his rent. Behind, were neat little garden plots attached to each house,
each plot being from one-twelfth to one-eighth of an acre in extent.
For such a house, so favourably situated, and with such excellent accommodation, including water and garden, the rent paid was only 3s.
a week. I could scarcely credit the woman's statement on her informing me of this, seeing that I had then but just come from visiting the
most wretched and squalid dens in the town, for which 3s., 3s. 6d.,
and 4s. a week were paid. I asked her if she would consent to go and
live again in the town at a less rent than she now paid—to which she
replied that not only would she not re-occupy one of the dens in the
town rent-free, but that she would not consent to live in one of them
again if she were paid for doing so. I could readily believe her, for the
family bore a good character—indeed, none are accepted as tenants
who cannot furnish ample testimony on this point. Many think that
this rule is carried too far, and that the society should confine itself to
dealing rigidly with those who turn out to be bad characters—for it
is quite possible that many who have previously borne an indifferent
reputation might greatly improve from the altered circumstances in
which they would find themselves placed. Benevolence should lend
its efforts to the improvement of the erring as well as to the encouragement and reward of the well-doing.

It was hinted to me that the speculation had not answered, and
that it was not likely to answer at the present low rents. Others objected, on principle, to letting the poor occupy houses for which they
paid inadequate rents. "Let them live in palaces, if you will," said they,
"but let them pay for them. There can be nothing worse for the poor
than to give them houses, either wholly or partially in charity—it para-
lyzes their exertions, and impairs their self-reliance." The objectors
did not find fault with the houses, but with the rents. The principle
on which they went was, that no man—no matter what might be his
station in life—should occupy a house for which he did not pay a rent
that was sufficient to make the house a profitable concern, in a commercial point of view. To give a poor man a good house on any other
terms was only to recall, to some extent, the evils of the old poor-

law; it was, in fact, virtually to give him relief out of the workhouse. Admitting, however, the force of this reasoning, the society has still a large margin for the enhancement of its rents, ere it brings them, should it see fit to adopt such a course, to a level with those paid for some of the most filthy and disgusting dens in the heart and suburbs of the town.

The family in question consisted altogether of ten persons—the father and mother, and eight children, boys and girls. The eldest daughter was out at service, which reduced the number at home to nine. One of them, a boy, worked sufficiently to maintain himself, minus his clothes; but supposing that he maintained himself entirely, there still would be eight at home, depending for support upon the wages of the husband and father. He was a farm labourer steadily employed in the better kinds of work, and earning about 13s. a week. Considering that nearly 25 per cent. of this went in the shape of rent, the wonder to me was how so many could be supported on what remained. The simple economy of this lowly household shows the value of thrift and management in a housewife. Mrs. —— told me that her first care, on receiving her husband's earnings, was to lay the rent aside out of them. The rent is paid weekly by all the tenants. "Sometimes I'm sore tempted to spend it," she said, "but I know that if I missed it one week it would be more difficult to pay it the next. Besides," she continued, "so long as we pay our rent I know that we can always have a good roof over our heads, which is a great comfort." Having done this, she then deducts the school fees for her children, amounting to about 3d. a week, and such small contributions as may be due by her to the coal and clothing clubs. With all these deductions, 9s. 6d. at least will still be left her. She then sits down and calculates what she thinks she will want for the week, setting down the price opposite each article. On adding up her little budget, should the sum total exceed the balance in hand, she next considers what she can best afford to strike off; and having struck it off, she again adds up, repeating the process until, at length, she brings her wants within the compass of her means. Her chief business for the rest of the week is to make such comforts as she can afford go as far as possible for the support of the family. With all her care, she cannot understand how she manages to provide for so large a number. "Why, you see, sir," said she, "I have to provide more than one hundred meals a week out of the 13s., after the rent and other things is taken out of it." This was a novel and a striking way of putting her difficulty. The number of meals required in a week, by a family of eight—the ninth in this case, as already shown, is maintaining himself—is 168, that is at the rate of three meals a day for each. The family consumes from 6s. to 7s. worth of bread a week, the remainder of the 9s. 6d. being laid out in the purchase of cheese, butter, vegetables, &c., according to their means. Sometimes, but very rarely, they have animal food. "My husband often comes home very tired," she said "and thinks it very hard sometimes that he can't have a bit of butcher's meat for supper. But then I tell him that if he works with his hands, I work with the head and hands too, so that there's not much difference between us." She then explained to me how much depended on the proper management of food. When she was confined, the bread did not go nearly so far, because the nurse did not know how to cut it right. "As I cut it, it goes far further," she said, "and yet my children don't look as if they wanted. Indeed, the poor things as are at school come home of a night so hungry, that I could not find it in my heart to refuse it to them, if it was in the house." I inquired what school her children attended. Two girls were at a female school, and the third child, a boy, went "to Mr. Pope's school." "I send him there," she said, "because they do get on so well. The little fellow comes home and tells us such queer things about the world being round like an orange, and people living on the lower side of it, just as we do on top." "Then your whole life is a continued contrivance?" I said to her. "O, yes," she answered, "it's one struggle from morning till night, and from one week's end to another. I hope I'm prepared for a better, but there's nothing now in this world that I care living for, except to see my poor children doing for themselves."

I have dwelt upon the circumstances connected with this family for the double purpose of showing how the poor can appreciate a dwelling superior to that to which they are generally accustomed, and how much the comforts of a labouring family depend upon thrift, management, and economy. If not the main difficulty, certainly one of the great difficulties, with which the poor have to contend, is their own want of management and forbearance. Anything that tends to destroy their self-reliance makes them, more or less, prodigal of their means. The old Poor-law did this to an extent which almost threatened the culinary art with extinction amongst the poor in some parts of the country. One of the results of the present law has been to necessitate, to a greater or less extent, the revival of this art or science. But amongst the labouring poor in the rural districts the women are still deplorably deficient in knowledge of cookery. Indeed, in general, they are ready to take offence, if you endeavour to point out to them more efficient and economical modes of proceeding in preparing their meals. In no place in which I have been are they so ignorant, in this respect, as in Kent. There are two reasons for this. One is, that their food is of a kind that seldom requires cooking—their staple diet consisting of bread, cheese, and butter, all of which they buy. The other is, that the females of a family are called so much from home to work in the hop garden, that it is next to impossible for them to give any due attention to their household duties. Thus, if a man requires a shirt, his wife, instead of making one for him, will go and purchase one at a slop-shop, where she has the privilege of procuring the worst possible article at the highest possible price. All this tends to confirm the opinion which I expressed in an early letter of this series, that it would be better for a labouring man and his family, even in an economical point of view, if his wife never left her home for out-door work, except in his own garden or allotment.

About Tunbridge Wells the labouring classes seem to be peculiarly destitute of anything approaching even to the idea of good management. There is much in local circumstances to account for this. In common with the poor elsewhere, they have, of course, the Union to look to, if they become destitute. The feelings with which this common resort of destitution is regarded by the poor are very different in different parts of the country. When the law is harshly enforced it is looked upon as a stigma to be upon the parish—a stigma in some cases equal to, and in others greater than, crime itself. When it is prudently but rigidly worked, relief is applied for, by the able-bodied, with reluctance, and only in the last resort. They then regard it as no disgrace to them, but as a legal right to which they are driven by overpowering necessity. In other places, where it is indifferently enforced, the feelings of the poor are in a transition state respecting it—whilst, wherever it is laxly administered, it is fast re-introducing many of the evils of the pernicious system which it superseded. The state of things at Tunbridge Wells illustrates this last position. There the law appears to be laxly administered; and not only do the poor readily fly to the Union, whenever they feel the pinching of want, but they are at no pains to stave off the necessity for so doing. Indeed many, who ought never to have been the recipients of relief at all, have been receiving it annually for years back. Some small farmers in the neighbourhood are in this predicament. When such is the case, what can be expected of the labourer? One old woman confessed that she did not see what a parish was for, unless it was for the poor to go to whenever they needed it—they, of course, being the judges of their own necessities. The law enjoins that no able-bodied man shall receive relief out of the workhouse except in certain specified cases, such as the illness of a member or members of his family. When such a man asks for relief, the guardians are, in too many cases, but too anxious to find an excuse for keeping him out of the house, and anything will suffice. If one of his children has a slight cold it will do. To give him relief out of the house is of course an evil, but a less one, in their estimation, than his breaking up his establishment and entering the house with his whole family, to become a permanent charge upon the rates. The poor are quick in discerning what the feeling is in this respect, and they take advantage of it. An able-bodied man is frequently deterred from asking for relief by his abhorrence of the workhouse; but if he can get it without entering within the walls, he will ask it frequently, and will take it as often as it is given him. The law contemplated that entering the workhouse should be made the condition of an able-bodied man's receiving relief; but, in many cases, the poor make the threat of entering it the means whereby they obtain relief out of doors. It is unnecessary to dwell upon the carelessness and improvidence which this is likely to engender amongst them.

Another cause of want of management, on the part of the poor about Tunbridge Wells, is of a more local kind, consisting of a too prodigal distribution of charity. Some charities, like some schools, are strictly confined to the adherents of the church; others are of a more liberal description; but they come in contact with each other, the same parties being frequently the recipients of relief from several charitable sources. This, it seems, cannot well be avoided, but its evident tendency is to make the poor look to other sources than their own exertions for support. When this is the case it is vain to expect either thrift, foresight, or good management on their part. And yet there is no class of society to whom good management is of so much consequence as to the poor. For, from the very circumstances of their position, they are compelled to purchase everything which they consume at a disadvantage. Their dealings are invariably with the small trader, and it is vain to expect him to sell either at wholesale or at ordinary retail prices. Something must be allowed him for his time, for every turn of the scale, &c. But the advantage which he takes of them is altogether disproportioned to his trouble and to his position as a dealer in small quantities. He sells them inferior articles at enormous profits, particularly when they get into his debt, which they too readily do. The evil of paying higher than others for their commodities seems almost inseparable from the condition of the poor.

In further illustration of the inroads which have been made upon the habit of self-reliance in the neighbourhood in question, I may mention a practice which prevails, and which puts many, who make no claim to be paupers, in the position of *quasi*-beggars. If a small tradesman or farmer meets with a calamity, a begging petition is immediately sent round to repair his loss. Nor is the calamity necessarily an unavoidable one. Thus a man will buy an old horse, say for £4, and in the course of a year work him to death. His petition goes the rounds, and he perhaps collects £10 to buy him a good serviceable beast. This is, truly, trading on other people's capital!

I have already stated that the efforts of the clergyman, seconded by those of other residents, are doing much to improve the condition of the poor in the parish of Brenchley. It is in contemplation to support the poor within the parish without going to the Union at all. This would be tantamount to a withdrawal from the Union. Brenchley may virtually withdraw from the Union, so far as the maintenance of the paupers in the workhouse is concerned, but it cannot repudiate its contribution to the maintenance of the expenses of the establishment.

There are numerous coal and clothing clubs in Kent, to which the poor are regular subscribers. After subscribing a certain amount they receive coal or clothes, or both, to the value of their subscriptions, and half as much again.

Allotments are not as general as they might be throughout the county. Wherever they exist, they are spoken of as being, in more ways than one, of the greatest possible benefit to the poor.

I have little room here left to say anything in respect to the intellectual and moral condition of the poor in the district under consideration. It unfortunately does not speak well for their habits generally, that all the establishments, such as beer-shops, which depend almost exclusively upon them for support, are in a thriving condition. As a set off to this, however, I must not omit to mention that, in many places, their deposits in the savings banks are large, regular, and increasing. Even at Tunbridge Wells this is the case. There can be no question that one of the greatest drawbacks on them, in a moral point of view, is the overcrowded state of their dwellings. This is partly owing to the want of cottages, and partly to the exorbitant rents which they are charged. To make good their rents they will take additional families into their dwellings, which, if it lead to no other evil, is bad in a sanitary point of view. But they are more prone to let their spare room to single lodgers, which is almost sure to lead to disastrous consequences. The evil reaches its height during the hop-picking season, as may be inferred from the fact, that it is almost invariably the case in Kent that the greatest number of illegitimate births which occur during the following year take place within the first two quarters of the year. On the whole, however, the evil in this respect is, as already said, not so great in Kent as in other counties, in which the sexes are not under the same surveillance whilst engaged in out-door work—that prolific opportunity for mischief. This is proved by the Reports recently made by the Registrar-General. Whilst in Kent the proportion of illegitimate births to every hundred births, in 1845, was but 6.1, in Suffolk it was 8.5; in Berks, 8.1; in Salop, 10.8; in Westmoreland, 10.2; in Cumberland, 11.1; in Wilts, 7.4; in Dorset, 7.1, &c.

I am in possession of several details respecting education in the hop-growing districts, but—with the exception of the extent to which education is more prevalent amongst the girls than the boys, owing to the constancy with which the latter are engaged in out-door occupations—there is but little difference between the educational system here and that described as existing in the counties already spoken of. Little has really been done, since the madman Thom marched his infatuated followers almost to the very walls of Canterbury, to rend the thick pall of ignorance which obscures the Kentish mind. I cannot quit this subject, however, without making a passing allusion to the praiseworthy exertions in behalf of education of the Rev. Mr. Pope, at Tunbridge-wells, who, amongst other things which he has done in this direction, has established a school there, which is largely attended by the children of parents adhering to all denominations, and which he has placed under the superintendence of a competent teacher. The universal testimony which was borne to me in favour of this school was fully corroborated by a personal inspection of it which I was afterwards enabled to make.

On the whole, then, in estimating the condition of the labourer in the South-east, it must be borne in mind that if he receives higher wages, he has higher rent to pay, and higher prices to give for his food. But he gets in the main a better dwelling, and a more nutritive diet. So far, therefore, he is in a better position, and is a haler and heartier man, than the labourer of the west. At present the labourer is suffering in Kent, as elsewhere, from want of employment; but the pressure upon the rates occasioned by this cause is not so great as in some of the western districts. With some very glaring exceptions, the poor-law has recently been administered in Kent much more judiciously than in many other parts of the kingdom. The expenditure for the poor in 1847, as compared with that in 1846, exhibited an increase of only 6 per cent. That was a year in which there was an increase in every county in the kingdom. In many it was above 10, and in one— Nottingham—it reached 19 per cent. The increase in Kent was 1 per cent. lower than the average increase throughout England, which was 7 per cent. In Surrey and Sussex the increase was respectively 8 and 5 per cent.

The Morning Chronicle, Wednesday, April 3, 1850.

To THE EDITOR OF THE MORNING CHRONICLE.

SIR—After reading your letter on Saturday, my family omitted meat two days at dinner, thereby enabling me to transmit 2s. 6d. to you for the poor woman at Tunbridge, who was unable to give her hard-working husband any all the week.

A TRADESMAN.

LABOUR AND THE POOR.

—◆—

THE RURAL DISTRICTS.

[FROM OUR SPECIAL CORRESPONDENT.]

HERTS, BEDS, HUNTS, CAMBRIDGE.
THE STRAW-PLAIT AND LACE-MAKING DISTRICTS.

Letter XXXIV.

The above-named group of counties forms what may be termed the East Midland district of England. The counties of Hertford and Cambridge are joined on the east by Norfolk, Suffolk, and Essex, and the southern portion of Hertford is bounded by Middlesex—while the western part of the county, together with Bedfordshire, Huntingdonshire, and a portion of the Isle of Ely, in Cambridgeshire, are contiguous to Lincoln, Northampton, and Bucks. The four counties together contain 1,476,545 acres, being not quite 200,000 more than the single county of Norfolk. Lincolnshire, Devonshire, and the West Riding of Yorkshire each contain a larger area than the whole of the four counties together. The area of the group is thus distributed: Herts, 400,350; Beds, 297,632; Hunts, 242,250; and Cambridge, 536,613 acres. There are 39 counties larger than Huntingdon, 38 larger than Bedford, 36 larger than Hertford, and 27 larger than Cambridge.

The population of the four counties has increased from 287,883 in 1801 to 488,151 in 1841, being at the rate of 68 per cent. in the four decennial periods. That of Bedfordshire in 1801 was 63,393; in 1841, 107,936. Cambridgeshire: 1801, 89,346; 1841, 164,459. Hertfordshire: 1801, 97,577; 1841, 157,207. Huntingdonshire: 1801, 37,568; 1841, 58,549. The number of inhabitants to each 100 acres was, in 1841, for Bedfordshire, 15.3; Cambridgeshire, 34.6; Huntingdonshire, 24.6; and Hertfordshire, 39; being in the case of Bedfordshire 15.3, Cambridgeshire 34.6, Huntingdonshire 42.8, and Hertfordshire 9.3 per cent. below the average of England and Wales. The number of persons returned as independent in each of the four counties was, in

Bedfordshire 43.1, Cambridgeshire 17, Herts 16.1, and Hunts 29.5 per cent. below the average of England and Wales; while the amount of real property in proportion to the population varies considerably in each of the counties—in Cambridgeshire, Herts, and Hunts it is above, and in Bedfordshire below the average. The proportions are, Bedfordshire 11.12 per cent. below—and Cambridgeshire, 24.27; Hunts, 27.19; and Herts, 0.21 per cent. above—the average. Pauperism, as indicated by the proportion to the whole population of the persons relieved in the quarter ending Lady-day, 1844, was, in the whole of the four counties, above the average of England and Wales; in Cambridgeshire it was 27.5; Bedfordshire, 26.9; Herts, 17.5; and Hunts, 8.9, above the average. And while pauperism is above the average in these counties, the returns of the deposits in the savings banks are, as might naturally be expected, below the average. In Herts the deposits were 46.2; Cambridgeshire, 44.5; Hunts, 32.7; and Bedfordshire, 23 below the average. The actual amount invested by depositors in 1847 was—in Bedfordshire, £111,705; Cambridgeshire, £140,527; Herts, £115,250; Hunts, £55,108. The average amount of each depositor was—Bedfordshire, £29; Cambridgeshire, £31; Herts, £27; and Hunts, £28.

Having thus alluded to a few of the more striking features of this group of counties, I will proceed to describe the nature of the employment and the condition of the greater proportion of its labouring population. Pillow lace, straw-plaiting, malting, and agriculture form the chief sources of employment for the people. In the counties of Herts and Beds, together with the neighbouring county of Bucks, the great proportion of the population are occupied in the straw-plait manufacture. The number of persons returned as thus employed in the two counties of Herts and Beds is 6,506; of this number there are in Herts, males above 20, 97—under 20, 239; females above 20, 2,840—under 20, 1,575; total, 4,751. Bedfordshire; males above 20, 83—under 20, 63; females above 20, 1,032—under 20, 575; total, 1,753. The number employed as straw hat and bonnet makers is, in Herts, 71; in Beds, 853; total, 924. The number of dealers and factors in both counties is 244. The district to which the straw-plait may be said to be confined is within a circle of about 12 or 14 miles round Dunstable, and within that area the whole labouring population may be said to be employed upon the straw plait. If you enter the cottage of one of the labourers, you are almost certain to see every individual present, from the youngest to the oldest, busily employed in straw-plaiting. Some of the more experienced members of the family plait with almost inconceivable rapidity—each individual straw appears, as it were, to know the exact place assigned for it in the plait.

In one cottage which I visited, a young woman was engaged on a twenty-straw plait, and at the same time appeared deeply interested in a conversation in which she was engaged with a stout, robust-looking young countryman, who was sitting near her, and who appeared in his turn far more deeply absorbed in the contemplation of his companion than with the intricacies of the seven-straw plait upon which he was engaged. Still, however, the work went on, to all appearance unimpeded, till my sudden and probably somewhat unwelcome intrusion caused a momentary suspension of proceedings. The young woman informed me that for the plait upon which she was then engaged she hoped to be able to get 5s. 6d. a score when it was finished, the score being twenty yards. "A good many years ago," said she, "my mother used to get 16s. a score for a fifteen-straw plait, but now we only get 5s., or 5s. 6d., for a twenty-straw plait like this. I learned to plait at the straw school. I was sent there when I was three years old—that's sixteen years ago—and I used to get a penny a day, and the missus used to have the plait and find us with straw. There was a great many other girls, and boys too, used to go to the school with me. I think there was more than twenty of us altogether. Last year I only got 4s. a score for this fine plait, but they are giving a little more this year. I got 5s. for my last, but I haven't sold any for some time—mother has been poorly, and I've been obliged to wait upon her a little. I've got three sisters, but they don't work at the very fine plaits. One of 'em works mostly at the five-straw, and the others I think do the seven-straw. If I could sit still and work at this plait that I'm on now, I could make, I dare say, thirty yards in a week, that would be 7s. 6d. Then the straw will cost me perhaps 1s., I dare say, because it's the finest, and they charge more for that, you know, than the coarse. The men bring the straws to the markets, all cut of a length, and ready for us, and they sell 'em in little bundles. Sometimes I buy a barn bundle, which costs me 6d.; but there is a good deal of bother in getting the straws, and peeling of 'em, and cutting 'em, and other things. I think it's almost as cheap to buy the little bundles at once. My father is almost always at work on the farm; he arnes 8s. a week now. He used to have 9s., but they've reduced him lately. Mother works at the plait, too. We all work at it. I don't think I've had plait out of hand for a month together in any year since I began it. Sometimes I don't make more than 3s.; sometimes as much as 6s. a week. I've got a savings-bank book, but I'm goin' to draw it out in the spring," said she—a blush at the same time stealing over her features. "So am I, too," said the young man, upon whose feelings the mention of spring appeared to produce a most exhilarating effect. "We're both a goin' to draw out, and we're a goin' to be married on the plait money. Ain't we, Mary? When I leaves off work at night I sets on to the plait; I am not very first-rate at it, but still I can manage to do a little bit. Well, I've yarned a couple of shillings or so every week for ever so long, and I've put it all away, and a little too besides; so, I thinks we may get on middlin' like. Do'ant you, sir, and do'ant you too?" again addressing himself to his affianced one, and accompanying his question by a salute, which, if not given in the most gentle manner, was, at all events, given heartily, and, but for the presence of a stranger, would doubtless have been favourably received. The cottage, I may add, was remarkably clean, though somewhat dilapidated, and everything about its internal arrangements bore evident marks of the industry and comforts of the inmates.

One of the largest dealers of the town of Dunstable informed me that plait was at least 25 per cent. dearer this year than it was last year, owing to the great demand which existed for it at present. Large quantities of straw hats and bonnets are now continually being exported to America; as many as a thousand dozen were sent off by one house on the day previous to my visit. The straw-plait manufacture has been for some time extending itself throughout the adjoining districts, and is taking the place of the lace work in many parts where pillow-lace was formerly manufactured. The complete failure of the Italian plait, large quantities of which were formerly imported from Leghorn and Tuscany, has also given an impetus to the trade. "The whole of the Italian plait," said a large dealer to me, "has gone completely out; what used to sell for 6s. a score once, is now not worth 1s. The straw has gone bad, somehow or other. The work is the same, but the material has got worse. There's nothing worth speaking of now brought over to this country from Italy." The straw which is grown in this portion of the counties of Herts, Beds, and Bucks, appears to be more peculiarly adapted for the straw plait than that of almost any other part of the country, in consequence of the peculiar fineness of its fibre and the delicacy of its colour, which are attributed to the chalky nature of the soil upon which it is grown.

The towns of Dunstable and Luton are the chief places in which the hat and bonnet making is carried on. The plaiting is chiefly confined to the surrounding villages, and the persons employed upon the plait bring it into the markets of these towns for sale to the dealers, by whom it is made up into hats and bonnets. Great numbers of the young women of Dunstable consider it *infra dig.* to work at the plait, and they look upon the plaiters as a totally inferior class of persons to themselves. In Dunstable one firm employs not less than 300 sewers nearly all the year round; another house, I was informed, employ about 250; altogether in Dunstable the number of sewers is about 1,000, and in Luton about 750. The hats and bonnets of the finest quality are usually made in Dunstable; in Luton, generally speaking, they are of a coarser and more inferior character. One young woman informed me that the lowest price which she ever received for making a bonnet was 5d.; she had, however, always been employed "in the better kind of plaits; there's a good many, though, that gets more than that," said she, "in Dunstable. Mr. —— gives for the very best bonnet 1s. 3d. The little 'Jenny Lind' hats we get 4½d. for. I dare say I could make three of them in a day. I never did much at them though; they're for summer wear. Them very large broad brimmed ones as the children wears they get 1s. 9d. for making, the finest quality, some 1s. 6d., some 1s., and so on. It all depends on the fineness of the plait; the coarser the plait is, you know, the less time it will take us to make it." One person, who employs a considerable number of hands, informed me that sewers could earn from 7s. to 20s. per week, and that few, if any of them, earned less than 7s., except in cases where they had but recently begun to learn. In the neighbourhood of Luton the poor people not unfrequently purchase the straw, plait it themselves, and make it up into hats and bonnets, which they sell themselves in the town upon the straw market days. One woman who was walking along the road with a quantity of bonnets, of a somewhat coarse character, informed me that she and her three children had done all the plaiting, that she had made up the bonnets which she had with her— a dozen in number—and she expected to get 6s. for them. It had taken her and her children nearly a fortnight to make them. Another woman told me that she had just sold a dozen bonnets for 3s. 6d., and that the straw for them had cost her 9d., to say nothing of the thread she had used for sewing the bonnets. Upon calling at another cottage, where I perceived the inmates were at work in plaiting and making bonnets, one of them stated to me, in answer to my inquiries, that she had earned last week, 7s.; the week before, 6s. 6d.; and for the four weeks previous to that, 7s. per week; that she was employed upon the best kind of work, and that there were very few who could earn more at it than she could. "It's quite impossible," she said, "for any young woman to earn a pound a week. If they were to sit up all night, and not go to sleep at all, they couldn't do it, and whoever told you so told you what was quite wrong." The very next person I inquired of informed me that "nobody couldn't arne more than 5s. a week at it." Such are a few of the apparently conflicting statements which were made to me upon the subject of the sums paid for straw hat and bonnet making. Whatever may be the amount of their earnings, however, the persons employed in the trade appear to be, one and all, greatly superior in their condition to any class of workpeople that I have hitherto seen. They have the appearance of being remarkably healthy and well fed, and they are comfortably and respectably attired. Last Christmas the holiday trains upon the Dunstable branch were all filled to excess with straw-bonnet makers, nearly every one of whom had parcels containing something in the shape of presents of various kinds for their friends whom they were about to visit.

The straw-plait affords employment, however, not only to the adults of both sexes, but to children of the most tender age. From the age of three years many of them are sent to the straw-plait school, where they are taught to plait; but in very few of them is there anything else taught. Probably, the worst feature in connection with this kind of work is, that it affords employment to children so young. As soon as they are able to earn a few pence during the week by their exertions, they are almost certain to be kept constantly to it, and no opportunity is afforded for giving any education to the children. "I've got," said one woman to me, "four children; three of 'em—that's all but Tommy, and he's too young yet—work at the plait, and they can't get much schooling. The three of 'em arnes about 3s. 6d. a week, and you know that's a great help to poor people like we." It is no doubt owing to this very general employment of the children that Hertfordshire and Bedfordshire have attained to the position of being the most ignorant counties in England. As one proof of the deficiency of education among the people, as compared with other counties, the proportion of persons who signed the marriage register with their marks in 1844 was in Bedford 53, and in Hertford 53—8 per cent. above the average of England and Wales. The children in the plaiting schools usually earn from 6d. to 9d. per week, their hours of attendance being commonly from about nine in the morning till four or five in the afternoon. So generally is the straw plait carried on in those parts of the counties of Beds and Herts to which allusion has been made, that you can scarcely meet a child walking along the road that is not engaged in plaiting. This employment has the effect of relieving to a great extent the pressure which would otherwise rest upon the agricultural labourer. I shall presently have occasion to refer more particularly to his condition; but were it not for the assistance which he obtains from the earnings of his family at the straw plait, his condition would not be one jot better than the great majority of his brother labourers in other counties.

The straw plait gives employment also to a number of other persons besides those who plait and make the hats and bonnets. There are bleachers, cutters, dyers, flatters, stringers, drawers, packers, &c. Their earnings vary from 5s. to 12s. per week. The first of these classes whose services are called into requisition in connection with the straw plait are the "drawers." Their duties consist in drawing out the straws from the wheat as it lies in the barn. The straw of wheat that has been threshed is useless for the purpose of plaiting, as it is always broken and bruised by the strokes of the flail. The "drawer," therefore, draws out the straws, and cuts off the ears of corn. He is usually employed by the farmers, and gets for his services a farthing per pound for the quantity of straw which he may draw. The material then passes into the hands of the cutters, who cut it into lengths of about six inches, each straw being usually cut into four lengths, each of which will be of a different degree of fineness—the lower part being the coarsest, and the upper portion, near the ear, the finest. The outer coating of the straw is then removed, and the straw thus prepared is made up into bundles, in which state it is sold to the plaiters. The services of the "dyers," "bleachers," and "flatters," come into requisition after the material has passed through the hands of the sewers, and has been formed into hats and bonnets. The "packers" are employed in packing the hats and bonnets for conveyance to their ultimate destination in London or elsewhere.

One other great source of employment for the people of Bedfordshire consists in making pillow lace. The trade in this article was once very considerable, but the introduction of machinery, and the extensive manufactures of Nottingham and other places, have reduced it so low that it has ceased, almost as if by common consent, to be considered as a means of subsistence. The number of persons returned as lace makers in 1841 in the county of Bedford was, males, above 20, 18; under 20, 9. Females, above 20, 1,880; under 20, 695; total, 2,602. In Herts the total number returned was but 84, and in Hunts 45.

I visited several of the poor persons who were employed in lace making. None of those whom I saw, however, were dependent upon lace for their support, nor could I find any person who was solely dependent for existence upon it. Indeed, it would be a difficult matter to see how it could be possible for any human beings to exist upon the amount which can be earned at lace-making. The first person whom I called upon resided in Ram-yard, in the town of Bedford. The house which the woman occupied was in the most wretched and dirty condition. Her children were unwashed and ragged; the few articles of furniture which were in the room were in the most dilapidated condition, and there was that close and disagreeable smell about the place which appears inseparable from dirty and slovenly habits. The statement of the woman was as follows:—

"This lace that I'm at work at is lace-edging; it is what is called a 'French ground,' and there are three stitches to a pin in it. I gets 2d. a yard for it from the lace-buyers, and it takes me, if I stick close to it, six hours and a half to make a yard of it, and then I must work as hard as I can to get it done. My two eldest girls work at it sometimes, but there's three others that don't do much. I can't sit to it all the week round, as I have got other things to attend to. Years ago we used to get double and treble what we get now for making lace; it has fallen down shockingly. This is the real British lace, pillow lace—all made with the bobbins; there's not a bit of machinery in the town; no, and I wish there never was none nowhere else—that I do. Now I can't make more than six yards in the week, do all I can; and that is a shilling—that's just what it is. If I can save it till it comes to a dozen yards, I should be able to get 2¼d. a yard, that is 2s. 3d. a dozen. They won't give us more than 2d. a yard for less than a dozen yards, because they've got to pay something to the lace-joiners, who join the pieces when they're less length than that. The lace is generally bought here at Bedford, but then it's mostly sent away to London or some other place. When we take half a dozen yards to the lace-buyers they make you take so much thread out of your money. I should have to take three-ha'porth of thread out of every shilling, that's one slip; and if I was to go to the draper's, or any other shop in the town besides the lace-buyer, I could get eight slips of the very same thread for a penny as he charges me three-ha'pence for one, so you see he takes a good profit out of the thread, besides what he gets out of the lace. I've got five children. My husband's at work, and earns 10s. a week pretty regular, at a shop in the town. He pays £7 a year rent for this house; there's three rooms in it upstairs, and two down here."

Another person upon whom I called was working upon "point ground lace." "I don't call it, though," said the woman, "anything else but lace edging. If I work as hard as can be, I can't make more than half a yard a day of it; it takes me two days to make a yard, if I am not called away to anything else. Then, sometimes when you have done a little bit of lace, you don't know where to sell it. They'll tell you sometimes they don't want it, to see if they can't get you to offer it 'em a little less. 'We've got plenty,' they'll say, 'more than we know what to do with—take it away.' And then when they do buy it, they make you take three ha'porth of thread out of every shilling they pays you for it. Some of 'em makes you take two penn'orth, one person only makes you take a penn'orth. They makes us have the thread, and if we don't take it they won't have the lace. I took some the other day to Mr. ——, and I says, says I, 'I've got some lace to sell.' 'Have you?' says he. 'Yes,' I said, 'but I don't want any thread. I've got a little at home that I want to use up first.' 'Oh, then,' he said, 'you may take your lace away, I don't do business in that way. If you don't want my thread I don't want your lace.' Since I can remember, we used to get ever so much better paid than we do now. Why, three years ago, when I first went into this pattern, they used to give me 7d., now they only give me 6d.; and many a time they've got it from me for 5d., and make me take their bothering thread out of it, too. I can always make a sight more money at charing than I can at the pillow. There is only one man in the town that gives you so much a yard, and no thread, for the lace; but then he gives you a penny a yard less than the others do. It's that wretched 'blond' stuff as has spiled all our trade. The ladies buys it because it looks well just for a time, but then it never washes, and then it's done for. My husband earns 10s. a week; he's at work in the town."

A third young woman whom I saw, said:—"I've been making lace for a long while as wide as my finger nails, and it takes between sixty and seventy stitches to make six head-pins; the rest of it is point ground, but it's very thick, and it takes me twelve hours a working very hard indeed to make a yard of it." "Aye, that it does," said another young woman, who sat next to her. "I'm sure I couldn't make a yard of it in a day, and I have been at it longer than you have too." "I get 4d. a yard for it," resumed the former speaker; "but then I don't have to take their thread, I can get it where I like."

A fancy lace-maker at Wotton, who was employed in making "neck-ties," said, "This neck-tie will take me about ten or twelve days to finish, and work hard at it too. It's to have—[and probably some fair reader will understand the amount of work required in an article of this description]—head-pins all round, fifty stitches to six 'head-pins;' and the 'scollopes' are to come in and out, and it's to have 'nooks' which run all round, and 'side edges.' Well, when I've done I am to have 5s. for it. Sometimes I work 'cap-strings,' 'veil-pieces,' and ladies' pocket handkerchiefs. There isn't many as can make these sort of things—they want a good deal of practice. I made a veil-piece, and I dare say it were sold for four or five guineas. I don't know what the rich folks give for such things, but it was a regular beauty. They told me it was for a weddin' of some lady in London. Lor' bless me, I was at work for two months at it, I do think. Well, when I took it home I thought I should have had a lot of money for it, and I was a goin' to do a wonderful sight of things with it when I got it. I know one thing I was goin' to do was to take my old man home a new flannel jacket, and I did mean to have a warm gown for myself; but I couldn't do neither. I bought a few little things for the young 'uns, and I paid off a little score at the shop, and it was all gone. They guv' me a sov'run for my veil. I've never made none since then, and I don't think I'll ever be bothered again with a fine thing like that."

Another person who lived in a small village, a few miles from Bedford, said that she was usually employed on "point ground edging." "The last time I went," says she, "to Mr. ——, to sell my lace, I saw one poor woman a crying in the streets, and I asked her what was the matter, and she said that when she went to sell her lace Mr. —— had bated her, and had got off 6s. from what she ought to have had 15s. for. He wouldn't give her more than 9s. for her lot. The poor woman said, she had depended on the money to pay her rent with, but they saw that she had got a good lot of it, and so they made her take what they liked for it. Mr. —— won't turn nothing away; he'll buy anything, if you'll only take his price for it. There's another person that has come round lately to buy, and he gives sometimes a farden a yard more than t'other; and then there's a sort of opposition like a'tween 'em when they both comes; sometimes we gets a ha'penny a yard more. One of 'em says he'll give a farden, and then the other says he'll give a ha'penny. There's one man, Mr. ——, he'll buy as much lace as you like to take him, and give you a ha'penny a yard more than t'others. He keeps a grocer's shop, but then he won't give you no money; he makes you take it all out at his shop. I generally take my lace to him; but then, sir, you don't always want grocery; there's a many things that you'd like to do with your money if you had it. The last time I went to Bedford I brought thirteen yards, as I wanted the money for it. Well, I got a ha'penny a yard less for it—that's 5½d. instead of 6d.; but they made me take sixpennorth of thread, that I could have bought for a penny anywhere else. They gave me 5½d. a yard for it; that was 6s. all but a halfpenny, and then the thread was 6d.—and that's 5d. more than it was worth—so 5s. 6½d. was all I got for my month's lace, for it was just a month that day since I began it. I walked there with my lace and walked back again. When I was a little girl, about ten years old, I used to get my mother ten shillings a week—now I don't get ten pence. My little girl arnes sixpence a week at the lace school, and I pay twopence-ha'penny a week for her lace-schooling. She don't larne nothing else there but to make lace. The girls as is about nine years old go there at daylight in the morning and come home about dark; and they arnes sixpence a week, but you pays twopence-ha'penny to the missus for larning of 'em. My eldest girl has larnt her thread, and she's a regular lace-maker now, and goes to it regular, but she only arnes 6d., sometimes 9d. a week. There's generally more girls at the school in summer than there is in the winter. The girls as is over nine go to the school in the winter at day-light; they work till nine or ten at night, and then comes home; them girls is about twelve or fourteen year old. In the summer they stops about as long; there's none of them arnes more than a shilling or eighteenpence a week; but they must work very hard, though, to arne eighteenpence. The missus of the school sets the little ones so many score pins to be done in the hour, and then when they're done she gives 'em some more. A very good hand can make, at the edging I've been at work at, half a yard in a day; not more than that, I'm sure they can't; I know I can't, and I reckon I'm a pretty good hand, for I've been at it all my life—that's more than forty year now come March. A few years ago they might have sold this sort of lace for eighteenpence or two shillings a yard; now you can't get more than sixpence. I have often only got fivepence. When my first child was born I could do a *fut* (foot) a day—that was six in a week, and six *fut* is two yards; and I used to arne three or four shillings at it, although I had my child to attend to. Now you can't arne as much as that in a month, without a child at all. I've got three children as works at the lace, and when all my three lace-makers and myself are at work at it, we can't get so much as I could make by myself when my first child was born, and I had to attend to it. I often look at the poor little children, and see how they makes 'em sit shut up in their room for eight or ten hours a day for their penny or twopence—for they can't arne more. I thinks often what a cruel thing it is for the poor little children. But then what are you to do with 'em, I argues—why, nothing? Where there's a parcel of girls, and no boys' money to help the poor people, they must be badly off; how can they help it? Some of 'em only arne 8s. a week on the farms, some only 7s. My husband is a horse-keeper, and he has to go at four o'clock in the morning, and doesn't come home till seven at night, and he gets 9s. 6d. a week. Then he has to go to the horses on Sundays, and he gets the extra 6d. for that; the 9s. is for the other six days—that's 1s. 6d. a day, and we pay 2s. a week for rent; so how could we do with three girls at home, unless they arned a trifle, if it's ever so small? There isn't nobody that works at the lace as hasn't got a husband to bring 'em home something as they can live upon what they arnes. The girls as isn't married, and works at the lace, are obliged all of 'em to have something from the parish to keep 'em from starving—or else they're not virtuous, and goes in the streets. It wants very nice hands, indeed, to make these fancy things in lace, and there isn't one in a hundred of them that gets anything of that to do. I know one young woman that is a first hand at it, and she's been a making lace 'ties,' and she told me as she only made 3s. last week, and half-a-crown the week afore, and she worked very hard, too, because she wanted to get some new things, to go and see her friends in. Where it is now, you see, sir, that lace has been so bad, is because a great many of the people are so low, that they're obliged to make this lace to get a little bit of money quick, like—that's where it is."

LABOUR AND THE POOR.

THE RURAL DISTRICTS.

[FROM OUR SPECIAL CORRESPONDENT.]

HERTS, BEDS, HUNTS, AND CAMBRIDGESHIRE.

LETTER XXXVI.*

In my last Letter some account was given of three of the principal branches of employment for the labouring population of these counties. I shall in the present communication proceed to a consideration of the fourth, and by far the most extensive, source of employment—viz., agriculture; and, after a brief description of the state of agriculture in this district, I shall proceed, in the subsequent Letters, to describe the condition of the agricultural labourer.

In Bedfordshire the surface of the country is broken up into a vast number of hills and dales. In the southern and in some of the central parts of the county the Chiltern Hills rise to a considerable height. In the immediate neighbourhood of these elevations the soil is, generally speaking, hard and sterile, and the country presents in many parts a dreary and monotonous aspect. Large quantities of this district are, however, constantly being brought under cultivation, and, by the adoption of an extensive system of drainage, have been rendered fertile and productive in the highest degree. From the centre, and towards the south-eastern part of the county, there is a considerable quantity of dairy land. The western portion of it is somewhat flat, and the soil is sandy, and I am informed that it produces very heavy crops of beans. What is called the Vale of Bedford is a peculiarly rich tract of land, and yields excellent crops of wheat and barley, and also considerable quantities of turnips. There is yet a large tract of land which remains unenclosed, and which would no doubt amply repay the cost of enclosure and cultivation. The north-eastern portion of Huntingdonshire, and the adjoining part of Cambridgeshire—which form what might almost be called a separate county, viz., the Isle of

---

* No Letter XXXV. was printed.

Ely—are composed of rich fen land, much of which is used for grazing. The fens in Hunts consist of about 40,000 acres, and in the Isle of Ely they extend over about 250,000 acres. The soil of the eastern and south-eastern portions of Huntingdonshire is principally of a clayey character; a great portion of the soil of the other parts of the county is a rich sandy loam, and the under stratum of almost the whole county, as well as of some parts of the adjoining ones, is a strong blue clay. The soils of Herts and Cambridgeshire also vary very considerably, but they partake in a great measure of the character of the adjacent counties. In the district about the town of Cambridge, the country is exceedingly flat. London clay is to be met with in considerable quantities in the county of Hertford.

Where such varieties of soil exist, the mode of agriculture will of course be found to vary very considerably. In many parts the land is exceedingly well cultivated, and the neatness and trimness of the hedges, and the comfortable character of the farm buildings, are sufficient to convince any person that their owners are enterprising and doubtless successful farmers. There is, however, no part of the whole of the four counties which can at all equal the excellent condition of the farming upon the property of the Duke of Bedford at Woburn. The farm, in particular, is indeed a model establishment, and upon a very large scale. The extent of the great farm is, I was informed, not less than a thousand acres. The farm-buildings are the most commodious and well-arranged that I have yet seen in any part of the country. In one portion of the extensive range of buildings is the engine-house, in which there is an engine of 25 horse-power employed in chaff-cutting, turnip-cutting, grinding linseed for the cattle, in threshing wheat and barley when required, and in various other ways.

The system of the box-feeding of cattle has been carried out to a considerable extent by the Duke of Bedford. The boxes are light, commodious, and well ventilated; their bottoms and sides are rendered perfectly water-tight, and the manure of the cattle is consequently not allowed, as in the majority of cases, to soak away or to be absorbed by the ground. There are three tiers of buildings for the cattle, in each of which there are double rows of boxes, with an elevated flagged pathway, of about four feet in width, down the centre of the building, the whole of which is kept admirably clean. At the time of my visit there were about 70 head of cattle in the boxes. The fatted stock had been sold off a few days previously, and their places supplied by others. One tier of the boxes was appropriated to Scotch, another to Devons, and a third to Herefords. Another portion of the farm buildings was occupied by cows and calves. There were about sixty cows in the yards, and twenty calves in the stalls. In an adjoining part of the building were two bulls, one of which was the finest creature of the sort that I ever saw, and his pedigree, as well as that of his companion, was carefully noted and preserved on papers which were posted over their respective stalls. The pigs occupied another part of the building; and as I looked at the care bestowed upon them, at the comfortable character of their abodes, and the quantity and quality of their diet, I could not refrain from contrasting it with the "piggeries" in which vast numbers of the labourers in one portion of the county of Cambridge, to which I shall have occasion to refer in a future letter, lived, moved, and had their being.

The system of feeding adopted by the Duke of Bedford for his cattle, is the one invented by Mr. Warnes, of Trinningham, whose exertions to extend the growth of flax I had occasion to notice in a previous letter. The cattle are not, according to this system, fed upon oil-cake, but upon linseed, of the refuse of which oil-cake is usually made. The linseed being first bruised, or ground, is steeped in water till it assumes the consistency of a jelly, in which state it is mixed with chaff and turnips, and given to the cattle, which thrive exceedingly well upon it. The meat which was displayed in the town of Bedford at Christmas time, and marked as having been fed by the Duke, looked remarkably well, and not so enormously fat as one has been accustomed, for some years past, to see Christmas beef. A few days previously to Christmas a great sale of stock takes place upon the farm at Woburn; none of it is sent to market, the butchers from all the neighbouring towns attending in large numbers to purchase the stock, which is annually sold by auction. As the cattle have not to be driven any distance to market, and do not receive the ill usage which they would necessarily endure in the course of a long journey, the meat is much superior in quality to any which the butchers could purchase in London or elsewhere. Hence the great competition which exists among the butchers of Bedford and other places to become the purchasers. "The Duke's meat" is one of the objects of their highest ambition, and at Christmas there was scarcely a butcher's shop in Bedford in which there were not to be seen large placards attached to the meat, with the words upon them, "Fed by his Grace the Duke of Bedford." I was informed that so great was the competition among the butchers, that at the auction several of them "bid against themselves."

One man actually bid four times against himself, so anxious was he that the beast should be knocked down to him. One of the bullocks was sold for as much as £35; the average price of the whole was, I was informed, £18. The purchasers appeared to be perfectly satisfied with their bargains, for, in returning home from the sale—perhaps somewhat warmed by the good things they had seen and enjoyed—they kept up an almost constant succession of "Hurrahs for the Duke of Bedford." On the farm at Woburn about thirty men and as many boys are kept constantly employed. To their condition and to the cottages of his Grace I shall refer in my next Letter.

But it is not only in the county of Bedford that great improvements have taken place with respect to agriculture. There are few parts of the country in which, perhaps, greater exertions have been made to improve and cultivate the soil than in the Isle of Ely, in Cambridgeshire. Only a few short years since, the whole of this part of the county was a desolate and dreary waste, almost constantly inundated by the upland waters, and perfectly destitute of anything like adequate means of drainage. Indeed, the whole surface was a series of stagnant pools, constantly producing exhalations which loaded the air with pestiferous vapours and fogs. During the last fifty years the whole appearance of this district has been changed. Mr. Marshall, the clerk to the union in the Isle of Ely, says: "The alteration which has taken place appears to be almost the effect of magic. By the labour, industry, and spirit of the inhabitants, a forlorn waste has been converted into pleasant and fertile pastures, and the people themselves have been rewarded by bounteous harvests. Drainage, embankments, engines, and enclosures, have given stability to the soil (which in its nature is as rich as the Delta of Egypt), as well as salubrity to the air. These very considerable improvements, though carried on at a great expense, have at last turned to a double account, both in reclaiming much ground and improving the rest, and in contributing to the healthiness of the inhabitants. Works of modern refinement have given a totally different face and character to this once neglected spot. Much has been performed; much, however, yet remains to be accomplished by the rising generation. The demand for labour produced by drainage is incalculable; but when it is stated that, where sedge and rushes grew but a few years since, we now have fields of waving oats and even wheat, it must be evident that it is very great."

Mr. Marshall then proceeds to show the beneficial effects which this improved system of drainage has produced upon the health of the inhabitants. Upon this subject he says:—"On reference to a very perfect account of the baptisms, marriages, and burials in Wisbeach, from 1758 to 1826, I find that, in the decennial periods—of which 1801, 1811, and 1821 were the middle years—the baptisms and burials were as under:—

Years.	Baptisms.	Burials.	Population in 1801.
1796 to 1805	1,627	1,535	4,710
1806 to 1815	1,654	1,313	5,209
1816 to 1825	2,165	1,390	6,515

"In the first of the three periods the mortality was 1 in 31; in the second, 1 in 40; in the third, 1 in 47—the latter being less than the exact mean mortality of the kingdom for the least two years. These figures clearly show that the mortality has wonderfully diminished in the last half century; and who can doubt but that the increased salubrity of the Fens, produced by drainage, is a chief cause of the improvement?"

The low lands both of Cambridgeshire and of Lincolnshire appear to have been the object of some attention in the early periods of our history. We are informed, by an old authority, that "one Geffrey Gaddesby, a late abbot of Selby, did cause a very strong sluice of wood to be made upon the river of Trent, at the head of a certain sewer called the Maredyke, of a sufficient height and breadth for the defence of the tides coming from the sea, and likewise against the fresh waters from the west part of the before specified sluice to the said sewer into the river of Humbre." Geffrey's successor, it appeared, pulled down the wood sluice, and made new ones of stone; but jurors appointed under patent of Henry V. pronounced the new ones not strong enough, and directed flood-gates of certain dimensions to be made, and also "one demmyng without the said sluice towards the river of Trent." One of the most important works of modern times in connection with the drainage of fen lands was the Eau Brink Cut, the proposition for which originated so early as 1724; but it was not until 1817 that an Act was obtained for the purpose of carrying out the works, which were finally completed in 1821. They have proved perfectly successful, having lowered the low-water line in the river several feet, and completed the drainage of upwards of 300,000 acres of land. In the year 1829, a work of a similar character was executed, under the direction of Sir J. Rennie, in connection with the river Nene, about five miles below Wisbeach, the effect of which has been to bring into cultivation 100,000 acres, which were formerly a complete stagnant marsh. The drainage of the fens in the eastern districts was formerly carried on to a great extent by means of windmills. In 1820, one of Watt's steam engines was employed for the purpose of draining a large fen, known as the Bottisham Fen, near Ely; since which time steam-power has superseded, to a great extent, the use of windmills. The principal of the fens in the eastern districts, now drained by steam power, are—

Name of Fens.	Acres.	No. of Engines.	Horse Power.
Deeping Fen, near Spalding, Lincolnshire	25,000	2	80 and 60
Marsh West Fen, Cambridgeshire	3,600	1	40
Misserton Moss, with Everton and Graingeley Cars	6,000	1	40
Littleport Fen, Ely (75 windmills formerly employed)	28,000	2	30 and 40
Middle Fen, Cambridgeshire	7,000	1	60
Waterbeach Level, near Ely	5,000	1	60
Magdalen Fen, near Lynn, Norfolk	4,000	1	40
March Fen district, Cambridge ..	2,700	1	30
Feltwell Fen, Brandon	2,400	1	20
Soham Mere, Cambridgeshire (formerly a lake)	1,600	1	40

Where the fen lands, as in most instances is the case, receive the waters from the surrounding high grounds, the mode adopted for draining generally consists in the formation of "catch-water drains," recommended by Sir J. Rennie, into which the smaller drains from the high lands discharge their contents. Main drains for the level are also formed, parallel to the "catch-water drains." Between the main drains the level is generally intersected with minor drains, which have a fall either way towards the main ones. The catch-water drains are constructed so as to discharge the water directly either into the river, or by means of sluices. The catch-water drain is also provided with sluice gates, by means of which their contents may be directed into the main-level drains instead of into the river; and thus, in dry weather, the irrigation of the soil is provided for by means of the waters from the surrounding high lands. If the drainage of the high lands be discharged through the catch-water drains, it is obvious that the drainage of the low levels will consist only of the rain water, which, in the eastern districts of England, seldom exceeds 26 inches in depth per annum—and a great portion of this will be carried off by evaporation and absorption. At Littleport, and in many other places, the surface of the fen district lying below the level of the river into which the waters are discharged, it is necessary to have recourse to steam-power to raise the water collected in the drains. At Bottisham Fen, in order to effect this, scoop-wheels have been brought into use, resembling under-shot waterwheels—but which, instead of receiving motion from the water, force it upwards, and are set in motion and worked by steam-power. Mr. Fairbairn has, I believe, within the last few years, adapted a form of bailing-scoop or alternating trough to the single-acting Cornish engine, for the purpose of raising the water. The length of stroke of the piston remaining the same, the length of the dip is regulated by connecting-rods at the end of the trough or scoop. I was informed that one of these scoops, which is in use, is made of cast iron boiler plates, is 25 feet in length and 30 feet in width, and raises 17 tons of water at each stroke. Mr. Glyn states as the result of his calculations, that a steam-engine of 10-horse power will be sufficient to raise and throw off the drainage-water due to a district of 1,000 acres of fens during the month, in about 20 days, working at the rate of 12 hours per day.

A Scene on the Fens

The central portion of this group of counties is at present entirely destitute of railway accommodation. The opening, however, of the Great Northern Railway will supply the want at present so generally felt throughout this district. The London and North-Western Railway passes through a small portion of Herts, and two branches from the main line supply the towns of Dunstable and Bedford. The Eastern Counties Railway affords communication with Cambridge, Huntingdon, Ely, and Newmarket, and also with the town of Hertford.

The total quantity of arable land in the four counties is about 505,000 acres, and of pasture about 358,000. The value of the produce of the arable land has been estimated at £7 per acre, and of the pasture at £6. According to this computation, therefore, the total value of the produce of the arable and pasture soil would not be less than £5,683,000. The number of persons returned in 1841 as farmers and graziers, in the four counties, was 7,700; of which number there were, in Bedfordshire, 1,458; Cambridgeshire, 3,341; Herts, 1,780; and Hunts, 1,121. The agricultural labourers amounted, in Bedfordshire to 12,861, in Cambridgeshire to 18,916, in Herts to 17,541, and in Hunts 7,712; making a total of agricultural labourers of 57,030. The total number of persons, therefore, engaged in agriculture in the four counties was 64,730. The number of persons who in these counties may be considered as dependent upon agriculture for their support cannot be less than four times that number, or about 256,520—being rather more than one-half of the entire population.

The towns of Hertford and Ware are the chief places at which the malting trade is carried on. The number of persons returned as maltsters in 1841 was only 221, and it is not stated, even with respect to these, whether they are the owners of the malt kilns or the persons employed in them. There are, however, considerably more than 221 persons employed as labourers in the malt trade; and as nearly the whole of them are employed as agricultural labourers when not engaged in malting, and as the census was taken in June, a period of the year when malting is suspended—I have no doubt that the small number of persons returned as maltsters is owing to their being returned under the head of agricultural labourers. There are in the town of Hertford 20 malt-houses, and in Ware not less than 90, with upwards of 100 "cowls." There is no town in England where the annual return of Excise duty on malt is so large as at Ware. Till within the last few years Kingston-upon-Thames contributed the largest amount. It is now, however, considerably distanced by the town of Ware. I was not able to ascertain the quantity of malt made in the town of Ware. When I applied to the Excise officers in that town they refused to furnish me with the information. I was informed, however, by other parties that the quantity was not less than 200,000 qrs. annually.

The malting season usually commences about the 1st of October, and continues till about the latter end of May, being about seven months of the year. During the warm weather but little malt is made—what is made being used almost exclusively in the brewing of porter. The houses in Hertford are most of them small, and few of them can wet more than 25 or 30 quarters at a time. In Ware, however, they are enabled to wet as much as 50 or 60 quarters in some of the houses. The manufacture of malt requires great care, and the temperature of the house is a point of considerable importance. As it is not possible always to obtain the required heat, which is about 75 deg., and as the regulations of the Excise require that only a certain portion of time should be allowed for the process, considerable loss frequently takes place from the parties being compelled to put the barley through its different stages before it is in some cases perfectly prepared, and before vegetation has been allowed to proceed to a sufficient extent. Several of the maltsters have complained much of the stringency of many of the Excise regulations, which they say are perfectly unnecessary for the protection of the revenue. The regulations are, that the barley must in the first instance be put into a cistern of not more than 40 inches in depth, where it is not allowed to remain more than 48 hours; it has then to be taken out, and placed in what is called a "couch," which must not be of a greater depth than 30 inches, where it must remain 30 hours. After it has undergone this second process, it has to be spread out upon the floors, where it may remain eight or ten hours; and from the floors it is finally removed to the kiln, where it remains for about 24 hours. I was informed that in several cases the malt had been spoiled, in consequence of the maltsters being compelled either to turn over the malt too soon, and so to stop the vegetation, or to let it go too far before they were allowed to turn it. In the latter case the malt turns sour, and can never be brought to have a good flavour.

The men employed as maltsters appear to earn very good wages while the malting lasts, and I had some difficulty in ascertaining from them what was the amount of their earnings. "Oh, indeed," said one of the men, "I'm not a going to tell you what I yarnes, 'cause if I did the masters would say at once—'Oh, here's these chaps a braggin' of what they yarnes; let us cut 'em down.'" Notwithstanding, however, the repugnance which he expressed to naming the amount of his earnings, he proceeded to make the following statement:—"The men as works by the week gets eighteen shillings or a guinea a week, and their sack-carrying money—that's three ha'pence a quarter that we charges the farmer for carrying in the barley; we won't let their men carry it in themselves, and we won't take it in unless they gives us three ha'pence a quarter. The farmers have tried ever so many times to cut us down to a penny, but it ain't no go. At the beginning of this season the farmers held a meeting about it, and they passed a fine lot of what they called resolutions, and then they drawed up some long rigmarole, saying that after the 1st of November they wouldn't give more than a penny, and they put the paper in the market-place to be signed; but we licked 'em, hang me if we didn't. Two or three days arter, a man came into this yard with a waggon-load of barley, and, says he, 'I've brought you some barley.' 'Have you?' says I. 'How much money have you got?' 'A penny,' says he; 'that's all master sent you.' 'Then you may keep that for pocket-money,' says I, 'and take your barley back again.' Howsomever, he forked out the other ha'penny, and we unloaded the barley for him. They've tried it on several times since, but it ain't no use. One man came a few days ago, and said he'd only got a penny; and I told him to take his barley away, for I wouldn't unload it for a penny, and so off he went to master and told him I wouldn't unload it. 'How much did you bring the men?' said master. 'Only a penny,' said the man. 'Well, how much barley does your master grow?' 'One hundred quarters.' 'Well, now tell him from me,' said master, 'that if he cuts the men down to a penny he'll only save 4s. 2d. on all his barley.'" My informant then went on to state that he had to be at the kiln from three o'clock in the morning till eight at night; that he was frequently obliged to sit up all night to "back up" the kiln, and in the middle of the day he sometimes snatched a few hours' sleep. "I get 8d. a quarter for making malt," said he; "then I have to pay two men 15s. a week each to shovel the malt, and sack it, and other things. I am 'the head man,' and have to employ and pay any one to help me. Them as I employ don't get no share of the sack money. I wet about sixty quarters every four days, and we are obliged to work all Sundays through, the same as t'other days. I've got two kilns to attend to, and I don't think there's any other man in Hertford could do the same as I do." According to his own statement, therefore, the earnings of this man must have exceeded £2 per week. The men who have charge of the malt-houses can scarcely be considered as labourers; from the position which they hold, they ought rather to be viewed as employers; and when the amount of responsibility which attaches to them, together with the many hours of labour which they undergo, and the fact that they are employed for only a few months in the year, are all considered, the amount of remuneration which they receive cannot be considered excessive. The earnings of this person were, however, above the average, he being a most expert and able hand. The quantity which is usually considered as a fair amount of work for one man is 25 quarters in the four days. In the towns of Hertford and Ware, and in several other towns in Herts, a considerable number of persons are also employed as brewers, whose wages average about 12s. per week, with an allowance of five pints of beer per day.

As the cost of food is a point upon which the comforts of the labouring classes depend to a great extent, I have made it my business to ascertain the retail prices of provisions in the different parts of the country to which my inquiries have been directed. Subjoined is a list of the retail prices of the chief articles of subsistence in the under-mentioned towns in the Christmas week of 1849:—

Provisions.	Norfolk (Norwich).		Suffolk (Bury).		Essex (Chelmsford).		Herts. (Hertford).		Beds. (Bedford).		Hunts. (Huntingdon).		Cambridgesh. (Cambridge).	
	s.	d.	s.	d.	s.	d.	s.	d.	s.	d.	s.	d.	s.	d.
Flour, per stone of 14 lbs.:														
Best	1	10	1	11	2	0	2	1	2	1	2	0	2	1
Seconds	1	7	1	9	1	9	1	10	1	10	1	10	1	10
Thirds	1	6		..	1	6	1	7	1	8	1	6	1	7
Bread, pr. 4 lb. loaf:														
Best		..	0	6	0	6	0	7	0	6	0	$5\frac{1}{2}$	0	$6\frac{1}{2}$
Seconds	0	$4\frac{1}{2}$	0	$4\frac{1}{2}$	0	5	0	6	0	5	0	$4\frac{1}{2}$	0	$5\frac{1}{2}$
Beef, per lb.														
Prime parts ...	0	7	0	7	0	$6\frac{1}{2}$	0	$7\frac{1}{2}$	0	7	0	7	0	7
Inferior	0	6	0	$5\frac{1}{2}$	0	5	0	6	0	6	0	6	0	6
Mutton, per lb.:														
Prime parts ...	0	$6\frac{1}{2}$	0	7	0	7	0	$7\frac{1}{2}$	0	$6\frac{1}{2}$	0	$6\frac{1}{2}$	0	7
Inferior	0	$5\frac{1}{2}$	0	5	0	6	0	6	0	5	0	5	0	6
Pork, per lb.	0	6	0	6	0	6	0	6	0	6	0	6	0	6
Bacon, do.	0	6	0	7	0	$7\frac{1}{2}$	0	9	0	8	0	$6\frac{1}{2}$	0	8
Fresh Butter, do.	1	0	1	0	1	1	1	0	1	1	1	1	1	1
Salt Butter, do. ..	0	7	0	6	0	8	0	8	0	8	0	7	0	8
Cheese, do.	0	7	0	5	0	8	0	8	0	8	0	$7\frac{1}{2}$	0	8
Potatoes, per stone of 14 lbs.—a pk.	0	8	0	$4\frac{1}{2}$	0	8	0	7	0	6	0	6	0	4

LABOUR AND THE POOR.

THE RURAL DISTRICTS.

[FROM OUR SPECIAL CORRESPONDENT.]

HERTS, BEDS, HUNTS, AND CAMBRIDGE.

Letter XXXVII.

The dwellings of the labouring classes in the above-named counties are, generally speaking, badly constructed, unhealthy, and over-crowded. Exertions have been, and are still being made to improve the existing state of things, but hitherto they have been inadequate to meet the pressing and growing wants of that portion of the community for whose benefit such exertions are required. The noble example set by the Duke of Bedford—to whose exertions in this respect I shall have occasion hereafter to refer—cannot fail to be productive of an enormous amount of good, not only to the tenantry of his grace, who may be immediately benefited, but also as showing to other landed proprietors the benefits which result from improving the physical condition of the labourer, and at the same time affording to them the advantage of extensive experience in the best mode of providing increased cottage accommodation of a suitable character for the labouring classes.

Mr. Lowe, the clerk to one of the unions in this district, in his report to Mr. Weale on the condition of the cottages of the agricultural labourer, says, "If we follow the agricultural labourer into his miserable dwelling we shall find it consisting of two rooms only; the day room, in addition to the family, contains the cooking utensils, the washing apparatus, agricultural implements and dirty clothes, the windows broken, and stuffed full of rags. In the sleeping apartment the parents and their children, boys and girls, are indiscriminately mixed, and frequently a lodger sleeping in the same and only room; generally no window, the openings in the half-thatched roof admit light, and expose the family to every vicissitude of the weather; the liability of the children, so situated, to contagious maladies, frequently plunges the whole family into the greatest misery. The children are brought up without any regard to decency of behaviour, to habits of foresight or self-restraint; they make indifferent servants; the girls become the mothers of bastards, and return home a burden to their parents, or to the parish." This description, although written some time since, is but too true at the present time.

Commencing with the county of Herts, there are in the towns of Hertford and Ware a great number of wretched and dilapidated two and three roomed houses in many of the back streets and alleys. There are also in the villages on the road between Hertford and St. Alban's, many miserable hovels. The town of St. Alban's, like those of Hertford and Ware, contains a great number of old and decayed tenements, many of which are densely crowded.

In the northern and eastern parts of the county which adjoin to Essex, Cambridge, and Suffolk, the cottages are of the worst possible description. Within a circle of about ten or fifteen miles, taking Saffron Walden, in Essex, as the centre, there is scarcely a resident proprietor, and the cottages are suffered to fall into ruin and decay. The principal owners of this kind of property are small tradesmen, whose sole aim and object are to extort as high rents as possible from the poor people, and to avoid the slightest outlay upon the property.

Proceeding from Herts into the county of Bedford, it will be found that the cottages of the labouring classes are also in a most disgraceful condition. In the town of Bedford there are several rows of small houses built back to back, without the slightest means of thorough ventilation. Perhaps the worst place of this kind, is one called Gravel-lane, where I was informed as many as forty persons died of cholera during the visitation of that disease. In another place called Beauchamp-row, fever is seldom or never absent. In the parish of Flitwick comparatively few of the houses are drained, dung heaps abound in the immediate vicinity of the dwellings, while the exhalations from a stagnant pond in the neighbourhood, in warm or foggy weather, are most injurious to the health of the inhabitants. In Toddington the cottages are equally as bad. In the Leighton Buzzard union many of the houses occupied by the people are perfectly unfit for dwellings; great numbers of them have no bedrooms, and the families are compelled to live and sleep in the same apartment, in which the bare ground forms the only floor. The cottages in the parish of Eddlesborough are as bad as it is possible for such places to be. The following description, given a few years since by one of the guardians of the union, is equally applicable to the present time:—"The poor have for some time been permitted to build hovels in the waste, and although some of them are much better than others, the whole of them, with the exception of one built by a wheeler, are without up-stairs rooms; in some instances these places are formed by being excavated in the banks, over which a lean-to roof is placed, and they are necessarily extremely damp. There are many cases of extreme wretchedness among the people, numerous applications for relief are constantly made, and the relief, however liberally or carefully bestowed, is never followed by any improvement or permanent benefit. Much immorality and crime invariably exist among these people, some of whom are quite lost to all feelings of decency and virtue, which must be attributed to the promiscuous intercourse of the sexes of all ages, numerous instances of which might be adduced." "In the hamlet of Egginton," says the same gentleman, "there are twelve tenements belonging to a charity, formed originally out of two barns; these are always inhabited by paupers of the lowest grade, and who, in their present condition, would find a difficulty in obtaining any decent cottage as tenant to a private individual. They are generally the resort of persons who are turned out of their houses for non-payment of rent, &c. Two only of the tenements have a room up stairs, and all except these two have dirt floors; the other ten tenements consist of one room each. In two or three instances this room is divided by a sort of partition put up by the inmates. The largest number of persons occupying one of these tenements is eight—a man, his wife, and six children, the eldest child aged 16, the youngest an infant. There is no bed in the house, the whole family sleeping on two heaps of straw, confined in two corners of the room by stakes driven into the ground. None of the tenements are ceiled. There are no back doors nor windows for ventilation; the filth is thrown out into stagnant pools in front of the building; the stench is at all times great, and in hot weather of course proportionably increased. With the exception of one, the tenements are occupied by families with children of all ages. The number of persons on the whole is fifty-five. In the parish of Soulbury, a building, formerly used as a workhouse, is now occupied by persons of depraved habits. One room is occupied by a man, his wife, and three grown-up daughters and a son; two of the daughters have bastard children."

In the town of Woburn there is a place called Cobb's-row, consisting of about twenty houses of two and three rooms each, almost every one of which contains a separate family. "The place," said one of the lodgers to me, "is filthy in the extreme. There are no drains to any of the houses, and all the slops and mess have to be thrown down a gutter in front of the houses. Sometimes when it is stopped up with rubbish, the landlord, who lives in one of the houses, comes out with a broom and a kind of rake, and scrapes down the gutter; and when the stuff has been left there for a few days, you may suppose what a pretty smell he kicks up. In hot weather we can't get a breath of air, for we dar'n't open the window because of the smell, and there we are shut up all the day, me and my wife and six children in one little poking room. Yes, and I have to pay 2s. a week, too, for the hole; and one of the duke's cottages, with two or three rooms in it, wouldn't let for so much as that. I shall try hard to see if I can't get in one of the next new ones that's built. There's no chance of getting into one as is built now, for they're never empty, none of 'em." Many other villages and places might be named where bad cottages exist, and to the whole of them one and the same description would be almost invariably found to apply, as they are damp, low, cold, smoky, dilapidated, and comfortless; while great numbers of the inmates are almost constantly afflicted with cartarrhal diseases, colds, inflammation of the eyes, dysentery, and frequently contagious and epidemic complaints.

The town of St. Ives is sadly deficient in good cottage accommodation. Many of the houses in the narrow courts and alleys leading off the Sheep-market are extremely old and incommodious. To the houses in many other parts of the town the same remark applies. I was informed that one great reason for the non-improvement of the dwellings in this town was, that nearly the whole of the town was copyhold, and that as soon as any improvement was made, the agent of the Lord of the Manor invariably caused a re-valuation of the premises to be made, and, as the fines are arbitrary, usually exacted one equivalent to several years of the improved rental. Of course, under such a state of things, no person will attempt to improve the property, and the Lord of the Manor will not allow any tenement which has once been erected to be pulled down. Hence the great number of decayed and ruinous places.

In many parts of the town of Cambridge the dwellings of the poor are also in the most disgraceful condition. I might refer to King-street and the alleys leading therefrom, to Christ's-lane, and other places. But perhaps the worst of all is a place called Falcon-yard. In one of the houses which I visited there were thirteen families residing. In a room on one of the floors lived a man, his wife, and five children. The eldest boy was sixteen years of age, the eldest girl, a little over fourteen, having been for several months a common prostitute, and three younger children, together with the parents, all slept in one and the same room: the eldest boy and girl and two other children in one bed on the floor, the father, mother, and one child, on a stump bedstead. The number of persons residing in this Falcon-yard, I was informed, was about 300. There are two privies for the use of the whole of the inhabitants, but as they are at a distance of about fifty yards from some portion of the premises, those of the inhabitants who have back windows to their rooms are in the habit of throwing all their refuse out of the windows on to a large dung-heap in the Red Lion-yard, the reeking steam from which is constantly penetrating the rooms. "Here," said one of the inmates of this crowded and dirty yard, "this is my grand hole that I pays sixteen pence a week for—this is where me and my husband and daughters sleeps; the bed is about as big as an old pocket handkerchief. I have been here four and thirty years." "I've got two rooms," said another person, "and here's our bed-room," opening at the same time a small door which led to a dark recess in which there was no window or light whatever. A piece of paper, however, was lighted, and I was then enabled to distinguish the form of a bedstead in one corner, and a heap of bed clothes on the floor in the opposite portion of this "black hole." The "Falcon," which gives its name to the yard was formerly a very extensive inn. There is an old-fashioned gallery which runs round the yard, and the different apartments round this gallery have been let off to lodgers at rents varying from 1s. 4d. to 2s. per week. Several of them are kept remarkably clean, considering the character of the place, but the majority are as wretched as it is possible to conceive. They are all of them very dark and ill-ventilated.

But the town of Ely and one or two of the surrounding villages perhaps bear a worse character than any other part of these counties. In a house in Broad-street, in which one of the inmates was suddenly seized with diarrhœa, the floor of the room (or ground rather, for there was no flooring or even brick to it), in which he lay, was about a foot below the level of the adjacent ground. At the back of the cottage was a large heap of pig and other manure, which reached to the sill of the window. The head of the old stump bedstead on which the sick man lay was close to the wall, and the filthy fluid of the dung heap outside was oozing through the wall, within a few inches of the bed's head. At one place in Benton-square which I visited, lay an old woman upon one of the dirtiest stump bedsteads that I had ever seen. Her person was disgustingly dirty, the wretched covering of the bed filthy in the extreme, while the stench of the room was almost overpowering. Myriads of animated existences luxuriated in the dirt and filth of the wretched bed and its occupant. The woman, I was informed, had not suffered herself—and judging from the dirty appearance of the other members of the family they had not pressed her much upon the subject—to be touched with soap and water for the last six years; and I was informed that no article of her wretched bedding had been cleaned or removed for the same period. She was one of the most notorious opium eaters in the opium-eating city of Ely. The exhilirating effects of her last dose had passed off, and had given place to that wretched lowness of spirit in which the life of an opium eater alternates. As the repulsive-looking hag sat upright in her filthy bed by the chimney corner, her uncouth and cadaverous features streaked by the various courses her tears had taken in her intervals of despondency, and which were some shades less dirty than the other portions of her face, with her tangled grey hair hanging over her shoulders, her shrunken neck, and withered arms which were exposed to view as she rolled up another pill of the filthy-looking drug, and raised it tremblingly to her discoloured lips, presented a spectacle more loathsome than imagination could conceive. The only articles of furniture in the room were an old chair or two and a rough-looking three-legged table. Her daughter, twenty-eight years old, was standing by the side of the fire, and two grown-up men—her sons, I was informed—were sitting upon an old form or bench in front of it; two dirty, ragged little urchins completed the number of the inmates. "I've been on this here bed six years," said the miserable old woman; "I fell down, and broke my hip, and it wasn't set. I've never been able to get out of this room, nor beyond the side of the bed, all that time. I won't go in the workhouse, I'd rather stop and die where I am." Adjoining the cottage, as if to see how much filth and stench could be accumulated in the smallest possible compass, was an enormous open cesspool, which formed the receptacle of the garbage and refuse of all the houses in the square. There was, perhaps, no labourer who earned more money when employed than the husband of this woman. The greater part of his earnings, however, was always spent either in opium or in drink. Within a few yards from this disgusting place was another cottage, with scarcely an article of furniture in it. The glare of a few expiring embers in the fire-place displayed at intervals damp and discoloured walls, a broken ceiling, patched-up windows, two broken chairs, a table, an old chest of drawers, and the shoeless feet, ragged clothes, and dirty faces of five young children, who sat huddled together around the hearth to enjoy the infinitesimal amount of warmth which the fire could furnish. The father was out of work, the mother was selling matches in the town. The eldest child only went to school, and that a Sunday school, but could not read. There was one bed for the whole family. In Walpole-lane there is a row of houses from which fever is never absent; the small piece of ground at the back of these dwellings can be compared to nothing but a wide-spread dung heap; a well, a privy, a pigstye, a muck-heap, and a stable, are all in immediate proximity to each other, and perhaps the most filthy of all the places, inasmuch as it receives a portion of the contents of each of the others, is the well which supplies the water for the use of the inmates. One hovel close by, consisting of but one room, in which was a large family, had on one side of it an enormous dung heap, on the other a pigstye, at the back a filthy ditch, and immediately in front the privy used by the whole of the inhabitants of the lane. In another part of the town, called Bug's-hill, the cottages are in the same condition. The rent paid for these dens varies from 1s. to 1s. 6d. per week. During the last few months there has not been less than forty-three cases of diarrhœa in these disgusting places.

As might be expected from the disgraceful condition of parts of the town the rate of mortality is fearfully high, compared with other parts of the country. Mr. Cole, one of the medical officers of the union, informed me that in those parts of the town to which allusion has been made, influenza, scarlet fever, or fever of a typhoid character, are seldom or never absent, and that smallpox, caused in a great measure by the neglect of vaccination, diseases of the respiratory organs, ague, and scrofulous affections, assume an aggravated form in these districts. Upon a comparison between the absolute mortality of Ely as a whole, and the absolute mortality of all England, it appears that the mortality of Ely is 26 1-11 for every thousand of the population, while that of all England is only 22. The difference of mortality between the city and the Fens is in the proportion of 29 for the city to 21.5 for the Fens.

Comparing the mortality of different parts of the city of Ely with each other, it appears that in those portions which may be called the "seats of disease," the absolute mortality is as high as 34.5, while in the most healthy parts it is only 23.5. The same gentleman informed me, as the result of his experience and observation, that while the preventible mortality of the Fens was only 9, that of the town of Ely was 16.75.

But it is not only in the city of Ely that bad and unhealthy cottages are to be found, the villages around it are equally as bad, and if possible in a worse condition. At a place called Welsh's-dam, near Chatteris, there are sixteen cottages, containing together a population of eighty-one persons, among whom there were last year not less than eleven fatal attacks of cholera, besides a number of cases of diarrhœa. The cottages are built by the side of an extensive dam, the upper part of which reaches to the tops of the windows of the cottages, and the houses are consequently damp and wretched in the extreme. At a place called Little London, situated on the Lynn road, there is a ditch, which runs close to the backs of the houses, and the refuse from the other houses, which constantly floats upon its surface, is borne into the very doors. Here cases of fever and dysentery are constantly occurring.

There is one village, however, within two miles of the city of Ely, called Witchford, which in point of filth would bear comparison with the worst place in any part of the kingdom. Along the entire length of the village, and within a few feet of the doors and windows of the houses, is a slough extending over nearly the whole width of the road, containing and retaining accumulations of decaying animal and vegetable matter, either thrown from the dwellings or flowing into it from the adjoining farm yards. The condition of the dwellings is wretched beyond description. Fevers of the typhoid character and scarlatina are never absent. In company with Mr. Cole, the union surgeon, I visited several places where fever was at the time most prevalent. In one cottage six of the family had been attacked with the disease. On going up stairs into the sick chamber—if a hole in the roof deserves the name of a chamber—I found four beds. The apartment containing them might be about 14 feet by 10 feet. The sides of the room were sloping, and the width of the ceiling could not be more than about six feet, while its length might be about the same. In one bed in this loft or room lay the father of the family, who had been confined with fever for six weeks, and in an adjoining bed lay his daughter, 12 years of age. The two other beds, and the unoccupied portions of those in which the victims of fever lay, were occupied by the wife and the five children during the night. The eldest boy was 14, and his sister 16 years of age. The condition of such a place, without the slightest means of ventilation—the dormitory of eight persons by night, and the sick room of two by day—can be more easily imagined than described. The fœtid atmosphere, the moans of the child, the fevered eye and hectic cheek of the father, the broken plaster of the ceiling and walls, the creaking door and gaping floor, the broken windows stopped up with divers coloured rags, all combined to produce a scene which for wretchedness and misery could perhaps not be surpassed in any civilized or even uncivilized part of the world. The room below was little if anything better than the one above. Through the dense smoke with which it was filled might be seen three sickly-looking children sitting by the fire—they were the other members of the family, who had so far recovered as to be able to be brought down stairs. Three, four, and five weeks had been the respective terms of their illness, and those only who may have witnessed the utter prostration of strength which follows a partial recovery from fever will be able to form any conception of the wretchedness which these children presented. When the first member of the family was attacked, the doctor gave directions that the others should not sleep in the same room. This injunction, however, was unheeded; the reason being, that they could not make up beds on the cold and damp brick floor of the lower room. Either the front or back door of the cottage was obliged to be left entirely open, in order to allow the smoke to escape, the chimney being wholly useless for that purpose. This was an industrious family; the husband had received 7s. a week almost constantly, and had not been out of work since the harvest until the time that he was attacked. During harvest he worked day work, and received about 18s. a week for three weeks; but what he earned went to pay the shoemaker's bill. One of the neighbours had kindly attended throughout the whole period of their illness, in order to render any assistance in her power. In the next cottage were two persons, one of whom sat shivering with ague before the fire in the lower room, and in the upper one lay the wife burning with fever. In the third cottage, sat by the side of the fire, with a child six months old on his knees, a labourer who had that day been compelled to give up work; he was another victim to the deadly fever. By the side of him sat his sister, a young woman of 17 years of age, so far recovered from fever as to be allowed to be carried down stairs. In an upper room, of about eight feet square, with sloping roofs like the adjoining cottage, were two beds so close that they touched each other, in one of which lay the wife of the man in the lower room, and the mother of the child he was nursing. She was in the last stage of typhus. At the request of the doctor who accompanied me I turned to open the window of the room, the close atmosphere of which was almost unbearable. While engaged in opening the window, the attendants had succeeded in raising the patient in her miserable couch, and as I turned round an involuntary shudder came over me as my eye rested upon the wretched spectacle. There was a death-like gaze in the eye of the woman that unmistakably told of the approach of dissolution; her gaunt and bony features, sunken cheeks, and discoloured lips, bore evidence to the intensity of the attack under which she was suffering. By her side, in the adjoining bed, had lain for three weeks previously the sister, who was then sitting down stairs, and at night, in the same room, and in the same beds with the fevered patients, had slept, through the whole period, the husband and little child, two grown up young men, and their mother. In the next cottage the whole of the family, with the exception of the mother, had had the fever, and both parents were at that moment suffering under a loathsome disease. In the fifth and last house, the inmates were complaining of colds and pains in their eyes.

There were living altogether in these five houses 37 persons. The rent was from £2 10s. to £3 per annum. The owner, a Mr. Ward, I believe, dwelt close by the property. From appearances in front of the houses I was prepared for such a state of things in the rear. But the worst that I had conceived fell infinitely short of their actual condition. Four upright pieces of wood, not more than four feet in height, with several other pieces laid transversely over the top, supported a quantity of loose straw, which was called the "thatch" of a place dignified by the name of a "privy," the ground being covered by the filth which flowed over out of a small hole intended as its receptacle. Within a few feet from this was the well containing the liquid which the people drank, its component parts being made up of the overflow of the privy, the refuse from the pigstye, the contents of a ditch into which the slops from the houses were thrown, and the spring of the well itself. The water presented a dull and turbid-looking appearance, and its smell was most offensive. Heaps of pig and other manure lay piled, in some cases against the walls of the cottages themselves, in others a few feet removed from them. At the back or front door of each stood a pail or pan, into which the refuse of the house was thrown, and when full, the contents were emptied into the ditch close by, the current of which being stopped up caused the most offensive of the contents to be deposited about the road, where they were either absorbed by the soil or flowed into the well. "The pig don't get on well," said the landlord of the place, "it belongs to them as as got the fever. It's no use my taking it as it is, for they owe me £3 for rent. I wish they'd manage to get it on a little better, for it won't fetch near what they owe me as it is—it's always a cryin' for wittles." "I suppose," said the gentleman who accompanied me, "you would rather that the pig 'got on' than that the people got well?" "The pig would be some security for the rent," was the business-like and unfeeling reply of the landlord. On my alluding to the disgraceful condition of the yard, he said— "The place is my own, and I suppose I may do as I like with it; and as for the privy, it is only two or three months since I went to the trouble of putting it up—the house is as healthy as any other in the place." In this opinion I entirely concur, for nearly every house in the village is in the same disgraceful condition, and I was informed that in hot and wet weather "the smell from it was most abominable." The village possesses admirable natural facilities for drainage. It is not situated, as many villages are, in the marsh or fen land; on the contrary, it is on the high lands. Reports have been constantly made on its sanitary condition to the guardians of the poor, but they have been, and still are, comparatively unheeded. The dread of incurring expense prevents anything from being done for the improvement of the place. Meanwhile the parish supports the sick by means of out-door relief; the expense of the first family alluded to having been in one week not less than 23s. 3d., exclusive of the charges for medical attendance.

LABOUR AND THE POOR.

THE RURAL DISTRICTS.

[FROM OUR SPECIAL CORRESPONDENT.]

HERTS, HUNTS, BEDS, AND CAMBRIDGE.

Letter XXXVIII.

In a former communication I referred to the sanitary condition of the agricultural labourer in these counties as respects his dwellings. I propose in the present Letter to give some account of his employment, and of his wages.

In those parts of the county of Herts which, from their proximity to the metropolis, may almost be considered as forming portions of its suburbs, it will be found that not only is employment more constant, but the wages are generally speaking higher than in most other parts of the county, being from 8s. to 10s., and in some cases as high as 12s. per week. The whole of that part of the county in the neighbourhood of the town of Hertford and Ware is studded with the dwellings of resident proprietors; the condition of the labourer consequently receives some share of attention, and employment is almost constantly to be obtained. In some parts, however, where there is a considerable extent of grass land, regular and constant employment cannot be found for the whole of the population. One gentleman, however, who has been a resident in the parish of Shenley for upwards of fifty years, and who has expended a considerable portion of his income during that time in improving the condition of the labourer and in affording him the means of employment, states that, notwithstanding there being a great quantity of grass land in his parish, and a considerable population, he believes "that but for the public-house nuisance, and its consequent temptation, not a soul in his parish would go to bed hungry or be badly clothed—that the higher the wages, the wife and children are nothing the better if beer-shops intercept the most of them." He adds, "I believe that in this parish there is one beer-shop to considerably less than a hundred souls." The same gentleman, still speaking of this parish, says "We have a police, very expensive, and of no use—no near magistrate—very little dissent, but not too much religion—and I think very little crime."

Throughout the greater part of the counties of Bedford and Cambridge, the average wages may be taken to be about 8s. for married, and from 5s. to 7s. for single men. The "horsemen" usually receive more. Happening to meet with one of this class of persons—a young man, apparently of about twenty years of age—I inquired as to his weekly rate of wages. "Oh," said he, "they be very poor indeed; they be only six shillings." I well knew, from what I had previously heard on the point of wages, that my informant was indulging in some reservation on the subject; and upon further pressing him as to the amount he received for "year's end"—a sum of money paid to the labourer at the end of the year—he proceeded with some amount of physical exertion to draw forth a watch from his pocket, about the proportions of a moderate-sized dial. "Why here, maister," said he, "d'ye see this? This is my 'year's end.' I give three pun' ten for this and the chain; a bran new slop cost me seven and sixpence; a new coat was two pun' ten, and that was just a little above my year's end." With his weekly wages and "year's end," his wages would, therefore, average about 8s. 6d. per week.

Upon the farm of the Duke of Bedford, at Woburn, the wages generally given are about 9s. a week for farm labourers, and from 10s. to 11s. for horsemen. In the fen lands of the Isle of Ely and Huntingdon the wages are about 8s. per week. In the Linton union, in Cambridgeshire, there are several parishes conspicuous for the wretchedness of the condition of the labourer, and the low rate of wages. In more than one of the parishes in this union the whole of the cottages have been pulled down, and the labourers, being compelled to live in Linton, have to walk considerable distances in going to and returning from their work. There appears to be a great desire on the part of some of the farmers to avoid giving the labourer more work than is absolutely necessary. I was informed of the case of a man, who was known to be one of the most notorious poachers in the district, and five of the farmers actually subscribed together 5s. a week to assist him in obtaining a livelihood, and to prevent his coming to the board of guardians; they at the same time well knowing that, as they would not give him work, he would make up the deficiency by poaching. "They're a screwin', close-fisted, hard set of fellows—that's what the farmers are all about here," said an old labourer to me. One of the most influential of the guardians told me that both himself and the reverend chairman of the board were constantly endeavouring to impress upon the farmers the necessity of affording some employment for the people. A determination upon the part of the chairman of the union to act strictly upon the principle of the poor-law, viz., the application of the workhouse test to the labourer as well as to the employer, has been attended with very considerable success. Upon one occasion of a meeting of the Board of Guardians, there was a farmer present who was notorious for the small amount of employment which he afforded to the people in his parish. While at the board it so happened that three families came up for relief who belonged to his parish, one with seven, a second with eight, and a third with nine children. What was to be done with them was the question put by the chairman. "Send 'em to the house," was the reply of the farmer. Orders for their admission were accordingly made out by the clerk. The farmer in question was the principal rate-payer in the parish to which the families belonged. "What will be the weekly expense to the parish of these thirty persons?" inquired the chairman of the clerk. "About five pounds a week," was the reply. "My share of the poor-rate won't be less than three pounds of that," said the farmer. "I can get 'em to work for me for 8s. a week; that'll be only 24s. a week. Call 'em in." The applicants for relief were accordingly re-admitted, and, to their great surprise, the father of each family, instead of receiving an order for the workhouse, was told that he would be employed on the farm at work of some kind or other. From that time to the present there has scarcely been an application for relief from an able-bodied labourer of that parish.

The "ticket system" is one that is very generally adopted in this and other parts of the county, as well as in the adjoining counties of Essex and Suffolk, and in some parts of Bedfordshire. Under this system no relief is afforded to any applicant unless he can show, by the production of his ticket, that he is unable to obtain work. Many opinions have been expressed as to the effects upon the labourers of this mode of affording relief. It has been considered by some that it operates unfairly towards the labourer, inasmuch as it compels him to take any work that may be offered to him, without reference to the amount of wages which may be paid for his labour; and that while on the one hand there might be found persons who would be willing to give the applicant employment upon some comparatively unproductive kind of work at a somewhat reduced price, and with the benevolent view of keeping him out of the workhouse, still there would not be wanting others who would make the application an occasion for effecting a reduction of wages. The refusal of the party to accept work at such reduced price would be attended with the refusal of all relief by the boards of guardians, and the labourer would be thus left entirely at the mercy of his employer. From all that I was enabled to learn, however, I could not ascertain that any great abuse of the system had taken place, the farmers generally contenting themselves by endorsing the certificate, of which the following is a copy:—

"THE FOLLOWING CERTIFICATE TO BE FILLED UP BY THE PAUPER'S LAST EMPLOYER.

I have employed ....
from .... to .... 18......... and discharged
him* .... his pay amounted to ....
      (Signed)
    * "State the cause, whether on account of illness, want of employ-
ment, neglect, &c."

The endorsement is as follows:—

"TO THE BOARD OF GUARDIANS OF THE SAFFRON WALDEN UNION.
"The bearer, ... of the parish of
.... has applied to us, the undersigned, for work, but we could not employ him."

I was informed that the guardians of the Caxton and some other unions had frequently pressed parties to accept the workhouse in cases where it was considered that the wages offered were inadequate to the maintenance of the applicant and his family; but in cases where the wages were clearly sufficient to prevent destitution, although probably below the usual rate, the guardians generally did not seem to consider themselves justified in disturbing the relations between the labourer and his employer. The number of able-bodied paupers in the Linton-workhouse is always considerably higher in proportion than in any other union in this district. In the quarter ending Christmas, 1848, the total number of inmates in the house was 195, of whom there were 85 able-bodied men and women; in the corresponding period of 1849, the total number of in-door paupers was 224, of whom 101 were able-bodied men and women; the number of old and infirm men in the house being 31.

By the drainage and cultivation of the fen lands in the Isle of Ely an enormous increase has taken place in the amount of employment.

In the parish of Littleport alone not less than 14,000 acres of fens have within the last thirty years been brought under cultivation, there being not more than 500 acres of high land in the whole parish. The increase in the population in this parish, consisting of persons from other parts of the country, was 35 per cent. during the decennial period between 1831 and 1841. There is not a sufficient number of persons to reap the harvest in these districts, and it is here that the Irish flock in such vast numbers about harvest time. There is no want of employment in this part of the county, and the rate of wages varies from 8s. to 9s. per week.

The condition of the labourer in the fen lands, so far as employment is concerned, presents a marked contrast to the southern portion of the county of Cambridge. In the parishes of Castle Camps and Shudy Camps there is probably a larger amount of distress and destitution to be met with, in proportion to their size, than, perhaps, in any other parishes in the Eastern or Midland counties.

The condition of the people in the former of these parishes has been alleviated to some extent, by giving them allotments of land at a low rent, and also by supplying them with fuel at reduced prices. The amount of benefits, however, thus laudably conferred by the few resident and charitable proprietors has by no means compensated for the want of employment and the low rate of wages. The resident rector of Castle Camps, in a letter addressed to me on the subject, states, "All the poor belonging to this parish have for several years, *as they were able*, had allotments of land, at a rate far below many of those of the neighbouring parishes; and with regard to all persons with three children and more, as well as the old people, they have had coals sold to them at half price for about four months in the year, and the widows for a longer period. But for a long course of years, and before I came here, a system has prevailed among those who had the power at Shudy Camps, of pulling down cottages, and preventing others being built; the result of which has been to drive so many families into this (Castle Camps) parish, that I believe the number of Shudy Camps people residing here at present is not less than one-third of the entire population, and the distress of some of these has been increased by their becoming union paupers. Among some of these there is the greatest distress, which I have no means of alleviating, for they are in a great measure abandoned by their own parish." While the parish of Shudy Camps has pursued this iniquitous system, and is reaping the benefit of it by shovelling the burden of its paupers on an adjoining parish, the rate of wages there is lower by 1s., or even more, per week than in the neighbouring parishes. As stated by the reverend gentleman above, many of the persons residing in Castle Camps are in the greatest possible distress. "My husband," said one poor woman upon whom I called, "only arned 3s. 6d. last week. I've got nine children; my eldest boy arns 1s. 6d. a week; but when the weather's bad he can't get that. Last week he was kept on all the week. If my husband was in constant work he could arn eight shillings a week, but then the work is so *chanceful* like, that there's no knowin' what he do arn. If it wasn't that we was able to get in debt a little, I don't know whatever we should do in the winter time. We try to get out of debt in harvest time, and whenever we can we give a shilling or so off as we can spare it. We pay sixpence a bushel for coals at the parish. They allows us to have 'em for that price. We have got a rood of ground. We pay 7½d. a month for it. We've got such a family that we eat nearly all the taturs off it soon after harvest, and can't save many for the winter. Sometimes my oldest girl arns a trifle at 'smocking,' that is, making smock frocks. She can get 1s. 6d. a week for that if she works hard and regular. Sometimes I can get a shilling or so at it, but there's nothing doing at that now. When I was confined with my last child the parish allowed me a shilling a week for my month and a little longer, for I was so poorly that I could not get about; I could not get strength nohows at all, and then I had to give the nurse something every week. I have one son as is married, and he has got one child and nothing to do. I expect he will have to go into the workhouse soon. They won't let such as we go into the house. The farmers gives my husband a day's work or two in the week, and then they think we can manage to keep out; but I'm sure we should all have perished if it hadn't been for the shopkeeper letting us have a little bread and flour. I don't like to go in debt no further than I can help; but I'm druv to it. If there's anything I should like more than another it would be to be out of debt, and then I should not care how soon I died; that I should not, for I'm sure my children would be all better off in the workhouse than they are now. As to meat, I seldom or never see a bit of it in this place." Another woman, whose husband had not been able to work for the last five years, received 3s. 6d. a week from the parish, and had seven children to support, the eldest of whom brought home from 1s. 6d. to 2s. a week, but had not been in work for the last two or three weeks.

At a third cottage which I visited, the father of the family had been out of work for many weeks; there were five children at home, the eldest girl being seventeen; none of the younger ones had either shoe or stocking to their feet; and they were all wretchedly clad. "We have not," the eldest daughter said, "tasted any bread for two days. We have had nowt but *turmuts* (turnips) to eat. We boil 'em for dinner, but the children are so hungry that they won't wait sometimes till they're *biled*, but eats 'em as they are." The whole of the family were about to emigrate to the Cape of Good Hope. "The papers had all been signed, and they expected to go every day." "My husband," said a woman who lived in the next house—a damp and wretched place, with a stagnant ditch close to it—"is out with a few mats, to see if he can sell 'em. He gets threepence a piece for 'em when he can sell 'em. He has had no work for three months. My eldest girl used to earn a little at smocking—about eighteenpence a week. She ain't had nothing to do at it though lately. I have not tasted a drop of tea, a bit of sugar, or a mite of butter for many weeks, and I can't eat the *turmuts*, they perish my inside so; so I has a bit of bread when most of the others has the *turmuts*." A few doors beyond was another family, consisting of five children, the mother of whom said—"My husband has not made more than half a week's work for the last two or three weeks. Sometimes we get a mite of pork, sometimes mutton. Last Sunday I got four penn'orth of mutton; but lor', when that's cut up into seven bits there isn't much of it apiece." Many other instances of a similar kind might be quoted from this place, but the tales of misery and privation vary so little in their general features that to mention more would be but to weary the reader for no practical purpose. We will, therefore, pass on to the adjoining village of Shudy Camps, where, if possible, the condition of the labourers is even still more deplorable, and their miseries more intense. I thought that in Castle Camps I had fathomed the lowest depths of misery. Not so, however; the wretchedness and misery of the agricultural labourer in this part of the county, appears to be an unfathomable abyss. Beyond the "lowest deep" there is always a "lower deep;" and I despair of ever discovering that point at which it may be said, "Thus far can misery go, and no farther; and here is the extreme verge beyond which humanity cannot exist." The tenacity of life among the agricultural labourers is almost incredible. Sheep, cattle, and pigs would not exist in many of the hovels where those who tend them live; and if these animals were to endure one-half of the amount of privation which the peasant undergoes—if their food were as scanty and as unsuited to them as is the diet of the labourer to him—if the cattle-shed of the oxen, and the stye of the pig, were not better provided with litter for them to lie upon than are the cottages of many of the labourers with bedding—and did they not afford better protection against the inclemency of the weather than do many of the miserable hovels of the labourer—the extent of mortality among them would speedily call forth, on the part of their owners, all the energies which self-interest and the love of gain could excite in them.

In Shudy Camps destitution and want appear to hold unrivalled sway over the miserable inhabitants. There is no resident proprietor in the parish, nor within some distance of the place, neither is there an individual residing in the place who is able to afford any assistance to the people. The hand of charity, which alleviates in some measure the distress of the agricultural labourer in other parts, is never opened in this village, and none but the relieving officer of the union, as he distributes the parish allowance to the sick paupers, enters, for purposes of relief, the miserable dwellings of the people of Shudy Camps. The roads to these parishes are impassable in almost all kinds of weather. After a few days of rain a strong current of water from the high grounds in the vicinity flows down the road with such impetuosity as even on some occasions to carry horses and carts away. On the occasion of my visit the water was from eighteen inches to two feet deep. The village itself, and indeed a great part of the country for several miles round, is the property of the Charterhouse. Not a farthing of the rents of the cottages or farms is spent in the place, or devoted to the purpose of giving employment to the people, or of improving the soil. The governors of the Charterhouse can scarcely be aware of the condition of their tenantry, or they surely would not leave them in their present wretched state.

Here are the accounts which two or three of the people gave of their condition. The first was given by a woman apparently about 40 years of age, whose sunken eye and hollow cheek told too plainly that disease and want had almost done their work upon her. She was so weak that she could scarcely support herself. The day was very cold, and her eldest son was just dragging in a small branch of a tree, which the wind had broken off. "I've six children at home, and two in the workhouse," said she. "My eldest boy here is turned of 14, and when he is at work he earns 4d. a day at stone-picking. My youngest child is a year and a half old. The boy that's in the workhouse is 16, and the girl is 18. When the girl was at home she used to do a little work at 'smocking;' but she's had nothing to do for a long time, so she went to the workhouse; it was the best place she could go to. My husband has 7s. a week when he is at work; nobody has more than 7s. now—some of 'em gets less. This week he has had three days and a half's work—the weather has been bad, he couldn't work any more; last week he had three days, and the week before he hadn't none. We don't have anything from the parish because there's none of us ill. They've wanted me to go in, but I'd rather stay out if I can manage to do it anyhows. I've had nothing but a bit of bread to-day. I went to the person as employed my husband for a day and a half last week, and I asked him to let me have the money, for I hadn't a bit of bread at home for the children; and he let me have eightpence, and I bought a loaf of bread with it and a little bit of tea, and we shall make shift with that till my husband comes home." She went on to say that latterly she had been subject to fits, and that she frequently fainted away because she had not victuals enough. "I go without so long," said she, "that everything gets swimming, and goes round with me, and then I can't stand up no longer, and goes off fainting like." The condition of the cottage was most deplorable. In an outbuilding attached to the dwelling— the clayey floor of which was damp and muddy—was one of those uncouth-looking wooden frames, which by courtesy are called bed-steads, upon which lay an indescribable collection of mud-coloured rags, which served as covering for one portion of the family; while in another corner of the room, but scarcely distinguishable from a heap of the clay of which the surface was composed, was the sleeping place of the remainder of the inmates.

In the adjoining cottage dwelt a family, ten in number, the eldest boy was 24. "I," said the eldest girl, "am 21; my youngest brother is a year and a quarter old. My father and mother and all of us sleeps up in the roof. My oldest brother arnes 7s. a week when he's at work, and my father arnes the same—he is at work on the roads this week. My brother's out of work now." "I haven't got," said another woman with tears in her eyes, who was crouching down over a few cinders in the fire-place, "a mite of food in the house, and I've just put the last twig of wood on the fire. I went to the clergyman this morning, and I asked him, for God's sake, to give me sixpence to buy a bit of firing with; and he said he could not afford it, and that he was as bad off as I was. I went out into the hedges, and picked up a few mites of wood. My husband is in pretty constant work, and gets 7s. a week, when the weather will let him work. I have had thirteen children, and I've got eight of 'em at home; some of 'em is in bed—they're warmer there than they would be up and about, for they've got no shoes to their feet. We get through a bushel of flour in the week, and that costs us 7s., but that's not enough for us sometimes. One of my boys arnes 1s. 6d. a week at 'bird scaring,' but none of t'others don't arne anything. One of my children has gone in the workhouse, so that saves us something. We've got a little bit of ground that we pay 5s. a quarter for; we've sowed it with a peck of wheat this year: we had a few taturs last year on it, but they didn't do us no good, the ground was new broke up."

A labourer, to whom I was speaking on the subject of his wages, said, in answer to a question which I put to him, "Live, sir! we don't live, we only breathes. How can a man and his family live on 7s. a week, and pay 2s. out of it for his rent?" "But," said I, "you do manage to live—what do you live upon besides your wages, which, you say, are not enough to keep you?" "Well, then, if you must know," said he, "we steal—we're forced to do it. Why if it wasn't that we 'bent the twig' sometimes, how could we live? Put some of the gentle-folk in our places, and see if they wouldn't do it, too. I was coming home the very last night of all by ——'s park, and I see a something run across the road. I huv'd a stone, and bless me if I didn't hit her, and I took her home, and no harm neyther; and now you may go and split on me if you like—I'd as soon be in gaol as out. I had but two days' work all last week, but me and the young 'uns had a hare for dinner for all that. Do they think they're to starve? I'm blessed if they shall if I can hev' a stone or"——(pointing to the hedge, and indicating by the motion of his hands the mode in which he would proceed in setting a snare). I was perfectly prepared for the answer of the man, as I had been given previously to understand that great numbers of the inhabitants were obliged to have recourse to poaching to eke out their existence. In point of fact, in many of the cottages which I have visited in different parts of the country, I have seen unmistakeable signs that the inmates do not live upon bread alone. Entering somewhat hastily into one of the cottages, I observed a great bustle among the inmates, and the eldest child was carrying into the out-house a shallow red pan or dish, upon which I could plainly see the greater portion of the body of a hare, while in another corner of the room lay a skin, which, from its apparent freshness, I have no doubt belonged to the hare off which they were dining. On casting my eyes towards the table, I saw the father busily engaged in turning the contents of the plates into an old hat, which the man afterwards proceeded, with an air of assumed indifference, to place upon his head. When the perturbation into which my unceremonious visit had thrown the family was somewhat allayed, the father of the family, which was five in number, proceeded to inform me that he had been out of work for the last week or two, and that the last time he was in work he made only three days in one week and four in the previous one. "If it wasn't," said he, "for what we pick up sometimes, I'm sure we should starve." The phrase "pick up" is one that is very frequently used among the agricultural labourers; and I have found that it is one that almost invariably applies to something from the neighbouring preserves. Speaking to some children at a short distance from this village, one of them said that they had had "a Jack Caw" for dinner. The naturalist would probably be puzzled to know what kind of creature was intended by a "Jack Caw." This creature, however, is neither more nor less than a cock pheasant, a hen of the same species being denominated a Jenny Caw. Each description of game, and even poultry, has its alias among the agricultural labourers. I was informed that the reason for giving other names to game and poultry was, to prevent the children from knowing what they actually were, and thus to render them incapable of telling to others the real names or description of food which they might have had at their meals.

In a number of other cottages which I visited I heard the same tale of want of employment and insufficiency of food, and saw the same kind of wretched dwellings and miserable inmates. I obtained from them an account of what they had had for their Christmas dinners, and the result was that six had had bread and potatoes—three, bread, potatoes, and turnips—two, apple puddings and potatoes—two, "a little bit of plum pudding" and turnips—and the remaining one had a piece of pork, turnips, and plum pudding. I had previously visited the workhouse of the union in which these villages were situated, and I learned that on Christmas day each inmate had eight ounces of roast beef, one pound of plum pudding, one pint of beer to every grown person, and half a pint to all under nine years of age. Each of the females had an extra quantity of tea and sugar, the old women had an ounce of snuff each, and the old men an ounce of tobacco. The breakfast of the men consisted of a pint and a half of gruel and eight ounces of bread, and that of the women of seven ounces of bread and the same quantity of gruel. The supper consisted of an ample allowance of bread and cheese. The snuff, tobacco, and extra tea and sugar, it must be stated, were the gifts of the Rev. Mr. Townley, the chairman of the union.

The following is a copy of the usual diet of the inmates of the workhouse:—

DIETARY FOR ABLE-BODIED MEN AND WOMEN.

		Breakfast		Dinner					Supper	
		Bread	Gruel	Beef	Pork or Bacon	Soup	Potatoes	Rice or suet pdg.	Cheese	Gruel
		Oz.	Pts.	Oz.	Oz.	Pts.	Oz.	Oz.	Oz.	Pts.
Sunday	Men	16	$1\frac{1}{2}$	5	..	..	16	..	..	1
	Women	14	$1\frac{1}{2}$	5	..	..	16	..	..	1
Monday and Friday	Men	16	$1\frac{1}{2}$	..	..	$1\frac{1}{2}$	12	..	$1\frac{1}{2}$	$1\frac{1}{2}$
	Women	14	$1\frac{1}{2}$	..	..	$1\frac{1}{2}$	12	..	1	1
Tuesday and Thursday	Men	16	$1\frac{1}{2}$	..	4	..	16	..	..	1
	Women	14	$1\frac{1}{2}$	..	4	..	16	..	..	1
Wednesday	Men	16	$1\frac{1}{2}$	..	..	$1\frac{1}{2}$	8	Rice. 12	$1\frac{1}{2}$	$1\frac{1}{2}$
	Women	14	$1\frac{1}{2}$	..	..	$1\frac{1}{2}$	8	12	1	1
Saturday	Men	16	$1\frac{1}{2}$	..	..	..	12	Suet. 12	$1\frac{1}{2}$	$1\frac{1}{2}$
	Women	14	$1\frac{1}{2}$	..	..	..	12	12	1	1

Old people of 60 years of age and upwards may be allowed 1 ounce of tea, 7 ounces of butter, and 8 ounces of sugar per week in lieu of gruel for breakfast, if deemed expedient to make this change.

Children under nine years of age to be dieted at discretion; above nine to be allowed the same quantities as women.

Sick to be dieted as directed by the medical officers.

The giving both gruel and cheese at supper is optional, and the Board of Guardians may discontinue either one or the other at their discretion.

LABOUR AND THE POOR.

THE RURAL DISTRICTS.

[FROM OUR SPECIAL CORRESPONDENT.]

HERTS, BEDS, HUNTS, CAMBRIDGE.

LETTER XXXIX.

The injurious effects of insufficient and unsuitable cottage accommodation for the agricultural labourers, referred to in my last letter, are to be seen not only in the wretchedness of their mode of living, but in many other phases of their physical, social, and moral condition. To this more than anything else, perhaps, is to be ascribed the almost total want of decency, and the low standard of morals, which are found to prevail in agricultural districts. Parents and children—boys and girls of all ages—are indiscriminately huddled together in their sleeping apartments. Not unfrequently one or more lodgers take their place in the promiscuous assemblage. It is impossible that in such a state of things feelings of decency or of modesty can be either nourished or strengthened, and these wretched abodes frequently become the nurseries of vice of the most frightful character. In the agricultural districts of these counties, cases of incest are of frequent occurrence, and numerous cases have come under my own knowledge in which mother and daughter have claimed for their children one and the same father. The number of illegitimate children born in these four counties in the last year of which I have the returns, was 1,231; and to the want of proper feeling induced by the scenes which were constantly occurring in their crowded apartments, is, no doubt, mainly to be attributed this enormous amount of vice. Speaking to several of the unfortunate females who obtained their livelihood by prostitution, as to the causes which had led them to the adoption of their wretched life, I have been struck with the fact that in many cases they belonged to large families, the members of which were in the habit of sleeping together in one crowded apartment. "I had four sisters and three brothers," said one of them to me, "when I left home; my eldest brother was seventeen; there were but two beds on the floor for the children, and we used all to sleep there together, and it is to that, more than anything else, that I can trace my ruin." Another said, "There were four of us, not counting father and mother, that had but one room to sleep in, and we had two lodgers with us for two or three weeks in harvest time, and that was the beginning of wrong with me, though I was only fourteen at the time." A third said, "If it hadn't been that we were all forced to undress ourselves before one another, and five of us to sleep in the same room, I do think—though perhaps that wasn't the only reason—that I should not have been leading the life I now am. If there had been no one else sleeping in the same room, I might perhaps have fallen into this way, but I don't think I should have gone wrong so soon." In several other cases similar statements were made, and in more than one the fearful depravity disclosed was such that I will not shock the reader by stating it.

The vast majority of the evils inseparable from the constant attendance on ale-houses and beer-shops are also in a great measure traceable to the comfortless condition of the labourers' dwellings. It not unfrequently happens that at the close of the day the agricultural labourer betakes himself to the neighbouring pot-house rather than return to his own home. In these places of resort he has a comfortable fire provided for him; he meets with companions for whom, unfortunately, in too many instances, he feels a greater sympathy than for the members of his own family; idle and dissolute habits are contracted, and many a nocturnal depredation upon the hen-roosts and game-preserves is planned within the precincts of such places.

In a former letter I endeavoured to point out the extent to which disease prevails in many of the badly ventilated and overcrowded cottages of the poor in one portion of the county of Cambridge, and I referred incidentally to the expenses incurred by the maintenance of the persons so afflicted. I have before me a return, in connection with the sanitary state of the dwellings of the poorer portion of the population, from which it appears that the annual loss of life from the effects of filthy cottages and bad ventilation is greater than the loss from death or wounds in any wars in which the country has been engaged in modern times. Of the number of persons receiving relief in England, upwards of 43,000 are widows, and not less than 112,000 are orphans. The greater proportion of deaths of the heads of these families occurred from removable causes—the average age at death of these persons being only 45, considerably below the average duration of life. In addition to the expenses incurred by the maintenance of the families and widows of those who have died from removable causes, considerable expense is incurred in the punishment of crimes, many of which have their origin in the condition of the dwellings of the poor—crimes principally of an agrarian character, which are concocted in the alehouse and the beershop. An increase in the comforts of the labourer's home would therefore have the effect of preventing a vast amount of crime of this character, and of reducing the expense incurred in its punishment.

But, in addition to these evils, the younger portion of the population are constantly brought up under noxious physical influences, and they will invariably be found inferior in physical power and general health, as compared with a population reared under more favourable circumstances. Of the great majority of children so circumstanced, it will not be too much to say that they will be found far less susceptible of moral feelings, and the effects of education—should they succeed in obtaining any—will be far less enduring and beneficial, than in the case of a more healthy population. It will not, therefore, be a matter of surprise to any person who may be acquainted with the generally bad and unsuitable character of the labourers' dwellings, that the prevailing characteristics of this portion of the population are improvidence, recklessness, intemperance, ignorance, and sensuality.

Many of the evils which affect the condition of the labourers, as regards their homes, might doubtless be reduced, both in intensity and amount, by the sufferers themselves, if they were disposed to use exertions for that purpose. Who that has seen heaps of manure and other filth close by the door of the cottages, and small stagnant pools of water immediately in front of them, or draining off towards the doors of the hovels, does not feel convinced that these nuisances might be abated if the inmates would only give themselves the trouble of setting about the task? With respect to the interior of the cottages, there are many of them in which the labour of an hour or so would lead to the increased comfort of the inmates. The rough and uneven floors might be made more smooth and level, the walls might be whitewashed, and an outlay of twopence would frequently purchase glass sufficient to supply the place of the broken pane, through which the wind is whistling to the annoyance of the whole family; the cold draughts of air from under and around the doors might be, in some measure, prevented: and a latch on the door would not unfrequently prevent the inconvenience and trouble of placing the table against it to keep it shut. But in the vast majority of cases nothing of the sort is ever attempted, and, most unfortunately, what the occupier fails to do the landlord generally leaves undone. Indeed one would almost imagine from their cottages, that the senses of the labourers were deadened, and that cold affected them not as it does others; and it is only when they are seen shivering over their handful of fire, and heard complaining of the want of it, that one is forced to the conclusion that in this respect they feel as other mortals. Use has, no doubt, enabled many of them to look with apparent unconcern upon the scenes of destitution which surround them. Familiarized with poverty and privations from their youth, they see not the misery, and feel not the wretchedness, of their situation. In their present condition, the great bulk of the labourers can scarcely be said to have any idea of the advantage of a change in their mode of existence, and they appear to be incapable of, and indifferent to, the employment of any means of improvement which may happen to lie even within their reach. Perhaps there is no sense which in the labourer appears more completely obliterated than that of smell. The effluvia from the dung heap, the drain, or the adjoining privy, or the closeness of the room, appear to give them no concern; they will sit, together with their families, unmolested by a stench which, in many cases, has compelled me either to apply my handkerchief to my nose, or hastily to retreat to the door for fresh air. In one case I inquired whether the smell of a dung heap, the steam from which was reeking through the windows, was not offensive to them—the answer I obtained was, "Oh no, we be used to it." There is also, too often, an utter want of cleanliness in their dwellings. There are, it is true, exceptional cases in which the places are kept surprisingly clean and neat, but of the vast majority of them it may be said that they are dirty and wretched in the extreme. "It is useless to try to keep the place clean," said one person to me, "the damp comes up through the floor and in at the door, and mucks everything all over as soon as you've made it a bit tidy; it puts you quite out of heart with the miserable hole, and then when it rains, it all comes down the walls— thick, black, mucky stuff, enough to *pison* you." But while there are improvements, many of which the labourers themselves could accomplish if they were so disposed, there is a large body of occupiers who would be but too happy to effect some substantial change in the character and condition of their dwellings, if it were in their power so to do. Unfortunately they have not the means nor the power of obtaining for themselves these beneficial changes. It is absolutely impossible for such labourers themselves to make such improvements in their cottages as they might wish to see effected, and it would be not only unreasonable but unjust to expect that they should expend any considerable quantity of either time, labour, or money in improving the property of the landlords, if the latter do not themselves evince an interest in the comfort of their tenants. There have been instances in which cottages have been built by the labourers, but they are mostly of a wretched character, and are chiefly to be found in the vicinity of commons and other waste ground. In respect to their cottages, the labourers are generally perfectly helpless, and they must still continue in their wretched and deplorable state, unless they receive the assistance of the wealthy and opulent landowners upon whose estates they reside.

But while there are duties which the landlord has to discharge in the great work of improving the condition of the labourer, there is another class, that of the tenant-farmers, who have duties not less important (though not involving a large outlay of capital) devolving upon them, which, if fulfilled, would be productive of incalculable good. I could refer to several cases which have come under my own knowledge, in which the duty of visiting and encouraging the labourer, and of evincing some sympathy for his condition, has been most grievously neglected. A gentleman, who has paid some considerable attention to the state of the labourer in the county of Bedford, states "that, great as are the efforts which are being made by one noble proprietor in this county, much, very much, remains to be done in this respect by others. A greater degree of sympathy between employer and employed is urgently desired. The exertions of the landlord, in erecting suitable dwellings, must be in a great degree neutralized, if they do not call forth corresponding exertions on the part of the tenant. Without wishing to press this point too severely, it cannot escape observation that whilst the wives of the squire and the clergyman may be found fulfilling their duties, and visiting and encouraging the humble tenants of the cottage, the wives and daughters of the farmers do not take their fair share in this unquestionable duty."

One of the great difficulties with which I have been constantly met by persons who were anxious to improve the condition of their tenantry, is that of building cottages of such a character as to insure a fair return for the outlay, and at the same time afford the necessary convenience to the occupiers. Upon this point I cannot do better than quote a portion of a letter written by the Duke of Bedford to Lord Chichester on the subject of cottage accommodation. "Cottage building," says his Grace, "(except to a cottage speculator who exacts immoderate rents for scanty and defective habitations), is, we all know, a bad investment for money; but this is not the light in which such a subject should be viewed by landlords, from whom it is surely not too much to expect that, while they are building and improving farmhouses, homesteads, and cattle-sheds, they will also build and improve dwellings for their labourers in sufficient number to meet the improved and improving cultivation of the land. To improve the dwellings of the labouring class, and afford them the means of greater cleanliness, health, and comfort in their own homes—to extend education, and thus raise the social and moral habits of these most valuable members of the community, are among the first duties, and ought to be among the truest pleasures, of every landlord. While he thus cares for those whom Providence has committed to his charge, he will teach them that reliance on the exertion of the faculties with which they are endowed is the surest way to their own independence and the well-being of their families. I shall not dwell, as I might do, on the undeniable advantages of making the rural population contented with their condition, and of promoting that mutual goodwill between the landed proprietor and the tenants and labourers on his estate which sound policy and the higher motives of humanity alike recommend." In a statement of the requisites of cottage architecture by Mr. J. C. Loudon, that gentleman concludes by saying, "In general, proprietors ought not to entrust the erection of labourers' cottages on their estates to the farmers, as it is chiefly owing to this practice that so many wretched hovels exist in the best cultivated districts of Scotland, Northumberland, and other parts of the country. No landed proprietor ought to charge more for the land on which cottages are built than he would receive for it from a farmer if let as part of a farm, and no more rent ought to be charged for the cost of building the cottage and enclosing the garden, than the same sum would yield if invested in land, or, at all events, not more than can be obtained by Government securities." These conditions are of course laid down on the supposition, that the intended builder of the cottages is actuated more by feelings of human sympathy than by a desire to make money by the cottages.

Cottage property does not, however, appear to be of so unproductive a character as is very generally supposed. There is no doubt that many speculators in this kind of property receive a much larger return for their money than any other class of owners. From a table appended to a recent sanitary report I have extracted the average cost of the erection of cottages in five of the counties to which my attention has been directed, and I have also calculated the per centage of return for the outlay. The results are given in the following table:—

County.	Average Cost of Erections.		Average Rent per Annum.		Per Centage per Ann. on Outlay.	
	Two Rooms.	Four Rooms.	Two Rooms.	Four Rooms.	Two Rooms.	Four Rooms.
Norfolk	£60	£105	£3 5	£6 0	£5 8	£5 7 0
Suffolk	75	120	4 0	5 10	5 4	4 2 0
Bedford	45	70	4 0	5 10	8 8	7 2 0
Hertford ...	55	85	4 0	6 10	7 2	7 0 6
Northampton	60	100	4 0	6 10	6 6	6 5 0

Of course this does not include any charge for repairs. That is an item which would, however, be represented by a very infinitesimal amount, for if the cottages were well and substantially built—as most of the recent ones have been in these counties—they would require very little repair for some time, beyond what the occupier will be bound to perform, and if they are old ones, or of an inferior character, the owner, in the majority of cases, would decline to incur any expense on account of repairs. The value of the land also is an item which is not taken into account, but after making deductions upon that score there will still be a margin left, which, though not so large as might be desired by the capitalist, is still sufficient to show that cottage property is not altogether valueless.

Many instances have come under my knowledge in which landed proprietors have erected cottages of the most commodious character, which they let at rents which it obviously would not answer the purpose of the speculator to let them for, and which, considering the amount of accommodation given, might be considered as below their actual value; and at the same time, while building new cottages and letting them at low rents, they will not, in order to prevent any increase in the number of fresh settlements, allow more than a certain number to be erected on their estates. The consequence of this is, in cases where they do not possess the whole of the parish or parishes, that the other owners of cottages in the same parish are enabled to obtain a much higher rent than they otherwise would. Mr. Twisleton, in speaking of the existence of this practice, says:—"In such cases the gentleman may be praised for his liberality, and the small owner of cottages censured for his covetousness; but in point of fact the former is, in one sense, the cause of the high rents."

But viewing the question apart entirely from all considerations as to the per centage which the amount of rent paid by the tenant may bear to the outlay of the landlord, the gain which would be effected to the employer of labour, by affording to the labourers suitable and convenient residences, would amply compensate for any deficiency arising from the amount of rent paid for the cottages. In many cases the labourer has to walk several miles to his work, and it is vain to expect that he will be able to perform for his employer such an amount of labour as he would if he had not the additional fatigue of going and returning a long distance to and from his work. In the county of Bedford alone there are 34 parishes in which agricultural labourers have to walk to other parishes to their work. In ten of these the labourers have to walk upwards of four miles, and in the remaining 24 the distance they have to go varies from two to three miles. Many cottages have been erected, which, though built without the expectation of a large return, prove in the results, as shown by an improved tenantry, that the money has been most profitably invested. But whatever may be the advantages, direct or indirect, to the employer, the benefits to the labourer are incalculable. He gains by the additional expenditure which may have been incurred by the landlord upon the external appearance and the internal accommodations of his dwelling. He has the benefit of the good roads in the neighbourhood of the cottage, and of an efficient system of drainage. The closer proximity to his work in which he is placed prevents much exposure to the extremes of wet and cold, and saves him from the additional fatigue which he was wont to undergo in journeying to and from his place of work. Instead of being compelled to take his meals in the neighbouring beer shop, he is enabled to take them at his own home with the other members of his family; and social sympathies are thus strengthened and fostered, instead of his being exposed to the contaminating influence of the beer-shop. The advantages, however, are not confined to the labourer himself, his wife and family are benefited by having constantly before them motives to neatness and cleanliness, in consequence of their living in the immediate neighbourhood of their employer, and being almost constantly exposed to observation; for it will be found an almost invariable rule, that the further the cottages of the poor are removed from public notice, and from the more public roads and thoroughfares, the greater will be the amount of their wretchedness. The chairman of the Bedford Union, whose statement fully and entirely coincides with all that I have heard and seen among the labourers, says, when speaking of the moral effects upon the labourer of improved tenements, "I have much pleasure in saying that some cases of the kind have come under my own observation, and I consider that the improvement has arisen a good deal from the parties feeling that they are somewhat raised in the scale of society. The man sees his wife and family more comfortable, he has a better cottage and garden, he is stimulated to industry, and, as he rises in respectability of station, he becomes aware that he has a character to lose. Thus one important point is gained. Having acquired certain advantages he is anxious to retain and improve them, he strives more to preserve his independence, and becomes a member of benefit, medical, and clothing societies, and frequently, besides this, lays by a certain sum quarterly or half-yearly in the savings bank. Almost always attendant upon these advantages we find the man sending his children to be regularly instructed in a Sunday school, and, where possible, in a day school, and himself and family are more constant in their attendance at some place of worship. I know of more instances than one, where, in consequence of encouragement of the kind above-mentioned to the father of a poor family, the children were regularly sent to school, and there became so much improved in character and learning that they are now filling situations of high respectability (one a confidential clerk in a large mercantile house in London), and are assisting to support their parents in a manner as delightful as it is creditable. A man who comes home to a poor and comfortless hovel after his day's labour, and sees all miserable around him, has his spirits more often depressed than excited by it. He feels that, do his best, he will be miserable still, and is too apt to fly for a temporary refuge to the ale-house or beer-shop. But give him the means of making himself comfortable by his own industry, and I am convinced by experience that in many cases he will avail himself of it."

In the decennial period between 1831 and 1841, the number of houses in these four counties increased in a greater ratio than the population. In 1831, the average number of persons to each house was 5.3 in each of the four counties. In Cambridgeshire and Huntingdonshire, the number was reduced in 1841 to 4.9, in Bedfordshire to 5.08, and in Hertfordshire to 5.2. The following table will show the population of each county, the number of inhabited houses, and the proportion of persons to each in the periods referred to:—

Counties.	Years.	Inhabited Houses.	Population.	Proportion to each House.
Bedford	1831	17,978	95,483	5.3
	1841	21,235	107,936	5.08
Cambridge ...	1831	26,712	143,955	5.3
	1841	33,095	164,459	4.9
Hertfordshire ..	1831	26,549	143,341	5.3
	1841	30,155	157,207	5.2
Huntingdonshire	1831	9,990	53,192	5.3
	1841	11,860	58,549	4.9

In the several counties in which my inquiries have been made, I have always felt a pleasure in recording any instance of individual exertions for the improvement of the condition of the labourer which may have come under my knowledge. The exertions of the Duke of Bedford in improving the condition of the dwellings of the labourers on various parts of his estates, and more particularly in the county of Bedford, have been, and still are, of the most extensive and admirable character. Impressed with a sense of his high responsibilities as a landlord, as evinced in the extract from a letter to Lord Chichester which I have previously quoted, he has, for upwards of three years, endeavoured to carry out an improved system of replacing the decayed and miserable dwellings on his property by others calculated to induce in the labourers higher notions of decency and comfort; and "he has, by so doing," says the Rev. C. Hartshorn, "given to the labouring classes an opportunity of proving upon whom the blame of bad habits for the most part rests, and it is not stating too much to say that already a visible preference has been shown for neatness, cleanliness, and decent habits, among all those who have been thus placed in habitations where the existence of such an amendment in their moral and domestic economy can be displayed."

The necessity which existed for carrying out upon a large scale a liberal system of cottage building will be best learned from the statement of the Duke himself. "My inquiries," said his Grace, "into the condition of the cottages on my Bedfordshire and Devonshire estates led me to the conclusions—first, that notwithstanding a very considerable annual expenditure upon them, many of them were so deficient in requisite accommodation as to be inadequate to the removal of that acknowledged obstacle to the improvement of the morals and habits of agricultural labourers, which consists in the want of separate bed-rooms for grown-up boys and girls; and, secondly, that the practice of taking in lodgers had led to still further evils among the labourers. The improved methods of cultivation, extensive draining operations, and general improvement in husbandry, requiring as they did additional hands, which are going on more or less in all parts of the country, the breaking up of inferior grass lands, and the conversion of woodland into tillage—especially since the passing of the Tithe Commutation Act—by giving work to many more labourers than were formerly employed, have caused a proportionate augmentation of their numbers, and consequently an increased want of cottage accommodation. To meet this increased want, and at the same time to improve the habitations of the labourers, I determined to re-build the worst of my cottages, and also to add to their number in those parts of my estate in which it appeared necessary so to do. I therefore directed my surveyor to prepare a series of plans of cottages suitable for families of different sizes and descriptions, and sufficient to satisfy the reasonable wants of the labourers and their families; and to be so constructed as that, avoiding all needless expense, the cottages should be substantial, and not liable to premature decay, or likely to require costly repair." In pursuance of these directions, plans were prepared by Mr. Hacker, the architect to his Grace, and during the years 1846-7-8, fifty-two cottages were erected according to his plans; in the course of last year not less than fifty-three; and instructions have now been given to build not less than 800 cottages in different parts of the Duke's estates.

Before proceeding to describe the character of the newly erected cottages and the condition of their tenants, I will endeavour to give the reader some description of the large establishment at Woburn-park, for the manufacture of every requisite for cottage building. An extensive quadrangular pile of buildings encloses the farm-buildings and the workshops, with its "office of works" and other appropriate offices. A roadway separates the agricultural from the manufacturing portion of the buildings. To the part devoted to agricultural purposes I referred in a former letter. In the centre, then, of one of these extensive ranges of buildings is the engine-house of the manufactories, with its tall chimney, opposite to which the chimney of the engine-house of the farm-buildings rears its head. The union here presented of the two interests which it has almost become a fashion to consider as rivals—agriculture and manufactures—is at once pleasing and instructive. The whole range of buildings, situated in a declivity, and surrounded with portions of arable and pasture lands, ornamental grounds, and thick shrubberies—the tall chimneys peering above the tops of the trees, pouring forth their wreathed volumes of smoke in the clear blue sky and springing up, as it were, from the midst of a stack-yard stored with agricultural produce—the noise of the various agricultural machines set in motion by the steam-engine, one employed in thrashing, others in chaff and turnip cutting, and in pumping water for the cattle; on the opposite side the noise of the saw-mill with its seven-bladed saw, worked by the second engine, and cutting up whole trunks, as if with the fury of a savage; the lathes engaged in turning different articles of wood and iron, and which, connected with innumerable bands, cranks, and axles, perform with perfect regularity almost any kind or amount of work which may be required; the sonorous sounds of the anvils of the smiths, the continuous clang of hammers in the carpenters' shops, and the chisel of the mason; the lowing of cattle, the bleating of sheep, the squeaking of pigs, and the chirping of birds; farming men in their smock-frocks; men with their teams, boys in their jerkins; painters, plumbers, and plasterers, in their respective costumes; the stoker black at the furnace, the engineer oily at his engine, and some two dozen of staid and demure-looking clerks, each busily engaged in his respective department— constitute together a scene which, whether for the novelty of its contrasts, or the interest which it is calculated to excite in the mind, is without a rival either in the more secluded agricultural districts, or in the more busy and populous seats of manufacture. The manufacturing engine, if it may be so termed—which, from its extreme beauty and the lightness of its construction, might be almost termed a model engine—is of 25-horse power. The furnace is almost entirely fed with pine-blocks, cut from the extensive woods at Woburn. A saw-mill, which, at the time of my visit, was, as I have said, working with seven blades, is constantly sawing the timber into blocks for the furnace, or into deals and boards of different thicknesses, as they may be required. In an adjoining-room is a powerful lathe, which is used for boring iron pump-barrels for the cottages in course of erection, or about to be erected. In the next department were sixty or seventy carpenters engaged in planing flooring boards, and in making doors, window sashes, and other articles for the cottages. The plumbers were at work on buckets for the pumps, preparing lead for the roofs, and pipes for the water. Smiths were at work in making ranges; and in the yard a number of masons were busily employed in fashioning into shape huge masses of stone. In addition to the workshops, there were a variety of store rooms for all kinds of materials—paint, glass, locks, bolts, handles, and every sort of ironmongery. Each department possesses its own establishment of clerks and superintendents; the whole being under the management of Mr. Hacker, the architect and engineer to his Grace. Upwards of 200 persons were employed in the different kinds of occupation relating to cottage building. Everything connected with the cottages is made or manufactured upon the estate, from the foundation to the chimney-pots, with the exception of the black Staffordshire tiles for the flooring. In my next I shall give some description of the cottages themselves.

LABOUR AND THE POOR.

———◆———

THE RURAL DISTRICTS.

[FROM OUR SPECIAL CORRESPONDENT.]

HERTS, BEDS, HUNTS, CAMBRIDGE.
THE COTTAGES OF THE DUKE OF BEDFORD.

LETTER XL.

Having in previous letters shown the necessity which exists for the improvement of, and increase in, the number of the dwellings of the labouring classes, and the efforts which have been made to meet the exigencies of the case, I intend, in the present letter, to refer more particularly to the exertions made in this respect by his Grace the Duke of Bedford, upon his estates in that county.

The cottages which have already been built are situated in several parts of the county of Bedford, at Cople Houghton, Regis, Millbrook, Ampthill, and at Woburn. At the latter place twenty-two have been built during the last year, the whole of which are inhabited. At one place in the town called "Brig-yard," there existed, up till a very recent period, a block of about a dozen cottages, of a most dilapidated character, which were not, however, the property of the Duke of Bedford. These have recently been purchased by the duke, and have been pulled down, and it is proposed to build new cottages in their stead, upon the same plan as those already erected in Woburn and other places, and which I will now proceed to describe. One of the rows of cottages which I visited was in the Leighton-road, just outside the town of Woburn, having a frontage towards the road. They are built in groups, or blocks, of four, five, and six cottages each, and at different elevations; the effect of their being so distributed is remarkably pleasing, and they present altogether a most attractive appearance. The designs of the cottages, although varying in some of their details, are generally of a plain Gothic character. Although an ornamental style is one which will probably not be expected to be indulged in by those who may feel it their duty to erect cottages for their labourers—the far

more important points to bear in mind being those of affording sufficient light, ventilation, and convenience—still, without overlooking
in the slightest degree these necessary requirements, these cottages
present a most attractive and picturesque appearance. Speaking of
the architectural details of these cottages, the Rev. C. H. Hartshorne,
President of the Northamptonshire Agricultural Society, says—"The
proportions are, without exception, satisfactory and just, the outlines
are undulating and broken; they show that much care has been bestowed to produce constant variety of elevation—a task requiring the
most consummate skill, where everything must come in its proper
place, every room receive its due share of light and ventilation, and
where only three rooms can be admitted into the formula for regulating the laws of permutation. Still they are diversified, especially
at Millbrook, by hooded porches, with single and cross loops, gables
projecting fifteen inches, eaves twelve, pendants, hip knobs, barges
floated in cement, rafters with moulded feet, water tabling, resting
on herring-boned bricks, rounded coigns, chimneys rising seven feet
above the ridge, panels and chequers of different coloured bricks,
formed both of the mild porous clay of Ampthill and of the stiff gault
from Marston Morteyne." The whole group has the appearance of being what they were intended to be—labourers' cottages; while there
is an absence of all meretricious ornament, there is, at the same time,
an air of lightness, comfort, and convenience about them which could
scarcely be supposed attainable in buildings of this kind. The cottages
are built of a red kind of brick, which is made in the neighbourhood;
the walls of the cottages are a brick and a half thick, and the edges
being rounded off at the doorways, give a neat and finished appearance to the buildings. One or two of the cottages are constructed with
hollow brick walls, and are supplied with tubes worked in the walls
close to the chimneys, for the purpose of diffusing the air in a rarefied
state throughout the whole of the building. The mention of "hollow
walls," "tubes," and "rarefied air," is calculated to convey the idea of an
enormous increase of expenditure. Not so, however; the contrivance
is perfectly simple, and what is more, effects a saving of twenty-five
per cent. on the brickwork. A slight increase of expense is incurred in
consequence, in the carpenters' work in the roofing, but to so small
an extent that it is scarcely worth mentioning. The front doors of
the cottages are grained to imitate dark oak. The roofs are of plain
tiles, with Staffordshire rolled edges. The window frames are formed
of cast-iron, painted of a lead colour, and contain small diamond-

shaped compartments for the glass. These lights or windows, from their being constructed of cast-iron, are far less liable to get out of repair than if made of lead; they are perfectly air and water tight, and are not liable to be bulged out by internal thrusts. Each block of cottages is supplied with iron spouting, and conducting pipes, connected with drains made water tight with cement, which lead to a large cemented tank sunk in the ground, capable of holding 5,000 gallons of rain water—sufficient, indeed, to last throughout the driest of summers. "We've never been without rain water yet," said one of the inmates of these cottages, "ever sin' I've been here, and I calculate that I save at least twopence a week for soap, through using it, instead of the hard spring water." In addition to the rain or soft water tank, each block or group of cottages is provided with a well of hard or spring water. An iron pump is connected with the well and the tank by two different suction-pipes, and is provided with two handles, one of which draws the hard, the other the soft water. The waste water from the sinks in the houses is conveyed by water-tight drains to a large cesspool or manure tank, at a distance from the houses. The covering to this can be removed at any time, and the cottagers have in turn the advantage of using the sewage thus collected on their gardens and allotments, which are in immediate proximity to the tanks.

The gardens in front of the cottages at Woburn are necessarily somewhat small, as the amount of frontage in the neighbourhood of a town is a matter of some consideration. They are, however, well stocked with flowers, herbs, cabbages, and other vegetables. There are no walls or fences in the front to separate a portion of the ground belonging to one of the cottagers from that of his neighbour. Where they are all honest, industrious and sober, as they appear to be here, such divisions are not wanting, and the ground, thus left open and uninclosed, instead of being divided into a number of small and uniform quadrangular spaces, has an appearance of extent and comfort which it would not otherwise possess. The yards at the backs of the houses are divided by low fences, and sockets are sunk in the ground, four on each side of the garden, to receive posts to which lines are attached for the drying of clothes. At the bottom of each garden, under the same roof, though in different compartments, is a wood and coal house, or barn, a place for the ashes, and a privy. Everything calculated to promote habits of cleanliness and of order has been attended to. In order to avoid the dirt which would be made by carrying wood or coals through the house to the barn, a roadway is constructed at the back for the purpose of allowing the fuel to be deposited at once from the carts into the barns. In the other cottages at Cople and the other places, there are, in addition to the compartments in the outbuildings, comfortable styes for the pigs of each cottager, and a spacious oven for the use of the inmates of each group of cottages. In Woburn, in consequence of the nuisance which it would cause, the tenants are not allowed to keep pigs, and they have no oven except one in their ranges, since they are not under the necessity of making their own bread, as is the case in some of the villages.

Having thus taken a survey of the general plan and arrangement of the cottages, together with their external appearance, I will request the reader to accompany me inside one of them, where one of the inmates—a bustling, active, middle-aged woman—will give us a cordial welcome, and act as our *Cicerone* over the place. We shall first enter into the sitting-room, the floor of which consists of black Staffordshire tiles, and the first thing which strikes the visitor will be the perfect cleanliness and order of the apartment. A milk-white muslin curtain hangs at the small window, the glass of which is without a smear or a speck of dirt; the walls of the room are as white as whitewash can make them and as dusting can keep them; the small range is highly polished with black lead, and the brasses glisten again with the fire; the hearth has been just whitened, the candlesticks on the mantelpiece newly burnished, and the thousand-and-one little nick-nacks in the shape of ornaments are settled in their appropriate places. It is about dinner time; the husband is expected home, and seven plates and a dish are placed before the fire to be warmed ready for dinner; a clean white table-cloth is on the table, and a little girl, eleven years of age, who has just laid aside her straw plait, is placing the well-cleaned knives and forks in order round the table; two other children are playing in the yard, and the other two will be home from school presently. "Oh, come in," says the busy little inmate of the cottage, "don't be afeard; and I'm not afeard, neyther, of any one coming in to see my place now, as I used to be afore I come here, though I wish you'd a come some other day, when I wasn't so littery, but you must take it as you find it, you know Saturday is always our cleaning-up day. 'Comfortable cottages?' Indeed they are; they're just the things for poor people like we. Lor, sir, if you'd only a seen we before we came here you would have seen a difference; we were up to our very noses in dirt and muck—now it's our own faults if we're so; but you know where there's a large family like ours it's not easy to keep things as we'd like. I've got five children; that's my eldest; she do a little at the straw plait, but not very much; my husband's at work in the farm, and he arnes ten shilling a week. 'Floor dry?' Why, yes, it's as dry as can be, always, in wet weather and all. We're obliged to whitewash the walls once a year; there ain't no plaster on 'em, you see, and I didn't like 'em at first so; but when I thought of how it used to fall down in the other old place, I thought it were a good job that we hadn't none of it here. The Duke's very partickler; he won't let us knock so much as a nail in the walls. It's a great blessing to the poor people that he's built these cottages, and I says, God bless him for it; that's what I says, and I'm sure the other people does so too. The little range we pays for at so much a week; here's the biler, and here's the oven. Oh, yes! we can get a bit of meat sometimes; here's a bit of pork. I expect my husband home presently to dinner. We get meat oftener now than we used to do afore we came here. I don't know how it is, but we do. My husband don't go to the beer-shop so much as he did, and he has more constant work, and the rent is not so much as we were forced to pay afore. Here's our little pantry, where we keeps our victual— shooks and shelves and all in it; and these windows at the top is some stuff—I don't know what they call it (zinc), and it is all full of little holes—see! that keeps it as cool and as nice as can be. (Three or four of the upper squares of the window of the pantry are filled with perforated zinc, instead of glass, and it is to the means of ventilation thus afforded that the poor woman alludes.) Here's the washhouse, where we does little odd things now and then—washing up plates—where we does the washing too; and here's the sink, where all the dirty water runs away to the great hole out there. Here's a copper and a dresser, and pegs for hats and 'that like.'"

From the lower rooms we will now proceed to the chambers, or sleeping apartments, noticing the stairs—for who can help it—leading up to the bedrooms; they will be found as clean and as white as it is possible for boards to appear. The floor of the bedrooms corresponds to the stairs; there are some homely-looking blue curtains around one of the bedsteads, which, as well as the bedclothes, are remarkably clean; the two other bedrooms—for there are three in the house—contain beds for the children. In one of the rooms only is there a fire-place, the other rooms being ventilated by means of a small orifice in the ceiling, partially covered with perforated zinc; there is a window to each room, and a separate entrance also to each of them. "My husband and me sleeps in that room," says our guide, "with the youngest girl, the two t'others sleep in this room, and the others here; so you see we're not obliged to pig altogether as we were in t'other place. Oh! that was a hole of a place. There were but one room in it for us all to sleep in, and it were under the thatch, and the walls used to be as wet as wet, in wet weather. We couldn't open the window there neyther, for if we did, we couldn't shut it again, and there was always a nasty close kind of smell with it. There isn't none of that here, is there? Sniff, so—don't be afeard," showing us at the same time how, by drawing in the air by our nostrils, we could detect the presence of anything impure in the atmosphere. "It's wonderful," continues our contented and somewhat loquacious guide, "what things people do invent now-a-days. They'd never ha' thought in my younger days of such a contrivance as that," pointing to the ventilator in the ceiling, "for giving fresh air to the room, but it does, though, even when you can't open the window. In the most brilingest weather it helps to keep the room cool, that it do. We never were so comfortable in our lives as we are now. We've got a nice lot of ground at the back, and we mucks it from the cesspool. It didn't do very well last year, because the ground was rather new; it will do better this year, I dare say. The rent we pays is sixteenpence a-week."

It may perhaps be thought, that in the description of this cottage I have taken an exceptional case, and one which may not be considered a fair sample of the condition of the tenants. It is, however, by no means a selected case; and I could refer, if necessary, to the whole of the other cottages which I visited as affording abundant proof that the exertions of his Grace to improve and to elevate the condition of the labourers on his estates in Bedfordshire have been attended with signal success, and rewarded with the warmest gratitude of those who have been the objects of his solicitude.

The cottages are built of various sizes—some consisting of two rooms, for aged or married persons without families—three rooms for persons of small families—and four for those of larger families. Extra three-bed-roomed cottages are also built for persons who may require such an amount of accommodation. None of the tenants are allowed to take in lodgers without the consent of the steward. In order, how-ever, to provide accommodation for single young men and others who may require lodgings, plans of several lodging-houses have been pre-pared, and it is proposed to erect several of them. They will contain six or eight rooms for lodgers, and two separate apartments for the person having the management of the house. The convenience of the lodgers will be as much studied in the erection of these lodging-houses as in those of the other kind of cottages already alluded to. Each apartment will be separate, and contain everything necessary to cleanliness and comfort.

The terms upon which the cottages are let may be best learned from the agreement which is signed by each of the tenants upon taking possession, and of which the following is a copy:—

"......, ..., of ...., in the county of Bedford, ... acknowledge that I hold of the Duke of Bedford the cottage in ...., in the said county, late in the occupation of ...., and now occupied by me, together with its yard, barn, and garden, and the right of pumping water from the tanks or wells, and depositing ashes in the ashpit respectively appropriated for the said cottage and .... other cottages, from the .... day of ...., one thousand eight hundred and .... from week to week, at the weekly rent of .... upon and subject to the following conditions—

"All taxes and rates (except land tax and property tax) to be paid by the tenant.

"The tenant at his expense to provide, and the landlord to fix, a three feet oven and boiler range in the living room, and an eighteen inch washing copper with its ironwork complete in the washhouse.

"The landlord to provide lime for limewhiting, and the tenant to properly scrape and limewhite the inside of the cottage throughout, once in every year at the least.

"The windows and pumps to be kept in repair by the landlord; and the cost of the repair of the windows, and a .... part of the cost of the repair of the pumps, to be repaid by the tenant to the landlord within one week after payment thereof shall be demanded by the landlord's agent.

"The tenant to clear out the privy once in six months.

"The tenant to clear out the ashpit once every .... weeks, the tenants of the said .... other cottages doing so in the intermediate weeks.

"The tenant to sweep the chimneys twice a year.

"Not to carry on any trade or business in the premises.

"Not to keep .... poultry, or underlet or take a lodger, without leave, in writing, from the landlord's agent.

"Dated this .... day of .... 18......   Witness,"

The rent is calculated at three per cent. on the outlay, and varies from 1s. to 1s. 6d. per week. A two-roomed cottage is 1s., three-roomed 1s. 2d., four rooms 1s. 4d., extra size four rooms 1s. 6d. According to this calculation, it would appear that a two-roomed cottage, which lets for 1s. per week, costs £86; a three-roomed, let at 1s. 2d., about £100; a four-roomed, at 1s. 4d., £116; and an extra size four-roomed cottage, let at 1s. 6d. per week, about £130.

Many persons who might be disposed to follow in the footsteps of his Grace, in improving the condition of the cottages of the peasantry, may very naturally ask at what expense have all these benefits been obtained? The answer to the question presents at first some difficulty. Nearly the whole of the materials of these cottages were produced or manufactured upon the premises of the duke. The bricks were made from his own land, the iron-work was manufactured in his workshops. They were built from the designs of his own architect, and by workmen paid by himself. These are advantages which probably do not come within the reach of every person who may be disposed to act in a similar manner. The nearest approximation to the cost of the cottages is, however, to be obtained from the amount of rent paid by the cottagers; but the price of labour and the value of materials will vary considerably in different parts of the country. In order, however, to furnish the necessary data for building cottages upon the same plan as those at Woburn and elsewhere, the Duke of Bedford has caused plans of the different styles of cottages, with the details of the various quantities required in their construction, to be printed for the benefit of those who may wish to profit by his experience. In a letter accompanying the plans which he presented to the Royal Agricultural Society, his Grace says, "The experience obtained in erecting the new cottages already built on my estate has enabled my surveyor to ascertain the quantities of each kind of material required for the construction, *separately,* of the cottages shown in these plans; and in the hope that this information may be useful to others, I have directed these quantities to be put in detail upon the plans. I have deemed it best not to have the prices added, as they vary in different localities; and to furnish, therefore, the prices of one locality would be useless, and might mislead. The quantities being given, it will be easy to add the prices they bear in other places in which the erection of cottages according to these plans may be desired. As the cottages of many landed proprietors may be, and probably are in a state similar to my own, it appears to me that the information founded on actual experience, which I have obtained on the subject of cottage building, may be acceptable and generally useful." Fully concurring in the opinion of his Grace as to the benefits to be derived from his extensive experience, I shall conclude the present letter with some of the details of the quantities used in cottages recently built by him.

The first table of quantities refers to a block of three cottages—the centre one with two bedrooms, the two others containing three bedrooms each, with the quantities included in the outbuildings, ash-pit, oven, well, pump, pigstye, copper, pantry, and dresser.

QUANTITIES FOR HOUSES.

38,830 building bricks
56 quarters lime
58 loads sand
10 bushels cement
3,190 6-in. paving squares
12,150 plain tiles
374 valley tiles
69 18-in. ridge tiles
21 bundles tiling laths
29 bundles plastering laths
2 cwt. 2 qrs. hair
6 small scrapers and stones
3 York sinks, with grates, waste pipes, and traps
$245\frac{1}{2}$ feet cube fir
2 feet cube oak
$65\frac{1}{4}$ 12-ft. 3 by 9-in. deals
3 solid door cases and ledged with hinges, latches, and bolts
3 ditto and ditto with hinges, latches, and stock-locks

6 small one-light solid window frames, with iron quarry lights to open, glazed, complete
4 one-light window frames, and ditto
10 two-light ditto, one each, to open, and ditto
2 three-light ditto, one each, to open, and ditto
Nails and screws
20 pairs cross garnett hinges
20 thumb-latches
36 iron cloak pins
10 chimney pots
4 bedroom stoves, fixed, complete
3 kitchen ditto and ditto
157 feet iron gutter and down pipes, fixed, complete
1 cwt. 2 qrs. paint
Labour
Cartage

QUANTITIES FOR OUTBUILDINGS, &C.

20,500 building bricks
24 qrs. lime
27 lds. sand
30 bus. cement
420 6-in. paving squares
10 12-in. oven   do.
6,950 plain tiles
160 12-in. shell drain tiles
133 18-in.   drain pipes, 6-ins. diam.
28 18-in. ridge tiles
8 1-3 bun. tiling laths
3 York man-hole stones
6 do. door-cills
6 prs. do. hook-stones, with iron hooks
6 do.   catch-stones, with iron catches
75-ft. cube fir
2 1-3 12-ft. 3 by 9-in. deal
3 small louvre frames
3 do. piggery feeding doors, with hinges, hasps, and staples

3 ledged piggery doors, with hook hinges only, and hasps and staples
3 do. privy-doors, with hinges, latches, and bolts
4 do. outer-doors, with hook hinges only, latches, and stock-locks
8 fencing posts, 3 ft. out of ground
8 drying posts, 7 ft. ditto
16 leng. rails and palings, 3 ft. high
2 hand gates, with hinges and latches
Nails and screws
1 oven-door and frame
3 com. closet apparatus, with supply cisterns, and service from pump to each
1 double pump, with suctions to draw from well and tank
2 qrs. paint
Labour
Cartage

The next table gives the quantities for a row of six cottages, with three bedrooms in each:—

QUANTITIES FOR HOUSES.

70,150 building bricks
99 qrs. lime
104 loads sand
20 bushels cement
6,540 6-inch paving squares
25,725 plain tiles
917 valley tiles
150 18-inch ridge tiles
45 bundles tiling laths
50 do. plastering do.
3 cwt. 1 qr. hair
12 small scrapers and stones
6 York sinks, with grates, waste pipes, and traps
668 feet cube fir
$4\frac{1}{2}$ feet cube oak
99½ 12-feet 3 by 9-inch deals
6 solid door-cases and ledged doors with hinges, thumb-latches, and bolts

6 ditto and ditto, with hinges, thumb-latches, and stock-locks
12 small solid window-frames, with iron quarry-lights, to open, glazed, complete
24 two-light window-frames, and ditto one, each to open
4 three-light window-frames, and ditto
Nails and screws, &c.
36 pairs cross garnett hinges
36 thumb-latches
72 iron cloak pins
18 chimney-pots
6 bedroom stoves, fixed, complete
277 feet iron gutter and down-pipe ditto
3 cwt. 1 qr. paint
Labour
Cartage

QUANTITIES FOR OUTBUILDINGS, &C.

34,800 building bricks
40 qrs. lime
46 lds. sand
40 bus. cement
720 6-in. paving squares
10 12-in. oven ditto
10,940 plain tiles
545 12-in. shell drain tiles
217 18-in. drain pipes, 6 ins. diam.
120 18-in. ridge tiles
16 bun. tiling laths
3 York man-hole stones
12 ditto door cills
12 prs. hook-stones, with iron hooks
12 catch-stones, with iron catches
302½ ft. cube fir
4 2-3 12-ft. 3 by 9-in. deals
6 small solid louvre frames
6 ditto piggery feeding doors, with hinges, hasps, and staples
6 ledged privy-doors, with hinges, latches, and bolts
6 ledged piggery-doors, with hook-hinges only, and hasps and staples
6 ledged outer doors, with hook-hinges only, latches, and stock-locks
28 fencing posts, 3 ft. out of ground
14 drying posts, 7 ft. out of ground
39 leng. rails and palings, 3 ft. high
6 hand gates, with hinges and latches
Nails, screws, &c.
1 oven-door and frame
1 double pump, with suctions to draw from well and tank
6 common closet apparatus, with supply-cistern and service from pump to each
3 qrs. 14 lbs. paint
Labour
Cartage

LABOUR AND THE POOR.

THE RURAL DISTRICTS.

[FROM OUR SPECIAL CORRESPONDENT.]

HERTS, HUNTS, BEDS, AND CAMBRIDGE.

LETTER XLI.

In a former Letter I referred incidentally to the extent to which opium is consumed among the labouring classes in the Isle of Ely. There is, probably, no habit which, in any part of these counties, has taken a deeper root among the labouring classes than has that of opium-eating in the districts where it prevails. This practice is at present confined almost exclusively to the fen districts of the county of Hunts and the Isle of Ely; in the high lands of those parts the custom prevails but to a very limited extent.

The practice is one which has grown up within a comparatively short period—the principal reason which I have heard assigned for it being the great extent to which persons are afflicted with rheumatic affections in the fen districts. In order to procure some little alleviation, numbers of the poor people have had recourse to opium as a means of lulling or of making them insensible to their pain. From those who had recourse to the drug medicinally as it were, the practice of taking opium has gradually spread to others who were anxious only to enjoy the temporary stimulant which it afforded. To such an extent is opium used in the district, that one druggist in Ely informed me that the average annual quantity sold by him for the last few years had not been less than 3 cwt. per annum. From two other druggists in the same place I learned that the quantity sold by them was not less than 80 or 90 lbs. in the year. In the town of St. Ives, one druggist informed me that he sold about 2½ cwt. in the year. In Wisbeach and Chatteris the quantity consumed is considerably more than in either of these towns, but I was not able to obtain any information as to the quantity sold in either of these places. In Whittlesea, also, the consumption of the drug is very large. "You may set it down," said a druggist to whom I was speaking on the subject, "as a ton weight per year for the fen parts of Huntingdon and the Isle of Ely." In New-market there is not more than one-eighth of the quantity consumed, as compared with Ely, and in Soham not more than a tenth. "My present stock of laudanum," said a druggist in Ely, "is forty gallons, and I never keep a less stock than that by me. I generally make my own laudanum; it takes 1 lb. 4 oz. of opium to make two gallons of laudanum, but I use only 1 lb. 2 oz. to the two gallons, the other 2 oz. being made up of certain *addenda* to render it more palatable to the people." The same druggist who informed me that he sold 2½ cwt. at St. Ives, told me that half a cwt. was sold as laudanum, the remaining 2 cwt. being consumed in its raw state.

The trade in opium is one which has increased very rapidly during the last few years, and the price has also fallen very considerably. A few years since, the price of laudanum was 6d. per oz., and of opium 2s. 3d. The present price of laudanum is in Ely 3d. per oz., in St. Ives 4d.; of opium, 1s. 4d. per oz. in Ely, and 1s. 6d. in Wisbeach. One great cause of the extent to which the drug is used is its comparative cheapness as compared with ardent spirits; the same effects may be obtained, I was informed, from a pennyworth of opium as from a shilling's worth of spirituous liquors. Indeed there is very little spirits drunk in these parts, for the opium appears to have almost entirely superseded it, and so deeply has the practice taken root among the people that the drug has come to be considered by them almost as an article of necessity. The more respectable of the labouring classes adopt as much secrecy as possible with respect to opium eating. It is a solitary vice, and is indulged in for the pure love of the effects which the narcotic drug produces. Many of the labourers or their wives, when they go to the shops to purchase it, state "that it is for the pigs, as they fat better when they're kept from crying." One plan very usu-ally adopted by them to avoid its being known what quantity they are in the habit of taking, is that of going to different shops alternately to purchase it. In too many cases, however, all sense of decency is en-tirely destroyed. While I was in one of the druggists' shops in Ely, a woman came in and asked for a pennyworth of laudanum. The quant-ity was weighed out, and she drank it off with the utmost unconcern. I was informed that many persons are in the habit of going to the shop, taking their pennyworth of opium or laudanum, and then calling for a pennyworth of alcohol, which is 56 degrees above proof; and this they swallow immediately after, to take away, as they say, the taste of the laudanum. The usual quantity taken by elderly women—who are principally the greatest opium-eaters—is 30 grains per day, that being a pennyworth. Many of them, however, will take considerably more than that. "Several persons," said a druggist at St. Ives to me, "have come into my shop and swallowed off at once two scruples of opium. I have been really frightened to see them take it in such quantities, I thought it would have killed them. When they came into the shop I have seen them look very bad, and have asked them if they were used to take it in such large doses, and they have said, 'Oh, yes!' But I certainly thought, by the ravenous way in which they took it out of the box, that they wanted to poison themselves." I was told of the case of one old woman at Wisbeach who was never content with less than ninety-six grains of opium in the day. There are several persons in Ely, who were formerly in a respectable position, but who have been reduced to the greatest possible distress through having fallen victims to this wretched habit. "Sir," said one of these persons to me, "I can't live without it; we have pawned everything and sold everything that we can lay our hands on to get it. There's such a craving for it that we can't get over, and it's hopeless to try to do without it. A little while ago a friend who knew us in better days gave us decent clothes, but before we'd had 'em three days they were all pawned. It's no use, we can't live without it." The opium that is principally consumed is the Turkey or East India drug; the Chinese opium is not so generally liked by the people; and they have also an objection to buying it when it is very hard; they prefer it "damped" or made soft, as they can more easily make it up into pills, in which form it is usually taken. Confirmed opium-eaters may be distinguished with the greatest ease, by the cadaverous and unhealthy appearance of their complexions, the filthiness and slovenliness of their persons and attire, their total disregard of everything appertaining to decency in their habits, and the dirty and disgusting character of their dwellings.

But the consumption of opium is not confined to the adult portion of the population, nor is it merely in its crude state, or as laudanum, that this drug is taken. The quantity of opium which is consumed in the shape of Godfrey's Cordial is incredible. "How many ounces of Godfrey do I sell in a week? Ask how many gallons of it are sold," said a druggist with whom I was conversing on the subject; "it is sold by the pailful about here." "If you want to reduce the rate of infant mortality in Ely," said another druggist, "you must make a common sewer to drain the place of Godfrey and paregoric, which are given to the little creatures to a frightful extent. I have frequently told the people not to give their children so much of it. I have even in some cases turned them away, without supplying them with the article." Each druggist appears to have his peculiar recipe for making Godfrey; they vary a little in some respects, but the proportion of opium is about the same in all cases. One ounce of Godfrey generally contains about a grain of opium, being about the strength of paregoric. Water, sweetened with treacle, a little aniseed, cloves, or peppermint water, are generally the other ingredients. One person gave me the following as the proportions used by him:—

> 1 drachm of essence of peppermint.
> 4 drachm of tincture of opium.
> 12 oz. of treacle dissolved in a pint of water.

When under the influence of this mixture, the children lie in a perfectly torpid state for hours together. "The young 'uns all lay about on the floor," said one woman to me who was in the habit of dosing her children with it, "like dead 'uns, and there's no bother with 'em. When they cry we gives 'em a little of it—p'raps half a spoonful, and that quiets 'em; sometimes when they're hungry, and the victuals isn't ready for 'em, we gives 'em a drop too." A sufficient dose of Godfrey for a child of three or six months old "to begin with," would be, I was told, "about fifteen minims." About harvest time the quantity of this mixture which is sold is considerably more than at any other season of the year; it is then given to the children to keep them quiet while the parents are at work, many of whom are in the habit of leaving a number of children in the care of some person while they are absent. "I always take care," said a young girl of about fourteen, who had been employed on several occasions to take charge of a number of children in the absence of their parents, "that they leave me plenty of 'stuff,' 'cause then, when they begins to cry, or gets troublesome, I shoves some of it in their mouths, and that stops 'em." During the period of gleaning the quantity sold is even greater than during the time of the harvest, as every person who is able to glean is anxious to get out into the fields. The children are then in many cases left without any person in charge of them, a sufficient quantity being given by the parents to keep them in a state of stupor till they return home. It appears that the habit, once commenced with children, is rarely or never discontinued; the moment the child recovers from its temporary stupefaction, it feels uneasy, and begins to cry; recourse is again had to the deleterious compound—the state of torpor again succeeds, to be followed again by the same treatment, to the almost total neglect of proper and nourishing diet—till nature can bear up no longer against the barbarous practice. "It is my firm belief," said a medical gentleman of St. Ives, "that hundreds of children are killed in this district by the quantities of opium which are administered to them in the shape of Godfrey's and other cordials." The practice of taking the drug is one that is never adopted by the Irish labourers who arrive in these parts to assist in the harvest. Several of the druggists informed me that they never remembered a single instance in which Irish labourers had purchased either opium, laudanum, paregoric, or "Godfrey"—but of tobacco they consumed large quantities.

Another practice, which almost by necessity in many cases exists among the labourers, is that of frequent attendance at the beer-shop. Vast numbers of them take their meals in the middle of the day in these places, in consequence of the great distance which they would have to walk to their own homes. But in addition to those who resort to the beer-shops to have their meals, there are great numbers who have not the excuse of distance from their dwellings to account for their very frequent attendance at such places.

As showing the extent to which attendance at the beer-shop is indulged in by the labourers, I may state that in the county of Bedford, which consists of 120 parishes, while there are 188 butchers' shops, and 259 bakers', there are not less than 883 public-houses and beer-shops. There are 57 parishes in which there are no butchers, 43 in which there are no bakers, but only 10 in which there is neither public-house nor beer-shop. The Chaplain of the Bedford County Gaol says—"To drunkenness and attendance at the beer-shop, directly or indirectly, I may safely say crime, in a great measure, in the county, owes its origin. Destitution, no doubt, occasionally leads to theft and fraud. But to what is the destitution in too many cases owing? Generally to drunkenness. This conclusion has been drawn from the statements of the prisoners themselves, and the vast number of public-houses and beer-shops throughout the county go to confirm it."

There exists, also, among the labourers a very general propensity to theft, when employed in the barns of their employers. For years past they have been in the almost constant habit of taking home with them at night in their pockets, or in small baskets, small quantities of wheat or barley. They seem to imagine that they have obtained a prescriptive right to these pilferings, and many a labourer who has been punished for the theft has indulged in the same offence for several years. I was informed of the case of one labourer, who had been punished for it, who stated that he had been in the constant practice of taking home small quantities of grain for the last twenty years; and that he always considered this as his perquisite. Many of the labourers consider it as almost amounting to a case of hardship, when a farmer, who happens to have his suspicions aroused, causes the men to be watched and apprehended by the police. They think that if he were to give his men fair warning of his intention not to allow such proceedings, it would have the effect of putting a stop to the practice. Sack stealing, also, is another custom of which the farmers complain sadly. Several, who have spoken to me, have stated that they lose every year from forty to fifty sacks. These articles, it appears, are almost universally taken by the labourers, either for the purpose of coverings for their beds, or for nailing up, to keep the wind out of their cottages. How far these practices might be put a stop to by a more liberal treatment of the labourers, and by improvements in their dwellings, is a question which might not be unworthy of the consideration of the employers of labour.

With respect to the actual amount of pauperism, the information which I have been enabled to collect shows a considerable decrease as compared with former years. The following table will show the total number of persons in each of the four counties receiving in-door relief—the proportion of the persons so receiving relief who are able-bodied male paupers—and the total amount expended for out-door relief, for the fifth week of the quarter ending Christmas, 1849, and also for the corresponding period of 1848:—

Counties.	No. of In-door Paupers in Week ending Christmas Quarter,		Decrease.	No. of Able-bodied Male Paupers receiving In-door Relief in Week ending Christmas Quarter,		Decrease.	Amount expended in Out-door Relief for Week ending Christmas Quarter,		Decrease.
	1848.	1849.		1848.	1849.		1848.	1849.	
Bedford	929	792	137	72	33	39	£535	£496	£39
Cambridge .	1,157	1,001	156	69	70		1,019	915	104
Herts	1,653	1,492	161	151	124	27	643	640	3
Hunts	414	373	41	27	16	11	319	314	5
Total Decrease			495			77			£151

Vagrancy exists to a very considerable extent in these counties. By a return recently presented to Parliament on the subject of vagrancy, it appears that the number of vagrant poor for one year (1847), relieved in the following counties was as under:—

Counties.	Males.	Females.	Males between 18 and 40.
Bedford	1,936	284	435
Cambridge	4,207	508	1,114
Herts	9,649	1,382	7,923
Hunts	1,387	101	482

In the three counties of Norfolk, Suffolk, and Essex, the numbers were as follows:—

Counties.	Males.	Females.	Males between 18 and 40.
Essex	13,318	1,370	4,411
Suffolk	4,327	478	1,780
Norfolk	1,949	240	1,294

The above numbers represent those only who were received into, or relieved by, the several union workhouses of these counties. There is, however, another class of vagrants, which consists of the professional beggars, few of whom probably are included in the above returns, as they would frequent their places of resort in the different districts, without applying for relief from the different parishes. The system which has been adopted in many parts of these counties, to which I shall have occasion to refer in a future letter, of placing the relief of vagrants under the management of the police, has tended most materially to diminish the amount of vagrancy.

Of the numbers given above, by far the greater portion may be considered as tramps, who were then traversing the country in search of employment. With the class of professional beggars, the counties of Hertford and Cambridge are almost overrun; and to the absence of a constabulary force in the county of Cambridge, is, no doubt, mainly to be attributed the large number of beggars who resort thither; and the proximity of Hertford to the metropolis may probably account in some measure for the large number in that county. At Cambridge, during term time, the beggars usually reap a rich harvest; indeed it is, in their vernacular, "a crack town." It is the head quarters for the beggars in the Midland and surrounding districts. It is also the grand centre for the Irish who come over to this country as reapers. They congregate in vast numbers in the town about the last week in July, go to mass at the Catholic chapel, and they separate to the different districts of the county on the morning of the following, or the evening of the same day. There are in the town of Cambridge thirteen lodging-houses, to which more or fewer of this class of persons resort at the close of the day; but there is one in particular, well known to every beggar within the British seas. Among the other lodging-houses of the town which I visited, was this favoured place of resort, or "boozing ken" of the professional mendicant.

The room in which the "company" were assembled might be, from its position, justly designated a cellar. A descent of about a dozen steps from the level of the ground conducted you to a small passage, having upon one side a door leading to the beer-cellar, which contained about twenty-four barrels of beer. The other door opened into a room of about 14 feet by 20, in which were assembled a group of the most miscellaneous characters which it could be supposed possible to collect together in one focus. There were 46 persons in all—men, women, and children of all ages. There was the member of the Spanish Legion, whose services were still unrequited by the Government for whom he would tell you he had fought; there were three who were on the "sea lurk;" two decent-looking artisans, with clean white shirts, their unfortunate "companions in distress, and their dear children, who had done nothing to deserve it." Close by stood a widow woman, who had been "trying to get a bit of bread by the sale of tattens and driz" (threads and tapes), and her companion, who went the same rounds with her, with a huge bandage round his head, and his arm in a sling, both of which were now laid aside. He had now recovered from "the fall which he received when engaged in building the new Houses of Parliament." There were the shoeless, the ragged, the dirty, the clean, the lame, and even the blind, young and old—one and all in their varied characters, suited to call forth sympathy or to impose upon the charitable and humane. In one corner of the room was a huge brown pan, technically called the "scran pot," filled with pieces of bread, beef, mutton, and other broken victuals, which the company had collected in the course of the day. Three or four children and an enormously large cat were gathered round the victuals, selecting some portions for their especial use; one of the children was busily engaged in tearing with his teeth the meat from off a rib bone of beef; another had a lump of bread and cheese; a third was "polishing off" some portions of a fowl; and a fourth was throwing at one of his youthful companions lumps of bread and pieces of meat, "for he would not eat such stuff as that." In another part of the room six men were engaged in playing cards, and four others in a game called "shove-halfpenny;" and a woman with a comfortable-looking flannel gown, who had been out on the "clean cadge," was employed in washing out the dress in which she had been out during the day, and which she wore over the flannel one. The other female members of the community were variously employed—some in repairing their "pal's toggery," some in patching up their own—two were engaged in making fancy doyleys, of various coloured worsted; one was knitting nightcaps; another, making dolls' dresses; and some were engaged in frying steaks or soles, or toasting bacon and herrings. The card-players were bawling; a ballad singer was practising; one or two women were singing different songs; the rest were talking. The confused noises—the fumes of tobacco, of onions, of gin, of the wash-tub, of broiled meat, fried fish, and toasted herrings—and the impure atmosphere caused by 46 persons in a small room under ground, heated by a large fire—rendered the place almost intolerable.

Among those present were one or more of each branch of the begging profession. There were "high-flyers," "slummers," "nakes," "dreary nakes," "shallow go nakers," "sea lurks," "croakers," "sneaks," "tattens and drizzers," "common frizzlers," "dreary grizzlers," "dance

bloaks," and others, to one or more of each of which class I was introduced by a friend who accompanied me. From several of them I
succeeded in obtaining some account of their mode of life. The first
to which I will refer was the statement of an Irishman, whose appearance was altogether most deplorable. He had no shirt, and his breast
was almost entirely uncovered; as for his coat, it is an abuse of words
to call the rags that hung together on him a coat; his knees protruded
through his trowsers, which hung in fringed tatters from below his
knees, and his feet were, of course, bare. "Sure then," said he, "it's
thirty years I've been on the cadge, and it's a long day, too. I never
had a home of my own since I came to this counthry. I have slept in
the boozing-kens in the counthry, many's the time; maybe it's been
in the prison I have, and in the workhouse, bad luck to 'em. It's five
days since I come to Cambridge; last week I made 14s., but there was
two days that I didn't go out, it was so cowld. To-day I only got 10½d.
and some grub (victuals). Sometimes I work a little in the summer
at raping, but not much; in the winter I always 'pad the hoof.' Sure
it's little money we'd get if it wasn't for that, and it's better than stale-
ing any day—they'd transport a man for that—but they only 'lumber'
you for a moon (a month's imprisonment) for t'other. I always work
the 'nake,' sometimes the 'dreary nake' [a naker is one who begs in a
ragged or ill-clothed condition; 'a dreary naker' being one who carries
on his operations without shoes or stockings, and this is called 'padding the hoof,' or 'padding it on the shallows.'] I never did nothing
with a 'slum' in my life, since I haven't the larning for that. When I
beg I tells the people anything that comes in my mouth. 'Sure it's a
cowld day, yer honner,' I says sometimes; 'For the love of God give
us a thrifle,' sometimes. When I can make ten or fifteen shillings a
week I'm satisfied. One good gintleman gave me 10s. a few days ago;
another gave me 7s. 6d., and one gintleman heaved a sovereign out of
his carriage and said, 'There, Pat, go and buy a coat.' Indeed I didn't
buy one, for this one does very well, but I wouldn't tell the gintleman
so. Sure, we're every bit as honest among ourselves as the rich folks
are. I come from Tuam, in county Galway. I don't know how many
times I've been 'jigged;' the last I had was two 'moons.' The last four
days I was on the cadge I made 10s. 9d. I got a lump of bread to-day,
but it's too hard for an ould man like me to ate; sure I put it in the
scran-pot when I don't want it, and the pigs gets it."

One individual, of considerable reputation for ability among the
fraternity, and whose usual occupation is that of "pushing the slum"

(begging petition), stated that he had had three "moons" of it for going out as a "croaker." He carried with him a petition setting forth that he was a farmer residing in Bottisham—that his cows had eaten a quantity of poisonous berries, which had "by some means got to the cavity of the brain," and produced delirium in the animals, which terminated fatally to the whole of them—and that that circumstance, joined with the badness of the times, consequent upon the repeal of the Corn-laws, had brought him to ruin, his wife to the grave, and his family to the workhouse. For this he was taken up as an impostor, and received three months' imprisonment. As soon as his term had expired he went to Hertfordshire, where he met with a "pal." As they were walking along the banks of the river Lea, some accident occurred to a barge coming down the stream, in consequence of which she sunk. The two travellers immediately dressed themselves as bargemen—had a petition drawn up, stating the cause of their distress to be the sinking of their barge in the river Lea—attached the name of the owner of the barge to the petition, as having given them a sovereign—and drove a very successful trade on the sunken barge, till they were apprehended, and got three months in Hertford gaol. Within three days of his liberation from Hertford gaol, the fellow was again in Cambridge gaol for being "asthmatical and subject to fits in the streets." Upon this occasion he was on the "shallow-go nake," and was standing up against a wall in Bridge-street, Cambridge, without shoes or stockings, and with nothing on but his trowsers and a tattered shirt, and a handkerchief tied round his waist. After having shivered and coughed for some time without attracting much notice, he fell down as in a fit. Dr. ——, of the town, came up, felt his pulse, and pronounced him an impostor. He was taken into custody, and received fourteen days' imprisonment. "Lankey Jack," said one whom I saw in another place, "is the most splendid fellow of any of us. He has never done a day's work in his life. He can do a'most any thing. He can come the 'sick dodge' better than any man I ever see'd. If you was to see him in asthma, you'd think he was going to die—he does it so first-rate. He's only four-and-twenty." To resume, however, the narrative of our friend's exploits. His fourteen days having expired, his next appearance before the public was in the character of a gentleman farmer. He was dressed in a hunting coat, top boots, and buckskin breeches; he hired a fine-looking horse, and went round to the various farmers and gentry in the neighbourhood with the following tale:—
"I have taken the liberty of calling upon you on behalf of a very old

and valued friend of mine, a gentleman who farms upwards of five hundred acres, within a few miles of this place. From various causes, which it is as unnecessary as it would be painful to me to mention, he is at present in embarrassed circumstances. His high sense of honour, and the feeling that any application for assistance from his neighbours and those who know him would be attended with disgrace, prevents him from calling personally upon you, and also prevents me from stating his name. I have headed the list myself with £10; several others have given various sums, and I should be happy to take your name for any amount you may feel disposed to give, the strictest secrecy being of course required on all hands." In three weeks he made £50 by this plan, but was finally taken into custody for the imposition, and received two months in Chelmsford gaol. Three days after his liberation from Chelmsford gaol, he again made his appearance in Cambridge, as a broken-down artisan. In this character he went to the house of a gentleman in the town, with a few knives and common articles of cutlery; and, making use of the name of a friend of the gentleman upon whom he called, he induced him to purchase some of his wares to the amount of 7s. 6d., in order to enable him to get to London, that he might enter the Hospital for Consumption, and also that he might see his sister, who was very ill, and who had been left an orphan a short time since in consequence of his mother dying of the cholera. Some inquiries were made, which led to the detection of the imposition; and on the following day—almost in a state of nudity, and afflicted with his favourite asthma—he was taken into custody, and again ordered to receive two months' imprisonment in Cambridge gaol, which term he had just completed at the time of my visit. He did not think that he should take to the "slum" again just yet, either in Cambridge or in Essex, for if he was "nailed," he would be almost certain to be "fullered" (fully committed). He was about to make his way to London, "to see how things were going on there."

The following somewhat interesting document, being a letter written by one of the fraternity to his brother and sister, will give the reader some insight into the social relations of some of these individuals, and will furnish some proof of the readiness with which they can adapt themselves to the situations in which they may be placed, and of the calmness with which they bear up under domestic calamities and bereavements of no ordinary nature:—

"Camebridge, June 9.

"Dear Sister and Harry—I send these lines hoping you are all well, which leaves me at present. I hope you received the last letter that I wrote in dick Loyds' letter from reding. I am going to Norwich from here. I have been doing pretty well lately, as I have taking entirely to ankeeing. I have likewise to inform you, that since I have left Reding that I have been a married man, but by some sad mistake I lost my wife yesterday. I hope the child is very well. I should like to have an answer, but I'm not settled in my mind when I shall be in norwich upon account of Whitsuntide been so near. I hope you are comfortable. I have nothing particular to mention here, no more than hoping you all are well. I have not been to epsom races, as I thought I should, because the mob that came from Bath races to reading gave me the frightables. I see captain carrotts togged himself out of Bath races; if I went I know how I should get on, I should work like blazes and nob the horrors for my trouble, so I am gust as well without, although my head is scarcely right this morning. I started from Reding to henly-upon-thames, from there to high wicombe, from there to chesam, from there to marlow, from here to tring, from there to Leighton buzzard; this is reckoned the best beer in England, and well I know it; from Leighton to Bedford, the county town for Bedfordshire, and from bedford to saint notes, where I got locked out from my dear wife, and was the occasion of me having the price of some fourpenny in the morning, as she begged the breakfast while I Laid down for an hour. She was a Lovely creature, but short of teeth, and troubled with saint antnony's dance, which please me very much to see when I had nothing to do. I am now single, but much against my will, until I reach norwich, where I hope I shall have the opportunity of once more embracing the charms of Matrimony. I have turned quite sure its all right, So no more at present from your affectionate Brother.

"N.B. I shall write again in about a week, when I shall expect an answer."

One of the women present, who was occupied during the day in selling "tattens and driz" (tapes and laces), informed me that she "had only made 2s. all day, and some few odd ha'pence." She almost always got more given her as charity than for the goods which she sold. Three men who were in the habit of working together as "sea-lurks," and dividing their earnings, told me they had had a very bad day, and only divided 2s. 4d. each. These individuals were dressed as sailors, and their tale was of course always of some disaster connected with the shipping interest, in which they were concerned, and had been either wrecked or cast away, or something of that kind. The "high-flyers" are generally persons of a somewhat higher grade in point of education. The two most noted of this class are called "Bath Josh" and "Soldier Fred." One of them dresses in an old hussar's jacket, the other in an old tattered red coat. Their principal employment consists in drawing up the "slums," or petitions, for those who may require their services in that capacity. The facility with which they can imitate the handwriting of persons is astonishing, and I was told of several instances in which gentlemen were for some time unable to pronounce the imitations of their names to be forgeries. The usual price for a "slum" varies from 1s. to 2s. 6d., the charge depending upon the length and character of the document.

After I had remained in this apartment some time, and the dinners and suppers of the various parties had been disposed of, it was suggested that they should have some singing. Accordingly a number of songs were sung, many of which, by a more select audience, might be considered objectionable; but the more obvious and indecorous the allusions, the more general were the marks of approbation of the company, males as well as females. On another occasion nearly the whole of the evening was occupied by the trial of a prisoner for murder—the company having formed themselves into a criminal court for that purpose. Seated in an elevated position on one of the tables sat the judge; he had on a woman's red cloak, a white collar turned over about his neck, an old grey Welsh wig upon his head, and a pair of woman's cuffs tied round his wrists. There was a small table with writing materials before his lordship, who conducted himself throughout with all the gravity peculiar to the high and important station which he filled. The prisoner was arraigned at the foot of the table, but was accommodated with a stool. On each side of the table sat the learned counsel, each of whom was robed in a woman's black dress, with white collars round their necks. On one side of the room sat the twelve jurors; opposite to them were the forms for the accommodation of those present who represented the public. The door was guarded by one who acted as policeman, and there was an usher of the court, with a wand of considerable dimensions, who kept silence while the proceedings were going on. I did not hear the opening address of the counsel for the prosecution, but from what I could gather, the unfortunate transaction arose out of a quarrel at a beer-shop. The prisoner and the deceased had been engaged in a quarrel, they had both left the house together, and the last time the deceased was seen alive was in the company of the prisoner. Witnesses were called who deposed to these facts, and the case for the prosecution being closed, several witnesses were called for the defence, who stated that the witnesses previously called were not to be believed on their oath. A policeman proved the former convictions of two of them. A witness who represented himself as a Jew, and who refused to be sworn as a Christian, and was directed to take the oath as a Jew, also gave it as his opinion that others of the witnesses were undeserving of credit. The prisoner's counsel, "oppressed with the importance of his duties, and having the life of a fellow-creature placed in his hands," pointed out with considerable ability several discrepancies in the evidence, dwelt at some length on the "hardship of hanging a fellow on merely circumstantial evidence," and concluded by impressing on the minds of the jury, "the saying of a learned judge, which could not be too often repeated in a criminal court, that it was better for a hundred guilty men to escape than for one innocent soul, like his client, to be hanged." The counsel for the prosecution having addressed the jury, the judge, in the most solemn manner, proceeded to charge the jury—pointed out discrepancies in the evidence, and several contradictions in the statements of the witnesses—told them to weigh well the evidence on both sides, and if they had a doubt upon their own minds "to be sure to give it in favour of the prisoner;" and he expressed his "perfect concurrence in what had fallen from his 'learned brother' as to the injustice and hardship of hanging an innocent man." The jury, after some consultation, found the prisoner guilty. The judge put on the black cap, and passed sentence upon him according to the regular form. The court broke up, and preparations were immediately made for carrying the sentence into execution. The crowd of gazers to witness the execution were assembled in the lower end of the room—the procession was formed in the adjoining beer cellar—the clergyman, the sheriff, the hangman, and other officials, were all represented—the culprit was led to a chair upon which he stood—the rope was adjusted and made fast to a hook in the ceiling. Everything was in readiness for drawing away the chair from under the man, when a loud knocking was heard at the door, and a messenger arrived with a reprieve, the announcement of which was received with the most rapturous applause; and the mock tragedy, with all its revolting features, ended by an order for an abundant supply of warm ale and gin, and other beverages.

LABOUR AND THE POOR.

THE RURAL DISTRICTS.

[FROM OUR SPECIAL CORRESPONDENT.]

HERTS, HUNTS, BEDS, AND CAMBRIDGE.

THE SPINNING HOUSE.

Letter XLII.

In my last Letter I endeavoured to give some account of a celebrated lodging-house in the town of Cambridge, well known among the members of the begging profession. I propose in the present to treat of another institution in the same town, the iniquitous proceedings connected with which were so strongly represented to me by several highly respectable and influential residents, that I feel I should not be fairly discharging my duty were I to omit giving the result of my inquiries with respect to it. The establishment has more than once been brought prominently before the notice of the public, in connection with the mode of treatment there adopted towards a very numerous class of persons residing in that town—I mean prostitutes. The institution in question is called "Hobson's Workhouse," but is more generally known as the "Spinning House." I endeavoured to obtain information from the University authorities as to its management, but my request to be furnished with copies of the rules and regulations was peremptorily refused. I was, however, enabled, notwithstanding this refusal, to obtain some information which I will now proceed to lay before the reader.

It appears that by an indenture of feoffment, dated 30th July, 1628, made between Thomas Hobson on the one part, and five members of the University of Cambridge, and six other persons described as of the town of Cambridge, of the other part, the said Thomas Hobson, "in acknowledgment of God's mercies and blessings upon his labours, and in testimony of his earnest and fervent wish to do good to the poor of the University and town wanting means to live upon, and settle themselves in some honest calling, and that they might thereafter be employed and set to work, and brought up and instructed in some trade or occupation, and thereby not only enabled to live of themselves, but by their labours become profitable members of the commonwealth, and helpful to others among whom they should live—and in consideration that there were then, at the only care, cost, and charges of the chancellor, masters, and scholars of the University, and the mayor, bailiff, and burgesses, in a great part erected and builded upon the property included in the said indenture, divers buildings and houses, intended only for the benefit and employment of the poorer sort of people of the said University and town—the said Thomas Hobson conveyed unto the partners of the second part certain messuages and tenements, upon trust that they should, within the space of four years, build, erect, and finish one or more convenient house or houses upon the premises, as well for setting the poor people of the said University and town to work, as for an house of correction for unruly and stubborn rogues, beggars, and other persons who should refuse to work; and also, in convenient time, should provide a sufficient quantity of wool and flax and other materials for setting of the said poor people to work; and should from time to time thereafter well and sufficiently maintain and repair the said houses to be by them erected, and all other the premises; and so of the same and every part thereof, and all rents and profits arising from the same, for and towards the uses aforesaid." Since the date of this indenture a considerable amount of other property has been bequeathed to the support of Hobson's Workhouse; and the wishes of the testators have been expressed in almost the same language. How far their benevolent objects have been carried into effect may be learned from the fact, that for the last half century the buildings have been used as a receptacle for profligate and disorderly women, and common prostitutes committed by the Vice-Chancellor; such persons being allowed to remain there not only in a state of complete idleness, but in a condition as discreditable to the authorities of Cambridge as it is physically and morally injurious to the wretched inmates themselves.

The Spinning House, or prison as it now is, is one of the most wretched and miserable places of the kind that I have ever seen. The direction of the founder, "that they should well and sufficiently repair the premises," is as unheeded as is the other part of his wishes with respect to the purpose and aim of the establishment. The building is in a most dilapidated condition; the walls are cracked, the arches over many of the windows are fractured, and some of them have already fallen in. The interior as well as the exterior presents altogether a wretched and desolate appearance. It consists of four wards, which contain together about sixty cells, with a day-room in each ward for the prisoners. To each of the wards there is a small triangular-shaped piece of ground, inclosed with high walls and iron gates. The length of these inclosures, or yards, is about thirty feet, their breadth at the lower end about twenty feet, and at the upper portion, or entrance, about six feet. The building—consisting of two stories, each containing a row of cells—is situated at the rear of other premises which face the road, and is enclosed upon each side by portions of adjoining tenements, thereby effectually excluding the admission of any fresh currents of air. The cells are six feet in width by about eight in length, and are each furnished with an iron bedstead, a straw mat, a flock bed, two blankets, and a counterpane. There are no glazed windows to the cells, the only light that is admitted being through an aperture of about three inches square in the iron shutters which are placed on the outside of the window frames. There are no means of warming the cells, either by hot air or by fires, as in other prisons, for there are no fire-places in them. "When the beds have not been slept in for some time," said the deputy-governor to me, "they are aired with the warming-pan." Such is the precaution, and such are the means adopted, for airing the beds, in cells where during the day the iron shutters are thrown open, and where there is no glass to prevent the admission of damp and wet. In winter the floors of the cells are often covered with the snow which drifts in through the casements.

With respect to the management of the prison—there are no means of classification or separation of the prisoners. In the day they are congregated idly together, and left without any control or efficient check upon their conduct; and they pass their time in occupations which, to hear them relate, as several of them did to me, would make the most depraved of beings blush. "It is," said one of the unfortunate creatures, who had upon several occasions endured the horrors of the place, "a dark, damp, filthy, dirty, wretched, badly-managed place. There is no order kept, and no one man can keep 'em in order. I was in twenty years ago; and I was put in when my last little boy was three months old—he is nearly three years old now—and it was as bad the last time as it was at the first. You are all huddled together, and sit among yourselves, talking and hearing all manner of bad language, blackguard stuff and slang, and doing the worst kinds of things. There was poor ——; when she went in she was as modest a girl as possible for one of her sort to be, and she would blush when she heard any bad language, but when she came out she was as bad as any of us. She used often to say that she got her education finished there. We call it 'going to college.'"

But the charity is not only diverted from the original purpose and intention of the founder, and wretchedly and disgracefully conducted, but even the regulations which have, within the last few years, and since a recent inquest on the body of one of the unfortunate creatures who came by her death in the place, been drawn up for its management, are totally disregarded. They are, in point of fact, a dead letter; and as they are posted up in different parts of the building, they seem only intended to mislead the unwary, or to blind persons to the real character of the place. As I before said, I was not able to obtain a copy, nor was I allowed to take one, of these regulations; but I could not help seeing that one of them was to the effect, that each inmate should have the frequent use of the bath. Upon my inquiring for the bath-room, I was shown to the kitchen of the establishment, and was pointed to a tub which was used for that purpose. The mode of using the tub, as stated by one who had used it many times, was—"The girls strip naked, and one of them gets into the tub, and then the others come and sluice you all over like pigs; and then, when one's sluiced, she comes out and sluices the others. It is such a beastly dirty place, you are smothered up with smoke and dust, and you are always obliged to have a good wash that way before you come out."

Another of the regulations requires that the deputy governor should read prayers every evening at eight o'clock to the inmates. This rule, like many others, is impracticable and unheeded. The deputy governor has to attend as porter to the establishment, and as he is uncertain when the proctor or his men may bring him another "canary"—for such he calls the prisoners—he is unable to leave his post as "porter" in order to assume the functions of "chaplain." The present deputy is literally a host within himself—he is the deputy governor, the gaoler, the cook, the attendant, the porter, the chaplain—he is the witness, as we shall presently see, against the parties—and, in addition to all these multifarious duties, he carries on the business of a tailor, on his own account, on the premises, the fact being notified to the public by a brass plate on his door. For the performance of his public duties, he is allowed £60 per annum, and is consequently obliged to have recourse to his own business in order to support himself. The least that could be expected from the authorities is, that they should provide suitable attendance and accommodation for those whom they deprive of liberty; and if their funds will not permit of their so doing, the next best thing they could do for the improvement of the morals of the town, would be to give up the establishment altogether, and leave the matter, as in other places, in the hands of an efficient police. The system at present pursued is totally inefficient for the repression of the evil which it is intended to remove. The terrors of the Spinning House, great though they may be, have not unfortunately much practical moral force. There are several females in the town who are well known both to the proctors and their men as persons of abandoned character, who are nevertheless allowed to continue their course with impunity; for they have been in the place so often, that the proctors will not take them any more. One of these individuals has been in, at different times, for not less than 103 weeks; and many others have passed nearly as long a period in it.

The proctor, arrayed in his gown and band, and accompanied by two men, perambulates the streets of Cambridge during term time, and occasionally out of term, armed with powers to arrest any female whom he may suspect of being an improper character; and many respectable females have been grossly insulted by these functionaries, and compelled to pass through the ordeal of an examination from which every modest woman would shrink with abhorrence. Proctorial laws, unlike other police laws, do not require that the person of abandoned character should accost any individual, in order to constitute an offence cognizable by the authorities; and in point of fact, the accosting of an individual, which in most places is made to serve as a criterion of character, is entirely overlooked. The form of trial—if it be not an abuse of words to apply such a term to the process which the prisoner undergoes previously to her final committal—is as repugnant to every principle of justice as it is opposed to the notions of every person who boasts of English customs and of English liberties. The Vice-Chancellor attends at a private room in the establishment every morning during term, to sit in judgment upon the presumed offenders. The public are not admitted; no friends of the prisoner are allowed to be present; all legal assistance and advice is denied; and the accused can call no witnesses. The proctor, or one of his men who arrested her, the gaoler, or the *multum in parvo* who acts as such, and the Vice-Chancellor who sentences her, are the only persons privileged to attend this extraordinary court of justice during the trial of the unfortunate culprit.

The proceedings are very secret, very simple, and very summary. The prisoner is brought in by the gaoler; her name, age, and address are entered in the minute-book by the Vice-Chancellor. The proctor or one of his men states that he saw her in such a street or place, and, "suspecting her of incontinence," he arrested her. The gaoler is asked if he knows her, or if she has ever been under his charge before; if he replies in the affirmative, the warrant of committal, for such period as the Vice-Chancellor may direct, is made out, and the prisoner is ordered to be removed. The warrant—though I was not able to obtain a copy of it—sets forth that the person therein named was brought before the Vice-Chancellor upon such a day, she "being suspected of incontinence;" and that, as he is "satisfied of the accuracy of such a charge," the governor is thereby directed to keep the said person in his safe custody for the period therein mentioned. The whole, therefore, that is necessary to obtain a conviction in this court, is to be suspected by the proctor or his men, and to be known by the gaoler. No evidence is required to prove any overt act on the part of the prisoner; it is not necessary that she should even accost any man in the streets, or be seen in his company. Although proceeding upon the most legitimate business through the streets, any female whom the proctor may chance to suspect of incontinence is liable to be dragged off to this sink of iniquity.

But it was stated to me by several who partly justified these proceedings, that the proctors and their men, from their extensive knowledge and intimate acquaintance with abandoned characters, would be certain not to suspect an innocent person. Unfortunately for this defence, numerous facts prove that even proctors are liable to err, like other men. I was informed by the editor of one of the Cambridge papers that he had had, a short time since, a somewhat severe struggle with the proctor to prevent his wife being taken off to this den while walking through the streets in the open day. I extract from the *Cambridge Independent* the following case, which occurred some time since:—

"THE PROCTORS AND THEIR MEN.—The following case has come to our knowledge from the lips of a most respectable female, who is naturally indignant at the treatment she received on Tuesday evening last from a proctor and his men. A few weeks ago she and her husband came to this town to embark in business, they having a competency. A shop not being available, the husband, who is a tailor, rather than be idle, obtained work at Mr. Parfitt's, in St. Mary's-passage. It is her habit to meet her husband in the evening, to accompany him home, and, as they have an appointed time, they wait for each other against St. Mary's Church. On Tuesday, the husband, having done work before the usual time, accompanied a friend to a house to have a small glass of ale. In the interim his wife came up, and before she had waited three minutes the proctor and his men came up, and the latter rudely thrust their faces under her bonnet, and, after a vulgar gaze, exclaimed, 'Who are you? what's your name?' Not aware of the existence of proctors or their men, and consequently ignorant of their high prerogative, she thought their conduct most insolent; but politely told them her name, and the occasion of her standing there. 'This must be inquired into' said the proctor, and she was taken into Mr. Parfitt's, and questioned. They detained her there about a quarter of an hour, asking her various questions. While this was going on inside the house, several persons had congregated around, they having seen the female in charge of the proctor. The husband, at his appointed time, came up, and looked for his wife, and seeing a crowd assembled, he inquired the occasion. 'Why the proctors have got a woman in that house,' was the answer. So, not seeing his wife at that moment, he entered his employer's to see what was going on; and, to his astonishment and dismay, he found his wife in an excited state, with the proctor and his men. On asking what it all meant, the proctor, with much dignity, said, 'We have been doing for your wife, what you ought to have done. We have protected her.' A conversation followed, during which the proctor said, 'take your hat off, sir, you don't know our power.' Both husband and wife were then allowed to go home, and the next day she was very ill."

Another instance of a similar kind took place shortly afterwards, in the case of a respectable and modest young woman, the wife of an exciseman in the town. The account which she gave me of the insult thus offered to her was the following:—"I had been out to a shop to make some purchases, and was returning home. When I was near St. Mary's-passage, some man stepped up to me, and, taking hold of me by my arm, said, 'the proctor takes you if you please.' I asked him what he wanted with me. I had never heard of the proctors or their men, and had only been a few months in the town. The man made no answer, but dragged me to the proctor, who asked me my name. I told him what it was, and he then asked me where I lived. I told him. I had just moved from there, and I then directly said, 'Oh, I have told you wrong, it is —— street.' I was so frightened I hardly knew what I said. The proctor said, 'Oh, I see how it is, you don't know where you live,' and turned round to the man and said 'bring her along.' I

was walking along crying between the men when I met Mr. ——,
who lives in the neighbourhood, and who had known me a long time
before I came here, and he said, 'My child, what are they going to
do with you?' I said I did not know, but that they had just taken me
from St. Mary's-passage. He then asked the proctor if he knew who
he had got there, and he said, 'Oh, yes, it's all right; she can't give any
account of herself.' I caught hold of Mr. ——'s arm and told him to
take me away, for I was very poorly and frightened. Mr. —— then
said, 'I know her very well; she is a respectable young woman, and
lives close by me.' The proctor then let me go, and Mr. —— and I
walked home together, the proctor and his men following us all the
way. When Mr. —— had seen me home, and was leaving the house,
the same men were standing at the door, and they asked him if what
he said was true. He said yes, and told them they had better go and
apologise to me for it. They said indeed they would not, and requested him to go back and do it for them." A day or two afterwards the
young woman pointed out the proctor to a gentleman who accompanied her, as being the person who arrested her, and when spoken
to on the subject, he replied, "Whatever was done, and all that was
done, I did it, and I am the proctor;" and refused to make the slightest
apology for the insult. Long established usages may reconcile persons
to the performance of almost any humiliating services, and it is upon
that hypothesis only that we may cease to wonder when we see such
duties so performed by gentlemen of education and of high literary
attainments.

From the arrest of these persons on suspicion, and their committal
without evidence, I will proceed to their treatment while undergoing
their punishment. Upon this point I am compelled to give the statements of the unfortunate creatures themselves, who have at various
times been incarcerated in the Spinning House. These statements
are, of course, to be received with due allowance and care. From the
manner, however, in which they were given, and the evident desire
of the narrators to state nothing but the truth, I believe that they are
in the main perfectly correct, and they furnish the strongest possible
proof of the worse than inefficiency of the present system. "I have
been in the Spinning House," said one of these females, "altogether
I don't know how many times. They won't take me now; they always
pass me in the streets as if they didn't know me. When they first take
you to the cage, they put you in the cell where the bed is. There is no
light and no seat in the place. The governor brings in the warming-

pan and warms the bed for you. They don't give you any supper the first night. We are kept in the cell till about nine o'clock the next morning, when the governor comes to us and takes us into the Vice-Chancellor's room—there's nobody there but the governor and the proctor, beside himself and us. The Vice-Chancellor says, 'Now let us hear what the proctor has got to say about this.' Then the proctor says, 'Well, sir, I was walking down such a street and met this girl, and I think she is an improper character.' 'Did she come quiet?' the Vice-Chancellor asks, 'Very quiet indeed,' perhaps he'd say, and then a paper is signed and given to the governor, who takes us back to our cells. There used to be 7d. a-day allowed for our keep, and the keeper used to buy the food. The allowance of food that they gave me last time was six ounces of bread for breakfast, two ounces of tea, about half a pound of sugar, and a pint and half of milk—that was for the week. Four days in the week I had for dinner five ounces of cooked meat and bread or potatoes; for the other three days a pint and a half of soup and five ounces of bread—that was, if there were more than three girls there—if there were less than four, it was twelve ounces of suet pudding. The supper was six ounces of bread and one ounce of cheese. I think that's about it. [This account exactly corresponds with the dietary table, a copy of which I took when in the Spinning House.] There is a blue striped cotton dress for you, if you like to wear it, but if not, you may wear your own. We sit all together in the day-room, and there's some very pretty conversation and goings on, you may be sure. [The young woman went on to give some account of the proceedings, but they were of such a character that I forbear to give publicity to them.] There is no place for us to wash at, except at the pump in the kitchen; and when I was there last they wouldn't give us any soap till we kicked up a row about it, and said we'd go to chapel dirty if they didn't let us have some." "I have been in," said another female, "17 or 18 times, I won't be sure which, but I always have a bit of a shindy with 'em. Once I had nearly every individual thing torn off me by the porter's men. When they got me in, they locked me up in the cell, and wouldn't give me any supper; and in the morning, because the other girls all said it was a shame to serve me so, they locked us up in the day room and would not bring us our breakfast till late in the day, so we sat and shied coals at the windows, and broke three hundred squares of glass, and they gave me and the other girls three months in the House of Correction for that."

"I have been," said another of these women, "kept in the place for 103 weeks altogether, and they won't take me any more, I think. When I kicked up a row there once, they put me in a large cell, in the top row, and kept me there for three days and three nights without any bed to lie upon—nothing but the bare floor. When I first went we used to be allowed to have anything we liked to send out for, if we had money, or anything anybody liked to send us, except liquors; but we used often to have gin and brandy sent in to us in bottles, marked 'bottled porter.' The last time I was in, the gaoler brought me a bit of bread in the morning, and I threw it at him, and said I wouldn't eat such stale stuff as that. About twelve o'clock he brought me a little sugar and a spoonful or so of tea. When the other governor was there we had no knives or forks, and we were obliged to take our victuals to our mouths with our fingers. I have often seen the girls dragged by the hair of their heads from the sitting-room into their cells, because they did not keep quiet. I have been served so myself many times. Once, when they took me in the streets, they tore nearly everything off me: the proctor twisted my arm almost out of its socket, and I bit a piece out of his. When I was in my cell the gaoler came to take me before the Vice-Chancellor, but I refused to go quietly. He then said, 'If you go quiet I will do all I can for you before the Vice-Chancellor.' When he got me in, he said, 'Now, you wretch, you shall have all that I can ever make him give you.' I was so enraged that I seized the inkstand and threw it at him. I could not get my shoes off quick enough before the proctor's men and the gaoler got hold of me, or else I would have thrown them at him, so I smashed some of the windows in the Vice-Chancellor's room with my fist, and cut it all terribly with the glass. At last they got me away and put me in the dark hole, where I lay curled up in a pool of blood on the floor like a snake, with my new black mantle over my head. I slept so all that night. In the morning I was so cold and in such pain that I began to cry, and asked him to forgive me; and he said, 'No, you wretch, you nearly killed me yesterday; I won't forgive you;' and he dragged me out of that cell, and put me in another, and said, 'You wretch, stop there; that's a haunted cell; there was a man cut his throat there.' I begged and prayed of him to let me out, and at last he said, 'I can't have the heart to keep you locked up any longer, although I was told to keep you locked up for twelve days and nights.' Then I was let out. When we were all together we made up our minds that we would get out of the place. The first thing we did was to break the pan off the fire-shovel, and that left it like a chisel. We set to work and got one brick out of the wall, and then we got some water and poured upon the mortar to soften it, and so we could remove another brick, and at last, by about two o'clock in the middle of the day, we had made a hole big enough for us to get through. The people who lived on the other side of the wall saw what we were about, and they hung up something over the hole to hide it, till we were ready to get out, and when we were all out we ran as fast as we could—the whole five of us, some with shawls and some without, but all covered with dust and mortar—up to Barnewall. Once when the proctor came to see us, he went into one of the cells, and we locked him in, and while he was there we called him a 'wretched prostitute,' and asked him if he was not ashamed of himself for following such a wicked course of life. One of us gave him a long lecture on the impropriety of his conduct, and when we let him out, we told him that if he was ever caught again he should be locked up for a longer time. The longest time I was ever in for at one time was three months."

"On one occasion," said another, "the proctor and his men came into my room, and said I must go with them. I said I was undressed, and could not go. They said that that should not prevent them taking me; so they called a coach, dragged me down stairs, threw a blanket over me, put me into a coach, and drove me off to the Spinning House; while the crowds of people in the streets were pelting the coach and the driver with stones and anything they could lay their hands on."

Several others who had been incarcerated in this hole gave me accounts of the neglect which they experienced while there; and one and all agreed in denouncing it as a wretched, dirty, and ill-managed place.

Before concluding my account of the condition of these four counties, it will probably not be uninteresting to the reader if I refer briefly to the leading social and moral features of these and other counties to which my attention has been directed. In order to enable the reader the more readily to ascertain the difference which exists in the condition of their respective inhabitants, in point of ignorance, pauperism, crime, improvidence, and illegitimacy, I have placed in a tabular form the per-centage, above or below the average of the whole of England and Wales—which average I have adopted as the standard—in which the particular features predominate in each county. I have included the counties of Northampton, Leicester,

Rutland, Nottingham, and Derby, to the state of which I shall have occasion to refer in subsequent letters, and also Norfolk, Suffolk, and Essex, already described in previous communications.

In the following table the first column contains the population of each county; the second, the per centage of ignorance in each county above the average of England and Wales, as indicated by the numbers of persons who have signed the marriage register with their marks, and who may be assumed to be incapable of writing their names. The third column contains the proportions of the youthful population receiving education, as shown by the results of the Church School inquiry, instituted in 1847. The fourth and fifth columns exhibit the per centages, above the average, of improvident marriages—that is, of marriages in which the males were under twenty-one years of age—and of illegitimacy, as shown by the returns of the Registrar-General. The sixth column shows the condition of each county so far as pauperism is concerned, and is calculated upon the proportion, to the whole population, of persons relieved in each county in the year 1847. In the last column is shown the amount of crime, as indicated by the gross criminal commitments of males to the assizes and quarter sessions during the same year. The numbers in the table under each particular head show the amount per cent. in each county above the average of the whole of England and Wales; and in order to simplify the table as much as possible, I have omitted all the fractional parts:—

	Population.	Ignorance above Average.	Proportion of Education to Population.	Improvident Marriages above Average.	Bastardy above Average.	Pauperism above Average.	Crime above Average.
EASTERN:							
Norfolk	412,664	38	1 in 10·5	21	53	29	17
Suffolk	315,073	42	1 in 9	24	27	36	7
Essex	344,979	42	1 in 9·5	35	below 19	50	17
E. MIDLAND:							
Herts	157,207	53	1 in 9	69	5	17	15
Beds	107,936	53	1 in 8	142	17	26	18
Cambridge ...	164,459	33	1 in 11	39	average.	27	below 1
SOUTH and E. MIDLAND:							
Hunts	58,549	38	1 in 8	122	below 18	8	below 18
Northampton	199,228	15	1 in 7	84	below 11	20	10
Rutland	21,302	below 38	1 in 7	below 14	9	3	1
MIDLAND:							
Leicester	215,867	below 2	1 in 10	104	below 23	18	25
Nottingham ..	249,910	1	..	31	18	below 26	below 15.8
Derby	272,217	below 13	..	below 16	39	below 44	below 39

It will be seen from the above table that those counties which are more exclusively agricultural in their character are the most ignorant and the most depraved. The average of the nine counties included in the Eastern, East Midland, and South-east Midland districts, which are comparatively destitute of manufactures, shows that ignorance is to crime as 6 to 1 *above* the average; while in the Midland counties, which are the seat of the great hosiery business, and also of iron and mining operations, the proportion of ignorance to crime is as 1 to 6 *below* the average. On reference to the two counties of Herts and Beds, it will be seen that there is an aggregation of every social evil. Vast numbers, as we have already seen, of the women and children of these counties, are employed in the light domestic manufactures of lace-making and straw plaiting, which appear to have the effect (among other ill consequences) of encouraging the evils of bastardy and of improvident marriages, with a consequent increase in the population—who in their turn become dependent upon a fluctuating and badly-remunerated trade, the effect of which is to be seen in a vast amount of pauperism and crime. Mr. T. Fletcher, in his valuable work on the Moral Statistics of England and Wales, states that "the most pauperized districts are those in which the farmers in the boards of guardians, and in the administration of the highway rates, still, in a sordid misconception of their own interests, use the public funds to the full extent of their ability, to keep up that excess of labour in the market—and, therefore, as they vainly imagine, that cheapness of it—which the farmers of Buckinghamshire and Bedfordshire find, without any such contrivance, among the poor peasantry of those counties, half dependent on their petty domestic manufactures of straw and lace." The proportion which ignorance bears to pauperism varies considerably in each group of counties. In the Eastern group the proportion of ignorance to pauperism above the average is as about 8 to 7, in the East Midland about 2 to 3, in the South-east Midland 1 to 2, and in the Midland about 1 to 3 below the average.

The proportion, however, which one particular form of evil may bear to another, and the connection which may fairly be supposed to subsist between these varied moral features, will, at all times, be liable to great fluctuations; and not unfrequently we find appearances which at first sight are seemingly opposed to long-established theories on the subject. Adequate employment will prevent the ignorant man from necessarily becoming a pauper, and a fair remuneration for his labour will often save him from the fate of a criminal. Comparative cheapness in the price of provisions and of the necessaries of life, combined with the means of employment, will often enable those who may have contracted improvident marriages to support themselves independently of the parish, and will prevent the issue of their ill-timed union from swelling the number of pauper children. The offspring of illegitimacy may be spared from becoming tainted with pauperism, when employment gives the parent the means of supporting it; and even should the pauper child become an inmate of the workhouse, yet, if shielded by watchfulness and attention from its contaminating influences, he may be rescued by institutions such as that of the Boys' Home at Norwich—a description of which I gave in a former letter—from the eventual disgrace of a felon.

LABOUR AND THE POOR.

THE RURAL DISTRICTS.

[FROM OUR SPECIAL CORRESPONDENT.]

COUNTIES OF NORTHAMPTON, LEICESTER, RUTLAND, NOTTINGHAM, AND DERBY.

Letter XLIII.

This group of counties constitutes what is generally known as the Midland district of England, and contains altogether an area of not less than 2,444,630 acres, according to the area assigned to the several parishes in the counties, in the Enumeration Abstract of the census of 1841. Commencing with the northern portion of the group, the counties of Nottingham and Derby join the southern part of Yorkshire; and a portion of Derbyshire, in the district of the High Peak, lies contiguous to Cheshire, a part of which also forms the north-western boundary of the county. The counties of Stafford and Warwick lie upon the western sides of Derbyshire and Leicestershire, and the south-western extremity of Northamptonshire. Portions of Oxfordshire and Bucks adjoin the southern extremity of the county of Northampton, while Bedford, Hunts, a portion of the Isle of Ely in Cambridgeshire, together with the western part of Lincolnshire, complete the eastern boundary of the entire group. The population of the whole of the five counties was, in 1841, 958,524, or about 40,000 more than that of the entire principality of Wales. As compared with the extent and population of the whole of England and Wales, they occupy about one-seventeenth of the whole superficies of the country, and they contain about one-sixteenth of the entire population. Viewed separately, there are 39 English counties larger than Rutland, 27 larger than Leicestershire, 26 larger than Nottinghamshire, 22 larger than Northamptonshire, and 21 of a greater extent than Derbyshire. In point of population the counties stand thus:—Northampton, 14th; Derby, 23d; Leicester, 29th; Nottingham, 34th; and Rutland, 40th. The distribution of the surface and of the population in the respective counties will be seen from the following table:—

	North-ampton.	Leices-ter.	Rut-land.	Notting-ham.	Derby.
Area of county in acres	646,810	511,340	97,500	525,800	663,180
Population (1841) .	199,228	215,867	21,302	249,910	272,217
Proportion to 100 acres	30·6	41·9	22·3	46·7	41·4
Number of inhabited houses	40,841	44,774	4,294	50,550	53,020
Average number to each house	4·8	4·8	4·95	4·94	5·1

The per centage of population to each 100 acres is below the average of England and Wales in each of the counties except Nottingham, where it is 8.6 above the average. For Rutland it is 48.1; Northampton, 28; Derby, 3.7; and Leicester, 2.6 per cent. below the average.

In order to show not only the present population of these counties, but also its rate of increase during the last half century, and the extraordinary fluctuations which have marked it, I have arranged in a tabular form the population of the respective counties at the time of each census, together with the rate of increase in each of them during the intervening decennial periods.

TABLE OF POPULATION, WITH RATE OF INCREASE DURING THE LAST HALF CENTURY, IN EACH OF THE FOLLOWING COUNTIES.

	1801.	1811.	1821.	1831.	1841.
Leicestershire, Population	130,801	150,419	174,571	197,003	215,867
Increase per cent..	...	16	16	13	9·5
Northamptonshire, Population	131,757	141,353	162,483	179,366	199,228
Increase per cent..	...	7	15	10	11
Rutlandshire, Population	16,356	16,380	18,487	19,385	21,302
Increase per cent ...	...	{ 24 persons.	13 per cent.	} 5	9·9
Nottinghamshire, Population	140,350	162,900	186,873	225,327	250,278
Increase per cent..	...	16	15	20	12·2
Derbyshire, Population	161,142	185,487	213,333	237,170	272,217
Increase per cent..	...	15	15	11	14·7

Upon looking over various parliamentary and official returns for information in connection with these counties, with respect to the more prominent features of their social organization, I find that, with respect to real property, the proportion is above the average in the counties of Northampton, Leicester, and Rutland, and below the average in Nottingham and Derby. The number of independent persons is, in each of the counties, below the average, as is also the amount of deposits in the savings banks. Pauperism is above the average in each of those counties in which real property is also proportionately high. Of the three counties in which mining and manufacturing operations are carried on, two (Nottingham and Derby) have pauperism below the average; while in the third (Leicester) it is above the average, although below the county of Northampton, which is more exclusively agricultural in its character, and where few manufactures, properly speaking, are carried on. The following table will, however, show the particulars for each county. The amount of real property is taken from a return made to the House of Commons in 1845; the number of independent persons in each county is from the Occupation Abstract of the census of 1841; the amount of deposits in savings banks, from returns presented to Parliament on the subject; the data with respect to pauperism are contained in the 12th report of the Poor-law Commissioners (1846); and the per-centages have been calculated on the population to which those returns refer in the various Poor-law districts:—

	North-ampton.	Leicester.	Rutland.	Notting-ham.	Derby.
Real property assessed to Property-tax	£ 1,252,100	£ 1,376,384	£ 156,980	£ 1,142,367	£ 1,379,025
Proportion per cent. above the average	16·51	18	36·62	below average 6·08	below average 15·26
Number of independent persons	3,788	4,377	416	4,818	5,193
Proportion per cent. below the average	32·2	27·7	30·3	31·9	31·2
Deposits in savings banks ...	£ 273,541	£ 196,929	£ nil.	£ 452,814	£ 358,389
Proportion per cent. below the average	14·5	43·2	„	18	12·8
Number of paupers relieved..	21,951	24,107	2,222	18,751	11,341
Proportion per cent. above the average	20·1	18·1	3·5	below 26·	below 44·4

Passing from these prominent features which mark the social condition of this group of counties, it will be necessary, before proceeding more into detail, to glance at the physical characteristics of the various counties. Commencing with Northamptonshire—its aspect is remarkably pleasing, its surface being broken up into numerous and diversified hills and dales. Unlike the neighbouring counties of Cambridge and Huntingdon, it contains none of those dreary and monotonous levels which fatigue the eye by the perfect deadness and sameness of their scenery. The inhabitants of Northamptonshire boast that the air is the finest and the most healthy in the country; and if one might judge from the great number of the nobility and gentry who reside within it, the opinion does not appear to be altogether unfounded. For a long period this county has contained the residences of great numbers of the nobility. Norden calls it, on this account, "the herald's garden." There are also many persons in various parts of the county who have attained an extraordinary longevity. I was informed at Naseby of one woman who died at the age of 93, and who at her death had living five sons and two daughters, whose united ages were 444 years. In the village of Earl's Barton there are four persons living in one cottage, whose united ages are 311; the husband of one of the inmates, aged 81, was at work upon the roads a few weeks since. In an adjoining village there are two or three persons upwards of 95 years of age. According to the returns made in the census of 1841 there were then living in the county 9,744 persons, between the ages of 60 and 70; between 70 and 80, 5,150; between 80 and 90, 1,268; and between 90 and 100, 66.

The greatest length of the county from north to south is about seventy miles—its breadth varying from seven to twenty-five. It presents one somewhat peculiar feature, to which reference has frequently been made—namely, that it is entirely self-supplied with respect to water. There is not a single stream which runs into it from any other county, while there are several which have their rise within its boundaries, and which run through other counties. Of these, the most famous—not so much on account of its magnitude as of the associations which are linked with it—is the Avon. The Avon well is situated in Naseby, at a short distance from the field of the memorable conflict between Charles I. and the Parliamentary forces. The owner of the plot of ground in which the well is situated has, within the last few years, shown his reverence for the name of Shakspeare by ornamenting the source of the classic stream. A circular well of about four feet in depth, and ten in diameter, receives the water from the spring, which flows in at the one side, and passes out at the other, by a subterranean passage, to pursue its way for a short distance, when, in conjunction with the Leam and other small rills, it continues its course by Stratford, and thence to its junction with the Severn. A plaster swan was brought down from London a short time since, and placed upon a stone pedestal by the side of the well. The cold sharp air of Naseby has, however, proved too much for it, and by the side of a portion of its body lies the once graceful neck of the classic bird. Another river, which takes its rise in Naseby, is the Ness. The periodical overflows of this stream frequently do considerable damage to the pastures upon the adjoining land. After a few hours' rain, the river will begin to overflow its banks; when the grass is unmown, it will receive great injury from the alluvial deposits left upon it by the waters, and the hay is in most cases rendered unfit for fodder, if not actually swept away by the force of the current. In 1848 the water of the river at one period covered an area of not less than from 8,000 to 10,000 acres. The annual loss by these floods has been estimated at £6,000. Within the last few years a committee has been formed for the purpose of adopting measures to prevent the recurrence of such disasters. The remaining rivers of the county are the Welland, the Ouse, and the Charwell. These facilities for inland navigation are greatly increased by means of the canals which traverse some portions of the county. The Oxford Canal joins the Grand Junction at Bramton, and the Union Canal leaves the town of Northampton, passes through the county towards Market Harborough, where it joins the Soar near Leicester, and so forms a connection with the Trent. The county is well supplied with good roads, and the Great Watling-street passes through a portion of it. The London and North-Western Railway enters it at a short distance from Blisworth, and leaves it at Kilsby, near Rugby. A branch from the main line at Blisworth runs along the eastern side of the county up to Peterborough—whence the Syston and Peterborough, the Eastern Counties, and the East Lincolnshire lines afford the means of communication to almost every part of the country.

The town of Northampton gives its name to certain tables which have been constructed with respect to mortality, and which form the data upon which the business of most of the Life Insurance Societies of this country is conducted. The Northampton Table of Mortality professes to show what number of persons out of 11,650, assumed to be born at the same time, attain to the ages of one, two, and three years, and to every year of age up to ninety-six, when it terminates with the death of the longest liver. The calculations were made by Dr. Price from the accounts kept at Northampton, during a period of forty-six years—from 1735 to 1780, both years inclusive—of the ages, at death, of 4,689 persons, who were buried within that period in the parish of All Saints. Calculations were also made upon the data thus furnished, of the value of life annuities, of insurances on single and joint lives, and of annuities payable on the survivorship of lives. These tables form the basis of the business of the Equitable, the Imperial, the Scottish Equitable, the Scottish Widows Fund, and many other English and Scotch insurance offices. The Northampton table has also been the basis of calculation for Friendly and Benefit societies; and the Government formerly sold annuities, to a large amount, on terms founded upon the data furnished by it; and legacy duties are still levied according to it under the 36th George III., c. 52. It is impossible to form any idea of the amount of money which has been, and is daily, distributed by calculations founded upon these tables— in the shape of premiums of insurance, life annuities, endowments, and life-interests in estates. One insurance office alone once stood engaged for the payment of upwards of seven millions sterling in the ensuing ten years, upon calculations entered into on the basis of this table. During the last few years a very general opinion has been en- tertained, that the mortality represented by the Northampton table is higher than that of the community generally. There appears, how- ever, to be no doubt, in the minds of those who entertain this opinion, that it was correctly constructed, and fairly represented the mortality of the people of this country when the data were collected on which it was based; and that the discrepancy between this and other tables, and between it and the experience of some of the principal offices, arises from the selection of healthy lives only by the latter and from the rate of mortality in one particular town having been taken as a criterion of that of the whole country—and also from the improvement of life which has taken place during the past and present centuries. Speak- ing of the Northampton table, the Registrar-General states, in one of his reports, that, "whether regard be had to its employment for the sale of life annuities, the valuation of life interests in estates and rever- sions, fixing premiums of insurance, adjusting claims for chances of survivorship by the great insurance societies, friendly societies, private persons, or the Government, the importance is incontestable of determining whether that table represents correctly the chances of life; whether the hypothesis upon which it was constructed gives an approximation to the truth, or is entirely false, and never represented the mortality of Northampton, of the inhabitants of All Saints parish, of lives insured, or of any other portion of mankind." The task of rectifying the complicated errors and the inveterate injustice running through the premiums, valuations, distribution of profits, and allocations of bonuses in offices that have used an erroneous table, is most laborious and difficult; but it is, perhaps, not beyond the powers of the actuaries now attached to the companies who are engaged in this branch of enterprise. At all events, future embarrassments may be prevented by the use of corrected tables. It would be out of place to enter here into any of the arguments which have been brought forward by the advocates of the various sets of tables of mortality now in use; but in order to show the necessity which exists for a speedy solution of the question, and for the formation of tables accurately constructed, and the advantages which would thereby be afforded to all classes of the country, I subjoin a table of the annual premiums required to be paid in order to insure the payment of £100 upon death, the premiums commencing at the ages of 20, 30, 40, 50, and 60, according to various tables. The tables referred to are the True Northampton Table, the False Northampton Table, a Table founded on the experience of the Equitable-office, and Dr. Price's Northampton Table:—

Age.	True Northampton Table.	Equitable Experience.	Dr. Price's Northampton Table.	False Northampton Table.
20	£1 10 11	£1 10 3	£2 3 6	£2 3 4
30	2 1 3	1 19 3	2 13 0	2 13 0
40	2 17 4	2 13 8	3 7 11	3 7 10
50	4 4 0	3 19 9	4 11 7	4 12 4
60	6 18 8	6 6 0	6 7 3	7 2 9

The origin of the registration of births, deaths, and marriages, and the publication of annual parish registers, are to be traced so far back as the year 1538. About that time the Church of England was declared to be no longer subject to the jurisdiction of the Pope, and Thomas Cromwell was appointed the King's Vicegerent for ecclesiastical jurisdiction. In the exercise of his functions he issued certain injunctions to the clergy, and among others one enjoining each of them to keep a book, or books, in which they should enter all births, deaths, and marriages within their respective parishes. In the year 1547 (the 1st Edward VI.) visitors were directed to enforce this, among other matters, upon the clergy. During a portion of the reign of Elizabeth, the clergy were required to make protestation that they would keep their register-books in a proper manner. Several of the canons also, which date their authority from the 1st James I. (1603), prescribe with great minuteness the mode in which entries are to be made in the registers, and they also order an attested copy of the same to be forwarded annually to the bishop of the diocese, or his chancellor. From inquiries which have been instituted throughout the country, it appears that 812 of the registers of English parishes commence in 1538, 1,822 between that period and 1558, and 2,448 during the ensuing 45 years, down to the year 1603. It is from this latter period that the Northampton registers date—the parish of St. Giles, from 1559; All Saints, from 1560; St. Sepulchre (for marriages), from 1566, and for baptisms and burials, from 1571; St. Peter, from 1578 for burials and marriages, and from 1596 for baptisms. The Northampton bills of mortality give for each year ending December 21, a list of the diseases and deaths in All Saints parish, and state the numbers, without distinction of sex, buried in the parish under two years of age, and between the ages of 2 and 5, 5 and 10, 10 and 20, and so on in decennial periods up to 100. They also set forth the aggregate number of males and females christened and buried at the churches of All Saints, St. Sepulchre, St. Giles, St. Peter, and nine other chapels or burial places within the town. The bills are presented annually to the "mayor, aldermen, municipal councillors, and the rest of the inhabitants of the town of Northampton," by the parish clerk. The bill usually closes with some appropriate piece of poetry, set round and adorned with skulls, bones, and hour-glasses. For six or seven years Cowper furnished the stanzas for the bills of mortality. In Grimshawe's edition of Cowper's works is a letter to Lady Hesketh, in which the poet gives an account of his first interview with the worthy parish clerk, who came to solicit him for "an effusion in the mortuary style." He says:—"On Monday last Sam brought me word that there was a man in the kitchen who desired to speak to me. I ordered him in. A plain, decent, elderly figure made its appearance, and, being desired to sit, spoke as follows:—'Sir, I am clerk of the parish of All Saints, in Northampton, and brother of Mr. C——, the upholsterer. It is customary for the person in my office to annex to a bill of mortality, which he publishes at Christmas, a copy of verses. You will do me a great favour, sir, if you will furnish me with one.' To this I replied, 'Mr. C——, you have several men of genius in your town, why have you not applied to some of them? There is a namesake of yours in particular, Cox the statuary, who everybody knows is a first-rate maker of verses; he surely, of all the world, is the man for your purposes.' To which the clerk replied, 'Alas, sir, I have heretofore borrowed help from him; but he is a gentleman of so much reading, that the people of our town cannot understand him.' I confess to you, I felt all the force of the compliment implied in this speech, and was almost ready to answer, 'Perhaps, my good friend, they may find me unintelligible too, for the same reason.' But on asking him if he had walked over to Weston on purpose to implore the assistance of my muse, and on his replying in the affirmative, I felt my vanity a little consoled, and, pitying the poor man's distress, which appeared to be considerable, promised to supply him." A copy of verses was accordingly duly forwarded per waggon, headed with the quotation from Horace—

> " Pallida mors æquo pulsat pede pauperum tabernas
>   Regumque turres."

After alluding in the verses to those who had left

> " The Nen's barge-laden wave"

during the preceding year, he addresses the well-known admonitory lines to those who remain—

> " Like crowded forest trees we stand,
>   And some are marked to fall,
>   The axe will smite at God's command,
>   And soon shall smite us all."

The following is a copy of the Northampton bill of mortality for the "year of grace" 1849—omitting, however, the verses on the subject of "Death," which were appended to the document:—

"To the Worshipful Francis Parker, Esquire, Mayor, the Aldermen, Municipal Councillors, and the rest of the worthy inhabitants of the town of Northampton, this Yearly Bill of Mortality is presented by their most obedient, humble servant,

John Wright.

" The Bill of Mortality within the Parish of All Saints, from
the 21st December, 1848, to the 21st December, 1849.

DISEASES, &C., IN THE PARISH OF ALL SAINTS.

Abscess	2	Dropsy	1
Aged	14	Fevers	2
Asthma	3	Fits	1
Brain Fever	1	Insane	1
Child Bed	1	Inflammation	13
Cholera	12	Paralysis	2
Consumption	20	Scarlet Fever	2
Convulsions	2	Teeth	2
Diseased in the head	2		

WHEREOF HAVE DIED

Under two years old	20	Forty and fifty	4
Between two and five	8	Fifty and sixty	4
Five and ten	3	Sixty and seventy	8
Ten and twenty	6	Seventy and eighty	11
Twenty and thirty	6	Eighty and ninety	2
Thirty and forty	9	Ninety and one hundred	0

"REGISTER OF BIRTHS.—All Saints, boys 117, girls 135, total 252;
St. Sepulchre, boys 140, girls 142, total 282; St. Giles, boys 63, girls 76,
total 139; St. Peter, boys 25, girls 10, total 35; Extraparochial, boys 53,
girls 42, total 95. Grand total 803.

"CHRISTENED.—All Saints, males 44, females 52, total 96; St. Sepulchre's, males 55, females 42, total 97; St. Giles's, males 47, females 41,
total 88; St. Peter's, males 15, females 8, total 23; St. Katherine's, males
10, females 18, total 28; chapel in King's-street, males 2, females 2,
total 4; Meeting in St. Peter's parish, males 10, females 15, total 25;
Wesleyan chapels, males 9, females 14, total 23; Commercial-street
chapel, male 1, female 1, total 2; chapel in Horse-market, males 3, females 3, total 6; in the whole town, males 196, females 196, total 392.
Decrease (from last year's bill) 31.

"BURIED.—All Saints, males 45, females 36, total 81*; St. Sepulchre's, males 65, females 63, total 128; St. Giles's, males 68, females
81, total 149; St. Peter's, males 11, females 9, total 20; St. Katherine's,
males 4, females 8, total 12; Infirmary, male 1, female 1, total 2; Roman
Catholic chapel,† males 3, females 5, total 8; chapel in King's-street,
male 1, female 0, total 1; meeting in St. Peter's parish, males 5, females
7, total 12; meeting in College-street, male 1, females 2, total 3; the
Friends' burying-ground, male 1, female 0, total 1; Wesleyan chapels,
male 1, females 2, total 3; Mount Zion chapel, Newland, male 1, fe-

---

*　4 Buried from the parish of All Saints at the parish of St. Sepulchre; 11 ditto at
the parish of St. Giles; 2 ditto at the parish of St. Peter.

†　Information refused.

male 0, total 1; General Cemetery, males 100, females 135, total 235; in the whole town, males 307, females 349, total 656. Increase 107."

LABOUR AND THE POOR.

THE RURAL DISTRICTS.

[FROM OUR SPECIAL CORRESPONDENT.]

COUNTIES OF NORTHAMPTON, LEICESTER, RUTLAND, NOTTINGHAM, AND DERBY.

LETTER XLIV.

The town of Northampton is one which, as well in early as in modern times, has occupied a somewhat prominent position. But, notwithstanding this circumstance, "every one" (to adopt the language of the Registrar-General) "must be struck with the small place which an English county town has in history, compared with the city States of Italy and Greece. Yet the population of Florence, Venice, Genoa, and once of Rome itself, of Sparta, Corinth, Athens, and Thebes, did not equal, or scarcely exceeded, that of some English cities and counties." The history of England itself is, however, in truth, the history of its towns and counties, of which the aggregate is the kingdom. With respect to the town of Northampton, there remains no trace of it in early British history. The Romans have left neither monuments nor name to mark the spot. Whether it was planted by Saxon families, or seized by their warriors from the Britons, when princes, druids, bards, and people were driven towards the west, is unknown; but there is no doubt that it was a town long before history shows it to us as the camp of hostile Danish troopers. For two centuries or more its people lived in the excitements, perils, and vicissitudes of war; it was burned down by Sweyn; and upon one occasion great numbers of its inhabitants were carried away captive. The conqueror divided its lands and houses among his followers; it was armed without by walls and a baronial castle, within by a Norman priory. It took its part in the struggle between the Saxons and Danes. The Saxon Chronicle calls the place Hampton, in the days of Edward the Elder. "In 917, after Easter," we are told, "the army of Danes rode out of Hamtune and Leicester." A mound to the south of the town shows the place of their encampment. The townspeople took a part in the conflict between the Montforts and Henry, and in the wars of the Roses. It was the headquarters of the Parliamentary army, and many of its people fell upon the field of Naseby. A portion of Cromwell's army marched through the town without shoes or stockings, and the townsfolk despatched 1,500 pair of their staple manufacture after him to Leicester. Northampton, with other towns, furnished its contingent of men and money for Cressy, Agincourt, and Blenheim. The Councils and Parliaments which have been held in the town, and the great political events which mark its annals, have all been duly chronicled by the local historians. "The presence of a flourishing place, that has records of eight centuries, revives the past events of its history; the rivers, the streets, the sites of old churches, the country, involuntarily recall the crowd of great or royal characters who have passed that way— Sweyn, Harold, and Tosti; Henry I., Henry II., and Becket; Richard the Lion-hearted, John and the great barons; the Montforts, Prince Edward and his hundred Crusaders; the Black Prince and Richard the assassin; Henry VIII., Elizabeth, and Burleigh; Charles I., Fairfax, and Cromwell, and, in these latter days, Victoria. Sweyn, with his predatory band, the first of the long procession of warriors, statesmen, and princes, burned the town to the ground; Victoria—then the Princess, now the Queen of a mighty empire—gave her name to a dispensary for the relief of the sick and the suffering. The two acts, the two persons—the relentless chief and the beneficent princess— characterise the epochs."

The town itself is situated on the south-side of the uplands from which the Avon, the Charwell, and the Nene flow down to the Severn and to the Wash. Fuller, speaking of its situation, with respect to a college which it was proposed to found in the town, says, "that it is a convenient place, where the air is clear and not over sharp; the earth fruitful, yet not over dirty; water plentiful, yet far from any fennish annoyance, and wood (most wanting now of days) conveniently sufficient in that age. But the main is, Northampton is near the centre of England, so that all travellers, coming thither from the remotest parts of the land, may be said to meet by the town in the midst of their journey." According to the Domesday account there were in Northampton at the time of the survey, 330½ houses, 35½ being empty, and 295 inhabited. Between that period and the 16th century, the town rose rapidly in importance. Leland, who was despatched by Henry VIII. on a tour of inspection, reports that "There be in the waulles of Northampton four gates. The Castle stondeth hard by the west gate, and hath a large kepe. The area of the residew is very large, and bullewurkes of yerth be made afore the castelle gate. Paroche churches in Northampton withyn the waulles be 7, whereof the Church of Al-Halowes (All Saints) is principall, stonding yn the Harte of the Toune, and is large and welle builded. There be yn the suburbes 2 Paroche Churches, whereof I saw one yn the west suburbe as I rode over the weste Brydge, fairly archid with stone under the which Avon itself, not yot augmented with Wedon water, doth ren. There is a Chapelle of St. Caterine, sette in a cemiterie in the toune longing to the Church of Al-Hallowes, where that paroche dooth byri. And I saw the ruines of a large chappelle without the North Gate." The preamble of the 27th Henry VIII., c. 1, about two years after the visit of Leland, shows that the condition of this town, as of some others, was such as to call for the operation of some stringent sanitary measures. The preamble recites that—"Forsomoche as dyvers and many howses messages and tenementis of habitations in the tounes of Nottingham, Shrewsbury, Ludlowe, Brydgnorth, Quynborowe, Northampton, and Gloucester, now are and of long time have bene in greate ruin and decay, and specially in the principal and chief streets there being, in the which streets have been beautiful duellinge howses there, well inhabited, while at this day much part thereof is desolete and void groundes, with piteous cellars and vaults, lying open and uncovered, very perilous for people to go by in the night without jeopardy of life." The act then proposes the following strong measure, which throws some light upon the tenures of that time:—"For remedy whereof be it enacted that if the *owners* within three years after proclamation by the mayors, sheriffs, or bailiffs, do not sufficiently re-edify and build the *houses*, it shall be to the *lords* of whom such vacant ground is holden, to enter immediately, and have it to them and to their heirs for ever." What might have been the effect of this measure in improving the town is not easy to determine; but about the middle of the seventeenth century we are informed, "that Northampton might well contend with the best inland city or town that is not seated upon a navigable river, for sweet and wholesome air, pleasantness of situation, plenty and cheapness of corn and butcher's meat, good ancient buildings, dry and commodious cellarage, broad and cleanly streets, a spacious market hall, fine and profitable gardens and orchards within the walls, while it was beautified and honoured with their standing." At the present time the town is, generally speaking, well built and clean; with the exception, however, of a few of the principal streets, the houses present a uniform appearance, the smaller ones being almost entirely occupied by persons employed in the staple trade of the town—shoemaking. There are several of the back courts and alleys branching off from some of the main streets, which call for the interference of the sanitary reformer. Among places of the sort might be mentioned No. 4 Court, and some others in its neighbourhood, leading out of Bridge-street, which are badly drained, ill-ventilated, and overcrowded. Cholera was more fatal in these places than in any other portion of the town. In Bull-yard, which consists of a square of small red brick cottages, tenanted by journeymen shoemakers, great complaints were made to me of the total want of drainage—the refuse from the houses having to be thrown into the court, or being collected in heaps till the scavenger comes once a week, and sometimes at longer intervals, to clear them away. In Bell-barn-court, there are a number of old and decayed rows of cottages, built back to back, without drainage and without ventilation; there is a small mockery of a garden in the front of each of the cottages. Northampton is well supplied with water, an engine and two reservoirs having been constructed in 1837, from which a supply is obtained in every part of the town.

The rate of increase in the value of real property in the town of Northampton has been very considerable. The annual value, as assessed to the income-tax in 1815, was £21,731—which, at the average price of wheat for the four previous years, would be equivalent to 4,515 quarters at 96s. 2d. per quarter; while the annual value of houses and lands assessed under the income-tax for the year ending 5th April, 1843, was £74,416—being equal to the value of 23,046 quarters of wheat, at 64s. 7d. per quarter, being the average price for the five years 1838-42. The population of the town, according to the census of 1841, was, males 14,026, females 14,095, making a total of 28,121. The number of deaths of all ages in the seven years 1838-44 was 4,816; the annual mortality per cent. being, for all ages, males 2.489, for females 2.396, and the numbers living to one death being for the former 40.2, for the latter 41.7. A great proportion of the population of the town are Dissenters. There are three Independent chapels in the town, two belonging to the Baptists, one to the General Baptists, one (as I was informed) to a "kind of Hyper-Calvinistic Baptists," one Unitarian chapel, two Wesleyan Methodists, one Wesleyan Association, one Primitive Methodist, one Millenarian, one Quaker's meeting-house, and one Roman Catholic church. There are also six churches in connection with the Establishment, in addition to a large licensed parochial school-room, in which service is performed.

The following table will show the number of children receiving education in the various schools in connection, more or less, with the Church of England:—

In Connection with the Church.	Sunday and Week Day.		Week Day only.		Sunday only.		Total of each School.	
Name of School.	Boys.	Girls.	Boys.	Girls.	Boys.	Girls.	Boys.	Girls.
St. Giles's Central Boys' School of the Northamptonshire Society for educating the Poor .	100	100	160	134	—	—	260	234
St. Katharine's Infant School..	—	—	67	67	—	—	67	67
Infant School	—	—	20	20	—	—	20	20
All Saints' Parochial	180	150	—	—	320	310	500	460
Grammar School	68	—	—	—	—	—	68	—
Infants' School	201	152	—	—	—	—	201	152
Blue Coat School	36	40	—	—	—	—	36	40
Yellow School	20	—	—	—	—	—	20	—
St. Katharine's Sunday School.	—	—	—	—	114	125	114	125
St. Giles's Sunday School	—	—	—	—	123	117	123	117
St. Peter's and Upton	—	—	—	—	47	50	47	50
Total	...	...	...	...	...	...	1,456	1,265

From this number, however, must be deducted 201 boys and 134 girls, who come under the head of "duplicate entries"—that is, they are entered as "Sunday only" in one school, and they also occur as "week-day only" in other schools. The number of boys and girls, therefore, receiving education in schools conducted upon the principles of the Church of England is 2,386. Another school is in course of erection in the south quarter of the town, in connection with the Church of England, which it is proposed to call "The Cholera Offering." In the new British school, which is chiefly attended by the children of the different sections of Dissenters, the number of boys is 273, and of girls 133. At the Roman Catholic day school there are about 150 children, girls and boys, about 100 of whom also attend the Sunday school at the chapel. At the Sunday school of the Wesleyans the average attendance of children of both sexes is about 340, and at the infant school 100. At the Sunday school the children are engaged during school hours in reading the Scriptures, spelling, and in learning the Wesleyan catechism. The Primitive Methodists have 20 children in their Sunday schools. The Wesleyan Association have no Sunday or week-day schools. The whole number of children attending the Sunday schools of the other sections of Dissenters does not exceed 250. The total number of children, therefore, receiving education—exclusive of pauper children, and of those in private schools—in the various Sunday and week-day schools of the town is as follows:—

Church of England	2,186
British Schools	406
Roman Catholics	150
Wesleyans	440
Primitive Methodists	20
Other Dissenters	450
Total	3,652

The number of children under ten years of age in the town amounted in 1841 to 9,958; under fifteen, to 14,782. The number of children receiving education is not more than one-third of those under ten years of age, and not more than about one-fifth of those under fifteen years of age. There is, therefore, ample room for further improvement in respect to education in the town.

Although it is an old saying with respect to Northampton, that you may know when you are within a mile of it by the noise of the lap-stones, it would still be wrong to consider the town solely as a place for the manufacture of boots and shoes. It is quite true that this forms the staple trade, and affords employment to the great majority of its inhabitants. The town is, however, the centre of one of the most flourishing of our agricultural counties. It forms the mart in which vast quantities of agricultural produce are disposed of, and a considerable trade is carried on in articles of furniture, clothing, books, and foreign produce. In addition to those engaged in the shoe trade, there were returned in 1841, 23 booksellers, 83 grocers, 65 drapers, 180 tailors, 88 curriers, 190 masons, statuaries, plasterers, and bricklayers, 165 carpenters and joiners, 59 painters and plumbers, 60 blacksmiths, and 85 innkeepers. There were also 23 brewers, 92 butchers, and 87 bakers. Of domestic servants there were 550 above twenty, and 368 under twenty years of age. With respect to the shoemaking portion of the inhabitants, in 1831 there were returned as shoemakers, males above 20, 1,322; in 1841 the number had increased to 1,821. There were also at the same time 442 males, and 346 females, under 20 years of age, engaged in the shoe trade. The whole number of males in the town above the age of 20 was 5,756, so that nearly one in three of the men is a shoemaker. The whole number of shoemakers in the county is 5,237, or about 1 in 10 of the males above 20 years of age. The proportion of shoemakers in all England is as 144,601 to 3,897,336, or 1 in 27 males of the age of 20 and upwards. In the town of Stafford, 899 in 2,704, or 1 in three men, are shoemakers; in Carlisle the shoemakers are only in the proportion of about 1 in 28, the numbers being as 205 to 5,784; in Bedford, the numbers are 212 to 2,272, or about one in ten. The sedentary occupation of the shoemakers, combined with their proverbial unsteadiness, has tended to increase to a considerable extent the rate of mortality among that class of persons. From the register which is kept at All Saints, I have extracted the annual mortality of the shoemakers of that, as compared with the whole district, and also with that of the country parishes in the sub-districts of the town. The proportion of shoemakers in All Saints is somewhat less than in the whole borough—the numbers being in 1841, 601, of whom 488 were twenty years of age and upwards. The mortality at the several ages in the seven years 1838-44, was as follows:—

Ages.	Number of Shoemakers in 1841.	Death of Shoemakers in 7 years, 1838–44.	Annual Mortality per cent. of Shoemakers in All Saints.	All Saints' Parish.	Country Parishes of Sub-District.
10–20	112	7	.893	.515	.474
20–40	304	25	1.175	.849	.820
40–60	141	13	1.317	1.606	1.229
60–80	42	18	6.122	6.257	5.893

From this it will be seen that the mortality among shoemakers between the ages of 20 and 40 is considerably higher in this than in the other districts at corresponding ages. Of 69 deaths, 31 were by consumption, and 8 by diseases of the heart—diseases to which this class of artizans appear to be peculiarly liable.

Before proceeding to give an account of the nature of the employment, and of the wages paid to the shoemakers of Northampton, there are one or two institutions in the town, mainly supported by the working classes, which, on account of the benefits derived from them, appear to be deserving of special notice. The first of these is the Northampton Artizans' and Labourers' Friend Society. The objects of the society are twofold—the establishment of a Provident and of an Investment fund. The mode adopted in carrying out the first-named is by the members paying a contribution of one penny per week to the society, which cannot be drawn out until the depositor shall have attained the age of 60 years, or in the event of his death, when the money is paid to his representative. These small deposits are allowed to accumulate, the depositors who are not in arrear with their weekly pence receiving an addition of something like 15 per cent. on their money. During the last twelve months the amount of the weekly pence paid into the Provident Fund was £64, to which has been added, by way of bonus and interest, a sum of not less than £10. Many of the members, however, prefer paying in more than the required penny per week; and the amount received during the year under the head of payments beyond the required sum was £184, which has been increased by about £11 of interest. The members, therefore, who have been regular in making their payments, have received a total addition of £21 to their deposits. Any member who may be in arrear with his subscription cannot, according to the rules of the society, receive any interest for his money, and this is one of the modes by which so large an amount of interest is added to the funds of the society. Persons contributing a penny per week to this fund are entitled to an allotment of the society's land, not exceeding a rood in extent. The society has at present about 50 acres, which is divided into 248 allotments, nearly the whole of the allottees being shoemakers in the town. The manner in which the land is cultivated is highly creditable to the poor people, many portions of it having produced extraordinary crops, and excellent vegetables. Meanwhile, the benefits afforded to the shoemakers, in drawing them for a certain portion of each day from their sedentary occupation to a more healthful employment, are shown in an improved state of health among them. By diverting their attention from the public-house and the beer-shop, a marked improvement in their moral condition has also taken place, and habits of temperance and sobriety have sprung up among them. The business of the society is conducted by a mixed committee, consisting of six gentlemen of the town and six working-men, who are members of the society, and who are annually elected by the members. Mr. Beckwith (one of the magistrates of the town), with whom the institution originated, and to whose laudable exertions is to be ascribed the position which it at present holds, informed me that he had personally inspected the homes of seventy of the oldest members of the society, and was surprised to witness the air of comfort and cleanliness which prevailed among them. "Their land," he says, "they value above all things, and will make the most extraordinary exertions in order to cultivate it properly and pay the rents punctually. Out of the whole number of allottees there is but one in arrear with his rent."

Another institution in the town that has also conferred great benefits upon the poorer classes, is the Victoria Dispensary. Upon the occasion of her Majesty's paying a visit to the Marquess of Exeter, she passed through the town of Northampton. The townspeople thought it a proper occasion for showing their loyalty by some public act of rejoicing. A considerable sum of money was accordingly raised with a view of giving to the poorer people a dinner of roast beef and plum pudding. In endeavouring to carry out this intention, the projectors were met by the almost insuperable difficulty of drawing the line as to the number or class to which the guests should be limited, and the plan of the dinner was abandoned. After some discussion among the committee, it was finally decided that they should establish a public dispensary, which, with the sanction of her Majesty, was called the Victoria Dispensary. The dispensary having been decided upon, and its title having been fixed, a new difficulty sprang up with reference to the principle upon which it should be conducted—a considerable number of the townspeople being in favour of making it a charitable institution, and another party being desirous that it should be on the provident principle. The latter plan was finally adopted. Each member of the society pays a penny per week; a man and his wife with their family pay twopence a week, for which they receive medical relief at the dispensary, every day in the week, if required. If unable to apply personally for medicine or advice at the dispensary, one of the medical officers of the institution calls upon them at their own homes.

The society met with considerable opposition at first; it is now, however, firmly established. There are 4,000 members on the books, their subscriptions amounting to not less than £10 per week. As showing the extent to which provident institutions are preferred by the more industrious and honest of the labouring classes, I was informed by the manager of the society that, when the cholera first broke out in the town, a requisition was sent to the mayor, requesting him to convene a public meeting to consider the propriety of opening the dispensary to the poor generally and gratuitously—so that all persons attacked with cholera might receive assistance. It was very generally thought that by doing so they would injure the interests of the dispensary, as many persons who were paying members might take advantage of the offer of gratuitous relief, and withhold their payments; but, to the surprise of the managers, they found that, in the four weeks that the dispensary was open gratuitously, they received an accession of 508 new paying members, and within a few weeks after, not less than 1,700 more. The poor set the greatest value upon the institution, as they feel a degree of independence in connection with it, which they would not were it conducted upon a merely charitable principle.

The Northampton General Lunatic Asylum is also an institution which appears to deserve special notice, on account of the very excellent manner in which it is conducted, and the great attention and kindness which are shown to the inmates, the great majority of whom are pauper lunatics. The Institution, which is beautifully situated upon some rising ground a short distance from the town of Northampton, was erected by private subscription in the year 1836, Earl Spencer contributing towards the expense of its erection the munificent sum of £7,000. The building itself is of a beautiful description of white stone from the Kingsthorpe quarries, and is tastefully decorated. In the interior of the house the arrangements are of the most complete and commodious character; galleries run round the entire building, of 14 feet in width and of 60 in length. Each department is heated by means of hot-water pipes. There are also 36 acres of ground tastefully laid out, belonging to the institution. In order to diversify the routine of life and to sweeten existence even in this asylum, various amusements are called into requisition. Occasionally musical parties take place in the house, in which the inmates take part. Several who had entered the asylum unable to read or write had made considerable proficiency in these branches of knowledge at the time of my visit—the schoolmaster being himself a patient, who appeared to take a great delight in his avocation. Even the higher branches of learning are not neglected. One of the patients is in the habit of teaching German to some of the inmates, and others are the willing pupils of an inmate who imparts to them his knowledge of Latin. No instrumental restraint is applied to any of the patients, the treatment pursued being strictly in accordance with the more enlightened and humane systems founded upon the virtue and efficacy "of a moral code of government, as adapted to meet all the exigencies of the insane." The Commissioners in Lunacy, in their report upon the institution, state that they "found one female with gloves upon her hands to prevent her picking her face; and, with that exception (if indeed it can be called so), no patient was under instrumental restraint at the time of our visit, and the use of such restraint is almost, if not entirely, unknown." This species of restraint has been superseded by various occupations and amusements which tend to amuse the patients. During the last year a handsome bagatelle table has been added to the men's gallery, and a considerable addition has also, I was informed, been made of standard books to the library. *The Morning Chronicle* and other daily newspapers are circulated in the house; and the letters which have appeared in *The Morning Chronicle* on the subject of "Labour and the Poor" have been read with the utmost interest by the inmates. Divine service is performed every Sunday, the average attendance at which is about 150; and the attention and decorum are such as would do credit to many a sane congregation. The number of inmates in the house has averaged, during the year, 250. Among the number of its inmates is Clare, the "Rural Burns," as he is called. The lot which had visited the father, as too many other farm labourers, has fallen upon the son. From his earliest life he was doomed to toil. For a considerable period he received nine shillings a week and his board on a farm at Helpstone; but his employer proposing to reduce his wages to seven shillings a week, he returned to the home of his father, who was then a helpless cripple and a pauper. The feeling with which he viewed the state of pauperism at home, and the apprehension which he entertained of its being his own lot, may be learned from one of his earliest productions—"The Village Funeral," in which the following lines occur:—

> "Oh may I die before I'm doomed to seek,
> 　　That last resource of hope but ill supplied,
> To claim the humble pittance once a week,
> 　　Which justice forces from disdainful pride."

His worst fears, however, have been more than realised. He is now a lunatic in this asylum, and the bitterest complaint which he made to me was of the injustice done to him by the public in not recognizing him, instead of Scott and Byron, as the author of Marmion and of Don Juan, and in refusing him the honour of having gained the battle of Waterloo. A volume of his poems, several of which are very pleasing, was collected and published previously to his affliction; and his then condition in life may be best gathered from one of his letters, with the perusal of which I was favoured, in which he says, "If I sink for want of friends, my old friend, necessity, is ready to help me as before. It was never my fortune as yet to meet advancement from friendship; my fate has ever been hard labour among the most vulgar and lowest conditions of men, and very small is the pittance hard labour allows me, though I always toiled, even beyond my strength, to obtain it." His parents, who were in a hopeless state of poverty, ended their days, I believe, in the workhouse; and it is extraordinary how the youthful poet should have found the means of acquiring any education whatever. By extra work, however, as a ploughboy, and by helping his father morning and evening at threshing, he earned the money which paid for his education, and from the labour of eight weeks he generally saved as much as would pay for a month's schooling. Clare was the writer, though not generally known as such, of the lines, "Here we meet too soon to part"—which, set to one of Rossini's most beautiful airs, were some time exceedingly popular. It is distressing to think of the struggles with which the peasant poet had to contend, but, still more so, to witness the melancholy wreck which he now presents, and the utter prostration of that noble intellect which, under happier auspices, might have obtained for its possessor a lasting and an honourable place in the Temple of Fame, instead of the forlorn position of a friendless lunatic in a county lunatic asylum.

LABOUR AND THE POOR.

THE RURAL DISTRICTS.

[FROM OUR SPECIAL CORRESPONDENT.]

COUNTIES OF NORTHAMPTON, LEICESTER, RUTLAND, NOTTINGHAM, AND DERBY.

THE BOOT AND SHOEMAKERS OF NORTHAMPTON.

LETTER XLV.

The chief seats for the manufacture of boots and shoes, in the county of Northampton, are the towns of Northampton, Daventry, Wellingborough, Higham-Ferrers, and Kettering. The villages round these towns are also nearly all, more or less, the site of the shoe trade. In 1841 the number of boot and shoemakers in the county was, males above 20, 5,237; under 20 years of age, 1,215; females above 20 years of age, 355; under that age, 214; making a total of 7,621. This return, however, does not fully represent the number of persons employed in this trade, the number under twenty years of age being considerably more than that represented in the returns made when the last census was taken. At least two-thirds of the children of those engaged in boot and shoe-making are employed in one branch or other connected with the trade. Assuming that the number of persons in this county dependent upon the shoe trade for their subsistence bears the same proportion to the numbers actually employed as in the case of the agricultural labourers, there will be found to be not less than 30,000 persons dependent for support upon this branch of employment.

The trade of shoemaking in Northampton is not exclusively confined to the natives of the county. There is generally a very large influx of "foreigners," or persons belonging to other parts of the country, who flock into the town at different times of the year, and who are, indeed, commonly considered the best kind of workmen. This class of persons usually visit the towns of Cambridge and Oxford about term time, and arrive in Northampton a little before Christmas, when the better sort of work is more brisk, and when there are generally more orders in the "bespoke" department. About the time of the meeting of Parliament and the commencement of the London season, these people flock to the metropolis, where they can almost always command work. They are, I was informed, generally speaking, "a very fuddling set of characters, and seldom or never are seen with a decent pair of shoes to their feet or a decent coat to their backs." A considerable number of them are Irish, and what are called by the craft "Irish Cockneys"—that is, Irish who have been for some time in England, but still not long enough to entitle them to the character of English. Many of them have picked up the trade by tramping about, by getting little odd jobs at the shops, and by seeing the work done by others at the lodging-houses where they have been in the habit of staying. There appears to be a very good feeling entertained by the "town hands" towards the Irish section of the "foreigners." "They are the best fellows going," said one of them to me, "for sticking up for prices." "The Daventry men," however, said the same informant, "are the greatest lot of scabs under the sun, and they'll ruin the trade, and the country too, if they are not put down. They have ruined the trade of Wellingborough already, and Northampton will soon follow." There is an association among the members of the trade, which has for its object the affording assistance to such of its members as may be on the tramp. Those who belong to the association are termed "flints," those who do not, "scabs"—hence the epithet applied to the men of Daventry. There are belonging to the association about 200 shoemakers, the great majority of whom are tramps. Upon their arrival in any town in which a branch of the society exists, the member receives, upon the production of his card of membership, a sufficient sum of money to pay for a night's lodging and his food. In London the sum allowed is 1s., in Northampton 9d., and in most other towns 6d. only. The society has endeavoured for some years to keep up the price of labour, but all their efforts have been ineffectual. "Two or three years since," said the secretary of the association, "we struck in one of the shops in the town. At the time we struck there they were paying 5s. 6d. for patent boots, blind rans, and now the same firm gets them made for 4s. 6d., stitched seats; and calf boots that they used to give 3s. 6d. for, they now give only 3s., and for many of them as low as 2s. 6d. Short boots that they used to give 3s. for, they have now made for 2s. 6d. and 2s. 9d. It was no use our holding out, for the 'scabs' from the country went in, and fetched the work out for whatever prices the masters liked to give."

In order to convey a complete view of the trade, I shall state the prices paid for each description of boots and shoes in the various stages of their manufacture, as well as for the preparation of the leather, so far as I have been able to ascertain them. With respect to the first stage, that of tanning, there is very little of that carried on in the county. There is but one tannery in the town of Northampton, and the material prepared at that establishment is almost invariably sent to London, where, I was informed, it can be purchased and sent back to Northampton at a cheaper rate than it can be bought in the town itself. Messrs. Gotch, at Kettering, who are large contractors for army boots, have a tannery in connection with their establishment in that town, at which twenty-four persons are usually employed. The common rate of wages paid ranges from 12s. to 16s. per week, the work being generally pretty constant.

The skins having left the tannery, the services of the curriers are next called into requisition. Many of the persons employed in this department are paid by the week, but the majority by the piece, or skin. The rate of weekly wages for a good hand varies from £1 to 25s. Where the person is paid by the piece, the amount of his earnings will depend, to a great extent, upon the quality of the skins upon which he is employed. The skins which are considered by the curriers as the best to work are those which are tanned at Stourbridge. A great deal appears to depend, not only upon the quality of the tanning which the skin undergoes, but upon the mode in which the beasts have been fed. The state of the hide affords a clear indication of the feeding of the beast; if he has not been forced, it will run regular all through, but if forced, it will be unequal and thick in the butt, and thin in the shoulder. A person who may have to work upon the Australian hides, although he may receive 3d. per dozen skins more, would not be able to earn so much by 5s. or 6s. in the week, as when employed upon the Stourbridge skins; this arises from the Australian hides not being well tanned. "Kips" and horse hides are the best kind of work; but of the latter there are none dressed in Northampton. The East India "kips" are also held in high favour by the curriers. A "kip" is a term originally applied to the skin of a half-grown beast, and in consequence of the similarity, in point of size and weight, of the English "kip" and the hide of the full-grown Indian beast, the term has been applied to the latter. There are also a considerable number of Petersburg "kips," but they are not so good as the English ones for working.

In order to arrive at a knowledge of the earnings of a currier who works by the piece, it will be necessary to follow the various stages through which the skins pass when under his hand, and the price paid at each process of preparation. We will take three dozen of 50 lb. skins, for example. The first operation which they will have to undergo is that of "shaving." For this a sum of 2s. 9d. per dozen is usually paid; for the Australian hides 3s. will be paid, but I am now dealing only with English ones. Upon an average, a good hand may shave three dozen of these skins in the day. After "shaving," the next process is that of "scouring" and "slicking," for which 6d. per dozen is paid—three dozen still constituting an average day's work. The great difference in price which appears to be paid in these two operations is explained by the fact that "shaving" is the most difficult part of the work, which none but the best workmen can perform; while many of the men who come into the shop to work at "table work," and who receive about 15s. per week, can perform the "scouring and slicking." The price of 6d. per dozen for "scouring and slicking" is only paid to the workman who undertakes the shaving and the whole of the processes connected with the preparation of the skins. For "setting and oiling," which are the next processes, the price paid is also 6d. per dozen, and the three dozen can be completed in about eight hours. This third operation, like that of "shaving," is one which requires some amount of extra judgment on the part of the workmen. The final process consists in the "making up," the price paid for which, not including "waxing," is 2s. 9d. per dozen; and it will take a day and a half to make up the three dozen skins, there being about half as much more work in "making up" as there is in the "shaving," although the same amount is paid for both operations. The "waxing" is usually performed by apprentices or boys. For the various processes, therefore, connected with the preparation of the three dozen skins, the currier will receive—

For " shaving " . . . .   8s. 3d.
    " scouring and slicking "   1s. 6d.
    " setting and oiling " . .   1s. 6d.
    " making up " . . . .   8s. 3d.
                                   ————————
    Total . . . .   19s. 6d.

The time employed being, in "shaving," one day; "scouring," one day; "setting and oiling," eight hours; and "making-up," one and a half days—which, at eleven hours per day, would be four days and two-and-a-half hours, being at the rate of 29s. or 30s. per week.

The leather having now gone through its various stages at the currier's, passes into the hands of the shoe manufacturers or factors, where the services of a class of persons called "clickers or cutters" are next required. Their duties consist in "casting," or cutting up the skins of leather into pieces of various sizes for the shoemakers. The earnings of the "clickers" vary in some of the establishments from 12s. to 18s. per week, the workmen usually being employed on the premises of the manufacturers. The leather having been cut into the required shapes and sizes, undergoes the process of "blocking." With respect to the earnings of this class of persons one of them informed me that he was paid, for "blocking" best calf Wellingtons, 4s. per dozen. There were, however, only two houses in Northampton which paid so high a rate as that, the usual price given being 3s. 6d. per dozen. For short Wellingtons the usual price was 2s. 6d. per dozen, one house in the town giving 3s. Best Clarences were paid for at the rate of 2s. 2d. per dozen, commoner kinds 2s. My informant also stated that he had "a strong lot of children, who assisted him," and with their help he could get through a dozen in about ten hours. To one of the boys who worked for him he paid 6s. per week. The cost of size, "dubbing," other articles, and wear and tear of materials, he estimated at about 2s. 6d. per week, exclusive of candles and oil. Blocking is almost always done at the houses of the workpeople.

After blocking, the next stage is that of "closing." The persons employed in this department are generally very young, the better description of work requiring excellent eyesight. The labour is particularly trying to the eyes, and impairs the eyesight very greatly. Lads and young men are frequently compelled to wear spectacles of great magnifying power, and I was informed of several cases where the workmen "used two pair of spectacles at once." Children are put to this kind of work at a very early age, some of the "closers" employing great numbers of them. The reason the children are more generally sent to the "closing" than to the "making up" branch is that they will be "out of hand sooner" at the one than at the other. At many of the closers they keep what is called "a factory of children." "At these places," said a shoemaker to me, "the poor little creatures go to work, many of 'em as early as four years old. They are so afraid of being late that they'll jump out of bed at four or five o'clock, and run to look at the church clock to see what time it is—there is always a light in the church clock. They give the poor little children very little wages, too—very often not more than a shilling a week—although they get through a deal of light kind of work in the day; and as they give 'em so little for their work, they are able to compete with other men, who won't have anything to do with the factory plan, but who work single-handed." The children do not receive anything for the first six months; after that period they receive from one to two shillings per week, and gradually rise to 8s. One young man informed me that he was eight years at work before he got as high as 7s. 6d. per week, and he was then seventeen years of age.

The first closer that I called upon was employed in closing "best patent Wellingtons, morocco legs and patent fronts," for which he would receive 4s. per pair; for short Wellingtons, of the same description, the price paid was 3s. Out of the sum which he received for closing the best patent Wellingtons, done in white silk, he would have to find the silk. It would take him and his wife "fourteen hours, without any 'hobbling,' to close a pair of boots of this sort, such as the aristocracy appeared in at their balls." "I don't think they know," said he, "all the sweat and blood which is spent upon their fine boots—they don't know all the aching heads and aching hearts endured by those whose fingers perform the labour for them; if they did, they would soon make the Legislature tell a different tale from what it has ever done. The tongues of some of the fronts of the patent boots contain an enormous amount of 'stabbing;' the 'flourishes' in some of them have twenty-eight stitches to the inch. In one pair which I made a short time since there were thirty-six to the inch. The flourishes consist of ornamental work in the upper part of the leg of the boot; they are never seen when on, as they are covered with the trowsers. It would take us two days to finish off a first-rate pair of this sort, working ten hours regularly every day. The tongue is first closed in the inside—there is then a row of stabbing to the lining which comes over the tongue to strengthen the work. That extra work would only be put in for the bespoke boots. If only intended for sale, of course so much regard would not be paid to strength." This person complained very bitterly of the system pursued by the manufacturers, of limiting the time for receiving and giving out work to the hours of nine and ten in the morning. The workmen are, he said, obliged to attend at that hour to take in their work, and receive other work in return. If they are after that time, they are not able to get any work for that day; they are locked out sometimes to the half-minute; and even when punctual, they not unfrequently have to wait a couple of hours before they can obtain their supply of work. I was informed, however, by several of the manufacturers, that it was absolutely indispensable that some certain time in the day should be fixed for taking in and giving out work, and that no more delay took place than could be expected where so large a number of workpeople were to be attended to.

The next person upon whom I called was employed in closing calf Wellingtons. The price paid for this kind of work, according to his statement, varied from 10d. to 15d. for "long Wellingtons;" for "short Wellingtons" from 10d. to 1s. It would take about three hours and a half to close a pair of the "tenpenny longs," and about four for the fifteenpenny ones. There were no "side rows" in the tenpennies; they were done either with thread or twisted silk, and the shilling ones were also done with twisted silk. For "patent circulars" the price paid for closing was 1s. 2d., and for "shooting half-boots" 1s. 6d. It was bad work, too, at that, as there was a great deal of "stabbing." Indeed, it was all "stabbing," except two or three seams up the front, one across the front, and one up behind. Then there were the coloshes that went all round the boots, and they had to be double-lined throughout. For closing calf "circulars," the price paid was 2½d., but out of that the "closer" had to pay ¼d. per pair for the lining to another person. Clarences were about the same price. For closing contract army boots, the price paid was 2¼d. It took about three hours to close a pair, four pairs in the day being considered a good day's work for the girls and young women who are principally employed upon them. Out of the 9d. per day so earned, the price of the thread would have to be deducted, and of course something for candles during the winter. The price paid for closing bluchers was from 2½d. to 3½d. per pair.

The leather having gone through these several stages of "blocking and closing," is now ready for the maker. The first person of this class upon whom I called was employed in making Wellingtons. His statement was as follows:—"The price paid for making Wellingtons is 2s. 6d. and it will take me fourteen hours to finish off a pair of them. The cost of candles will be about 7½d. per week, as I have the patent ones. Then there is the 'grindery'—that consists of hemp, flax, wax, paste, heel-ball, gum, ink, and bristles. The welts are sown to the upper leathers with hemp, and the welts and soles are put together with a finer kind of thread. Then we have to find the awls and knives, which are almost always breaking. The expenses of grindery and candles at this time of year would be about 1½d. to each pair of boots, and when we have to black the soles the ink would be about a halfpenny. I have frequently made double-sole Wellingtons, with small spriggs, for 2s. 6d., and I believe that there are a good many of them made at 2s. a pair. I sometimes work upon 'Clarences' when the trade is slack, which is always the case just before and after Christmas. It is brisker now than it has been for the last four years at this time of year. I have 2s. 1d. for making Clarences, and that has been the standing price for that description of goods for the last four years. For some Clarences they give as much as 2s. 6d. a pair, but then they are made smarter, with 'bevelled waists,' and it takes me as long to make a pair of them as it would to make a pair of Wellingtons. But patent Wellingtons they give as high as 4s. for, but there's a strange lot of time spent in making them, the work is so exact. Patent 'short boots' are 3s., extra patent 'shorts' 3s. 6d., best calf 'shorts' about 2s. and 2s. 3d. There are some of the masters in the town who give less money for all descriptions of goods, because they are made up for the cheap markets in London and other places. The persons who buy the boots know nothing at all about the quality of the leather or the kind of work that's put in 'em. There are many boots of this kind made in the town that will soak up as much water as a sponge in wet weather, and twelve pair of 'em wouldn't last out the year for any one purchaser, nor last so long as one good, substantial, well-made pair would. 'Cheap, cheap!' is the cry with everybody now-a-days, and they must have cheap shoes, too; no matter about the poor cobbler as makes 'em. But they have to pay dearer for 'em in the end. That's some satisfaction to us. We have the laugh at 'em, although they don't think it. We knows our customers, and we puts our work in according. There's several of the masters in the town who have shops in London, and other large places, where they sell nearly all they get made. People often think that there's no art in making shoes. Why, it's a trade that you're never perfect in, you're always larning. There was one old man at Wellingborough, who was ninety years old, and when he took home some work one day they found fault with it and the old man said, 'Well, I've been all my life making shoes, and now I can't please my master I'm sure it's time I gave over; we must be always a'larning and I'm getting a'most too old to larn now.' The usual mode of giving out the work to the men is this—they give you out the stuff for half-a-dozen pair, that is for the bottoms, and then, when they are at all slack, they will give you out the tops, one pair at a time, and make you go and dance upon 'em every time you want 'stuff.' Then, when they're at all slack, they have a custom of changing nearly all their hands—at least two thirds of them are discharged and fresh ones taken on; this is done to see if they can't get some superior article produced to what was produced before by those who were employed, because it is thought that, when men get on fresh, they will do their best to keep their situations. This is a system that ought to be put a stop to, for in my opinion, if it is not, it will not only be the ruin of Northampton but of all England. There is no such thing as middlemen in our trade. We get the work direct from the manufacturers and take it home to them. Some time since they used to make you take some of the wages out in bread or flour or such like, but it is only with the smaller and lower manufacturers that that plan is adopted now. There are a great many 'short boots' got up in the town—sprigged bottoms—for 1s. 7d. and 1s. 8d. per pair, and they'll take a man a good hard day's work to make a pair of 'em. They used to make best and seconds, but now they have got no best, for they call them all 'seconds,' and only pay 'seconds' price for them. They have them now made with 'stitched seats' instead of 'blind rans.' Two or three years ago, when you used to stitch a pair of seats, they gave 6d. a pair extra, but now, if they give you a pair of seats or blind rans, they take 6d. off."

A person employed in making strong bluchers said that he received 1s. 4d. for making. It took him about six hours to make a pair, and he could get through twelve pairs in the week. "But where you can get one man," said he, "who can do that, you will find ten as cannot. You will find more men as can make about six pair, and so on. It's all owing to the person's ability. I have been at work now near forty years at it—ever since 1813—before the Peace. Such things as I am making now I used to get 2s. 8d. for in those days. I would much rather do these boots now at 1s. 4d. though, than I would do 'em for 2s. 8d. in the war time. A bit of stuff in those days to make a man's shirt would be half-a-crown, and a bit of stuff for a girl's frock half-a-crown a yard, and now you can get a bit of calico for 4½d. that would last you quite as long, and a bit of print for a dress for the girls for almost nothing. I profess myself to be a 'strong-blucher man.' I have made bluchers for as low as 10d. or 1s., and could get as much money then out of 'em as I can out of these at 1s. 4d., because the work is not so particular, as they are only for the cheap trade. I take it that my grindery and candles is about 2s. a week. I pay 2s. a week for the house. I have eight children. This boy here pays for his board, and another boy pays for his living, too; so there's only six on 'em for us to keep."

"The Oxford shoes that I'm a making," said another person who was employed upon them, "are the best work as is of the kind. One man in the town gives 2s. 6d., but the one that I am at work for only gives 2s. 2d. If I was to work ever so hard, I could not make a pair under eleven hours. I have been at work in the trade for sixteen years. 2s. 6d. was the highest I ever knew to be paid for this kind of goods. It is oftener five than six pairs that I make in the week. I have made six pairs, but had to work pretty well night and day at them, though. They want 'em done so uncommon well now for the money. I have four children; one of them works with me, and I reckon her to count for a shilling a week. My wife works at the blucher closing, and gets 2½d. per pair."

A fourth shoemaker, upon whom I called, said: "I generally work upon the best work, such as 'circulars;' the price paid for them is 1s. 10d. per pair. What I am now at work upon is the common 'split kip bluchers.' I get 14d. for them, and can make a pair in about nine hours, if I work hard. About three years ago I used to have 2s. a pair for the circulars; but the trade has fallen off dreadfully. I don't have very good health; indeed, I never feel well. I am often obliged to leave my seat and go to bed, as I have such a giddiness come over me. The doctor says it's all owing to the sitting. I don't drink much myself; there's a many in the trade that do though, and they will have it, if they can get it. When I am able to work, I generally am at work before daylight, and about this time of the year we generally light up about five in the afternoon—so that, if you work until ten, it will take a shilling a week for candles. It's allowed on all hands that, one with another, we don't earn so much as farm labourers; take 'em all through, I don't think we make more than 7s. a week. I could make, I dare say, seven or eight pair in the week." "It is no use your saying that," said his wife, a sickly-looking woman, who was sitting by, "he can't make more than six pairs, sir, and then he'll have to work hard; if he makes more than that he has to go to bed. We don't have much meat; sometimes I buys a sheep's head and make broth of it, and that lasts us two or three days. We've had a good bit of trouble in our way, and are always behind; and for the last six or seven years we've had a confinement and a burial every year, and the expense of that is enough to pull any one back."

"What I am at work at," said a young man upon whom I next called, "are called 'turn rounds,' or 'sew rounds;' they are a kind of 'pump,' or morning slipper. They are sewn all round at once, and then they are turned, and we have to fit in the in-soles after. It takes about two hours and a half to make a pair of them, but then I am obliged to have a lad to sew them." [There were four young lads then at work with him, varying in their ages from six to ten, the eldest of whom received 4s. per week.] "The price paid for 'sew-rounds' is 8d. per pair. The work is rather slack just now. Then there is another sort of 'pump,' which we call the 'spring heel.' We get 9d. per pair for them, which is only a penny more than for the others, although there is at least threepennyworth of work more in them. There is another sort that we get 1s. a pair for. They are called 'sailor's top-piece pumps,' or 'high heels.' We have three extra substances to put upon them for 1s. We used to get 1s. 3d. a pair for them. When trade gets at all flat the men get a very short answer from the manufacturers; they care nothing at all about the men so long only as they just want them. If we go into the shops they say, 'Oh, we've got nothing to do, don't come bothering here;' but no sooner do they get a little brisk or busy than they lay on as hard as they can, and they'll sack you directly they begin to get slack. There is also a sort of boot called 'the shipping,' which cannot be made too light, as a great many of them are sent to Jamaica and other hot countries; they pay about 1s. 4d. for them, and the same for middle sole strong bluchers."

Having called upon persons engaged upon each of the principal kinds of men's boots, I next proceeded to obtain some information as to the prices paid for ladies' boots, and was directed to "a womans-man," who resided in one of the back rows in Bell Barn-yard. The following was the statement I received:—"For slipper pumps, leather, the price paid is 1s. per pair; patent, of the same description of slipper, 1s. 1d. per pair. Some persons can make a great deal more than others at this kind of work. I don't consider myself at all a fair judge of what a person can earn, for I am always ill; I have been troubled with the liver complaint for years. Some years ago I could make 15s. or 16s. a week, now I don't do more than about 8s., but it's oftener between 6s. and 7s., and even 4s. and 5s." Within a few doors of this person lived another person also engaged "in the ladies' department." He said, "I am now making double soles, top-pressed heels, copper spriggs, patent goloshed ladies' walking boots; the price paid for them is 1s. 5d., for 'pumps' of the same kind 1s. 1d. For the best kind of work they give 1s. 8d., and for the same sort as the 1s. 1d., they give for the best 1s. 5d. and 1s. 3d. The same sort of ladies' walking boot, for which they pay me here 1s. 5d., I could get 1s. 10d. for in London. For stabbing the goloshes round the top they pay 5d., and for putting the boots together 5d. Patent slippers, lastings, kid, or anything of that sort, the usual price is 1s., for the best 1s. 2d. It will take a good hand about eight hours to make a pair of the best walking boots. I could make a pair of pump slippers in about 5½ hours. I hardly close my eyes sometimes for a week together, owing to a pain in my chest from stooping over my work. I have often sat on my stool till I am ready to drop at the work. I seldom or never go out except for a little walk on Sundays, and for weeks together I have never been out to the top of the court. We have an association among ourselves, called 'The Shops Meeting Society.' The object of the society is to give relief to members who are upon the tramp; it is only for ladies' shoemakers. There are very few members of the society. In this town we allow them 6d. and a bed, in London 1s. and a bed. The members are only allowed to draw for one night; there is no relief between Northampton and London. In Daventry we give 3d. and a bed, and the same in Coventry; in Birmingham 6d. and the price of a bed. If this society were well supported, it would be impossible for a master to reduce his wages; because if he were to attempt to do so, to any member of the society, the member would receive a free card and travelling money to go upon the tramp, and he would go to some town where he could get his full wages."

Binding is the next and final process through which the boots and shoes pass. The quantity of binding done appears to have fallen off very considerably of late years. The wife of one of the ladies' shoe-makers told me that she did a little at binding and lining, but not so much as she did some years ago. She used to get three-halfpence per pair for silk lining, and five farthings for thread; but there was not one half of the lining done now that there used to be, because of the "double vamps and quarters," which were now used so much, and which was all done by the "closers." The "stabbing" had been the utter ruin of the trade, and "the double quarters" had quite "floored" the woman's work. "I could once sit down and make my 12s. a week by lining, and now I don't get 6d. at it." Another person employed in "binding," informed me that she got 1d. per pair for binding "cir-culars;" that before she was married, she used to have 2½d. for the same articles. For women's cloth boots she was paid 1½d. per pair for doing the binding, buttoning, and lining, while, eight years ago, they used to pay 2½d. for the same kind of work. There used formerly to be a good deal done in binding the buttoned cloth boots, but they were now all done by the closers, who run a "beading" round the tops instead of binding. The "beading" was stabbed on by the closers, the price paid being 1d. per pair, while the price formerly paid for the binding was 5d.

LABOUR AND THE POOR.

THE RURAL DISTRICTS.

[FROM OUR SPECIAL CORRESPONDENT.]

COUNTIES OF NORTHAMPTON, LEICESTER, RUTLAND, NOTTINGHAM, AND DERBY.

THE BOOT AND SHOE MAKERS OF NORTHAMPTON.

Letter XLVI.

A practice, which during the last few years has sprung up in connection with the boot and shoe trade of Northampton, is very generally complained of by the numerous class of artisans employed in that trade, and is one which, if not checked, would, I was informed, prove the ruin "not only of Northampton, but of the whole country." In this case, at all events, it is not the large capitalists of whom they complain, but persons of their own condition, who, by their petty and oppressive conduct, prove the truth of the adage that "servants generally make bad masters." It appears that a somewhat numerous class among the shoemakers of Northampton, who, either from drunken and disorderly habits, or from inability properly to perform their work, have been refused employment at the principal manufacturers of the town, have set up for themselves as small masters and employers of labour; and, encouraged in too many instances by the less respectable of the manufacturers and boot vendors of Northampton and London, they have introduced into the town, though not exactly in the same mode, all the mischiefs and injustice of the sweating system which exists in connection with the slop-sellers of the metropolis. The evils thus introduced among the shoemakers of the town are not, however, solely attributable to members of their own craft; but in a great number of cases these petty masters know nothing whatever of the trade, their occupation being that of keepers of small provision and chandlery shops, who endeavour to eke out their weekly profits by the high prices which their unfortunate workmen pay for the provisions which they are virtually compelled to purchase of them. These small tradesmen are in the habit of getting the work done at prices less than those usually paid by the respectable manufacturers; and, unfortunately, the helpless condition of many of the shoemakers, owing to their intemperate and improvident habits, makes them fall an easy prey to the rapacity of this class of persons, for, in the first moment of slackness of trade among the manufacturers, having no resources whatever upon which to fall back, they eagerly catch at anything in the shape of employment, heedless of the remuneration which they may receive, or of the injury which they thus inflict upon their more sober and industrious brethren. These small and unprincipled tradesmen, too, finding that there is then an abundance of labour in the market, regardless of the ability of the workman, take the opportunity of grinding all applicants for work down to the lowest possible scale. The position in which such a person is placed, between the factor on the one hand who purchases his articles, and the workman on the other who produces them, renders it absolutely necessary for him, if he would continue to carry on his trade, to get the work done at the lowest price; and thus, upon the producer, as is too often the case, falls the greatest and the most crushing part of the burden. The system itself is a most unnatural and artificial one. The factor who purchases the boots and shoes of the middle-man—for the small tradesman can be looked upon in no other light—is content to give a trifle over and above the amount for which he could himself get the articles made, because he first obtains a profit upon the leather, which he compels the middleman to purchase from him. The middleman, too, is content to give a higher price for the leather than that for which he could purchase it elsewhere, inasmuch as the excessive amount thus paid by him is more than counterbalanced by the extra price which he charges upon his provisions, and which, in his turn, the unfortunate workman is compelled to take of him. The benefits derived by this system to all but the unfortunate artisan are, first, to the middleman, who obtains a profit upon the sale of his goods to the factor. He gets the work done at considerably lower prices than those usually paid, and charges them to the factor at something over the usual rate. He has, therefore, a direct profit upon the labour of those whom he employs, and a second source of profit is found in the forced sale of provisions at increased prices to the workman. The factor is benefited, inasmuch as he is spared the trouble and expense of giving out, preparing, and receiving the work from the workpeople; and although he may pay even more than the full price for the labour, still he gains by the increase of price at which he sells his leather to the middleman. The unfortunate workman, the victim of the cupidity of both, suffers by a reduction of his wages and by the high prices which he is compelled to pay to his employer for the necessaries of life.

"There are also some men," said one of the shoemakers to me, "who cannot get work from the manufacturers, and who will get a bit of leather, and make two or three pairs of boots and sell them then and there for ready money. They will often sell Wellington boots right out for 6s. 6d. a pair to the manufacturers, all ready for the feet; aye, and some of the boots are good ones too. I could buy some made with really good leather and French town lasts for that price. This practice prevails to a great extent throughout the town, and causes great injury to the regular trade; for the manufacturers are always ready to buy them, because it saves them the trouble of giving out the work, and they can get 'em done cheaper too that way." Another shoemaker, speaking upon the same subject, said, "Sometimes they get two or three men to help 'em to make the boots, and so make up the boots and shoes at lower prices than the regular employer can get them made for. Some of them will buy the split kip and offal leather, get the blocking, closing, and everything done, and sell a pair of Bluchers for 2s. 6d., or Clarences for 3s. 6d., and Wellington boots they will get up and sell as low as 6s. The large manufacturers besides get an extra profit on the leather which they sell, as the workman has to take a good part of his charge for the boots out in that material. The work which is got up in this way is of the worst description, and anything does in the shape of leather, for they are only meant for the cheap London markets. Mr. —— and Mr. ——, of London, send down their leather, and get nearly all their stock made up in this way."

I called upon one of the small tradesmen who was in the habit of getting boots and shoes thus made up for the larger manufacturers, and who kept a small chandler's shop, not being an operative shoemaker himself. The statement, which he gave me with some unwillingness, was as follows:—"I get the boots and shoes made up, and sell them to the manufacturers. I get all sorts made up for them. Those which I sell the most of are the long Wellingtons and short Wellingtons, mostly of split kip and calf. I do nothing with the 'patent.' I get 9s. 6d. for a pair of best calf long Wellingtons; 7s. 6d. for 'kip long Wellingtons;' for calf short Wellingtons the same as the 'long kips,' and about 6s. 6d. for the 'short kips.' The manufacturers make me take half the amount out in leather. They charge me a trifle more for it than I could buy it for anywhere else. For stout calf Clarences I get 5s. 6d. and 6s.; what we make is generally of inferior calf and damaged leather. For stout Bluchers the price they give me is 4s. 6d. and 5s. The manufacturer makes a profit upon the leather, and, of course, I make a little on the shop goods. I don't compel the men to take any portion of their wages out in chandlery; but if I can sell them the things as cheap as anybody else, I think it is the least they can do to deal with me. I make about 60 pairs in the week. There are several little men like me who get the work made up in this kind of way. The price I pay for making 'calf-long Wellingtons' is 2s. 6d., for 'calf short Wellingtons' 2s. 3d., 'calf strong Bluchers' 1s. 8d., 'calf strong Clarences' 1s. 8d."

There appears some discrepancy in the statement of this person and those of the workmen whom I had previously seen. I am, however, disposed to attach the greater weight to the statements of the workpeople themselves, not only on account of the evident unwillingness with which the former gave his statement, but also because the amount which he informed me he paid to the workpeople was, as I subsequently learned, considerably overstated. One man who was employed by this same person informed me that the price paid for making "split kip Wellingtons" was 1s. 10d., and for "calf Wellingtons" 2s. Another of the persons who was at work under this grinding system, told me that he made Bluchers for one of the small men at 1s. 2d., and very often for 1s. 1d. He also informed me that he had plenty of the work, such as it was. He usually worked from five or six in the morning till ten or eleven at night, during which period he could not make more than three of the shoes he was then at work upon. The work was a very common kind—sprigged-bottomed stout Bluchers. He used to get 1s. 9d. a pair for the same goods a few years ago. It was all owing, he said, to the little masters trying to undersell the big ones in the market, and they did not care how the poor shoemakers suffered for it. Many other statements of a similar character were made to me by the shoemakers; but as no practical end would be answered by introducing them, I will refrain from wearying the reader by their recital.

The rate of wages does not appear to vary very considerably in other parts of the county from that paid in the town of Northampton. At Daventry the prices are usually considered to be somewhat lower than in most other parts. At Wellingborough the same prices are paid. A great deal of the better kind of work is done in the small villages in the neighbourhood of Northampton, as the persons residing there are found to be more steady in their habits, and greater reliance can be placed upon them by the manufacturers than upon those in the towns. At a village within a few miles of Higham-Ferrers, the complaints were loud and universal with respect to the conduct of one manufacturer. He keeps an extensive store, and all those who are employed by him, though not directly compelled to buy their provisions of him, are still expected to lay out their money with him. "He does not say exactly," said one of the men, "you must spend so much with us, but if you don't do so, he'll look very blue at you; and the next time you go, very likely there will be no work for you. I can buy a half-peck loaf for a halfpenny less than his. We pay a halfpenny more with him for almost every sixpence that we lay out; his candles are a halfpenny a pound more than anybody else's in the place, and so is his meat. The prices which he gives are 4s. for 'long Wellingtons, double sole;' 3s. 3d. for 'pump-sole Wellingtons.' Last week I made some water-tight lace boots, 'clinkered' all round, for 1s. 5d. the pair. He makes some of the 'army' for the contractors, and pays us 1s. 1d. for 'brown-edge pegged-heel Bluchers.' For patent button boots he pays 2s. 9d., and for closing and stabbing, 1s. I am now at work on cloth boots—sprigged, they're 1s. 10d.; if not sprigged 1s. 9d., and 5½d. for closing and stabbing. For best Clarences he gives 2s. 2d. 'sprigged'—2s. 1d. not 'sprigged;' common ones of the same sort 1s. 10d. and 1s. 9d.; for common Bluchers, No. 5, double backed, some 'tipped' and some 'sprigged heels,' 1s. 6d. No. 6 Bluchers he gives 1s. 2d. for; they are quite common things, very strong, and sprigged; for the 'split kip Bluchers' he gives 1s. 1d."

In addition, however, to the great quantities of boots and shoes which are manufactured in the county of Northampton for the retail trade of different parts of the country, a considerable quantity of army, navy, and convict boots are also made. The principal seats of the manufacture of these kinds of goods are Higham-Ferrers and Kettering, with the surrounding villages, including Raunds, Rowell, Broughton, Burton, Isham, Athlenburgh, Frendon, Woolaston, and others. In the Kettering district, however, by far the greater number are made. The number of hands constantly employed by one establishment in Kettering is about 650. Of this number there are "tanners" 24, "curriers" 12, "cutters or clickers" 16, "closers" 250, "makers" 350. About 200 of the makers are employed in the town of Kettering itself, the remainder in the surrounding villages. Almost the whole of the work done by these hands consists of the army and contract work. The wages paid to the tanners are 14s. per week, or, with two pints of table beer per day, 13s. per week. The best hands of the curriers receive 26s. per week; inferior, from 18s. to 20s.; clickers, 18s. per week. The price paid for making boots for the regiments of the line has scarcely varied during the last twenty years. The contracts are in comparatively few hands, and they are generally taken for a number of years. These regiments are not supplied by Government contract, but through their respective clothiers. A person who has been employed on the usual contract army boots for the last thirty years informed me that the price paid for making them varied from 14d. to 17d. If sprigged round the bottom, the price paid was 17d., and for the last twenty years he had received the same price. It would take him eight hours, "and work well," to make a pair of sprigged boots. It was good work for him to make nine pairs in the week, and that was allowing nothing for meal times, and reckoning twelve hours a day. The nine pairs of boots would be 12s. 9d., the grindery would cost him about 1s., and in the winter the candles would be about 7½d. He had belonged to a benefit club for the last thirty years, and had only "declared on" for three weeks during the whole time. Last June he was taken ill, but could not get on the club, as he was not clear of the box—had not paid up his subscriptions.

The "short Wellington" is the kind of boot made for the artillery—the price paid for making them, exclusive of closing, being 1s. 8d. per pair. The convict shoes are generally made by special contract, and although taken at lower prices as compared with the regiments of the line, there has been little or no alteration in the price paid for making. Mr. ——, who is a large contractor in Kettering, informed me that whenever they obtained the contracts for the convict boots, they gave the men the same price for making as they would for other goods of a similar character. For strong nailed shoes, such as those required for the convicts, the price paid was 1s. 3d. This kind of shoe was first introduced about ten years since, the amount then paid being 1s. 3½d., the difference during the ten years having been but to the extent of one halfpenny. For shoes of the same kind and the same make required for the shops, the price paid was the same as before the reduction took place—1s. 3½d. Several of the persons employed on convict shoes informed me that their earnings averaged from 10s. to 12s. per week, according as they stuck to their work. For shipping goods made in this establishment, which consisted partly of low shoes and bluchers, the prices paid were, for shoes 1s. 4d., and for Bluchers 1s. 7d. For nearly all kinds of shop goods the prices remained the same as during the last twenty years. The number of pairs of boots and shoes of all kinds made by 356 men in Mr. ——'s establishment during one week, was slightly under 2,800, or nearly eight pairs to each person employed—which, at an average price of 1s. 3d. would give 10s. per week as the earnings of each person employed.

At Higham-Ferrers there is also a large contractor for the army boots, who manufactures about 1,000 pairs of boots and shoes during the week, the prices paid being precisely the same as those above named. The work is usually given out by the manufacturer once in the week for the surrounding villages, and it is brought home in small donkey carts, which the workmen join together to hire, and which convey the work of one or more villages. One of the workmen is deputed from each village to go with the goods, receive payment for them, and bring back other work for the workpeople.

Higham Ferrers, Northants.

The physical condition of the shoemakers in the country parts is far superior to that of those who reside in Northampton and the larger towns. They have nearly all of them small plots of ground, in which they spend some portion of their time, and during the harvest great numbers of them go out to work in the fields. They are also, generally speaking, more healthy, sober, and contented than the shoemakers of the larger towns.

It is almost impossible to convey an adequate idea of the utter wretchedness and dirty appearance of the places in the larger towns in which many of the shoemakers live and carry on their operations. There is a general resemblance throughout the whole of them; and, although the details may differ in most cases, a description of one or two of them will suffice for all. On opening the door, which almost invariably leads directly into the room, the first thing that meets the eye is a quilt or coverlid, rarely clean and mostly ragged, which is stretched across that portion of the room adjoining the door. Arriving at the termination of this drapery, and looking round on the other side, will be seen, sitting in the recess between the window and the chimney, upon a low stool, an individual with a face as black as the presence of dirt and a long absence of soap and water can make it. It is, however, but a small portion of the face of this personage that can be seen; his hair generally covers his forehead, or hangs down the sides of his face, when not confined, as in some cases it is, by a band which is worn round the head; his chin, upper lip, and the lower part of his cheeks are almost completely concealed beneath the exuberance of his beard and mustachios, the crop of which is seldom, if ever, disturbed more than once a week; indeed several whom I saw had a three weeks' growth. Among the shoemakers it will be found, almost as a general rule, that where there is an excessive development of beard, there will be found a corresponding diminution in the completeness of the attire. The elbows protrude out of the coat, the knees through the trowsers and leather apron, and the toes out of the boots. The remaining parts of the man's person are covered with a quantity of rags, which originally were of divers colours, but which, through the constant application of grease, paste, ink, heelball, and other articles, which are included under the head of "grindery," have, in some cases, become a polished jet, and in others a dirty black, only exceeded in intensity of dye by the flesh of the wearer. By the side of this lugubrious specimen of humanity will be found his small table, containing his various articles of grindery and tools—a miscellaneous collection, consisting of broken awls, pieces of glass, blades of knives, pieces of brown wax, ends of candles, small brads, paste, bristles, wax-ends, and other articles of a similar kind, which constitute the stock of a working shoemaker. Thus equipped, the son of Crispin, with his head bent low over his work—giving him the appearance of a person doubled up into the smallest possible compass—and a pair of huge spectacles before his eyes, pursues his avocation, accompanying the blows of his hammer by some fragment of a song which he picked up at the last meeting of his "free and easy," or which he may have under rehearsal for one of those vocal entertainments in which the genius of the great body of Northampton shoemakers delights to revel. On the other side of the fire-place, if he is a married man, will frequently be seen a female, who, in point of cleanliness and tidiness, has no pretensions to the title of his "better half." She will be found at work either at the "closing" or "binding." If not engaged in either of those occupations, she will most likely be employed in washing a few articles of clothing, in a pan or small tub, which is mostly placed upon a chair, or upon the table, amid the articles of the breakfast service which have not yet been removed, even though it be past noon. Indeed, so highly do many of the shoemakers' wives appear to value time, that, in order to avoid any unnecessary waste of that precious commodity, the tea and dinner services are usually allowed to remain from one meal to another. If there are any children at home, they will be certain to be found—whether male or female—occupied in some department of the shoe trade; and it is scarcely necessary to state that, in point of cleanliness and decency of attire, their condition is not many degrees superior to that of their parents. The apartments of the shoemakers may generally be classed under two heads—they are either scantily furnished, or filled with the wrecks of broken furniture. Under the former class, an inventory of the goods and chattels would include an old small round table, a couple of chairs, and, if there are children, perhaps as many stools as there are occupants for them. In several instances that came under my notice there was no table—the stool or table containing the tools and various articles of grindery being used as the dining-table of the family, and an old tea-board placed upon a chair containing the articles of crockery used at the meals. In one place a dish with some potatoes and turnips was placed upon the floor, the wife and children sitting round, eating out of the dish with spoons, and the father taking his portion of the meal in his usual place in the chimney recess. A great proportion of the homes of this class of workmen bear witness to the dissipated habits of their occupiers, and, in the ruinous condition of the furniture, tell too plainly that the owners were "quarrelsome when in their cups." In such places as these the chairs are without bottoms, and many without backs; the face of the Dutch clock in the corner is broken, the looking-glass on the wall contains about a tithe of its original quantity, and portions of its frame are gone. Shakespeare and Milton are headless as they stand upon the mantel-piece; the fragments of crockery which abound in the place are varied in their character, and in the amount of injuries which they may have sustained; but all have suffered more or less in these "clashes of arms," which, upon various occasions, have disturbed the propriety of peaceful neighbours, and called for the intervention of the police.

There are, however, to be found among the shoemakers of Northampton, cases which contrast most favourably with the condition of many of their fellow labourers. Where temperate and provident habits have been formed, there the home of the shoemaker will be found to present features of domestic comfort, for which we may search in vain the dwellings of his improvident and intemperate neighbour. In such a place will be found a small collection of books—thumb-worn, it is true, and not so clean, perhaps, as many a more fastidious person might desire, but showing that their contents have been well perused. Indeed, the whole appearance of a place occupied by a workman of this class presents a scene of order and decency, as complete and as perfect as could be expected under the circumstances in which he is placed.

Politics generally run somewhat high among the great body of the shoemakers. In times of political excitement, if accompanied by slackness in trade, the shoemakers generally occupy a prominent position. "We are the most radicallest set of fellows, and Northampton is the most radicallest town in the kingdom," said one of the craft to me. Of cheap literature also they are great patrons, about 200 dozen of penny weekly publications being usually sold in the town during the week. It is one of the great boasts of the shoemakers that their trade has produced more celebrated characters than any other trade in existence. Whitier, the celebrated American shoemaker-poet, has written some verses which are particularly popular with the shoemakers. One person upon whom I called, when enlightening me upon the antiquity and mysteries of the craft, and the number of its celebrated heroes, recited, with evident feeling, the following lines, as near as I was enabled to collect them:—

> "Let foplins sneer, let fools deride,
>   We heed no idle scorner;
> Free hands and hearts are still our pride,
>   And duty done our honour.
> We dare to trust for honest fame
>   The jury time empanels,
> And leave to truth each noble name
>   Which glorifies our annals.

> "Thy songs, Hans Sach! are living yet
>   In strong and hearty German,
> And Bloomfield's lay, and Gifford's art,
>   And the rare good sense of Sherman.
> Still from his book a mystic seer
>   The soul of Behmen teaches,
> And England's priestcraft shakes to hear
>   Of Fox's leathern breeches."

The principal source of amusement to the shoemakers appears to be the "Free and Easy," or the "select concerts," usually held at some public-house or beer-shop. The prices of admission to these species of entertainments usually range from twopence to threepence, for which sum a ticket is usually given, by virtue of which, in addition to the right of admission, the holder becomes possessed of a title to "refreshments during the evening." Each person present at the Free and Easy is expected to "favour the company with a song" when called upon by the chairman for the time being to do so, and the great point of ambition with those who frequent these convivial meetings is "to give something new." The demand which this species of emulation among them produces for "Vocal Gems," "Minstrel's Companions," and a host of other cheap song-books, is very considerable. One bookseller in the town informed me that he sold on an average about twenty dozen of penny and twopenny song-books in the week. A demand has lately sprung up for a sixpenny song-book, on the ground of its containing more new songs than the cheaper editions; and he who is disposed to invest sixpence may be almost certain of finding something new with which he can astonish at the next meeting some of his less fortunate compeers. I was informed by one of the shoemakers that it not unfrequently happened that, after the vocalist had spent a week or more in the rehearsal of "something new," a more fortunate competitor for the honours of the club obtained the precedence in point of time, "and took the identical song out of his mouth." Actuated by a laudable desire to discharge the important duties of his office impartially, the chairman, upon such occasions, decides upon "hearing both sides;" and the company are thus afforded an opportunity of pronouncing an opinion upon the merits of the respective parties.

The material condition of the shoemakers might be equal to that of any body of operatives in the kingdom if they only paid a little more regard to their own best interests. The money which they spend in drink, and the time which they uniformly waste in each week, would go far to increase their comforts and to mitigate their distress. Monday is a day which they invariably devote to idleness and to the honour of their tutelary saint; and many a worshipper of St. Monday, after having spent the night at the station-house, loses the following day in explaining to the authorities the cause, and paying the penalty, of his intemperance or riot. The number of shoemakers taken by the police during the year ending Dec. 31, 1849, on charges of being "drunk" and "drunk and disorderly" in the town of Northampton, was 211; of these a proportion of 5 out of 7 were taken on Monday nights. The total number of charges of all sorts in the town of Northampton for the same period was 583. Deducting from these the number of "drunk" and "drunk and disorderly," the number remaining for other offences would be 372; and of these the greater number was furnished by shoemakers, and consisted mainly of charges arising out of drunkenness, such as assaults, embezzling of leather and boots, and other minor offences.

There does not appear to be any great want of employment among the shoemakers, either in the larger towns or in the surrounding villages. In the workhouses of the unions which comprise the principal portions of the shoemaking districts of the county, there was not, at the time of my visit, one able-bodied shoemaker. The following were the numbers of persons in the three unions of Northampton, Wellingborough, and Kettering, in the first week of January, 1850, and also for the same period of 1849:—

	Northampton Union.		Wellingborough Union.		Kettering Union.	
	1849.	1850.	1849.	1850.	1849.	1850.
Able-bodied men	29	27	9	4	28	14
Aged, infirm, and idiots	32	37	31	29	21	22
Boys above nine years of age	35	23	26	21	12	7
Boys under nine years of age	14	10	17	7	29	12
Able-bodied women ..	36	26	30	25	36	24
Aged, infirm, and idiots	14	12	31	29	15	18
Girls above nine years of age	23	30	12	18	10	10
Girls under nine years of age	21	27	10	11	19	10
Infants	9	5	8	8	7	8
Totals	213	197	174	152	177	125

This shows a total decrease, in the three unions, of 89—of whom 48 were able-bodied, and 22 were boys above nine years of age, who were able to work at shoemaking or at other occupations. In the Kettering Union the poor-rates were 1s. 2d. in the pound, while two years previously they were as high as 3s. The amount of out-door relief, including vagrant charges, was lower than it had ever been since the formation of the union; the amount for the week ending January 5, 1850, being £45, as compared with £51 in the corresponding period of 1849. The establishment charges, which consist mainly of relief afforded to the irremovable poor, under the Poor Removal Act, was for the week ending January 5, 1850, £4 10s. 5d., as compared with £10 5s. 2d. in the corresponding period of 1849. The charge for the relief of vagrants for the quarter ending Christmas, 1850, was £6, against £16 14s. 2d. in the same period of 1849, the numbers relieved having fallen from 1,491 to 650. In the Northampton Union, the amount of out-door relief for the week ending Dec. 25, 1849, was £75 8s. 4d.; for the same period of 1848, £76 7s. 1d. The total amount of out-door relief for the quarter ending Christmas, 1850, was £978 16s. 7d.; for that ending Christmas, 1849, £1,068 10s. 10d. Vagrant charges had also fallen in the same period from £20 9s. 3d. to £4 18s. 10d.

LABOUR AND THE POOR.

THE RURAL DISTRICTS.

[FROM OUR SPECIAL CORRESPONDENT.]

COUNTIES OF NORTHAMPTON, LEICESTER, RUTLAND, NOTTINGHAM, AND DERBY.

Letter XLVII.

Rutland is the smallest of all the English counties, its area being but 97,500 acres, and its population amounting only to 21,302. With the exception of a small manufacture of parchment and glue at Barrowden, there are no manufactures carried on within it, the employment of the people being exclusively agricultural. The total number of agricultural labourers in the county is 2,612, of whom 2,152 are males above 20 years of age, and 420 under that age; 40 females also are returned as agricultural labourers, of whom 39 are above 20 years of age.

The surface of the county is beautifully varied. The soil, generally speaking, is good, the greater portion being red land and heavy clay, which produce excellent crops of wheat. The Valley of Catmose bears a high character for its fertility and productiveness. A large portion of the land of the county is laid down in permanent pasture; the parts which are under tillage being generally cultivated upon the Norfolk system. In some districts the farming is as wretched as can well be conceived, while in others, where a greater amount of confidence appears to subsist between the landlord and tenant, the land exhibits the highest state of cultivation. The Earl of Gainsborough and Mr. Finch are held in high esteem for the fairness and liberality of their conduct towards their tenants. Land of the best quality lets at from 35s. to 45s. per acre. There appears to exist in many parts a feeling of misunderstanding between landlord and tenant, owing to the refusal of the former to grant leases, or even agreements, upon fair and liberal terms; and this has no doubt tended to retard the progress of cultivation, and to affect most injuriously the interests of the labourers. One highly respectable farmer residing in the neighbourhood of Oakham, and who held about 300 acres of land, informed me that he had been a tenant upon the same farm for 28 years, and had thorough-drained every foot of his land, laid out upwards of £500 in improving the farmyards, built waggon hovels, repaved the barn, and laid down a new barn floor. He had also, upon another farm of 120 acres belonging to the same landlord, stubbed up all the old hedges, put down new quick rows, carted stone at his own expense a distance of five miles to drain the land with, and had never received one farthing, nor even a post or a rail, from his landlord to assist him in his improvements; and yet he had just received notice to quit, because he would not submit to an increased rental, the rent he then paid being 44s. per acre. "I have made repeated application," said this enterprising farmer, "for some remuneration, but have never been able to get any. I have made land which was all but worthless before, and which would not have kept a sheep to the acre, remarkably good land. I have thoroughly drained it from end to end, and it now grows as good crops of turnips and wheat as any in the county, and I shall now have to leave it without the slightest compensation for all this outlay of my money." At Whissendine a system has been adopted for several years past than which nothing can be conceived more injurious or annoying to the tenant and the labourer. The greater part of the property in that neighbourhood belongs to a noble earl, and the whole of the tenants, as well as the cottagers upon the property of his lordship, constantly receive notices to quit, while several of the best farmers upon the estate have already given up their lands in disgust. The lands are let very high, and a surveyor who was recently employed to go over the farms, with the view of raising the rents, reported that they were "let at their full value, and would not bear raising." I endeavoured to ascertain, if possible, the cause of this extraordinary conduct, but the only explanation I could get was "that it was all done for his mere caprice." As might be expected from such a course of policy, the labourers in the parish of Whissendine are as wretched as can well be imagined.

The proportion of labourers to each 100 acres does not indicate anything like surplus labour in the county, it not being more than 2.8; and even in those parishes which have the largest proportion of labourers, and into which the evicted of other districts have been driven, ample employment could be afforded if improved systems of cultivation were adopted. On the part of many of the farmers, however, it is almost hopeless to expect that any such improvements would be made. Without the necessary capital, their hands are completely tied up; and while they realise their highest ambition, that of being considered large farmers, they have the mournful satisfaction of gazing upon large tracts of land badly cultivated, ruinous farm buildings, and other infallible indications of want of capital or energy, a pauperized and discontented body of labourers, who, instead of subsisting upon the fruits of their labour, are kept from starvation by parish allowances which swell the rates and help to crush the unfortunate occupier. Numbers of persons in this condition were mentioned to me. One farmer, occupying 350 acres of wretchedly cultivated land, employs two men; a second, holding over 600 acres, does not employ sufficient hands to perform the necessary work upon a farm of half that size; a third, with 400 acres, employs two men and a boy. There are many parts of the county to which these remarks do not, however, apply. In some of the parishes there is no complaint whatever on the ground of want of employment. Among parishes of this kind might be mentioned those of Market Overton and Cottesmore, where the land is well cultivated and held by intelligent and persevering farmers.

In some respects, the labourer may be considered better off than formerly in this county, in consequence of the cheapness of provisions; but, unfortunately, while there are many who are deriving benefit from the reduction of the prices of the necessaries of life, there are not a few who, being unable to obtain employment, are entirely shut out from the advantages which their more fortunate brethren enjoy. In the parish to which I have just referred (Whissendine) the labourers are greatly impoverished. The number of persons receiving in-door relief in the Uppingham union, for the week ending the 10th of January last year, was 127; for the corresponding period of the present year, the number was 114. The amount of out-door relief for the same period of 1849 was £42; and for 1850, £48 19s. The extreme laxity with which the principle of the poor-law appears to be carried out in this and in the Oakham union, has led, notwithstanding the reduction in the price of provisions, to this increase in the amount of out-relief. The returns, however, of the sums expended for in-door and out-door relief do not afford an adequate idea of the amount of distress in the county. The guardians of the poor, anxious to avoid applying the workhouse test, lest they should be burdened by the support of the applicant for relief and his family, have recently had recourse to a plan similar in character to a mode of relief which was productive of so much mischief under the old poor law. One of the guardians, who expressed himself to me as decidedly opposed to the plan, told me that at the last meeting of the board twenty-five of the applicants, who had the largest families, were set to work on the roads, there not being work then for half that number; while those with smaller families received an order for the house.

Probably there is no county in England in which the injurious effects of the present law of settlement are more severely felt. The fact of the county being so purely agricultural in its character, and there being no manufactures upon which the labourers can fall back, render more striking than they would otherwise be the mischiefs produced by the operation, or rather the abuse, of the present law. It is impossible to describe the injuries inflicted upon the agricultural labourer under the present law of settlement. The due cultivation of the land is impeded by the restrictions which it places upon labour. The difficulties thrown in the way of obtaining labour prevents the application of capital for the improvement of the land, and the consequent employment of the labourer. By increasing the expenses connected with the relief of the poor, it tends to swell the amount of poor rates, places an additional burden upon the farmer, and in the same proportion deprives him of the power of employing a fair amount of labour. The social and moral evils caused by the influx of large numbers of labourers into towns and villages, where there is no sufficient accommodation for them, and where they are compelled to crowd together in large numbers, are not the least of the evils produced by the existing law. The scenes of contention and confusion continually arising in this and in the other counties which I have visited, and which, in accompanying the relieving officer in his visits, I have had frequent occasions of witnessing, are almost impossible to describe. Most undignified contests ensue between the representative of the authorities and the recipients of the relief, as to the parish to which they belong, and from their heap of straw or wretched sick-beds, they not unfrequently vent the most horrid curses upon the administrators of the law. In the five counties the names of which stand at the head of this letter, there are not less than 1,284 parishes; and the labourer has to contend, hopelessly and unfriended, against the constant manœuvres of interested parties in these parishes who strain every nerve, and have recourse to every expedient, to send him over the country in quest of a home and a settlement. While the number of parishes is 1,284, the number of unions, however, is only 44. The labourer thus has, in these parishes, 1,284 enemies, who have an interest more or less in banishing, or otherwise placing obstacles in the way of his comfort and happiness. The substitution of union for parochial rating and chargeability, such as exists in one of the unions of Norfolk, would in these counties, if not entirely remedy this state of things, at least reduce the number of the conflicting interests against which the labourer has to contend in the proportion of 1,284 to 44. "So long," said a gentleman to me, who has been a county magistrate upwards of 20 years, and had had considerable experience in the working of the poor law, "as this parochial chargeability exists, and the power of removing English poor is vested in the parties whose interest it is to remove and banish them from their homes; the scenes of suffering and distress which have been constantly brought under your notice in these counties will continue to exist." The mode in which the labourer most usually suffers from this law is by landowners, or cottage proprietors, getting the poor man out of his dwelling and out of the parish before the expiration of the five years which would give him a legal settlement, if not already possessed of one. Having thus driven the poor man out of the parish, and being relieved from all fear of his becoming a burden upon them, they will still, if they have need of his services, give him employment, and in order to perform which he will have to walk frequently very long distances. There are also many of the landowners who will not allow any increase in the number of cottages upon their estates, and others who destroy what few do really exist, and others who, more slowly, but not less effectually, accomplish the object of clearing their estates of labourers and paupers, by allowing all their cottages to sink into decay, without making the least exertion to prevent their ruin, and when, through age and neglect, the wretched hovels fall down, no new ones are erected in their stead.

One labourer, whose cottage had been pulled down in an adjoining parish, had been forced to seek a residence in Oakham, for which he was compelled to pay £8 a year; and as he could not get employment out of the parish from which he had been evicted, he was, at the time of my visit, compelled to walk four miles every day to his work. Another poor man, in the same union, was receiving out-door relief on account of the large number of his family, and of his bad state of health, brought on by not having, as the medical officer informed me, "adequate support to enable him to go through the labour which he had to perform; he lived at a distance of four miles from his work, not being able to procure a residence nearer. He was driven out of his parish, as a considerable number of other labourers were, in consequence of the reduction of the number of tenements; a system which is still carried on to a great extent by the landlords, in order to prevent, as much as possible, settlements being effected in their parishes." In the parish of Exton, I was informed that a very large reduction had also been made in the number of cottages, and the expelled inhabitants resorted to Greetham parish, about two miles distant, in which there are a number of small freeholds. This influx of labourers from the adjoining parish is most injurious to the parish of Greetham; "the foreigners," said one of the occupiers, "don't get so regularly employed as the natives, and it's quite natural that we should not feel much interest in them; we think that they might as well go a little further as settle upon us." The occupier, however, is not, unfortunately, the only party who has cause to complain of this state of things; neither does the mischief stop with the unfortunate evicted labourer. By causing in one parish a large surplus of labour, an opportunity is afforded to parties so disposed to effect a considerable reduction in the wages of the labourers, and thus the selfishness of one or more unprincipled proprietors may produce an incalculable amount of distress; first, by destruction of the health of the labourer consequent upon increased fatigue in going to and returning from work; and, secondly, by a reduction of wages in those districts to which the unfortunate victims of his selfishness are compelled to resort. Another precaution is also taken in the parish of Exton to prevent any additional settlements being made. If the occupier of one of the houses upon the estate has a son or a daughter married, and is unable to obtain a residence in the parish, he is strictly prohibited from taking them to live with him, although he may have ample means of accommodating them. It appears to be an understood rule in this and in some other parishes, that if any person affords an asylum to a new comer, or to a newly-married couple, he is not to receive employment from any farmer in the parish; and if he should succeed in obtaining employment from one over whom control cannot be exercised, he is threatened with ejectment from his dwelling. "The consequence of this conduct," said my informant, "is, that persons thus situated are compelled to live together in any hole or corner they can find, and some of the wretched hovels which they inhabit are so crowded that they are compelled to live together like pigs."

When a man is once expelled from his parish, "he might as well," said a gentleman to me, "ask for the teeth of the employers, in other parishes, as for work, the answer invariably given being 'we have enough to do to employ our own labourers—go to your own parish.'" An instance of this came under my knowledge in the case of a labourer who had resided for 26 years in the parish of Whissendine, and had been unemployed scarcely a day during that period. The poor man had a large family, and was considered, therefore, a fit object for transferrence, if possible, to some other parish. He received notice accordingly to quit, left the parish in which he had resided upwards of a quarter of a century, and had to establish his character and obtain employment in some other place, where the employers would no doubt be equally as anxious as the people of Whissendine to avoid the risk of becoming burdened by additional labourers.

Having by this means reduced the amount of pauperism in any given parish, the only expense which will fall upon it will be its portion of the establishment charges, which include the expenses of management of the union workhouse, salary to the schoolmaster, and charges for irremovable poor and for vagrants. In the Uppingham Union these establishment charges for the half year ending 29th September, 1849, were £453, the total expenditure for the same period being £2,384. The proportion of the establishment charges to be borne by each parish is decided in the following manner:—As the total average expenditure for any three years is to the total amount of the establishment charges, so is the average for each particular parish to the amount required, which in many cases is a mere trifle—in one parish in the county of 1,550 acres, and another of 840 acres, not being more than £1. It is in order to obtain this minimum amount of rating in other parishes that so much injury is constantly inflicted upon the honest and industrious labourer.

Another practice adopted by many of the farmers to prevent the poor from obtaining relief, is by promising the applicant that they will give him work upon their farms. The applicant, deceived by this offer, and barred by it from obtaining relief, has one or perhaps two days' work given him, when he is discharged, to do the best he can till the next board day, when he is handed over to the tender mercies of another of the guardians of the poor. "I've been at work," said a poor man to me, "for the last twenty years. My master discharged me, as he said he could not afford to keep me any longer. I've got five children, and I was obliged, for the first time in my life, to go to the board. While I was there, one of 'em said to me that, sooner than I should go to the workhouse and be parted from my family, he would find some job for me. I went to him after the board was over. I asked him what I could do, and he told me that he should be glad to employ me, but he had not got the means. I told him how he had promised to give me work, and at last he gave me a day's threshing and discharged me, so I had 1s. 2d. to live on till next board day; and they've served me so two or three times since that." Another poor fellow, who was out of work, and who had occasion to apply for relief, was ordered to receive four loaves of bread, on the ground of the illness of his family. Some members of the board, who chanced to be absent when the order was made, heard of this order for relief having been given, and they insisted that work should be found for the man by some of the occupiers in the parish. He applied again the next board day, and was told that he must go and look for work. He stated that he had already been unsuccessful in his application for work. He was referred to several persons, and told to go and inquire for work there, and if he could not get any to return to the board. The poor man had to walk two miles to the residence of the persons mentioned, and when he returned, as might almost have been expected, the meeting of the board had broken up. He contrived to subsist until the next board day, when he again presented himself, and was told by one of the guardians that he should have some work upon his farm. He went accordingly, had two days' work and was discharged. In this manner he had been bandied about through nearly the whole list of the guardians, and when, nearly worn out with this treatment, he applied to the relieving officer, who had no power whatever in the matter, he was told that nothing could be done for him so long as work was offered to him.

It would seem almost superfluous, after what I have already said on the subject, to add anything with respect to the condition of the dwellings of the labouring classes. Some of these places are, however, so extremely wretched as to deserve some more especial notice.

In the town of Oakham there are several rows of very bad and unhealthy cottages. Perhaps the worst places of this character are John's-court and Bull-lane. The former are built without any regard to proper ventilation. They have no back premises, and but a few feet of court yard in the front of each. In Bull-lane the cottages are in a most disgusting and filthy state, and are almost unapproachable, in consequence of the almost continual overflow of cesspools intended as the receptacle for filth and refuse of all kinds. At Greetham a row of cottages of a very incommodious character have been run up by a speculator, who lets them at a rent of £6 per annum; the ground attached to the cottages is merely nominal, and does not deserve mention; the cottages have three rooms and a small kitchen, and many complaints have been made of their damp and unhealthy character. But of all the miserable places which it has hitherto been my painful lot to witness, none have exceeded, or perhaps equalled, several cottages in Hambleton. These hovels upon approaching them have the appearance of large heaps of manure, which having lain upon the ground some time have become marked here and there with patches of vegetation. They are sunk so low in the ground that no part of them is visible but the thatch. The descent down to the entrance of these dreary abodes is in a bed which the water, as it drained from the higher parts of the ground, has worn for itself. The mud walls of these hovels are cracked and bulged in all directions, and are only prevented from falling by some poles which are placed against them. At one stage of this water-course, by which the inmates descend, is the door of one of these hovels, on passing through which a continuation of the same system of surface drainage will be seen, which terminates in a hole of about two feet deep and of about the same width, by the side of the fire-place, from whence the water is baled out of the window, or rather through a hole in the wall, for there is no window to the place. There are several other smaller holes, or cesspools, in the flooring of the place which receive the water from the roof or which runs down the sides of the walls. The persons who inhabit this place—for there are human beings who reside here—are seven in number, the eldest boy 22, the second 19, the third 16 years of age; the eldest girl 17, the next 13 years of age, and the father and mother. The place already described is the sitting room; the sleeping apartment is in the loft of this building. Of the ten stairs or steps which lead up to this dormitory, four are completely gone, and the remainder threaten every minute to fall by their own weight. There are four beds in this loft, where all the family sleep except the eldest boy, who sleeps with his grandmother in the next hovel. An old counterpane hangs before the place where the small window once was inserted, and a tub and one or two pans were standing in the room to receive some of the water that was falling through the roof at the time of my visit. The grandmother lived in the next cottage, the condition of which was, if possible, much worse than the adjoining one. The ground on the outside of this cottage was so formed that the water discharged itself from the surface through the remnants of the window, and so on to the floor, thence by means of a shallow channel slowly oozed towards the cesspool or reservoir, as in the other cottage; and the grandmother, who was "going of 83," was engaged with a basin in ladling the water out of the hole and carrying it out of doors. By some neglect on the part of the old lady the reservoir had overflowed and had quenched the few embers which had been smouldering upon that portion of the ground set apart as the fire-place. The upper part of the wall of this building had fallen down to the extent of nearly one-half of the sleeping apartment in the loft. "I've been obliged to make an old quilt, sir," said the poor feeble old woman, "to hang up over this hole, lookye," said she, lifting up the quilt at the same time, "you can see all out of it. I puts the tub here, to catch the water as comes a-through. I've been here the best end of forty years; it's been very bad, it has; worse than this. Green was kind enough to stop the water, or else we used to sit up to our ankles in water to eat our vittles. It is very bad indeed, sir, and I should like to have a little done to it, so that I might live in it the rest of my days. The other cottage, where my daughter lives"—the one just described—"is much better than this. My grandson is a very notable and ingenious young man, and put up some sticks, to keep it from falling, but my wall has fell down. My other grandson, as sleeps with me here, is a very steady young man, indeed; it is wonderful to see how steady he is. I am too ould now to do much—I can't waish my clothes now, except this old flannel that I wears round me, and I have to put 'em out to be waished. I have three shillings a week from the parish, and a loaf, because I can't waish my clothes. When it do rain, sir, the water comes in through the window, and down the wall, and runs into this hole. When it's full, I lades it out, and throws it out of the window, and then it runs away through Dexter's yard" (the Dexters being the next door neighbours). "It is so damp and cold that it's made me hard of hearing, and has hurt my poor eyes, and nobody knows what I've went through in this house but the Lord and myself." Cottage No. 3 of this group, inhabited by a man, his wife, and six children, was in an equally disgraceful state; the earthen floor, saturated with the rain that had poured in from every opening, was a mass of soft, clayey mud, and the foot-prints in the floor, receiving the water that drained into them, formed a variety of dirty-looking puddles. The wretched people who live in these hovels are unable to obtain other residences in the parish, there being none to let, and out of their parish it is equally impossible, as the dread of their becoming chargeable to the parish would prevent any person from taking them in. The cottages are the property of Mr. Finch, who generally bears a good character as a landlord. They are almost within sight of his beautiful residence, and he has been repeatedly informed of their condition, and his reply has as often been to the effect that they were so thoroughly worthless he did not care what became of them. The parish, acting as middleman, rents the cottages of Mr. Finch, and lets them at an increased rent to the poor families, making a profit upon the transaction of £1 per annum, but refusing to expend a single farthing upon their repair.

LABOUR AND THE POOR.

THE RURAL DISTRICTS.

[FROM OUR SPECIAL CORRESPONDENT.]

COUNTIES OF NORTHAMPTON, LEICESTER, RUTLAND, NOTTINGHAM, AND DERBY.

LETTER XLVIII.

The population of the above five counties includes a large proportion of persons employed in the three great branches of British industry—mining operations, manufactures, and agriculture. One of my colleagues, in his letters on the Manufacturing Districts, has already described the condition of the miner, and of the operative engaged in manufactures. Upon me, therefore, devolves the task of dealing with the third and remaining branch of employment—agriculture—and of setting forth the condition of the labourers employed therein.

Dividing the population of these counties into the two great divisions of agriculture, and commerce and trade—the latter including manufactures and mining operations—the number of persons employed therein will be seen from the following table, the materials of which are taken from the "Occupation Abstract" of the census of 1841:—

Counties.	Farmers and Graziers.	Agricultural Labourers.	Nurserymen and Florists.	Total engaged in Agriculture.	Total engaged in Commerce, Trade, & Manufactures.
Northampton	3,315	21,792	624	25,731	26,859
Leicester ...	3,669	12,770	653	17,092	41,554
Rutland	616	2,629	71	3,316	1,955
Nottingham .	3,787	15,926	645	20,358	51,373
Derby	6,991	11,776	566	19,333	51,675

The total want of anything like statistical information on the subject of agriculture presents, at the very outset, an almost insuperable difficulty to any attempt to form an accurate notion of the value or extent of agriculture in any part of the country. Even with respect to the quantity of land under tillage or in pasture—information upon which might so easily be collected through the machinery of existing institutions—no authentic account can be obtained. A few years since some most valuable statistical tables were published by the late Mr. Marshall, which contained, among other matters, a statement of the superficies in statute acres of each county, showing the proportion of each in a state of tillage, in pasture, in wood, and unproductive; but a note appended to the table states that these proportions do not profess to be founded on very accurate data. But as the proportions there given have, upon various occasions, been adopted as correct, and as there does not appear to be any more trustworthy information to be obtained on the subject from official sources, I shall avail myself of them, in order to give the reader some idea of the annual value of the agricultural produce of these counties. The following are the proportions assigned by Mr. Marshall to each county. No figures are given with respect to the county of Rutland; and with regard to Leicestershire, nothing is set down under the head of "wooded and unproductive":—

Counties.	Tillage.	Pasture.	Wood and Unproductive.
Northampton	290,000	235,000	123,000
Leicester ...	65,000	450,000	—
Rutland	No account.	No account.	No account.
Nottingham .	200,000	100,000	235,680
Derby	100,000	400,000	156,640
Total	655,000	1,185,000	515,320

Estimating the average produce of the arable land at £7, the pasture at £6, and the wooded at 10s. per acre, the value of the agricultural produce of these counties, exclusive of Rutland, would be—

Arable	£4,585,000
Pasture	7,110,000
Wooded	257,660
Total	£11,952,660

From the proportions of arable to pasture land which exist upon a number of farms in Rutland, it will not be too much to assume that five-sixths of the whole of the county is pasture—the remaining one-sixth being divided between the arable and the unproductive, and the latter amounting to about 5,000 acres. The proportion for the county of Rutland would therefore be 11,250 acres of arable, 5,000 wooded and unproductive, and 81,250 acres of pasture. The value of produce of the arable land would be, at the same rates as above, £78,750; pasture, £487,500; wooded, £2,500; being a total of £568,750; which, added to the above, would give as the value of the agricultural produce of the whole group of counties £12,521,410.

As it is evident that, upon the state of agriculture, the mode in which it is carried on, the systems of cultivation adopted, the character of landlords and tenants, and the relations existing between them, must depend to a great extent the condition of the labourer, it will be necessary, before proceeding to review his condition, to glance at a few of those more prominent features which, in each county, so materially affect his means of employment, and his social and moral condition.

In Northamptonshire the character of the soil is exceedingly varied. In portions of the Spelhoe hundred there are to be found stiff loam, and light porous red earth; in Overstone, there is red land upon a subsoil of stiff clay; in Wymersley, strong clay and sandy soils are to be met with; in the neighbourhood of Hardingstone, strong clay, with black and red loam, are frequently seen in the immediate neighbourhood of each other. At Horton, and many other places, there is some very strong clay, and at Thorpeland a rich sandy loam. Generally speaking, the soil is of a kindly and productive character. The county is more generally noted as a stock-breeding and feeding than as a wheat-producing one, although in many parts very excellent crops of wheat are raised. The extensive cultivation of green crops, caused by the necessity for producing an increased supply of food for cattle, has completely revolutionized the systems of farming previously adopted in this county; and the old adage, "No food, no cattle; no cattle, no dung; no dung, no corn," appears to be fully and completely appreciated in many parts. There is probably no part of England in which the farmers are more keenly alive to the necessity of making greater exertions in order to meet the present altered state of circumstances in which they are placed by the recent changes in legislation, than in the county of Northampton. The great extent to which drainage is being carried on, the reduction to decent proportions of those high and unsightly hedge-rows which formed harbours for birds and vermin, and the removal of the large ash and other trees which luxuriate in the hedge-rows, to the deterioration of the crops in their immediate neighbourhood, sufficiently attest the improvement which is taking place. These signs of progress, together with the erection of new and commodious farm buildings, show that many of the landowners also are not insensible to the duties which they owe to their improving tenants at the present period. Foremost amongst the members of this class deserving of special notice on account of the liberal and en-lightened policy which they adopt towards their tenants, is Mr. Lewis Loyd. That gentleman is, I believe, at present the largest landowner in the county. Nearly the whole of the land between the towns of Northampton and Kettering belongs to him, including the parishes of Abington, Little Billing, Thorpelands, Overstone, nearly the whole of Sirwell, Pitchley, Weston, Great Moulton, Fotheringay, and other places. The whole of this property, so far as the farming portions of it are concerned, is under the management of Mr. Beasley, who, on account of his abilities both as a practical farmer and as an able and ef-ficient agent, is held in the highest esteem among the tenants. Of the whole of the farms on the extensive estate of Mr. Loyd it is not too much to say that they are in an excellent state of cultivation. Through-out the entire estate the hedges will be seen to be low and neatly trimmed—or, in cases where sufficient time has not elapsed since the purchase of the property to make these improvements, great num-bers of men are employed in effecting them. Right and left, heaps of drain tile are observable upon the land, ready for being placed in their proper position; watercourses, which had for ages pursued their zigzag course, are diverted into direct channels of uniform width, and the ground previously wasted by the tortuous direction of the currents is made productive and fruitful. Old, decayed, and crooked hedges are stubbed up, hedge-row trees are felled, the land is laid out with due regard to the convenience of cultivation, and new quick-hedges are planted so as to give a more regular and uniform appearance to the farms.

The course adopted by Mr. Loyd towards his tenants, in respect to improvements of this kind, is, I believe, unparalleled in any part of the country. Any of his tenants who may express a wish to have his land drained is directed to make application to Mr. Beasley, his agent, on the subject—who, after deciding as to the mode and extent in which the draining is to be performed, furnishes the necessary drain tiles and the labour for making the drains, free of all cost whatever to the tenant, the latter being only required to cart the tiles to the land. If the tenant desires the removal of unnecessary timber from his hedges, or that the enclosures should be laid out upon any more convenient plan, the necessary arrangements for surveying the land are made, and the quick or the new hedges, together with the labour necessary for removing the old and planting the new ones, are all found free of charge to the tenant, who is only required, as in the former instance, to cart the materials to the land. In all cases, too, in which the tenant complains of farm buildings being incommodious in their arrangements, or insufficient in size, new ones, built of brick and fire-proof, are erected; upon the same plan as the other improvements, new farm houses are built, where required by the tenants; and where it is found that there is not sufficient cottage accommodation for the labourers, cottages also are erected upon the same liberal system. The principle which appears to guide Mr. Loyd, with respect to the assistance which he affords to his tenants, is one which many years since was adopted by the late Earl of Leicester towards his tenantry in Norfolk. At that period his lordship received much undeserved censure, because, as was alleged, "he had built gentlemen's houses for his tenantry." The answer—if it were necessary to give any answer to such a charge—was readily to be found in his desire to place his tenants in that position to which their capital or industry entitled them. His usual language to a tenant was, "If you will keep an extra yard of bullocks, I will build you a yard and shed free of expense." Such is the principle upon which— but, if possible, to a greater extent—Mr. Loyd appears determined to act. The effects of such a liberal system are already to be traced in a contented, energetic, and skilful tenantry—in well-paid and well- employed labourers, whose homes are comfortable, and whose condition is one of comparative happiness—and in enormously diminished poor-rates, pauperism, degradation, and crime.

The late Marquess of Northampton afforded considerable assistance to his tenants by improving the condition of their farms—having given them, free of cost, 700,000 draining tiles during the last few years. The property of Earl Spencer has also been managed for some years in a similar mode. The Duke of Grafton, Sir C. Knightley, and Mr. Stafford, M.P., have likewise rendered great assistance in drainage works and other improvements, charging 5 per cent. on the outlay, in the shape of additional rent.

But while in many parts, and more particularly within ten or fifteen miles of the town of Northampton, the farms are generally as well managed as perhaps those of any county in England, instances are not unfrequently to be met with in which the most wretched kind of farming exists. The farm buildings are old and crazy, and the cattle stalls are open and exposed to all the changes and inclemencies of the weather. The straw yards contain no appliances for saving the liquid manure, but, on the contrary, its vital essence is allowed to evaporate in the air, or to waste itself in the pool of stagnant water adjoining the wretched buildings. From the small quantity of stock which is kept, it is next to impossible that the straw should be converted into really efficient manure; and in point of fact, the contents of the straw yard are little more than trampled straw, saturated with rain, and partially decayed by the combined action of the atmosphere and the exhalations from the soil. What return can be reasonably expected from the application to the land of such materials—termed, by courtesy, manure—it is difficult to ascertain; and nothing but an inveterate adherence to the antiquated habits of one's ancestors, or a deficiency of capital, can account for the folly of supposing that manure, deprived of the little wheat-making properties which it ever possessed, could be successfully applied to the land.

Speaking of the agriculture of Northamptonshire, Mr. Hillyard, in the preface to a small work published by him on the subject, in 1834, has the following remarks, which apply with equal, if not with greater force to the present state of things in this county:—

"The general agriculture of this kingdom has, no doubt, greatly improved within the last thirty years, and the county of Northampton has fully shared in such improvement, although it cannot be justly said to have made such advances in this most important science as not to be still capable of much greater improvement. Necessity is a powerful spur to industry and contrivance—a truth sufficiently proved by the fact that the greatest improvements in farming were begun on the poorest soils. Necessity compelled the occupiers of such soils to exert themselves to the utmost, and to become good farmers to gain a maintenance. Nature has been kind to this county, and given to the greater part of it a very productive soil; and therefore formerly too much was left to nature; art and great exertion were not much needed to raise such crops as enabled the farmers to live; the case, however, is now widely different; with the most productive soil, great exertion is absolutely necessary. In former times, old persons have often said to me, 'there is no farming like the old farming.' Such prejudices have died with them;

the present generation of farmers are more enlightened; they are not, as their predecessors were, opposed to all suggested improvements of cultivation."

Although this may be generally true with respect to the majority of the farmers of Northamptonshire, still there are many of them—happily they are not by any means the majority—who refuse to adopt any of the recent improvements in agriculture, or to depart from the old system of cropping their land, which, although venerable from its antiquity, has been completely exploded by all good farmers of modern times. "The mania for green cropping," said one of these rural antiquarians to me, "is just like the railway mania—it will ruin all that have anything to do with it." Upon a subject of such vast importance as that of an improved system of cropping the land—and upon the adoption of which the interests both of the consumer and of the producer, whether farmer or labourer, so greatly depend—while I am anxious to avoid the appearance of expressing any opinion of my own, I am desirous of laying before the reader the modes adopted by some of the best farmers in the county. The most beneficial results have attended the introduction of the system of green cropping into the previously existing modes of cultivation. Indeed, upon the successful cultivation of the turnip must depend, in a great degree, the prosperous condition of farming; and more especially is this the case in Northamptonshire, Norfolk, and other counties in which large quantities of stock are reared or fed. With respect to the value of turnips in feeding cattle, one intelligent farmer in the county who had paid considerable attention to the effects of feeding his cattle upon them, informed me that the produce of his five acres of turnips, averaging 20 tons each to the acre, returned him, in the shape of meat, about 6s. to each ton of turnips consumed. Taking the crop to be of the weight of 100 tons, this would give, at 6s. per ton, £30 as the value of the crop, independent of the value of the manure. The value of crops of this nature must, of course, be always dependent upon the character of the soil, its previous state of cultivation, and other circumstances of a similar character. To any person acquainted with the first principles of chemical science, apart from any knowledge which he may or may not possess on the subject of agriculture, it would be obvious that a rotation of green with the white crops would be attended with success. If such a person were told that one of the properties of cereal crops was to impoverish and weaken the land, by the large quantities of ammonia consumed in their growth, it would surely not require a very extraordinary amount of that "practical knowledge" with the want of which many of the best friends of agriculture have been taunted, to enable him to come to the conclusion that the next best course to adopt would be to endeavour to restore, if possible, some portion of the lost virtues of the land, or to produce some crop less exhaustive in its character. In order to effect this renovation, various systems of rotatory cropping have been adopted, which have been modified from time to time in such manner as the benefits of experience or the light of science may have pointed out. The ammonia which is withdrawn from the soil by the cereal crops is endeavoured to be replaced by the application of manure, and the larger the quantity of nitrogen which it contains the more completely will the quantity previously absorbed be replaced. By numerous experiments which have been made upon various occasions—and the results of which have been published from time to time in the proceedings of the Royal Agricultural Society—it is proved that leguminous plants contain nearly a double amount of nitrogen as compared with straw crops, and that they will consequently, when consumed by cattle or sheep, leave behind, in the shape of manure, an increased quantity of nitrogen, which will be available for the supply of the deficiency caused by the cereal crops. If this be the fact with regard to the properties of leguminous plants, and if the value of the turnip crop be as was stated to me by the gentleman above referred to, there cannot be much reason to doubt that the adoption of this system—leading as it would to an increased cultivation of the soil—would benefit the farmer by its profitable returns, and the labourer by affording him the means of increased employment.

But several of the farmers with whom I have spoken on the subject have gone completely to the other side of the question; and, admitting the advantages which an increased growth of green crops, for the purpose of feeding stock, would confer upon the land, they believe that the land would be stimulated to too great an extent, and would produce straw rather than wheat. Whether there exists sufficient grounds for believing that such would be the effect, is a point upon which I have heard many conflicting opinions. The more general opinion appears to be, that these effects, if produced at all, would be only upon a very small scale, and that upon the very best class of lands; but that, with respect to the great bulk of the land, there was but little ground for fearing the result of an increased application of really efficient manure. Upon this part of the question an eminent agricultural chemist states that, when the farmer shall have ascertained correctly the constituent elements of the plants, and the sum of the ingredients which they draw from the soil, "he will be able to keep an exact record of the produce of his fields in harvest, like the account book of a well-regulated manufactory—and then, by a simple calculation, he can determine precisely the substances he must apply to each field, and the quantity of these, in order to restore their fertility. He will be able to express, in pounds weight, how much of this or that element he must give to the soil in order to augment its fertility for any given kind of plants. These researches and experiments are the great desiderata of the present time."

The rotation of crops generally pursued in the county of Northampton is the four-course shift. The uncertainty attending the clover crops at intervals of four years only, has, however, caused some modification of the plan. I was informed of three different modes adopted upon different farms to obviate this difficulty. Upon one farm the plan adopted is the following:—First year, fallow, one-third mangold wurtzel, one-third potatoes, and one-third carrots, to be all carted off the land for home consumption; second, wheat; third, beans and peas; fourth, turnips, to be partly eaten on the land and partly carted off; fifth, wheat; sixth, barley, prepared for by growing mustard seed to plough in, or by a dressing of nitrate of soda; seventh, clover and grass seeds; eighth, wheat. Three crops of wheat are thus obtained within the eight years by this system, and of clover only one crop. Another course, which is also one of eight years, is, first, potatoes; second, wheat; third, white turnips and mangold wurtzel; fourth, wheat; fifth, swedes; sixth, barley or oats sown down; seventh, seeds; eighth, wheat. Under this system three crops of wheat are grown in the eight years and one of seeds. The turnips are all eaten upon the ground, the potatoes and mangold wurtzel being carried off. A third course, which was recommended at a meeting of the Agricultural Book Club as having been most successful, was one of six years: first, tares, and fallow for turnips, the latter being sown after the tares; second, barley, with seeds; third, the seeds mown; fourth, wheat; fifth, beans; sixth, wheat. In the fourth year it was recommended that the land should be broken up immediately after harvest, and well manured for the beans. Some persons adopt the plan of sewing broad clover on one turn, and Dutch clover, or rye grass, on the next. Trampling the seeds with sheep is also adopted in some parts of the county.

As might be expected from the fact of the quantities of cattle and sheep either fed or reared in the county, considerable attention has been paid by the farmers to the improvement of the quality and breed of their stock. In the Northamptonshire Agricultural Book Club the subject has been frequently discussed. The sheep most generally fed are a cross Leicester. Of cattle, the Durhams or short-horns appear to be the most in request for feeding. The Marquess of Exeter and Sir C. Knightley are extensive breeders of Durhams. Mr. Stafford breeds both Durhams and Herefords. Earl Spencer has some fine sheds of cattle, principally Devons; but perhaps there is no one in the whole county, who, for the quantity of land which he holds, keeps so large a quantity of sheep and stock as Mr. Beasley, of Overstone, who is the steward both to Earl Spencer and Mr. Lewis Loyd. The extent of his farm is about 700 acres, and he has recently added to it the land of the late Mr. Hillyard—a gentleman well known in the agricultural world by the number of works which he has written and published on the subject of agriculture. When I visited his farm there were upon it altogether 170 beasts and 890 sheep. When the arrangements upon the new farm are completed, Mr. Beasley intends to keep 200 head of cattle and 1,400 sheep. I shall have occasion in my next letter to refer to the extensive works of drainage and other improvements carried on by this gentleman, and to the amount of employment which he affords to the people. A number of steer calves are purchased every year, so that a constant succession is kept up, in the straw yards and stalls, of yearlings and two and three year old beasts. A bull, called the Lord Warden, belonging to Mr. Beasley, was purchased for the sum of £400, at the sale of the late Earl Spencer's stock, and is one of the most perfect specimens of his class that I ever saw. Several of his calves have been sold at enormous sums; the "Usurer" sold for 400 guineas; the "Upstart," a yearling ten months old, for 200 guineas; another, purchased by the Earl of Ducie, realized 200 guineas; and Sir Thomas Cartwright gave 180 guineas for another. The sheds for the cattle are all fire-proof, built of red brick with rounded edges, and have a pleasing appearance. They are well sheltered, and are constructed with a view of affording the greatest amount of convenience.

The rent of land in Northamptonshire varies considerably. The lowest may be taken at about £1 per acre, the highest at from 35s. to 40s.—not, of course, including land in the neighbourhood of towns and villages, which is generally let as accommodation land, at high rents, varying from £3 to £5 per acre. If from such elements it might be allowable to strike an average, the sum would probably be about 30s. per acre.

The farms, generally speaking, in the county are not, compared with those in Norfolk, what might be called large, the greater number of occupations being from 100 to 500 acres. In several parts of the county there has been for several years, and still continues to be, a desire on the part of some proprietors to enlarge the size of the farms held by their tenants. Upon the estate of the Earl of Cardigan the farms are increasing in extent—his lordship having, as I was informed, expressed his determination not to let any of his property in farms of less than 500 acres; and as the smaller tenants go out, their farms are consolidated with others. With respect to the tenure of the land, the general mode of letting is from year to year, and comparatively few leases are granted; but latterly there has been a pretty general desire to grant leases on the part of Lord Spencer, the Duke of Grafton, and many of the landowners. One of the tenants of the Duke of Grafton informed me that he had made repeated applications for a lease, but had been as often refused. His Grace had, however, very recently intimated to him that he might have a lease of his farm; but as no abatement was proposed to be made in the rent, the tenant now refuses to accept the lease. Mr. Lewis Loyd grants leases to each of his tenants requiring them, upon very liberal terms.

In my next I propose giving some account of the condition of the labourer in this county.

LABOUR AND THE POOR.

THE RURAL DISTRICTS.

[FROM OUR SPECIAL CORRESPONDENT.]

COUNTIES OF NORTHAMPTON, LEICESTER, RUTLAND, NOTTINGHAM, AND DERBY.

THE AGRICULTURAL LABOURER OF NORTHAMPTONSHIRE.

LETTER XLIX.

The condition of the labourer will be found almost invariably to be a reflex of the character of the employers of labour in any particular district; and in exact proportion to the intelligence and ability, to say nothing of the humanity, of the owners or occupiers of land, will be found to be the comfort, happiness, and contentment of the peasantry. A more striking instance of the truth of this proposition is, perhaps, not to be found than in the case of the labourers at Overstone, who obtain the means of employment upon the property of Mr. Lewis Loyd, and upon the farm of Mr. Beasley, the steward to that gentleman.

When in the neighbourhood of Overstone, I availed myself of the opportunity of visiting what most certainly deserves to be styled the "model farm" of Mr. Beasley. On a farm of about 900 acres, upwards of 200 of which were grass lands, there were employed, at the time of my visit, in the month of January, fifty-six men and seven boys, between thirty and forty of whom were employed in draining operations. About 200 acres of land had, within a short period, come into the possession of Mr. Beasley, and some additional employment was consequently afforded by the alterations and improvements which were being carried on in connection with the newly-acquired farm. The wages paid to the labourers were—to one, 13s. per week; to four, 12s. each; to one, 11s.; the wages of the whole fifty-six, some of whom were paid by piece work, averaged 10s. per week; and those of the boys from 3s. to 9s. per week. Upon several farms in Moulton, the adjoining parish, the number of labourers employed averaged two men and a boy to about 150 acres. One man was employed to look after the horse, one to thrash, and a boy to help occasionally. The poor-rates in Overstone were 4½d., in Moulton 1s. 0½d. in the pound, but would have been considerably higher were it not for the circumstance that nearly one-half of the persons employed by Mr. Beasley belonged to Moulton parish. "Although," said an elderly man to me, "there's a sight of shoeing (shoe making) done in Moulton, there's a many of the poor people that does farm work; and if it wasn't for Squire Loyd and Mr. Beasley, there's a many of 'em would have been dead afore this of starvation. There's no knowin' the good as they do in employin' the poor people; it's far better than charityin' of them, because they feels independent when they work for what they gets. Last week (Christmas) Mr. Beasley had a bullock killed, and gave all his labourers a dinner of roast beef and plum pudding, and a sight of beer with it; and Mr. Knight, his managing man, had dinner with the poor fellows."

The system of cropping adopted by Mr. Beasley is the "four-course shift." The farm is laid out in twelve fields, so that, according to this mode of cropping, there would be three fields of turnips, three barley, three wheat, and three clover or other green crops. The increase which has taken place in the productiveness of the land since it came into the hands of Mr. Beasley, has been prodigious. The average crop of wheat while under its former occupier was 2 quarters to the acre; and Mr. Beasley was informed that that was the greatest amount which it would be possible for him to raise—the land being of a very inferior quality. These predictions have been so far falsified under his able management that an offer has been made to, and refused by, Mr. Beasley to purchase 70 acres of his wheat at 6 qrs. to the acre. His turnip crop averaged 20 tons to the acre upon land where, a few years since, such a thing as a turnip was unseen. I referred in my last letter to the quantity of stock kept upon the farm, which produced more manure than it is thought expedient to apply to the ground. Not a farthing has been expended by Mr. Beasley upon artificial manures. Some salt occasionally sown with the wheat to strengthen the crops is the only article applied to the ground in addition to the home-made manures. There is a small steam-engine of six-horse power on the farm, used for thrashing or chaff cutting. The cost of fuel for the engine, for nine days, is 36s. The machine will cut, with one box, about six bushels of chaff, at three-eighths of an inch in length per minute. The expense of cutting, including fuel and men's wages in feeding the machine, is about one farthing per quarter. The usual price paid for cutting by hand is 3d., and in some places 4d. per quarter. When used for thrashing, the engine will thrash about 30 quarters in the day, and would take about seven men to feed it. The wages of the men would be—7 days, at 1s. 8d. per day, 11s. 8d., and the cost of fuel 5s., making a total expense of 16s. 8d., or about 6½d. per quarter. The price paid for thrashing by flail is 3s. per quarter. For the 30 quarters, therefore, the price paid would be £4 10s., but by engine 16s. 8d.—showing a saving in favour of engine over manual labour of £3 13s. 4d., or equal to the daily wages of 44 men at 1s. 8d. per day. But notwithstanding this enormous saving of labour in this department, the number of men employed on the farm in proportion to the land far exceeds anything which I have hitherto seen, with the exception of the farm of Mr. Warnes, in Trimingham, where the growth and preparation of flax afford the means of employment to a considerable number.

An accurate account is kept by Mr. Beasley of all sums received and expended upon the farm. The system of keeping the accounts is complete and effective. One portion of the set of books is devoted to "The State of Stock," and the pages are ruled in columns with the following headings:—"Stock brought forward," "Bred," "Bought," "Sold," "Died," "Number Remaining." The following page is ruled in like manner and headed, "Dead Stock," and shows the quantities of "Wheat," "Barley," "Oats," "Beans," "Peas," which have been either "Winnowed," "Bought," "Sold," "Consumed," or "Sown." The weekly receipts and expenses occupy another folio. Then there is "The weekly state of labour." A column is devoted to each day in the week, in which, opposite each labourer's name, is entered the nature of the work upon which he was employed and the amount paid to him at the end of the week. The whole of these accounts are made up at the end of each week, and the totals carried forward to the "general balance sheet." It is an invariable rule to sell the produce of the farm within the year. With an average sum of £29 paid in wages every week, it may perhaps be a matter of surprise to many persons, who consider it impossible for farmers to cultivate their land with profit at present prices, to hear that, at the end of the last year, upon this farm of 700 acres,

<pre>
The total receipts were £3,455 16   5
Total expenses 2,796   2   6
                                                  ─────────────
Leaving a gross profit of £659 13 11
From which deduct interest on capital
    of £5,675 at 5 per cent. 283 15   0
                                                  ─────────────
Leaves a net profit of £375 18 11
</pre>

But this is not all. The value of 600 fleeces which were not sold during the year have been added to this amount, which, at the rate of four to the todd, and at 28s. per todd, the present price, would be equal to £210.

Upon comparing the quantity of live stock at the end of the year with that of the corresponding period of the previous year, it appears that there was an increase in the number of cattle of 59, of sheep 281, and of pigs 37. The salary of the manager of the farm, and an addition to his salary of 10 per cent. upon the profits, was also included in the expenditure of the year.

To the net profits for the year, therefore, exclusive of interest at 5 per cent. upon invested capital, must be added the value of the 600 fleeces, the difference in value of the live stock, and the 10 per cent. allowance to the manager upon balance over expenditure. Before leaving Overstone it may be as well to state that a great number of cottages have been recently erected for the labourers. These cottages consist of two sleeping rooms in the upper part, a sitting room, a small wash house, with oven and other conveniences, a small out-house or "barn," as the poor people call it, for containing fuel, a pig stye, and to each cottage a rood or more of land, which is let at the rate of 30s. per acre—being the same price as that paid by the farmers for their larger quantities. There is a school in the village well attended, the cottages are cleanly and comfortable, and the people contented and happy.

In nearly all parts of the county of Northampton considerable quantities of aolitic limestone are to be met with, and the great majority of the cottages in the county are built of this material. Many of them are extremely old and have an exceedingly primitive appearance. In no place, perhaps, is this more the case than in the village of Naseby. The cottages in this place look almost as though they had risen out of the kealy earth upon which they are built, and of which they are generally formed. The Rev. H. Lockinge, late curate of Naseby, in a small account which he published of the place, says—"The village in general bears a rude and primitive appearance, education has been until very lately disregarded, its expansive plain unenclosed, and its roads, especially in the winter season, almost impassable. In short, I am inclined to believe that, were we to remove the many improvements effected during the last few years, the historian might have the pleasure of contemplating the place very nearly as it appeared when the decisive conflict brought the Sovereign to the scaffold, and left its details recorded upon our annals in streams of blood." He states, however, that he received from the people of the village during his ministry repeated proofs of attachment and respect, and to the best of his knowledge not one of his parishioners had been either accused or convicted of any serious crime.

In the village of Raunds the cottages are old, and many of them wretchedly inconvenient, and few places present a more miserable or dilapidated appearance. An open water-course, of considerable width, runs through the very centre of the village, which acts as the sewer of the place. One of the cottages which I visited consisted of only two rooms and a small "lean-to," with no garden or back premises whatever. The family consisted of seven children, and the father, mother, and grandmother. In the lower room sat the husband and two children busy at shoe making; in another part of the room the grandmother and two children, sitting on the bedside, were making pillow-lace—an article for the manufacture of which Raunds is greatly famed. The eldest daughter was washing out some clothes by the side of the fire-place, and the mother preparing the dinner. The other children were playing together on an old stump bedstead. It is needless to say that the small apartment, as well as the inmates, were wretched and dirty in their appearance.

There is scarcely a cottage in the place in which, to a greater or less extent, the same inconvenient crowding is not found to exist. The contrast of the employment of the male and female members of the family is striking—the one employed in the dirty and heavy occupation of shoemaking, the other seated close by, patiently fabricating the most beautiful lace; and it is a matter of surprise how, in the midst of so much dirt, the patient and ill-requited lacemaker can contrive to keep her elegant fabric so clean as she does. Of many of the cottages in Rotten-row and Litchfield-row I shall not be speaking in too severe terms when I say that they are entirely unfit for human habitations, and are alike a disgrace to the village and to their owners. They have one room above and one below; there is a step down of about a foot or eighteen inches to obtain an entrance into these places, and in the doorway there is not room for a full-grown person to stand upright. The rooms are exceedingly dark and wretched, and have earth floors. Few of them are water-tight, and the walls are stained with the streams of water that find their way through the dilapidated roofs. The rent of these wretched habitations varies from £2 10s. to £3. "They are like graves for the living," said a thin sallow-looking young man, in a hoarse and hollow voice, who was sitting in the chimney corner in one of these wretched hovels. "You may say, at all events, that you've seen a man and his wife, and six children, buried alive in Rotten-row." A sort of kinship, I was informed, exists throughout the whole village; nearly every inhabitant is related in some way to every other—the people seldom marrying out of their own family or connections. One of the more intelligent of the inhabitants of the place informed me that he thought "some of the people were a little backwarder, perhaps, than some others, but, taking 'em altogether, he thought they were as shrewd, and as drunken, as most other people of their condition."

In several of the "close" villages, the labourers suffer to some extent in consequence of the destruction of cottage property by the owners of the land, who are anxious to prevent any persons obtaining settlements, or becoming burdens on the parish. I was informed that this had been the case more particularly in the parish of Orton, where at present there was not a single pauper, in consequence of their having been forced into one or other of the adjoining parishes.

In the parish of Glendon, the whole of which is owned, I believe, exclusively by two proprietors, there are not more than two or three cottages, and the whole of the labourers employed upon 1,490 acres are compelled to reside in Kettering, Rothwell, and the surrounding villages. In several other parishes there is an equal deficiency of cottage accommodation. In the parish of Steane there are 1,360 acres and four houses only; in Warkworth, 2,370 acres and six houses; in Fawsley, 1,550 acres and four houses.

In the parishes of Blakesley, Gayton, Blisworth, and Whittlebury, cottages of an improved description have been built or enlarged for the labourers, with a most salutary effect upon the health and moral habits of the people. Their appearance is clean, decent, orderly, and healthy; and I was informed that applications for medical relief were rare, and that there was a marked love of home, and an attention to its wants and comforts, which had had a most ruinous effect upon the beer-shops in the villages. At Church Brampton and Chapel Brampton, the property of Earl Spencer, twenty cottages have been erected for the labourers, which, from their beautiful appearance, look more like gentlemen's villas than the residences of labourers. The cottages, ten in number, in each of the villages, are built in the Gothic style, of stone obtained from the neighbouring quarries of Duston and Harlestone. The cottages are detached, and to each pair there is a small scullery at the rear of the premises, built in a style to correspond with the dwelling. These sculleries can be seen from the road through the openings between the cottages, and, from their situation in the background, give a pleasing appearance to the whole group. There is also a barn or outhouse, with a loft overhead, a pigstye, and a dust-bin. To each cottage there is about a quarter of an acre of garden ground in the rear. A lawn, unbroken by any division or fence, extends along the front of the whole range of dwellings, and a number of flower beds of various and fantastic shapes, formed in the green turf, are planted with evergreens and choice flowers, and the whole agreeably relieved by raised mounds and patches of grotto work. This pleasing addition to the cottages was laid out and stocked by the late Earl Spencer, the tenants being only required to keep the place in order. The cottages themselves are exceedingly commodious; they consist of two lower and two upper rooms, well provided with cupboards and other conveniences. The sitting-room of each cottage is paved in large diamond squares, alternately black and white, and has a range fitted with oven and boiler. In the scullery there is a copper, an ironing-stove, and a large oven used for baking bread. Each of the cottagers had one or more pigs in the stye, a good stack of fuel, and occasionally a barrel or two of home-brewed beer. The sleeping rooms were remarkably clean and airy. The whole appearance of the cottages and of the inmates was such as to show most convincingly that the efforts which had been made to better the condition of the poor people had been attended with complete success. The cottagers were extremely pleased that so much care had been taken by the noble earl to increase their comfort, and, however it may be considered by some persons that unnecessary expense had been gone to in the erection of these abodes, such feelings are by no means shared by the tenants. As they conducted me over the different parts of the cottages and gardens, it was evident that they felt no small degree of pleasure in doing so, and while they expressed their feeling of gratitude to their benevolent landlord, they were "glad that God had put it into his heart to give the poor folks something to be proud of."

Several other cases might be instanced of the exertions made by the resident proprietors in improving the dwellings of the labourers. The village of Cranford is a remarkable instance of the good that may be thus effected. The Rev. Sir C. Robinson is the rector of the parish, and the proprietor of a considerable portion of it. All the old cottages have been pulled down, and given place to new and more commodious ones. In order to obviate some of the evils which necessarily arise from the indiscriminate herding together of members of the family of both sexes and of all ages, a lodging-house is in the course of erection for the elder boys and unmarried young men of the village. This arrangement is one which promises to be attended with beneficial results.

The amount of employment which is afforded in this county by the boot and shoe trade—many of those who work at that trade being occasionally employed as farm labourers—and the small amounts earned by the various members of the family by lace-making, tend to prevent to a great extent that fearful distress and privation which are to be met with in other parts where the labourer does not possess these adventitious aids. Added to this, there exists in most parts of the county a desire to give as much employment to the labourer as possible. The consequence is, that comparatively few persons are unemployed. In several parishes there are no labourers without work; and in Little Billing, I was informed that those persons who were old and infirm received from the farmers a sufficient sum to keep them from becoming chargeable on the poor lists. In the various unions of the county the number of able-bodied paupers is comparatively small, and even of these it is not too much to say that many are idle and dissolute characters, against whom the workhouse test affords no protection whatever. While in the Northampton union, an individual was pointed out to me who had obtained an order to go into the house. After a short and turbulent residence there, he came out, broke some windows in the town, received a month's imprisonment, again obtained an order for admission into the union, and upon the third day was complaining of the quality of his food, and that he had not received his "whack." He succeeded in creating a disturbance in the house, the police were called in, and he received twenty-one days' imprisonment for the offence. Again and again he has gone through the same routine.

While on the subject of the Northampton Union Workhouse, I cannot pass without notice the very excellent dietary table of that establishment. I believe, in that respect, it is equal, if not superior, to any in the country. The breakfasts throughout the week consist of, for the men, 7 oz., women, 6 oz. of bread, and a pint of milk, or 1½ pints of gruel. On three days of the week the dinner consists of 5 oz. of cooked meat, 12 oz. of potatoes, and 2 oz. of bread for the men, and 10 oz. of potatoes, and 2 oz. of bread for the women. On three other days of the week the allowance for men and women is 1½ pints of soup and 3 oz. of bread. On Saturday the men have 14 oz., the women 12 oz. of rice or suet pudding; 7 oz. of bread and 1½ oz. of cheese constitutes the supper. People above 60 years of age, and women employed in washing or other laborious work, are allowed 1 oz. of tea, 4 oz. of butter, and 4 oz. of sugar per week. The master of the workhouse filled me a basin from the soup which was boiling in the coppers for dinner on the day of my visit, and I have no hesitation in declaring that it would have given satisfaction to many an epicure in such matters. The gruel, also, I was told, was equally good, but I had not the opportunity of testing it by the same satisfactory process. Its quality may be judged of from the ingredients, which are in the proportion of 2 quarts of new milk, 2 quarts of water, and 1 lb. of best wheaten flour.

A mode of ventilation of workhouses, suggested by Sir J. Walsham, Bart., one of the Poor-law Inspectors, has been attended with great success in those establishments in which it has been employed. The ventilation is effected by means of zinc tubes, of about three inches in diameter, perforated with numerous small air-holes towards the bottom of the tubes. These tubes are carried across the ceiling of the rooms, and taken through the external walls of the building, where they terminate by convex perforated ends. Moveable caps are provided to cover the ends of the tubes in extremely cold weather, to which a small chain is attached so as to be ready for use when required. One of the great advantages of this mode of ventilation over those now in general use is, that it is placed entirely out of the control of the paupers, and they are unable to impede that ventilation which is absolutely necessary in buildings of this kind, where so large a number of persons are congregated under the same roof. In one of the workhouses which I visited, the tubes were applied with the most complete success, in the first instance, to a sick ward devoted to persons afflicted with loathsome diseases; the air of which was formerly so tainted, that very few of the guardians would venture to visit it. They were afterwards applied to the dining-hall, and the master of the workhouse stated that while, during the previous winter the people would perspire freely when eating warm food, even with four or five windows and a door or two open, at present, with the tubes, and every door and window closed, the air was sweet and comfortable, and no perspiration whatever was seen. There was also a complete absence of that close and disagreeable smell which I have found to exist in most of the other workhouses which I have visited. The master of another workhouse stated that since the introduction of the tubes there had been no case of fever or sickness worth mentioning, and that there had been a marked improvement in the health and appearance of both children and adults.

Returning from this digression to the condition of the labourer, the next point to be considered is his wages, which vary from 8s. to 10s. per week. I have already stated the rate of wages paid upon Mr. Beasley's farm. Upon Earl Spencer's farm about twenty men are constantly employed, the wages paid to married men being about 10s. per week; to single men, 8s. Two men, who look after the cattle, receive 12s. per week; the shepherds, 14s.

A considerable number of Irish reapers are employed for the harvest. They are generally considered as excellent hands, but require a good deal of looking after. Beer is not generally found them; a certain sum is given them per acre, and those of them who are disposed to have beer find their own. The majority of them prefer milk to beer, and usually have a quantity of milk boiled for them in the farm-house in the morning when they commence their work.

The diet of the labourer is generally better than that of the labourer of the Eastern counties. The comparative absence of animal food from the diet of the labourer even in this county, has for a long period been a subject of regret to persons who felt an interest in the comfort and well-being of the poor. Mr. Hillyard in 1834, stated—

> "Long have I regretted that in this county, which is capable of producing animal food in abundance for all, the agricultural labourers, who, from being always in the air, need more of it than any other class of people, should so long have had the least. While every person of right feeling must sympathise in this feeling of regret, it cannot fail to be a source of satisfaction that the present comparatively cheap price of provisions has brought to the poor man's door many of those necessaries, to say nothing of the comforts of life, of which for many years past he was so completely destitute."

The following were the prices of the principal articles of consumption in the chief towns of the undermentioned counties at the period of my making the inquiries:—

	Northampton.	Leicester.	Rutland.	Nottingham.	Derby.
Flour, per stone :					
Best	1s. 10d.	1s. 10d.	2s. 4d.	1s. 11d.	1s. 10d.
Seconds	1s. 8d.	1s. 8d.	2s.	1s. 8d.	1s. 8d.
Bread, per 4 lb. loaf :					
Best	5d.	5d.	5d.	5d.	5d.
Seconds	4½d.	4½d.	4½d.	4½d.	4½d.
Beef, per lb. :					
Prime parts	6½d.	6d.	6d.	6½d.	6½d.
Inferior	4d. to 6d.	5d.	5½d.	5d. to 6d.	5½d.
Mutton, per lb. :					
Prime parts	6d.	6d.	5½d.	6½d.	6d.
Inferior	4d. to 5d.	5d.	5d.	6d.	5d.
Pork, per lb.	5½d.	6d.	5½d.	5½d.	6d.
Butter, per lb.	9d. to 1s.	1s. 1d.	9d. to 10d.	10d. to 1s. 1d.	9d. to 1s. 1d.
Cheese, per lb. ...	6d. to 8d.	7d. to 10d.	5d. to 8d.	6d. to 8d.	5d. to 7d.
Bacon, per lb.	7d. to 8d.	8d.	8d.	7½d.	8d.

I also obtained from the principal unions of the counties in this district the contract price of provisions for the quarters ending the two last years. I give the result in the following tabular form:—

	Peterborough.		Leicester.		Oakham.		Nottingham.		Derby.	
	1849.	1850.	1849.	1850.	1849.	1850.	1849.	1850.	1849.	1850.
Flour, per sack of 20 stone	40s. 0d.	33s. 4d.	39s. 0d.	32s. 0d.	33s. 6d.	28s. 11d.	39s. 0d.	29s. 6d.	33s. 4d.	30s. 6d.
Bread, per cwt.	11 8	10 6	11 8	9 11	11 8	10 6	11 8	10 6	11 8	10 6
Oatmeal, per cwt.	18 8	14 0	18 8	13 2	16 4	14 0	14 0	12 6	16 0	14 0
Beef, per stone (14 lbs.) .	6 $8\frac{1}{2}$	5 3	6 5	5 3	7 7	5 10	5 0	4 8	6 5	5 3
Mutton, per stone	6 $8\frac{1}{2}$	5 3	6 5	5 3	7 7	5 10	7 0	5 8	6 5	5 3
Cheese, per cwt.	56 0	56 0	56 0	46 8	65 4	56 0	no contracts	no contracts	60 8	51 4
Butter	93 4	84 0	112 0	112 0	109 8	107 4	...	...	121 4	112 0
Potatoes, per bushel ...	0 10	0 8	...	1 4	...	...	...	...	4 4	2 0
Coals, per ton	19 0	15 0	8 8	7 6	12 2	9 $10\frac{1}{2}$	9 0	8 3	8 9	7 9
Milk, per gallon	0 7	0 6	0 6	0 $6\frac{1}{2}$	0 7	0 6	0 $6\frac{1}{2}$	0 6	0 $6\frac{1}{4}$	0 $6\frac{1}{4}$
Soap, per cwt.	53 7	51 4	45 0	45 0	46 8	42 0	49 6	48 0	48 0	44 0
Candles, per dozen lb. .	6 0	5 0	4 9	4 6	5 6	5 3	...	...	...	...

LABOUR AND THE POOR.

THE RURAL DISTRICTS.

[FROM OUR SPECIAL CORRESPONDENT.]

COUNTIES OF NORTHAMPTON, LEICESTER, RUTLAND, NOTTINGHAM, AND DERBY.

LEICESTER.

LETTER L.

The county of Leicester, lying upon the north of Northampton, having Lincolnshire and Rutlandshire for its eastern, Notts and Derby for its northern, and Staffordshire for its western boundary, extends from north to south about thirty, and from east to west about twenty-five miles. The area of the county is 806 square miles, and consequently 515,840 acres—although the area assigned to the several parishes in the enumerator's abstract amounts to no more than 511,340 acres. The public are informed, however, in the official blue books, that no attempt to reconcile this apparent contradiction has been deemed attainable. In the face of this declaration, it would be idle for me to attempt to account for the discrepancy of 4,500 acres.

Like most of the other counties of the Midland district, Leicester contains spots upon which many a gallant field has been fought, the issues of which have had an important bearing upon some of the important events in the early history of the country. It was on Bosworth Field that the leaves of the Roses of York and Lancaster were finally strewn—that Richard died, and Richmond conquered. The town of Leicester was stormed and taken by Rupert in the Civil Wars, and after the defeat at Naseby it was the resting-place of the fugitive Charles. At Ashby Castle, Mary Stuart passed many of her long and weary hours of captivity; and a short distance from the town are the meadows—sloping gradually down on all sides to the level ground—described in "Ivanhoe" as the scene of the celebrated passage-at-arms. Near Lutterworth may be seen the High Cross, erected by Anne at the restoration of peace, which, while it commemorates that auspicious event, has upon its pedestal an inscription in Latin of which the following is a translation:—"If, traveller, you search for the footsteps of the ancient Romans, here you may behold them; for here their most celebrated ways, crossing one another, extend to the utmost boundaries of Britain; here the Venones kept their quarters, and at the distance of one mile from hence, Claudius, a certain commander of a cohort, seems to have had a camp towards the street, and towards the fosse a tomb."

The surface of the county is varied and uneven in its character. The hills in the neighbourhood of Charnwood Forest, and in the north-west part of the county, rise to a considerable height. Many of them have an almost mountainous appearance; in many parts they are bare and barren—and the rocks project abruptly and peremptorily from the surface. But the general aspect of the county is fertile and pleasing, and the air well tempered and healthy. The Soar and the Wreke are its principal rivers, the former of which is navigable from Leicester to Loughborough, and thence to its junction with the Trent. At Melton Mowbray the Trent is joined by the Oakham Canal, which thus forms a connection between Leicester, and Oakham, in Rutlandshire. A portion of the Grantham Canal runs through the north-eastern, and the Ashby-de-la-Zouch Canal along the western, part of the county. The Midland system of railways affords ample means of communication between all its more important districts, as well as, by its connection with other railways, with almost every part of the country.

At Barrow-upon-Soar there are some extensive quarries of limestone, the qualities of which are such as to render it admirably adapted for works in water. Iron stone is obtained in considerable quantities from the neighbourhood of Ashby Wolds. Mount Sorrel appears to be entirely composed of a red kind of granite, so hard as to prevent its being worked except with the greatest difficulty. In the neighbourhood of Ashby-de-la-Zouch, and in many other of the eastern parts of the county, large quantities of coal are obtained; from Staunton Harold some valuable lead ore, and from Swithland large quantities of slates.

In the eastern and south-eastern parts of the county, and adjoining to Rutland, there are rich and extensive tracts of grazing land. The land upon the banks of the Soar and the Wreke is, perhaps, some of the richest in the county, both in respect to meadow and arable land.

In Charnwood Forest, which was enclosed in 1806-7, the land is generally of an inferior quality, the principal crop grown upon it being oats, and upon some of the more favoured spots turnips are grown. In the north-eastern districts the soil is, generally speaking, poor, and is principally used for dairy purposes, large quantities of Stilton cheese being made in the neighbourhood of Melton Mowbray. About Lutterworth there is some excellent pasturage, as well as in the neighbourhood of Market Bosworth. Near Loughborough also the land is very good, and the railway in that neighbourhood runs for several miles through a tract of land capable of producing in the largest quantities almost all kinds of grain. The county has long been famous for its breed of large black horses, and its horned cattle and sheep, considerable attention having been bestowed upon the improvement of the various breeds. The fleece of the Leicester breed of sheep is particularly valuable for the wool trade.

As in the adjoining county of Northampton, there appears to be a general spirit of improvement abroad among the farmers of this district, and they seem fully alive to the necessity of increased exertions to meet the altered state of circumstances in which they are placed. While animated by this desire for improvement, they appear to have, generally speaking, little or no fear of the result of their exertions. In consequence of a very general system of green cropping, an enormous increase has taken place in the quantity of stock kept upon the land. I endeavoured, but without success, to obtain some approximation to the number of cattle and sheep annually disposed of in this and the adjoining counties. No accounts are kept of the number of cattle sold in any of the principal markets of Northampton, Leicester, Nottingham, or Derby; nor could I succeed in obtaining, although I made application for it, the number of cattle or sheep conveyed annually upon the Midland Railway to the markets of the metropolis. For six months in the year Smithfield is supplied almost exclusively from these counties, and the quantities annually sent must be very considerable. The introduction of green crops into the mode of cropping has superseded almost entirely the necessity for the fallows, which are now rarely adopted except upon stiff land which has by neglect been allowed to become foul. Upon several farms of a light soil which I visited in the neighbourhood of Loughborough the usual practice is to grow "dills," or tares, which can be got off in time to sow turnips, so that they are enabled by this means to obtain two crops within the year off such portion of the land. The increase of food thus obtained by the growth of turnips and other green crops has led to a very great increase in the quantity of stock kept. One farmer informed me that since he had adopted the system he had increased his stock by 20 per cent. Another said that where he had but 30 head of cattle, he had now 43, and considerably better crops of grain, owing to the increased fertility given to the land by the application of additional manure. A third farmer had recently obtained the consent of his landlord to plough up some of his grass lands in order to extend the system of cropping adopted upon the other parts of his farm. A corresponding increase in the amount of labour has also taken place upon these farms.

Within the last fifty years large quantities of light land have been brought into cultivation, which formerly grew nothing but a kind of gorse. Enclosures have also been made to a very considerable extent, and almost the whole of the land which has been enclosed is of first-rate quality. Vast tracts of land, which formerly grazed only a few sheep in the summer, and afforded food for rabbits in the winter, now bear, in many cases, good crops of grain—while the turnips produced afford the means of keeping double or treble the number of sheep which formerly roamed over these uncultivated tracts, and consequently a vast field has been thrown open for the employment of the labouring population. In several parts of the county the old plan is still adhered to of ploughing with four or five horses ahead; ploughing in pairs is, however, the more general rule. The Duke of Rutland, Mr. Packe, Mr. Wilson, and a few other landowners, have for several years past afforded assistance to their tenants in draining and improving the land and in erecting farm buildings. The general rule appears to be to give the drain tiles, and to charge 4 per cent. upon the outlay for the erection of sheds for cattle.

Upon the light lands the shift generally adopted is "the four course"—seeds, wheats, turnips, barley. Various "shifts" are in use upon the strong lands. A gentleman living near Queensborough, and farming about 260 acres of strong land, informed me that the course adopted upon his farm was "the five course"—seeds, wheat, beans, wheat, fallow. Another course in use upon strong land is, seeds, beans, wheat, oats, turnips. In some cases of a light or sandy soil, the grass is laid down for two years, and two white crops are taken in succession. The strong clayey lands produce fine wheat and beans, and land of this kind prevails more or less in nearly all parts of the county. There is scarcely a part of the county in which are not to be found, nearly equally distributed, alluvial soil, light sand, and

Ploughing

strong, clayey land. The alluvial soils produce every kind of grain and pulse in the largest quantity and of the best quality, the depth of soil being in many places very considerable.

The general tenure of the land is from year to year; the exceptions to this rule are but few. There are in various parts of the county considerable portions of land belonging to the Church and to public charities; these are frequently let upon leases for lives. Many of the landowners are at present disposed to grant leases if required; but, however strongly these may have been previously desired by the tenants, they think the present is not a fit time for entering upon fresh engagements of that nature. The existing mode of tenure is far from giving satisfaction to the agriculturists as a body, and the land in many instances is not so well farmed in consequence. Several of the farmers have expressed to me very strong opinions upon the subject. "Nothing can be more unjust, or more injurious to the interests of the farmers and the labourers," said one gentleman to me, "than the present state of things with respect to tenure of land in this county. The tenant has no claim for unexhausted improvements by virtue of his agreement. And unfortunately many of the farmers never think about agreements upon entering upon the land; their only desire is to get it at as low a rate as possible, and trust to Providence for the rest." No compensation whatever is given for the extra feeding of stock, for the use of artificial manures, or for the feeding with oil-cake—the only allowance made being for the value of the wheat crops. Farms are generally quitted upon Lady-day, and for the crop of wheat which is sown by the out-going tenant he is allowed for the carting of manure, the working of the land, the seed which he sowed in autumn, and the taxes and rates upon that portion of the land for the half year previous to his giving up possession. For the land laid down in grass the outgoing tenant is allowed the cost of the seed, but only upon the production of his seed bill. The tenant has no claim for any draining, whether with turf or tile, which he may do upon his farm. In some few cases the agreements contain clauses giving compensation for unexhausted improvements. Notwithstanding the improvements which have taken place, I only express the opinion of numbers of the best farmers of Leicestershire, when I state that the land generally is not cultivated so well as it would be if the tenant possessed a certain tenure, and a claim for compensation for the extra capital expended by him in the amelioration of his farm. Cultivation is cramped and crippled by the existing system, a due amount of labour is not employed, and the land is not brought into that state of fertility which it would be under different circumstances. Many of the farms have been in the occupation of the same families for a great number of years. One person informed me that he had been sixty years on his farm, and that his family had held it before him for upwards of a hundred years.

I defer to a future occasion an account of the effects of preserving game upon the interests of both occupier and labourer; but while upon the subject of agreements and compensation to the tenants, I cannot avoid stating that, in many of the agreements, no compensation is given to the tenant for damage done by game. In case of such damage, a valuation is sometimes made, and the tenant is paid the amount awarded to him. In connection with the game-laws there is one point which was very strongly represented to me as being a source of peculiar annoyance to the farmers—viz., a species of surveillance kept over their farms by means of gamekeepers, who, in the exercise of their duties, have the right of traversing them at pleasure, and who are stated to be in the habit of reporting to their employers anything which they might think would afford satisfaction to the one, or give annoyance to the other. To persons of independent feelings such conduct must be doubtless a source of perpetual annoyance.

The county of Leicester is, I was informed, the most heavily rented in the kingdom, with the exception of Middlesex. Some of the best alluvial lands, on the banks of the Soar and the Wreke, are let as high as £3 per acre. Most of the other land is let at prices varying from 25s. to £2 per acre. The best feeding and permanent grass lands are let at from £2 to 50s. per acre. In the neighbourhood of Lough-borough the average rental of the land is about 30s. per acre. There are, however, some portions of cold, wet, clayey land in the neigh-bourhood of Holwell which lets at about 15s. per acre; and "dear at that," said a person occupying about 50 acres of it; "there's not food enough on it to keep a sheep to the acre." The farms are not generally what might be called large; there are a great number of them which range from 100 to 150 and 200 acres, and comparatively few so large as 500 acres.

One of the effects of the extreme apathy on the part of many land-lords in their refusal to assist the tenants is most strikingly seen in the ruinous condition of the majority of the farm buildings of the county. Not only is no assistance given to the tenant in erecting these essentials of all good farming, but the uncertainty of the tenure very naturally prevents the occupier from exerting himself to erect them. Except in special cases, the tenant would receive no compensation whatever for his outlay upon the farm buildings; and, as if to add still another difficulty in the way of the tenant increasing the productive-ness of his farm by the extension or improvement of his buildings, he is strictly forbidden to disturb the soil for the purpose of laying the foundation of any structure without special leave of his landlord. This injunction certainly appears somewhat unnecessary, when it is known that, in addition to his uncertainty of tenure, the tenant will receive no compensation for the buildings which he may erect, at the time of giving up the farm.

While the condition of the farm buildings in many instances reflects discredit upon the landlords, the increase in the number and the improvement in the quality of the agricultural implements place the character of the tenant-occupier in favourable contrast with that of the owner of the land. The implements most in use are Crossgill's clod crusher, Biddel's scarifier, Garret's horse hoe, portable steam threshing machines, and many improved winnowing machines. Steaming apparatus is very generally employed for preparing the chaff and food for cattle. In sowing nearly all kinds of grain, the Norfolk drill is very generally employed. Mr. Wilson, of Ripton, has very recently put down two steam-engines upon farms in his own occupation. Mr. Thomas Glover has invented an implement, the use of which promises to be attended with great success—viz., a turf-paring plough. It has gained prizes at all the meetings of the agricultural societies at which it has been exhibited; and in ploughing-up grass lands has proved of great service to those who have employed it.

The mode of assessing farmers to the income-tax is one which gives great dissatisfaction, and numerous complaints were made to me upon the subject. "We are assessed," said one farmer to me, "at half the rental, when over a certain amount, and if the rental you pay does not suit the commissioners, or they think it too low, they will raise it to any sum they please. They will rate you upon the average rental paid by your neighbours, without any regard to the quality of the land. Some time since I was re-assessed, because the commissioners thought I did not pay enough, and they charged me upon the average rental of the land in the parish, the greater part of which was accommodation land, and let at double and treble what it would have been worth if it had been further from the town. It is bad enough in all conscience to make us pay income-tax upon half the rental, when we're losing money, but to double our rental, and then make us pay income-tax upon it, is adding insult to injury."

In the neighbourhood of Melton Mowbray, and within a circle of about ten miles of it, large quantities of cheese are made by the farmers, principally "Stilton." In the neighbourhood of Holwell, Kettleby, and Broughton, the land is of a mixed character, consisting of a reddish kind of earth, and a cold, wet clay, by far the greater proportion being pasture land. I was informed by a gentleman that a few years since there were not more than thirty or forty acres under plough in the whole lordship of Holwell. That quantity has, however, considerably increased within the last few years, as a great deal of the grass land has been broken up. The amount of stock kept upon dairy farms is trifling, when compared with the numbers kept upon some of the plough-land farms in Norfolk and Northampton. The calves are usually reared on the farm, and when the cows cease to yield a fair quantity of milk they are sold, their places being supplied by others which have been reared upon the farm. The whey from the cheese is given to the pigs, a considerable number of which are usually kept on dairy farms.

The past year has been extraordinarily favourable to those concerned in the management of dairy farms in this part of the county. I was informed by several farmers that there had not been such a plentiful grass year for many years, and the quantity of cheese produced had, of course, been proportionately large. The quantity produced upon one farm of 123 acres was about twenty dozen cheeses, of about 12 lbs. weight each, being very nearly a ton and a quarter in the year. It must not, however, be supposed that the whole amount of produce of this farm was a ton and a quarter of cheese. Only about one-half of the land was laid down in pasture, the remainder being under tillage, and cropped upon the three crop and fallow system. With respect to the tenure of land in districts where dairy produce is raised, and the system of culture or management enjoined upon the tenant, the usual plan appears to be to require certain proportions to be mown every year. Upon one farm of 58 acres there were 13 acres which were to be mown every year, 12 acres under tillage, the remaining 33 acres being permanent pasture. The proportions required to be mown appear to be perfectly arbitrary, and are not settled with regard to any definite rule.

There are, however, a great many instances—and probably in this part of the county they would be found to be the majority—in which no conditions whatever are contained in the agreement; always excepting of course that most important one, to which all others indeed are subsidiary—the payment of the rent. Several persons here told me, when inquiring as to the conditions of their agreements, that they had but one—which was, to pay the rent at the audit.

Upon several of the dairy farms, turnips have been introduced among the crops, and where the tenants have been unfettered by any agreements they have taken up portions of the pasture and grown turnips for the sheep, and feed them off the grass lands; and by this means they have been enabled not only to improve their grass land by giving to it a better kind of manure, but also to keep up an increased quantity of stock upon the larger supply of food which they thus obtain from the soil. Where the tenant is bound down to mow a certain proportion of his land every year, he is to a great extent debarred from improving his farm or increasing his stock.

Assuming the proportions of pasturage and tillage in the Midland counties as given in a former Letter to be correct, it would appear that Leicestershire contains 65,000 acres of arable and 450,000 acres of pasture land. The annual value of the agricultural produce of the county, taking that of the arable land at £7 per acre, and of pasture at £6, would be—

$$
\begin{array}{llr}
\text{65,000 acres of arable, at £7} & \dots\dots & \text{£455,000} \\
\text{450,000 acres of pasture, at £6} & \dots & \text{2,700,000} \\
\hline
 & & \text{£3,155,000}
\end{array}
$$

There are 3,669 farmers and graziers in the county; the average value of the produce of each farm would therefore be about £850. The total number of agricultural labourers of all ages in the county was, in 1841, 12,664, and the amount raised, in proportion to each labourer employed, is about £250. The wages of the labourer, and his condition, will form the subject of the next letter.

In 1814 the annual value of the property in the county of Leicester assessed to the property tax, under each of the schedules, A, D, and E, was—

$$
\begin{array}{llr}
\text{Schedule A} & \dots\dots\dots & \text{£951,908} \\
\text{Schedule D} & \dots\dots\dots & \text{319,608} \\
\text{Schedule E} & \dots\dots\dots & \text{5,829} \\
\hline
 & & \text{£1,277,345}
\end{array}
$$

while the actual annual value of real property assessed to the property and income tax for the year ending April, 1843, was £1,376,384. The rental of the whole county, according to the property tax returns of 1815, was £702,402, being at the rate of 27s. 3½d. per acre, with the exception of Rutland and Middlesex the highest in the whole country. According to these returns the rentals of the several counties in which my inquiries have been made were as follows:—

	Total Rental of County.	Average per Acre of whole County.
Norfolk	£931,842	13s. 11d.
Suffolk	694,078	14s. 2d.
Essex	904,715	18s. 5½d.
Herts	342,350	20s. 3d.
Beds	272,621	18s. 5d.
Hants	202,076	17s. 1d.
Cambridge	453,255	16s. 6d.
Northampton	696,637	21s. 5½d.
Leicester	702,402	27s. 3½d.
Rutland	99,174	28s. 10d.
Nottingham	534,992	20s. 0d.
Derbyshire	621,693	18s. 11d.

The rental of Middlesex was then £349,142, or 38s. 9d. per acre. The increase which has taken place since the period at which these returns were made may be judged of by the accounts which I have given of the rent at present paid for land in these counties.

LABOUR AND THE POOR.

——◆——

THE RURAL DISTRICTS.

[FROM OUR SPECIAL CORRESPONDENT.]

GLOUCESTERSHIRE, MONMOUTHSHIRE, HEREFORDSHIRE, WORCESTERSHIRE, AND SHROPSHIRE.

LETTER LI.

In previous letters I have examined in considerable detail the condition of the labouring poor, first, in the counties of Bucks, Berks, Oxford, and Wilts, and afterwards throughout the southern portion of England—commencing with the western group of counties embracing Devon, Cornwall, Somerset, and Dorset, and thence proceeding eastward through Hampshire, Surrey, Sussex, and Kent. In the case of each group I have described the industrial, social, and moral features common to all the counties comprised in it, and likewise—as, for example, in treating of the mines and fisheries of Cornwall, and the hop-growing districts of Kent—the special characteristics which distinguish particular localities, and which exercise a marked influence over the condition and habits of the working population. I now proceed to notice briefly the circumstances of the agricultural labourer in Gloucestershire, Monmouthshire, Herefordshire, Worcestershire, and Shropshire. The district comprised by these counties extends from the mouth of the Severn to the borders of Cheshire, which lies conterminous with the only portion of Wales that is not bounded by them to the eastward. These counties constitute one of the finest agricultural regions in England, the soil being throughout extremely fertile, and drained by the two systems of rivers whose trunk channels are the Severn and the Wye. The surface in some places, as near Tewkesbury, presents large level tracts surrounded by a framework of low hills, whilst at others it is a succession of gentle undulations, which are brought to their very summits under the dominion of the plough. There are points, too, at which it is broken by prolonged ranges of hills, which attain a very respectable elevation, such as the Cotswold and the Malvern hills, and some of the ridges which intersect the southern half of Shropshire. These are, more or less, cultivated for some distance up; but in the higher altitudes the farmer is superseded by the shepherd. The agriculture of the district is of a varied character, dairy and feeding farms being found largely intermixed with the arable tracts. There is also a good deal of orchard ground to be met with, particularly in some parts of Gloucestershire, and throughout the whole of Herefordshire. In Herefordshire, hops are also largely raised, as they are likewise in Worcestershire, but to a less extent.

The aggregate population of the five counties was, in 1841, about 1,115,000. According to the census of the present year, it is now only a few hundreds less than 1,200,000—the distribution being (in round numbers) as follows:—Gloucestershire, 419,400; Monmouthshire, 177,100; Herefordshire, 99,100; Worcestershire, 258,700; and Shropshire, 245,000. The decennial rate of increase in each county during the last twenty years is shown by the subjoined table:—

RATE OF INCREASE PER CENT.

	1831 to 1841.	1841 to 1851.
Gloucestershire	11	6
Monmouthshire	34	17
Herefordshire	2	3
Worcestershire	13	13
Shropshire	5	1

The respective densities of the population in the several counties are at present as follows:—in Gloucestershire, 56 persons for every hundred statute acres; in Monmouthshire, 50; in Herefordshire, 21; in Worcestershire, 56; and in Shropshire, 28. As the average for England and Wales is 49 individuals for every hundred acres, it follows that Gloucestershire has seven more than the average; Monmouthshire, one more; Herefordshire, twenty-eight less; Worcestershire, seven more; and Shropshire, twenty-one less.

The relative proportions between those engaged in trade, manufactures, and commerce, and those employed in agriculture, in each county, as stated in the Occupation returns of 1841, will be afterwards considered. In that year, the number of agricultural labourers in each was—in Gloucestershire, in round numbers, 24,700; in Herefordshire, 13,000; in Monmouthshire, 9,000; in Shropshire, 22,500; and in Worcestershire, 19,300—making a total of 88,500. From computations similar to those already made in former portions of my inquiry, it appears that the number engaged in agricultural labour in each, and dependent on such labour exclusively for support, was—in Gloucestershire, about 90,000; in Herefordshire, about 35,000; in Monmouthshire, about 22,000; in Shropshire, about 80,000; and in Worcestershire, about 60,000; or in all, about 287,000.

In considering the state of the agricultural poor in this district, I shall deal very generally with the subject. So closely does their condition resemble that of the corresponding class in several of the counties which I have already described, that to adopt any other course would be but to occupy space and exhaust the reader's patience with unnecessary repetition. In some parts of Worcester, and along the eastern side of Gloucester, the state of the labouring poor is almost the counterpart of what it is in Oxford, and the western portion of Bucks. But in by far the greater portion both of Worcester and Gloucester, in the more purely agricultural sections of Monmouth, and throughout almost the whole of Shropshire and Hereford, it approximates more to the condition of the labourer in Somerset, Devon, Dorset, and Wilts. The comparison exhibits a striking resemblance as regards the physical, intellectual, and moral state of the poor in all these counties. In the amount of wages paid in them, in the house accommodation and diet of the poor, and in the means provided for their intellectual improvement, there is but little difference to be observed amongst them. The same causes are everywhere producing the same results. Fitful and precarious work produces scanty receipts, from which follow multiform privations. It also gives rise to an involuntary idleness, which too frequently ripens into habitual indolence. Such is the case in Dorset, Devon, and Somerset; and so it is also in Gloucester, Worcester, Monmouth, Shropshire, and Hereford. The inadequacy of the house accommodation afforded to the poor, and the consequent overcrowding of their dwellings, are the same, or very nearly the same, in all. It is obvious that the consequences must be the same as regards both the physical and moral state of the poor—whilst in all the evil is aggravated by a profound and seemingly hopeless ignorance.

It was my desire, in searching for material for such details as I might lay before the reader, to ascertain and elucidate such points of difference as might exist between the counties now in question and some of those which have been already considered. But the difficulty was to find any such diversities appertaining to the subject in hand. Not, for instance, that Gloucestershire does not differ from Wilts in some of its most important interests, and in the direction taken by a portion of its industry—but the moment you approach the consideration of the condition of the agricultural poor, the contrast between them ends, and the resemblance begins. And so with them all. The general statement, therefore, which I am about to make, and the details with which I shall illustrate it, will, unfortunately, have more of truth than of novelty in them. Indeed, I regret to say that they will be, with few exceptions, but too similar to the melancholy accounts which it has already been my duty to make public.

In dealing with the subject, in connection with the counties in question, I shall first advert to the condition of the poor in those of Gloucester, Monmouth, and Worcester. I shall afterwards treat of it in connection with Hereford and Shropshire.

This grouping of the counties is suggested by local circumstances, which have their source more in art than in nature. The five counties are each highly agricultural, but the agriculture of the first-named group rests on a broader basis than that of the second, owing to the other interests which have developed themselves in them, and to the different centres of industry and activity to which those interests have given rise. If the effect of this state of things is not very widely felt by the agricultural labourer, still there is no question that it has, in the localities more immediately affected, considerable influence on his condition. Such is the case in Worcestershire, with such places as Kidderminster, Droitwich, and Worcester; in Monmouthshire, with the mining interests existing in and around it; and in Gloucestershire, with such places as Tewkesbury, Cheltenham, Gloucester, Stroud, and Bristol. Neither in Shropshire, nor in Herefordshire, particularly the latter, are any such causes in operation. In these counties, therefore, the labourer's condition must be considered almost exclusively in connection with the chief interest, that of agriculture, to which he has to look for support.

In illustration of the difference in this respect between the two groups, it may be well here to mention that it appears, from the Occupation Abstract of the census taken in 1841, that the relative proportions of persons engaged in trade, manufacture, &c., and those employed in agriculture, were—in Gloucestershire, as 15.1 to 7.2 per cent. on the whole population; in Monmouthshire, as 13.1 to 6.5; and in Worcestershire, as 16.7 to 10.1. Thus, in the first two cases, the proportion of those engaged in trade, &c., was more than double that of those employed in agriculture; whilst it was also about 60 per cent. greater in the last-mentioned county. The mean proportion

     Labour and the Poor Volume VII.

between the three counties would stand thus—14.8 to 7.9, or very nearly double, in favour of those engaged in trade, &c. In Herefordshire, on the other hand, the proportions are reversed. In that county the ratio is 14.6 engaged in agriculture, to 9.9 employed in trade. In Shropshire they may be said to balance each other, being 11.7 as regards agriculture, and 11.9 as regards trade. The mean proportion between the two is 8.8 employed in agriculture, and 7.3 engaged in trade. Yet in the first-mentioned group, where the body of consumers, as regards agricultural produce, is so much larger than that of producers, it will be seen that the comparatively large trading and manufacturing industry there developed has but little effect on the average condition of the rural labourer throughout the counties in question—the effect in this respect of the different centres of industry comprised within them being confined to a somewhat limited district. The reason of the slight influence which they have on the average rates of wages throughout the counties generally in which they lie, will be presently considered.

A large proportion of the cultivated area of Gloucestershire is devoted to the purposes of pasture. As in Somerset, perhaps the greater part of the grass land of Gloucester is held as dairy farms. The rest is applied to what is, in farming operations, held as the higher purpose of feeding. Vast tracts along the range of the Cotswold hills afford little more than pasturage for sheep. In Monmouthshire, the proportion of grass land appears to be smaller than in Gloucestershire, whilst it is more regularly interspersed among the tracts that are arable. In Worcestershire, the grass land cannot, perhaps, be said to predominate; but it almost seems to divide the county with that which is under the plough. On the grass lands of this county, feeding is the exception to dairy farming, the latter being the rule. It is not to be denied that some of the finest specimens of cattle are bred upon the grasses of Worcestershire; but dairy farming seems much more prevalent of the two. In the three counties, the greater proportion of the land now under grass has been so for many years past. The consequence is that, in most of the parishes in which this species of land is found, the pressure of population is moderate as compared with what it is in some of the adjoining parishes devoted to the plough—provided the latter are not in the neighbourhood of a town or some large village, into which the poor have been gradually driven. This is particularly observable in some of the southern parts of Gloucestershire, where considerable tracts are found unbroken by arable land, the comparative scantiness of the population being indicated by the paucity of cottages. Grass land requires the expenditure upon it of but a small amount of labour, as compared with arable. With the exception of haymaking time, when, for a short period, there is a brisk demand for work, there is scarcely anything to be done upon it which the farmer and his family cannot themselves perform. If the farm is very large, a little extra work is required, but a large proportion of that extra work devolves upon women, whose duties keep them pretty closely confined to the dairy. Some arable has recently been converted into grass land, but in no case, of course, without throwing some amount of labour out of employment, and driving the labourer either into the workhouse, or from the parish.

As in other portions of the south and west, many of the farmers here are threatening to abandon entirely the cultivation of grain, and betake themselves to what now appears to them, as they say, the less onerous and more profitable operations of the dairy. Many of them sigh deeply over the days that are past, when they could buy lean Scotch cattle, and, after fattening them, afford to sell them at their cost price—the farmer looking for his profit to the manure and the grain crops which they enabled him to raise every second or third year. But this was a system, they contend, which could only succeed when fostered by high prices. Present prices, they assert, will not pay them for raising grain on any conceivable system. With wheat at less than 40s. a quarter, they say that there is nothing for them to do but to give up the land altogether, or else adopt a cheaper mode of turning it to account. If they take the former course, they may escape all difficulty, but if the latter, what are they to do with the unemployed labour which they will then find upon their hands? If isolated farms were only here and there thrown into grass, the evil might not attain a very great magnitude. But if large tracts together are so dealt with, it will be quite a different matter. There will then be no adequate outlet for the unemployed labour, which will exist on these tracts, and which must be supported from the rates. The farmer may, therefore, find that, if he derives any advantage at all from the change, he may, after all, buy that advantage too dearly. What he saves on the one hand, he must disburse on the other. This consideration has a salutary influence on the deliberations of some of them, who are brought to confess that the only alternative really before them is the abandonment of the present, or the adoption of an improved, and therefore, nominally, a more expensive system of cultivation. They are all the more impressed with this belief when they consider that the produce of the dairy is now about as liable to foreign competition as is that of the field. American cheese is a formidable rival to "double and single Gloucester;" and its appearance in the market has so affected the price of the commodity, that the poor man may now be said, in view of former prices, to get every third cheese that he consumes for nothing. But if every farmer in Gloucestershire were to turn dairy-man, even present prices could not be maintained. A large additional home supply would materially lower the market price of cheese both home and foreign, for a fall in price would not drive the American produce from the market. What would they gain, in such a case, by quitting the plough for the milk-pail? This is precisely the question which the wiser amongst them put to themselves; and as they cannot satisfactorily answer it, they acknowledge that the only course for them, if they would continue to be farmers at present prices, is to throw themselves upon an entirely new style of farming. But the difficulty with most of them is the want of capital for this purpose. There are others amongst them, who, in contemplating becoming dairy farmers, only look to the fact that such a system would be attended with less outlay to them—as if it followed that, in these times of competition, the way to obtain remunerative profits from land was to diminish the expenditure upon it. I have before briefly alluded to this subject, and if I again advert to it, it is because I consider that any views entertained by the farmers, which may in any degree affect their future operations, are an important element in the question of the condition of the labourer.

On the grass lands the circumstances of the latter are not much better than they are in the western part of Wilts. This is particularly applicable to Gloucestershire and Worcestershire. In the former, he is, of course, better off on the dairy farms in the immediate vicinity of Bristol, Cheltenham, and Tewkesbury, and in the latter, chiefly in the neighbourhood of Worcester, which is the centre of a very large dairy district. But even in these favoured localities his wages scarcely reach on the average 7s. 6d. a week. In some cases he has his privileges, such as a free barn, a small garden plot, and the means of keeping a pig; but in a vast number of instances he has no privileges whatever. In the more rural districts in which grass lands abound, his weekly receipts are still lower. The little difference which exists between him and the labourer in the arable districts in this respect, is, if anything, in favour of the latter—who, in the neighbourhood of some of the places named, is on the whole paid at a slightly higher rate, and is more generally found in possession of some or all of the privileges so frequently spoken of.

Owing to the different rates which I found prevailing, I had some difficulty in ascertaining the average wages of the ordinary farm labour in these counties. Had I confined my inquiries to a given radius around the large towns, I should have put the average at about the same as that which I found prevailing in Devon, viz., from 7s. 6d. to 8s. a week. Had I, on the other hand, restricted my researches to the more sequestered districts, it would not have risen higher than that prevailing in the south-west of Wilts, which was, when I visited that county, about 6s. 6d. a week. But, taking the three counties through-out, about 7s. a week will be about the fair average of the wages paid in them. This brings them in this respect to the level of Dorset and Wilts. But some districts are far less favourably circumstanced. For a considerable distance around Monmouth—throughout the cold and "hungry" tract in Gloucestershire, extending from Tewkesbury almost to the county of Oxford—and in Worcestershire along nearly the whole of the Hereford boundary, with the exception of the imme-diate neighbourhood of Great Malvern—I found 6s. a week not only a common rate, but the general rate of wages prevalent. If there is any difference between the rates in Monmouthshire and the other two counties, they may be regarded as a shade higher in the former, taking the average of the whole county. It must be remembered that comparatively few of the labourers have house-rent included in their wages. Out of the wretched remuneration which they receive they have to pay their rent, and purchase their fuel and clothing, unless private benevolence steps in and supplies them with these necessar-ies. This pittance, of course, does not represent the entire means of a family. The wife and children of the labourer, here as elsewhere, betake themselves to the fields—the one when she should be at home attending to the duties of her appropriate sphere, and the others when they should be at school, picking up the slight elements of knowledge which a parish school can impart to them. A boy of seven is useful at the business of "keeping birds," and he is sent at once into the field, where he remains all day, scaring away the crows, at 4d., 6d., and sometimes, but not often, 1s. a week. When he gets a little older, he becomes more useful, and attends to the cattle, when his wages are raised a little. At about thirteen or fourteen he is considered fit to "go with the horse," when his remuneration may be from 1s. 6d.

to 2s. 6d. a week. During harvest he is generally useful, when he commonly receives the highest rates ever paid to boys. It is then, too, that the women are of most service in the fields; but there is work in the fields for them, at 7d. to 8d. a day, during many periods of the year. The scanty means of a family may thus, during some portions of the year, be increased to from 10s. to 12s. a week, but the whole increase thus effected will still not make them exceed from 8s. 6d. to 9s. a week on an average throughout the year. The cost at which the additional shilling or two is secured to the poor man has been already considered, in speaking of the evils of the absence of women from their homes to labour in the fields.

But if house rent is not always included in the earnings of the labourer, it is his misfortune that beer or cider is. All the counties in question are cider producing counties—Hereford particularly so, which produces a large proportion of the cider consumed in the other four counties. The practice is almost universal in the three more immediately under consideration, of including a daily dole of cider as part of a labourer's wages. In summer the average quantity received per day by an adult is about three pints, which the farmer reckons at from 1s. to 2s. additional in the shape of wages. This he might fairly do, if taking the beverage instead of the money were optional with the labourer. But this it is not, and, whether the latter wants it or not, or whether he puts any or no value upon it whatever, he is compelled to take it, his money wages being reduced in proportion. He cannot leave the cider and get an additional shilling or two added to his wages. If he objects to the cider, the farmer treats it in the light of a gift, and says, "Very well, these are your full wages (viz., the money rate), if you do not take the cider into the bargain it is your affair." But when he takes the cider, and asks for higher money wages, the farmer then treats the beverage not as a gift, but as part and parcel of his earnings. If the labourer demands more than 7s. a week, the farmer then tells him that he is already receiving 8s. 6d., as he drinks, at least, 1s. 6d. worth of cider in the week in summer time. During winter the consumption is less. The poor have no remedy against this injustice. In giving the average rates of wages, I have confined myself to the money rates. Cider included, the amount would be, throughout the counties, about 17 per cent. higher. But this per centage the labourer is compelled to take in a shape which renders it of no use whatever to his family, and, in too many cases, very pernicious to himself. Boys and women have also their allowances of cider whilst at work. The boys generally consume all they get, but two-thirds of what the women get is drunk by their husbands. It is by drinking it occasionally in such quantities that numbers of them come at last not to wish for any change in the system. They not only look for their cider in the field, but they also spend a portion of their scanty money earnings in still further pandering to the taste which they have acquired. In Somerset and Devon, I found many labourers who would willingly compound their cider for an addition to their money wages. In the counties now in question, I also found some who would do so, but the great majority would prefer that things remained as they are. Near Newent, I was told by a farmer that when he proposed a change to his men, one or two accepted it gladly, but the rest declined it; and not only so, but begged him not to make it, so far as they were concerned. Their reason was, that the taste was now so settled upon them that, if the cider were not given them in the field, they would inevitably repair to the beer-shop for it—an alternative which they wished to avoid. The taste which had thus acquired such a dominion over them had been instilled into them from their boyhood, and those who are now boys are having it instilled also into them, so that, when they become men, they also will become slaves to it. If a reform in this respect is attempted, it is with the boys that the effort should be chiefly made. Near Tewkesbury, Mr. Woodward, whose farming operations are conducted on a scale similar to those of Mr. Huxtable in Dorset, compels his labourers to accept money instead of cider in the winter time. He may thus gradually bring them round to doing so also in summer. His labourers are thus more highly paid than those around them. I visited several of them. The men told me that they found it hard for a time to do without their drink; but that the rations (tea and sugar) which their families consumed were better on the whole than the cider. Their wives certainly thought so.

I also found prevalent in these counties that most pernicious practice of paying less to single than to married men. The result is the same as that to which the provisions, in respect to cottages, of the old poor-law gave rise. It is one of the most active causes that operate in favour of early and improvident marriages.

Alexander Mackay

Alexander Mackay was born in Inverness, Scotland, circa 1808 and became an accomplished and highly respected journalist and author. He began his career in journalism in Toronto, Canada, spending a number of years there following his decision to emigrate. A printed account of his voyage to Canada can be found in Charles Dickens' Household Words, entitled An Emigrant Afloat, in which he describes his journey across the Atlantic. Deciding to return he found employment with *The Morning Chronicle*, preferring journalism over law, having practised in Canada and being called to the bar on his return. He was sent out by *The Morning Chronicle* to the United States as their correspondent and afterwards published his own widely-acclaimed "Western World" detailing his travels around America during 1846 and 1847.

Following his Labour and the Poor investigations he travelled to India in 1850 to investigate the viability of expanding the cotton producing areas and trade in the East Indies. Ill health forcing him to return prematurely he sadly passed away at sea during his homeward journey. The following is an article from his long-time employer:—

The Morning Chronicle, Thursday, May 6, 1852.

THE DEATH OF MR. ALEXANDER MACKAY.

—◆—

It is with sincere regret that we record the death, on his way home, of Mr. Alexander Mackay, the author of the "Western World," and lately the commissioner in India of the Manchester Chamber of Commerce. Mr. Mackay was for many years connected with this journal, and we cannot withhold from his name the tribute due to the memory of an able coadjutor and of a valued friend.

By Mr. Mackay's untimely fate an opening career of great promise is cut short. Endowed with high mental qualities, possessed of a clear intellect and acute and rapid powers of reasoning—a keen observer, and an instinctive lover of truth—Mr. Mackay added to these gifts a most amiable disposition. These powers had been ascertained, and were in the act of being applied to important public purposes, when the climate of a hot country, acting upon a naturally delicate constitution, cut him off—not, however, before he had to a great extent completed his task.

Alexander Mackay was the son of Mr. Mackay, a much respected banker in Inverness, and was born in that town about 1820. He was educated at the neighbouring town of Elgin, and afterwards at Aberdeen. Family arrangements led him first to Canada, where he was destined for the colonial bar, and for some brief space practised with repute. Journalism, however, seems to have had more attraction for Mr. Mackay than professional practice, and accordingly he soon became the conductor of a highly respectable newspaper in Toronto. After residing in Canada for several years, and travelling over a great portion of the provinces and the States, he returned home in search of a wider sphere than could be afforded by colonial life. He was speedily engaged in connection with this journal, and so highly were his acuteness and logical abilities estimated, that he was sent out again by *The Morning Chronicle* to the United States, for the purpose of examining the diplomatic bearings of the treaties as to the Maine boundary, and observing the feelings of the American public on the question. His letters upon these subjects were replete with most valuable information, and with clear and logical reasoning. Not long after his return, Mr. Mackay published his "Western World," the great ability and comprehensive grasp of which were at once acknowledged. The book was indeed pronounced to be the best and the most complete work ever written upon the Transatlantic Republic. Its success was great and immediate, and the volumes became at once a standard authority upon that most important subject. The author's connection with this journal was prolonged for some time afterwards. As one of our Special Correspondents, engaged in investigating the condition of the English rural population, Mr. Mackay rendered important services to the question of Labour and the Poor, while his versatile pen was frequently and successfully turned to other topics of general literary and political interest. After the settlement of the corn-law question he devoted himself to the topic of the suffrage; and his pamphlet upon our system of representation, with its analysis of the constitution of the House of Commons, became a text-book with a large class of Reformers on the question of which it treated, and was repeatedly quoted in the House of Commons. From that period Mr. Mackay determined to devote himself to political life. He joined the Reform party, and delivered many able speeches at public meetings in the metropolis upon the franchise question. He had before him the hope of ultimately entering Parliament; but he consented for a time to withdraw from home politics, and to accept from the Lancashire cotton interest a mission to India, to investigate the possibility of extending the growth of the plant in our Eastern possessions. Somewhat more than two years ago he departed full of hope and spirit. He died on his passage home. The subjoined extract from one of our Manchester contemporaries will give additional particulars, besides showing the high character Mr. Mackay had earned for himself in the East. Our melancholy task is over when we again express our heartfelt sorrow at the loss of a highly promising author, a rising politician, an accomplished gentleman, and a most amiable man.

[FROM THE MANCHESTER EXAMINER AND TIMES.]

It is with feelings of deep regret that we announce the death of Mr. Alexander Mackay, the Indian commissioner appointed by the Manchester Chamber of Commerce. Mr. Mackay left this country on the 20th December, 1850, under the most favourable auspices—being accredited and recommended to the Chamber of Commerce of Bombay by the Chambers of Commerce of Manchester, Liverpool, and Glasgow, and carrying with him the full confidence of the mercantile and manufacturing public connected with the cotton trade. The object of his mission also received the unanimous approbation of the British press, and we have reason to know that it was regarded with good will by the leading members of the administration. The main purpose of his appointment was to ascertain by an unbiassed but minute investigation, on the spot, the real obstacles which prevent an ample supply of good cotton being obtained from the East Indies, and the causes which impede the extension of our commerce with that country.

The mission was one requiring great industry, intelligence, and sound judgment, on the part of the individual selected for the arduous and responsible undertaking; and it was peculiarly fortunate for the interests represented by the body with whom the mission originated, that they were able to secure the services of a gentleman so eminently qualified in every respect to carry out their views. Mr. Mackay's inquiry embraced a multitude of details, all bearing on the main subject of the mission—such as the means provided by the Indian Government to promote the internal as well as the export trade of the country over which they rule—the nature of the roads by which the produce of the interior is brought to the coast—the means of inter-communication between neighbouring districts—the state and man-agement of docks, piers, quays, &c.—the condition of the agricultural population, and the circumstances which tend to stimulate or repress their industry—the nature of the land tenure, particularly with refer-ence to the security of the cultivator—the amount and kind of taxa-tion, and the mode of levying and collecting it—all departments of inquiry requiring minute and impartial personal observation.

On his arrival, Mr. Mackay was cordially received by the Bombay Chamber of Commerce, and every facility afforded to him for the pro-secution of his inquiries, which were continued during the whole of last year, and the results of which have been from time to time trans-mitted home. The influence of the climate of India was, however, too much for a constitution not naturally robust, and he was compelled to terminate his labours sooner than he had anticipated, and endeav-our to regain his health by leaving the country. In a letter addressed to the Bombay Chamber of Commerce, dated March 30th, he men-tions his intention of returning to England, but, at the same time, states that before disease had disabled him, he had succeeded in tra-versing the greater portion of the cotton field of the Presidency, and that he had from actual observation arrived at important conclusions as to the condition, wants, and prospects of the cotton trade in the great district in question, and that he hoped, on his return home, by the aid of renewed health, to make the information he had gathered conducive to the common benefit of India and England.

These anticipations, alas! were not destined to be realised. He left India on the 3d of April, but his strength gradually failed until the 15th, on the evening of which day he breathed his last. We are told that he suffered little until within half an hour of his death, and that up to that period he retained the full use of his faculties, having, previous to his dissolution, made his will and confided his papers to the care of a fellow-passenger, to be transmitted to his brother in Inverness. These and other details are contained in a letter (given below), addressed by Mr. Arthur Latham, a mercantile gentleman, who was on board the same vessel, to Mr. Bazley, the president of the Chamber of Commerce. With the regret inseparable from the untimely fate of Mr. Mackay is mingled a feeling of satisfaction that the main object of his mission has not been left unaccomplished.

          "At sea, on board the Hon. Company's steamer
Aydalia, April 17, 1852.

"My dear Sir—You will no doubt have heard from Mr. Alexander Mackay, that his health having seriously suffered in India, he was about to leave the country by the steamer of the 3d inst., in the hope that the change would benefit him. This, however, was not to be. His strength gradually failed, until the evening of the 15th, when the doctors suppose that an abscess of the liver burst into the lungs, already diseased, and suffocation and consequent death ensued. I am glad to say that he suffered little until within half an hour of his decease, and until then also retained the full possession of his faculties. The captain has confided to me his papers for delivery to Mr. Thomas Mackay, of Inverness, whom he has left his sole legatee and executor, under a will drawn up a few hours before his death. These I purpose to send by the first steamer to Messrs. Arbuthnot, Ewart, and Co., of Liverpool; and I have suggested to Mr. Mackay that on their arrival he should select those of a private nature, and arrange with those of Mr. Mackay's friends on whose behalf he came out to India as to the disposal of the remainder.

"It is at Mr. Mackay's own request, made when all hope was at an end, that I now address you; and any further information respecting this sad affair I shall be most happy to afford you, on your addressing me a line, to the care of Messrs. Arbuthnot, Ewart, and Co., where I expect to be about three weeks or a month hence.—

          Meantime I am very truly yours,

                    "Arthur Latham.

"Thomas Bazley, Esq., Manchester."

Shirley Brooks

Charles William Shirley Brooks was born in London in 1815. After initially studying law he decided upon a literary career path and became a highly respected and accomplished man of letters.

His association with *The Morning Chronicle* included summary writer in the House of Commons, investigations into the Rural Districts as part of their "Labour and the Poor" series, and their follow-on "Agriculture and the Rural Population Abroad" series in which he travelled to and reported on Southern Russia, Asia Minor, Syria, and Egypt.

Shirley Brooks became synonymous with *Punch*, the famous London-based satirical magazine. He contributed regularly to *Punch* from 1851 onwards, being responsible for the popular "Essence of the Press" reports, before finally becoming editor in 1870 following the death of Mark Lemon.

The following is a piece published shortly after his own death that appeared in the *Gentleman's Magazine* in 1874, written by a long-time friend and son of Douglas Jerrold, the fellow journalist and *Punch* contributor:—

Gentleman's Magazine 1874.

SHIRLEY BROOKS.

BY BLANCHARD JERROLD.

I PROPOSED to offer to the reader a literary portrait, to discover all the habits and qualities of mind that made the subject of this outline—a figure of a man of letters not often seen in this country. But the materials have not reached my hands, and the task will probably fall to the share of some one better able to discharge it. Yet, to fill up the picture I had in my mind's eye, it is necessary that the painter should have had a long and sympathetic knowledge of the subject of it. A surface view of Shirley Brooks has been already taken by many hands. My intention was to show how in him we boasted in England a thorough man of letters; an artist who dwelt incessantly in art; a literary man for ever steeped in books—thinking books and talking books. All his outward expression took a literary form. I feel certain that when he had once put the law aside for letters (a transaction of his early youth), he never thought for a day of getting away from his bookshelves. He was a literary man of the old, gay French type, and appeared to be quite unconscious that there were paths in life less steep to climb than his. There was a serene content in him, which stood by him through all the fortunes of his career. He would parry a disappointment with an apt quotation, and close a transaction with a *mot*. He had a bright memory and an alert intellect; so that his wit and humour were perpetually fed and enriched from the ample stores of his reading. He was no recluse, for ever setting his heel towards the faces of men; but a joyous, sociable dweller in the midst of his kind. Yet he seemed to be always just clear of his study. He had always something fresh, dug from his shelves, that he made to sparkle on the topic of the hour. A happy illustration of a homely incident delighted him. You could not get him out of literature, in short; and in this quality of thoroughness he resembled, I repeat, an old French type of *savant* that is now unfortunately passing away. The kind of literary man whom such editors as M. de Villemessant produce are to the old *homme de lettres* what the Italian image boy is to the sculptor. Shirley Brooks threw the grace and learning of his art about freely, for the very love of it. It belted him, as the atmosphere belts and encloses the earth. And there are abundant evidences of this lying far and wide among his hosts of friends. I hoped to be able to submit many of these to your readers, in addition to my own store; but they are not yet to hand, so I must be content either to hand mine over some day to another, or wait till such time as I may be in a position to do justice to the quality that, to my mind, was the noblest in the mind of Shirley Brooks.

His books are the most notable events, or should be, in the life of an author. When we have said that Shirley Brooks was the son of an architect, that he was born in 1815, in Doughty Street, where Dickens lived for years; that he came of a gentle stock; that early in life he was articled to his uncle, Mr. Sabine, a well-known gentleman of Oswestry; that after having pursued his legal studies in London to some purpose he forsook the law for letters; and that thenceforth he steadily rose to the place of honour in which death found him in the midst of his books and papers, working cheerily among those whom he loved—his life is told. He travelled less than any man of his mind and means I can remember. He went to Southern Russia, to inquire into the corn trade there for the *Morning Chronicle*, and his pleasant letters home were afterwards published in the *Home and Colonial Library*, under the title of "The Russians of the South." We passed a few weeks together at Boulogne during the two or three summers when my father, Dickens, Gilbert à Beckett, and others—all gone now!—took their summer rest there; and he made a few holiday trips to Paris. I remember a chatty evening, full of his bookish sparkle, over a dinner at Philippe's, which he thoroughly enjoyed. But Shirley Brooks was as essentially a London man as Dr. Johnson. He was driven once or twice to the waters of Harrogate, and he had a liking for a Scotch trip; but no liking for any place was half so strong in him as that which he cherished for Fleet Street and Covent Garden. He would go into the country for a few days under great persuasion; and when he got there he chafed till he returned to his morning papers, his voluminous correspondence, his own armchair, and his familiar books—all set in his own methodical way, and not to be touched by strange hands on any account. But he was at home, he was at his ease only in the thick of London. When his family and all his friends were far away fishing, shooting, yachting, he would remain contentedly in town; and after his long day's work was done, he would issue from his pretty home in the Regent's Park, and walk happily through the quiet streets to the Garrick for a gossip, or to his favourite hotel under the Piazzas, where he and Mark Lemon would laugh like boys, over a plain dinner and a glass of punch.

Lemon had the higher animal spirits, but Brooks had the keener tongue, the more cultured mind, the finer grace. Lemon's fun bubbled from his loving heart. His eye compelled your laughter as much as his lip. You were aglow in his presence. Brooks was the well-bred gentleman, methodically genial—a sayer of good things you thought over. He was, as I have said, immersed in literature always, and could never be rid of his reading in his conversation; whereas Lemon was rather a man of the world, part of whose business lay in the pleasant ways of letters. Both were men of the old-fashioned, courteous address. In their denials they appeared to be conferring a favour. To the humble they were gentle; and they had their reward in the zeal with which all people in a printing house, an hotel, or their home pressed to serve them.

Let me note an instance of the effect which Shirley Brooks produced on those with whom he came in contact, viz.: the esteem in which he was held, throughout his life, at Oswestry, where he passed a few years of his youth, as his uncle's articled pupil. When it became known that I should endeavour to present to the readers of the *Gentleman's Magazine* a faithful sketch of my old friend (I met him for the first time in 1846) I received a letter from Mr. Askew Roberts, editor, I believe, of *Bye-gones*—the *Notes and Queries* of the Cambrian border, in which he testified to the deep impression Shirley Brooks's death had made in Oswestry. "As a boy," he says, "I remember the keen delight we always felt when Mr. Brooks came amongst us and took an interest in our sports. We all loved him, and I have felt it indeed an honour for so many years to be favoured with communications from him. Although we Oswestrians have only had hasty glimpses of Mr. Brooks of late years, his death—to all who remember his residence here—has been like that of a friend." Shirley Brooks had the faculty of holding people close to him. He had a princely memory. He never forgot a face he had seen, nor the circumstances under which he had seen it. The tenacity of his memory was indeed extraordinary. In March, 1873, he wrote to Mr. Roberts:—

> I want to ask you, who know all about Welsh affairs, a *domestic* question. It is partly suggested by what his sceptical Grace of Somerset said about Welsh coal. All the coals we get, no matter what one pays (they are *cheap* now, 28s.), are more or less bad. But it has been borne in upon my mind, as the Quakers say, that there is corn in Egypt, that is to say, coal in Wales, which must be good, and which may be supplied somewhere in London. Do you happen to know how this is? ... I remember that in the old days in Oswestry we used to have coals for almost nothing, and the late Minshull "the poet" (but I fancy this man had died before your time) wrote—
>
> > "And jaggers may by way of toll
> > Fling now and then a lump of coal."
>
> It must be quite forty years since Minshull wrote the doggrel.

This faculty of retention, applied industriously to literary pursuits by a man of fastidious taste, produced the thorough man of letters it was my ambition to describe to the readers of the *Gentleman's Magazine*. Mr. Roberts tells me he has often been absolutely amazed at the wonderful memory Shirley Brooks had for little things. Here are two examples:—

> Some one having given an epitaph in our *Bye-gones* column, Mr. Brooks wrote to say he could find a more dismal one in Oswestry Churchyard, and indicated the spot—giving, almost complete in his letter, the whole eight lines that composed it! And a few months earlier, noticing a discussion in the *Advertiser* about a brooch, bearing the date at which the "twelve Apostles" became a political bye-word in Shropshire, he wrote and said, "I was in Oswestry at the Cotes and Gore contest, which was three years before 1835, the date of the brooch, and then I heard the term, 'Lord Clive's Twelve Apostles' applied to the members as they had been in olden times; (for later, and before the Reform Bill there were two or three Liberals): I remember being remonstrated with for repeating the phrase, as profane!"

Traces of his sojourn in Oswestry are to be found in the "Gordian Knot" and the "Silver Cord." St. Oscar's, in the former work, is a vivid description of Oswestry; and Mr. Henry Cheriton is a faithful portrait of Mr. Sabine, the author's uncle, with whom he lived, and whom he assisted in his charitable work in the local Sunday schools.

In his early time—say about 1842-5—Shirley Brooks signed his articles, which were appearing in *Ainsworth's Magazine*, Charles W. Brooks: his second literary signature was C. Shirley Brooks: and finally he became Shirley Brooks. His full name was Charles William Shirley—the latter being an old name in his family. His early magazine papers, which brought him into communication with Harrison Ainsworth, Laman Blanchard, and other known men of the time, were of various kinds. One—"A Lounge in the Œil de Bœuf," was a brilliant dialogue among the courtiers of Louis the Fourteenth. A second was an account of an excursion of some English actors to China, brimming over with humour. Then there were dramatic papers—some of remarkable power—as "Cousin Emily" and the "Shrift on the Raft." These drew marked attention upon the young writer; and soon he was the centre of a strong muster of literary friends, who welcomed his beaming and handsome English face, and found pleasure in the wit and grace of his society.

His house became the resort of many men who were then rising, and have since risen, in the realms of literature and art. Angus Reach was his intimate friend; and they worked together for years on the *Morning Chronicle*—to which paper Brooks contributed the summary of Parliament during five Sessions—an experience that stood him in good stead afterwards in *Punch*. Albert Smith took many a hint and wise bit of advice from his friend Shirley Brooks. And then his life took a dramatic twist. It was probably his friendship with Charles Kean and Keeley that led him to the stage, and to the production of the delightful comediettas which brightened the reign of the Keeleys at the Lyceum Theatre. "Our New Governess," "The Creole," "The Daughter of the Stars," and "Anything for a Change" are light and bright pieces that deserve a more grateful public than they have obtained. Some day a manager will open the acting edition of them, and find that there is very seldom any dramatic writing produced now-a-days equal to that to be found in "Our New Governess."

But I have only touched on the literary activities of Shirley Brooks. His graceful pen—grace was his special quality—was a nimble one. Contributions to provincial papers, leaders for the *Illustrated News*, for the *Era*, for the *Home News*, travelled in copious streams. And here let me note how kind that brave and busy hand was: how tenderly it fell on a child's head, how it drew animals to its caress, how warmly it pressed a parting friend. For years that hand toiled every week in a certain paper—giving the entire pecuniary result to the widow of a dear friend. First, the friend fell ill, and remained for many many months unable to work. The brain had lost its balance. It was a mercy when the spent writer died. All this time Shirley Brooks quietly stood by; did the sick man's work for him, and, the sick man dead, continued the weekly task as his offering to his friend's widow. There was real heroism in this sustained toil, given regularly away until it was wanted no longer, that I never permitted myself to forget whenever I heard men forming an estimate of Shirley Brooks.

Not a demonstrative, nor in any way a gushing or sentimental man, Brooks was hearty. But his heartiness had been polished; and he was to the unceremonious, bluff, and fast folk of the present day, somewhat ceremonious and modish. His manner always reminded me of that of a fashionable physician; and, by the way, he affected doctors—and they affected him. I think it is Mr. "Original" Walker who has observed that a gentleman is a man of education who will take a polish. My dear friend Shirley had taken that polish.

In the society of ladies, I have been always told, he was delightful. His fine presence and gallant bearing, his lively talk that assumed considerable knowledge in his listeners, and in this sometimes flattered them vastly; and above all, his gracious and sympathetic method of approach, bespoke the man who had enjoyed the advantages which the constant companionship of cultivated gentlewomen gives to a man. It is the bloom upon the polish. Shirley Brooks could pay a compliment in the old, respectful style, and turn the corner of a mistake or an awkward incident with a special grace that was all his own. Be it observed that there are hundreds of illustrations afloat of the points of character I am endeavouring to submit to the reader; but I have them not at hand, and I am writing far away from the friends who could pour them into my basket. So that my estimate must be taken on my own good faith, and my faculty of observation that ranged over twenty-eight years. Some twenty of these years ago Shirley Brooks had invited a certain gentleman and his daughter to one of those joyous parties of his which, alas! there are few alive to remember to-day. In his letter he had omitted to give the number of his house. This being requested, he made an elaborate drawing of his street door—

writing, "This is that side of my door on which I am least anxious to see you."

But it is impossible to convey a complete idea of the admirable writer about whom I am merely making a few notes, without his letters. For he was a great and careful letter-writer. How he found time to carry on the correspondence in which he indulged was a mystery to the friends who knew the amount of "copy" he was in the habit of throwing off every week. He read everything of mark that appeared; he kept a thoroughly literary diary, which, I believe, will presently see the light of print. He was fond of society, and a diner-out of the old school; he had always time for a gossip; he was well posted up in every event of the day; and yet he found time to write sparkling, witty, and kindly letters about nothing and everything, by the hundred. In some he frolicked like a schoolboy; in others he would set seriously to work to solve or illustrate some literary subject that had accidentally turned up. He would enter upon a long correspondence to serve a friend. You never found him exhausted; seldom tired. If you caught him lounging by the dainty conservatory he had in his house, after a long day upstairs in his study, he would be reading the last *Quarterly*, or dallying with a novel by one of his friends—but he would brighten for a talk, and be sure to shine in it. When he had finished his correspondence for the day, after his work, he would take his letters to the post himself. It was his orderly way. You could see his methodical mind in the precise writing, the unbroken lines, the absence of any sign of haste from his shortest notes. His books and pictures were arranged with extraordinary neatness. He had photograph albums of friends, with their autographs and characteristic bits from their letters contrived with exquisite care under each. One letter of his, which I happen to have under my hand, is a good example of his unsleeping watchfulness over all about him, over the welfare of a friend, over the success of any undertaking in which he was concerned. The opening paragraph refers to some domestic joke we had in common:—

4th Monday in Lent (March 24), 1873.

My dear William,—I can write to you. The consciousness of innocence sits upon my brow, and also flutters over my inkstand; which I consider a rather fine image.

The C. K.* memorial will, I hope, be a success. Routledge began it, and is very energetic. It ought to be something artistic, at Windsor.

---

* The memorial to Charles Knight, of which Shirley Brooks was honorary secretary.

Some folks are pushing about an "educational tribute," &c., but I think we need not flavour *everything* with the smell of corduroy. 'Tis quite dominant enough already. You *ought* to be on the committee.

I was going to write to L. by order of E., to say that the latter, who, with Reginald, has been about Italy, and has seen all the sights, is making her way to Paris, and greatly hoped to find you there. I fear this hope will be blighted. I cann't send you her address, tho' I write to-day to Naples, as she will have left that before L. could write, but if I get a Marseilles address, I will send it.

Do you know Mrs. L. R.? She is a young artist of great merit. Frith and Tom Taylor prophesy a great career for her, and she is studying in Paris—having exhibited many pictures here, at the Academy, &c. It would be very kind if L. or you, or both, would give her a call, if you can. I subjoin the address. I know not what part of Paris it is in—you will. If you go, say that you are friends of mine, and that Mrs. Brooks will call on her when she comes. You will like her—she is very bright.

No news but those you read in the papers. They say to-day that Jessel is to be Master of the Rolls at once.

If M. Doré is in Paris, I beg my best compliments to him. Do you see Plimsoll wanted, or wants, him to paint a picture on the coffin-ships? And wouldn't he do it grandly!—Kindest regards.—Ever yours,

SHIRLEY BROOKS.

I may note that M. Doré declined the subject—deeming it a political one, on the merits of which he was not competent to pronounce judgment with his brush.

Some—I trust many—under whose eyes these lines will fall will remember Shirley Brooks in his latter days, when the hard-fought fight had been won, and he had come out of it, his whitening hair being the only scars of the struggle. He never looked braver, handsomer, nor happier. He was as deep in his books, as familiar with his ink, as ever; but now he had his acknowledged place in the literature which he loved. The steel at Napoleon's side was the same on the eve of the battle as on the morrow of victory; but on the morrow it was the sword of Austerlitz. How cheerily and kindly, in the heyday of his complete success, Shirley Brooks gathered his circle of friends about him, none who ever stood under his roof-tree will forget. That was a pleasant house in Kent Terrace, by the Regent's Park, where so many men whose names are household words were wont to gather and be wisely merry. How many years have I seen out and in, sitting with hosts of friends round the mahogany tree of our dear friend! How many times has his manly and kindly voice said "God bless you all" to us, as the bells of the New Year broke through the stillness of midnight! He stood at the head of his table last New Year's Eve, his friends crowded about him—the background his books and pictures; watch in hand. His happy English face, ennobled with silver hair, never looked fuller of the intellectual light that he had trimmed and burned—a student always—for nearly forty years. I remember that a sad feeling came upon me as I gazed at him, with his watch in his hand counting the dying seconds of the last New Year's Eve he was destined to see. For he reminded me of my father in his study at Kilburn Priory, on *his* last New Year's Eve, when he spoke so solemnly and slowly, as though in the midst of our revel, Death had whispered to him. The scattered flakes of white hair were the chief resemblance between the two; and it was these that revived the old scene in my mind—for I was struck with what appeared to me to be the almost sudden whiteness of my friend.

But no sad memory, no melancholy foreboding, was apparent on the night when, for the last time, Shirley Brooks blessed his guests, and wished them a happy New Year. All the old friends were there. Frith, Tenniel, Edmund Yates, Du Maurier, Burnand, Mrs. Keeley, Crowdy, J. C. Parkinson, Sambourne, and many others; and among the welcome strangers was Mark Twain, who proposed the health of the host in a speech brimming with his peculiar humour. Shirley Brooks replied quietly, and with a little fatigue in his manner. It was late, and he abhorred late hours. He had been an early man all his life; and to this good habit he owed that prodigious power of work which astonished his friends, who knew that he had never been a robust man.

Less than two months afterwards he was upon his death-bed. He was busy with his duties to the last hour of his life. On the morning of the day on which his eyes were closed for ever he looked over the forthcoming number of *Punch* and made some suggestions. He was at peace with all the world. He had blessed his wife for the loving care with which she had watched over him. His boys were at home with him. And he turned gently on his side, and fell into his long sleep, leaving hosts of friends to mourn him, and not an enemy that I ever heard of, to assail his memory.

Index

415

For information on these and other titles available please visit:

DittoBooks.co.uk